Studies in Eighteenth-Century

VOLUME 8

Studies in Eighteenth-Century Culture VOLUME 8

EDITED BY *Roseann Runte*
Dalhousie University

PUBLISHED for the
AMERICAN SOCIETY FOR EIGHTEENTH-CENTURY STUDIES
by THE UNIVERSITY OF WISCONSIN PRESS

Published 1979
The University of Wisconsin Press
Box 1379, Madison, Wisconsin 53701

The University of Wisconsin Press, Ltd.
1 Gower St., London WC1E 6HA, England

Copyright © 1979
American Society for Eighteenth-Century Studies
All rights reserved

First printing

Printed in the United States of America

LC 74-25572
ISBN 0-299-07740-3

Editorial Committee for Volume Eight

JUDITH COLTON / Yale University
ALAN S. FISHER / University of Washington
MILTON KLEIN / University of Tennessee (Knoxville)
ADRIENNE D. HYTIER / Vassar College
JAMES GRAY / Dalhousie University
ERIC ROTHSTEIN / University of Wisconsin
HENRY SNYDER / University of Kansas

Readers

Paul Alkon, English, University of Minnesota
Owen Aldridge, Comparative Literature Studies, University of Illinois—Champaign
Paula Backscheider, English, University of Rochester
Ehrard Bahr, Germanic Languages, University of California—Los Angeles
J. M. Beattie, History, University of Toronto
Peter Boerner, Comparative Literature, Indiana University
Laurence Bongie, French, University of British Columbia
Patrick Brady, French, Rice University
Gwen Brewer, English, California State University—Northridge
James Brown, French, Dalhousie University
Vivian Cameron, Art History, Nova Scotia College of Art and Design
Charles Carroll, Music, St. Petersburg Junior College
Arthur Donovan, History, West Virginia University
Irvin Ehrenpreis, English, University of Virginia
Robert Ginsberg, Philosophy, The Pennsylvania State University
Donald Greene, English, University of Southern California
Roger Hahn, History, University of California—Berkeley
Thadd Hall, History, State University of New York—Binghamton
Richard Heitzenrater, Perkins School of Theology, Southern Methodist University
Patrick Henry, French, Whitman College
Kathryn M. Hunter, English, Morehouse College
Robert Hunting, English, University of Maine—Orono
Margaret Jacob, History, Baruch College, City University of New York
Regina Janes, English, Skidmore College
Michael Keen, Director, Atlantic Geoscience Center, Bedford Institute of Oceanography
Gary Kelly, English, University of Alberta
Merrill Knapp, Music, Princeton University
Charles Knight, English, University of Massachusetts—Boston
Victor Lange, Germanic Languages, Princeton University
Kenneth Leffek, Dean, Graduate Studies, Dalhousie University
Jeanne Monty, French and Italian, Tulane University
Richard Olson, Humanities & Social Sciences, Harvey Mudd College
Richard Popkin, Philosophy, Washington University

Leonard Ratner, Music, Stanford University
Walter Rex, French, University of California—Berkeley
Jack Richtman, French, State University of New York—Albany
Ronald Rosbottom, Romance Languages, Ohio State University
English Showalter, Romance Languages, Rutgers University—Camden
Phillip Stewart, Romance Languages, Duke University
Damie Stillman, Art History, University of Wisconsin
Constant Stockton, History, Wisconsin State University
Gerald Straka, History, University of Delaware
Giorgio Tonnelli, Philosophy, State University of New York—Binghamton
Virgil Topazio, Dean of Humanities and Social Sciences, Rice University
Robert Uphaus, English, Michigan State University
D. P. Varma, English, Dalhousie University
William Williams, History, University of Maryland
Raymond Whitley, English, Mount Saint Vincent University

Contents

Preface ix
    ROSEANN RUNTE / Dalhousie University

Elite versus Popular Mentality in the Eighteenth Century
ASECS Prize Essay 3
    HARRY C. PAYNE / Colgate University

The World between the Literate and Oral Traditions in
Eighteenth-Century France: Ecclesiastical Instructions and
Popular Mentalities 33
    HARVEY MITCHELL / University of British Columbia

Pessimism Surpassed: New Colleges as Bastions against
Barbarism in Colonial America 69
    MARGARET W. MASON / Hood College

Elihu Palmer, Radical Deist, Radical Republican: A
Reconsideration of American Free Thought 87
    RODERICK S. FRENCH / George Washington University

Binding and Dressing Nature's Loose Tresses: The Ideology
of Augustan Landscape Design 109
    CAROLE FABRICANT / University of California, Riverside

Rochester's Sexual Politics 137
    REBA WILCOXON / Vanderbilt University

Mr. Locke and the Ladies: The Indelible Words on the
Tabula Rasa 151
SHERYL O'DONNELL / University of Arizona

Mary Wollstonecraft's Letters Written... in Sweden:
Toward Romantic Autobiography 165
MITZI MYERS / California State University, Fullerton

Sir William Temple's Views on Science, Poetry, and the
Imagination 187
CHARLES H. HINNANT / University of Missouri, Columbia

Friends and Enemies in Verses on the Death of Dr. Swift 205
JAMES WOOLLEY / University of Pennsylvania

Ironist and Moralist: The Two Readers of Tom Jones 233
WILLIAM PARK / Sarah Lawrence College

Sterne as Editor: The "Abuses of Conscience" Sermon 243
MELVYN NEW / University of Florida

Kant: Origin and Utopia 253
WALTER MOSER / Université de Montréal

Rudolf Erich Raspe: The Geologist Captain Cook Refused 269
RUTH P. DAWSON / University of Hawaii

Regnard and Collin d'Harleville on Legacies by Bachelor
Uncles 291
PHILIP KOCH / University of Pittsburgh

Voltaire, "Lexicographer of the Enlightenment" 313
VIRGIL W. TOPAZIO / Rice University

The Physiocrats and the Encyclopedists 323
JEAN A. PERKINS / Swarthmore College

The Useful Myth of Gothic Ancestry 337
MARK MADOFF / University of British Columbia

Strawberry Hill: Architecture of the "as if" 351
DIANNE S. AMES / Temple University

Executive Board, 1977–78	365
Institutional Members	367
Index	369

Preface

An eighteenth-century editor might well begin this preface by saucily vaunting the Bill of Fare in the hope of titillating the readers' appetites so they would seek to feast their eyes on the following pages of the proposed menu. However, the editor of this volume of *Studies in Eighteenth-Century Culture* lacks the desire to retain the readers from the delights of a bountiful repast, the presumption to entice them to consume a menu which in itself provides sufficient incentive for careful reading and gratification for the discriminating palate, and finally, both the inclination and the talent to imitate Fielding for more than one paragraph.

The articles appearing in this volume were selected from papers presented at national and regional conferences of the American Society for Eighteenth-Century Studies. They cover a wide range of topics and disciplines. To summarize the diversity of the contents would be a task similar, in a microcosmic way, to attempting to reduce the complexities of the many facets of the Enlightenment expressed by artists, authors, and philosophers in both the Old and New Worlds, to a simple formula. It is perhaps ironic to note that in this very diversity lies a key to the fundamental unity of this volume, a dissonant oneness, a parallel for which can be discovered in the shadowy recesses of the Enlightenment, in the contrast between the rational and the irrational, progress and tradition, reality and imagination, truth and illusion. The eighteenth century can be divided in a system of philosophical and artistic dichotomies. Inherent in this organization of incongruous couples (whether they represent thesis and antithesis or action and reaction) is the revelation that, living in a state of constant flux, man is uneasy and seeks to resolve the seeming paradoxes of divergent ideas and of living in an imperfect present prescribed by tradition while thinking of perfection and aspiring after the future.

The authors whose essays appear in this collection have all perceived some aspect of this duality. They have observed its physical manifestations—the presence of two classes (elite and popular) and two traditions (oral and literate)—and its philosophical expression—liberty and reason vs. oppression and irrationality, the mechanical world vs. utopia, actualism vs. catastrophism, the theories of the Physiocrats and those of the Encyclopedists, or the debates between the neptunists and the vulcanists. The authors have also explored the literary or artistic expressions of duality: type vs. individual, fancy vs. judgment, statement vs. demonstration. The authors have sought to elucidate the nature of these incongruous pairs by explanation, situation or resolution. The use of papier-mâché in the construction of Walpole's castle is explained as the architectural metaphor for the conflict between illusion and reality. The problem of nature, seen at once as a coy yet seductive maiden, a promiscuous yet chaste consort, is linked to a series of opposites—freedom/restraint, capturer/captive, definer/defined—and is situated in the basic conflict of male/female. The establishment of colleges in America is seen as the solution for the social and moral oppositions of civilization vs. barbarism and virtue and knowledge vs. vice and ignorance. Voltaire's alphabetical writings are the resolution of possible conflict between form and expression. The eighteenth-century woman, affected by Locke's empiricism in her thought and by patriarchal doctrines of traditional women's roles in her lifestyle, provides an example of a human irony. Fielding, both a natural historian and a believer in Providence, reconciled wish and belief with double irony in his writings.

By positing two readers (self and other), two interpreters, two classes, or two modes of thought, some of the authors in this volume have sought to refine and interpret these antitheses. Rochester is seen to unite all roles in one being: male/female, conquistador of sex/servile slave of love. Sterne the writer and Sterne the editor become one in their serious concern for brilliant style and precise diction. Other authors have hesitated before models which split the world so neatly and have reacted to them by presenting triads, as in the essay on Kant, or by multiplying the structures which gain in charm and richness through their defiance of any single system, even that of duality, as in the study of Mary Wollstonecraft, which illustrates both the loosely thematic and the linear structure of her *Letters*.

This volume begins with the ASECS prize essay, a study of elite perceptions of and interactions with the popular mind. Harry Payne's judicious treatment of numerous problems—including literacy, philosophy, class distinctions, morality, and work—indicates new horizons for the scholar, who will thereby gain a more complete understanding of the difficult notion of popular culture. Harvey Mitchell's paper, which follows, deals with oral traditions as reflections of primitiveness, clashing with the literate or semiliterate views of the clergy. The conflict between the French language and patois is symbolic of the one between civilized and uncivilized traditions. This contrast evokes that posited by Margaret Masson, who investigates the symbolic importance of higher education and the college movement it inspired in early America. The evangelical, philosophical, and political arguments for the creation of institutions of higher learning were founded on the contrast between civilization and barbarism. Roderick French, dealing with an early American, Elihu Palmer, examines the radical-deist-militant republicans in relation to the question of the continuity of political radicalism. This paper addresses a neglected phase in the history of philosophical naturalism.

The next four articles all deal with women. The first two seek to discover how women are perceived and the second two, how they perceive the world. Carole Fabricant illustrates the way bonds between women and landscape, as they were commonly viewed and treated by poets, painters, and estate planners, were fundamentally connected with larger aesthetic and ideological concerns in eighteenth-century England. Reba Wilcoxon discusses the theme of choice and the various roles assumed by Rochester (sexist, egalitarian, and "ironic" libertine) and concludes that Rochester, the poet, rejected the enslavement of either sex. Sheryl O'Donnell eloquently expresses the dilemma of eighteenth-century English women who believed in Lockean concepts but lived in a traditional society. Mitzi Meyers finds contradictions in the personality of one woman, Mary Wollstonecraft, radical idealist and realist reformer.

The papers in the following group are related by field. While they all deal with English authors, they are divided by a large span of time, the number of problems treated, and the authors' critical approaches. The first essay deals with a theory of literature, the second and the third with literature as expression, the fourth with literature as revision. In this sense, we move from a future orientation and a speculation of possible influence exerted, to a present tense and an interpretative analysis of meaning, to a past perspective where the eighteenth-century author's creative process is viewed from the perspective of his own corrections. Charles Hinnant examines Sir William Temple's contribution to poetic theory in the light of a clarification of that author's scientific attitudes. James Woolley demonstrates the manner in which Swift's "Verses on the Death of Dr. Swift" emphasizes a particular kind of friendship. That satirist's relationships with Queen Caroline and Mrs. Howard are explained within the contextual framework of the poem. William Park relates the concept of double irony as expressed by Empson to the role of the two readers, ironist and moralist, in *Tom Jones*. Melvyn New deals with Sterne's editing of the "Abuses of Conscience" sermon read by Corporal Trim in the second volume of *Tristam Shandy*. The alterations illustrate both the subtlety of Sterne's prose and his painstaking care in choosing the exact word to express the nuances of his ideas.

Walter Moser explicates, in terms of discursive and textual choices, the constraints which result from the encounter of origin and utopia in Kant. Ruth Dawson relates the circumstances of the life and the works of Raspe, scholar and delinquent, a sedentary geologist whose theories were at some times very advanced for his epoch, and at others, rather naïve.

The three papers which follow, may, like those in English, be grouped nationally and geographically. These essays treat literature as a form of philosophic expression, and philosophy or economic philosophy. The first and the last deal with comparison and contrast between two authors or two groups. In both cases the contrasts are highlighted by the difference in approach (caricature vs. character portrait, the pragmatic vs. the theoretic), while the comparative aspects are based on the similarity in subject matter or question treated. The article on Voltaire is not devoid of comparisons and contrasts, for without them it would indeed be difficult to capture what Faguet has termed Voltaire's "chaos of clear ideas." However, the unity of the essay is itself reflected in the discipline demanded of Voltaire by his choice of the alphabetical form. Philip Koch compares the bachelor uncles in Le Légataire universe; and in Le Vieux Célibataire; discovers that their roles are similar but that their individual portraits differ, the former representing a type and the latter an individual; and concludes that the more complex character evolved during the eighteenth century by a progress of continual refinements. If Voltaire's Dictionnaire philosophique opened doors for his readers, Virgil Topazio offers us a synthetic perspective on Voltaire's alphabetical writings. He describes how Voltaire sought to cover a great variety of subjects with clarity through his choice of form and style. Jean Perkins, in her essay on the Physiocrats and the Encyclopedists, discusses the often divergent, yet sometimes parallel positions of these two groups. Placing them in both a philosophical and historical perspective, her explanation is clear and comprehensive.

The final two papers in the volume deal with the Gothic. The first, by Mark Madoff, deals in a historically orientated fashion with the Goths and the relics attributed to them. He declares that they acted as symbols of racial pride, communal disintegration (or revival), and internal revolution. Dianne Ames interprets the gothic architecture of Strawberry Hill as a metaphor. The house is seen as a scrapbook where objects represent ideas and where the use of papier-mâché is an extension of print. These devices were employed for the pleasure that they would produce for the beholder.

It is on the note of pleasure that it is appropriate to conclude both this volume and this preface. Many eighteenth-century authors stated that they had a dual purpose in writing: to amuse and to instruct. Two centuries later our goals have not changed, and they are reflected in each individual essay. The Editorial Board and the Editorial Committee worked very diligently in selecting and editing the contents of volume eight. The authors, who provided the thought-provoking articles contained herein, were most cooperative in respecting deadlines and format. I thank them all most sincerely and take great satisfaction in inviting you to partake of the substantial entrées on the menu.

ROSEANN RUNTE

Dalhousie University
November 1977

Studies in Eighteenth-Century Culture

VOLUME 8

Elite versus Popular Mentality in the Eighteenth Century

HARRY C. PAYNE

In most places at most times the elites of European history have nurtured a sense of distance between themselves and their "inferiors." In the eighteenth century this general, unfocused, largely implicit sense of distance became a pervasive, explicit sense of polarity between the nature of the nonelite—"the people"—and that of the elite.[1] To be sure, the masses had evoked sympathy, concern, anger, and frustration from the intellectual and social elite in earlier times; no observer in republican Rome or Reformation Germany could entirely ignore the nature of the mass of men. But the people as a clear and distinct social category—defined by its economic function and precursor to what the nineteenth century would call the "working class"—entered systematically into perceptions of high culture only with the age of the Enlightenment.

In France the word *peuple* itself underwent a distinct evolution, first noted by the moralist Abbé Coyer in his *Dissertation sur la nature du peuple* (1755). At one time, Coyer observed, the *peuple* included "the most useful, the most virtuous, and consequently the most respectable part of the nation," including farmers, artisans, merchants, financiers, lawyers, and philosophers. Rising social pretensions among robe nobil-

From *Historical Reflections / Réflections historiques*, 2 (Winter, 1975-76), no. 2, 183-208.

ity, men of letters, financiers, and the like had gradually robbed the word of that meaning; even the status of artisans of luxury goods had come into doubt, since their hands "no longer resembled those of the *peuple.*"[2] Though Coyer emphasized only what he considered a regrettable rise in pretension, he recorded an important fact in social thinking: the word *peuple* had evolved from a juristic category with no semblance of economic realism to a rough denotation of a socioeconomic class. *Peuple* had come to be used most of the time as Voltaire chose to use it—as those "who have only their hands to live by." Coyer's analysis struck a responsive chord and was often quoted.[3]

Nowhere else in Europe did language record such a striking change, though the German word *Pöbel* did mirror some of the French connotations, and the English words *mob, multitude,* and *vulgar* do appear with much greater regularity. Still, everywhere in Europe there was a marked increase in talk about the nature and condition of those who had little else but their labor. This talk may have betrayed a growth in pretentiousness, as Coyer insisted, but this masked a substantial growth in the realism of social analysis. Between 1650 and 1780 the focus of social analysis shifted from juristic concerns of honor and privilege to the sociological concerns of the economic relations among men, from the aristocratic, legal categories of Loyseau to the administrative, economic categories of Turgot.[4] The world of elite culture debated the nature and future of the dependent majority of men over a range of issues and sentiments unprecedented in European history. The concerns were many and often peculiar to the world of the eighteenth century: Can the elite and the people share the same religion, or must there continue to be a "double truth"—one for the elite, one for the masses—in all civilized societies? Is it useful to deceive the people, even for its own good, or must one speak to it truthfully at all times? Should the people be educated, or will popular education rob society of its laborers? Can the popular mind apprehend the same truths as the enlightened mind, or must it be taught in a special way? Does the people have the moral sensibility to serve fairly on juries, even if, as many thought, the peasant valued his wife and child less than his cow? Why does the people gather at hangings—because of its "natural" cruelty, its having been hardened by its burdens, or its understandable, indeed admirable sensitivity to the lot of one of its own? Can the people at any place or any time be trusted with political responsibility, or will it always be the unwitting tool of political exploiters? Why does the mob dump grain in the river when it claims to be the starving victim of hoarders? Can there be equal happiness in all estates, or is misery the inevitable child of hard labor?[5]

The debates reflected a mixture of sympathy and scorn, realism and naïveté, humanitarianism and cruelty. The debates were real—there was little consensus on what should be done to and for the people, though the weight of public opinion moved perceptibly toward the more humane alternatives. The people itself emerged in the perceptions of *philosophes,* moralists, and their readers as a clear, albeit stereotyped, social object worthy of study and concern.

The "people" of the eighteenth century, for all its many guises— "mob," "vulgar," "multitude," "poor," *Pöbel, misérables*—still possessed certain identifiable, relatively constant characteristics in the eyes of the literate elite. Above all, the people appeared as something apart, as a group with little in common—except biology and emotions—with the readers and writers. Typically, Charles Duclos could exclude the masses, with no sense of doing anything extraordinary, from his considerations on contemporary *moeurs:* "Except for the *bas peuple* which thinks only of its basic needs, and has few notions as to anything else, the rest of mankind is everywhere the same. Proper society [*bonne compagnie*] is independent of legal status and rank, and is to be found only among those who have feelings, who have just ideas and genteel feelings."[6] So, too, Le Mercier de La Rivière, in other contexts quite sympathetic to the people's lot, could speak of the people in the starkest terms: "Their blindness places them lower than brutes [who at least have sure instincts], making them more miserable than animals, more difficult to lead, and more tempestuous." Like children in their gullibility, he continued, men of the people dwell in "a state of habitual delirium; ... ignorance differs in no way from madness, when you consider each according to its disastrous effects."[7] The litany of scorn is almost endless. But beneath that scorn lies a stark, realistic perception: work sets men apart, making the laborer's mind and character different from others. Work could be, as moralists often pointed out and as the article "Travail" in the *Encyclopédie* repeated, a source of "health, subsistence, serenity, common sense and virtue." But ancient myth, as the same article indicated, made work the child of Night and the grandchild of Chaos. In an age which cherished the sense of light and order, the man condemned to live by his labor enjoyed a separate and unenviable lineage.

Perceiving the people as a class apart, those moralists, political economists, and philosophes who spoke for and to the elite mind attributed certain characteristics to the popular mind. Collection of information about the life of the poor was increasing in the eighteenth century, but the elite's perception of the people rested less on disciplined observation than on random glimpses and traditional assumptions. The popular mind was associated with the passions and the senses, Plato's realm of appearances. Though the empiricism of the age insisted that all knowledge came to all men through the same simple functions—the senses—the elite ideal, be he Addison's "sociable man," Voltaire's *honnête homme,* or Wieland's "Cosmopolitan," was distinguished by his ability to step back from immediate experience, observe it, criticize it, master it, and then use it for future actions.[8] Indeed the emphasis of prevailing philosophies on the power of environment in shaping *l'homme machine* only underscored the depth of difference between elite and people. "If one divided all human knowledge into two parts," Rousseau wrote in *Emile,* "one common to all men and the other unique to educated men, the latter would be quite small compared to the other."[9] Rousseau could find solace in this notion, but to most the increment from the latter appeared to make all the difference in the world. Limited to its economic world, deprived of the proper environment—the *Bildung* of Weimar classicists—the people seemed locked into the realm of immediate appearance; and when it tried to move beyond, it almost always seemed to do so in a superstitious, irrational way. Precisely because all it had was sense experience, the people seemed, philosophes argued, to crave the wondrous and the spectacular, to crave sensual excitation in its broadest sense rather than the cool pleasures of reflective reasonableness. This desire for the wondrous explained to some the source of popular superstition. In the latter part of the century, many men of letters ceased to share the general scorn for the popular mind and looked to its supposed naturalness as an alternative to the abstract, unspiritual, critical empiricism of the Enlightenment. But even those who, like Rousseau, Herder, and Wordsworth, perceived the people with kinder eyes still assumed that the popular mind was both more concrete and sensual than the "abstract" reasonableness of the Enlightenment ideal.[10] A curse to Voltaire seemed a blessing to Rousseau, but none doubted that the people were closer to the world of the senses than the educated elite.

More ominously, the people seemed morally as well as intellectually deficient. The seemingly mindless violence of the crowd often caused despair and wonder in the minds of the "enlightened." None were prepared to attribute sensible "moral economy" to the crowd's behavior, though philosophes would often see some justice in their cause.[11] Usually philosophes assumed that crowds were the tools of elite leaders, manipulated by flashy rhetoric and specious signs to endanger peace and order. Though some—mostly the same who could see virtue in the closeness of the peasant to the senses—saw peculiar virtues in the people, especially the peasant, the weight of elite opinion fell heavily to the side of its moral weakness. The more perceptive did not blame the people for its misery and consequent moral insensitivity, but they still could not avoid their judgments.

Intellectually and morally limited, the people appeared, in a more general sense, overwhelmingly passive. Even when appearing as a force in history—especially in the realm of antique Rome and Greece—it functioned primarily as the tool of leaders, the pawns of Caesar. The eighteenth-century elite lacked any sense that the people was arbiter of its own destiny.[12] To this elite, the people was the tool of its sense experiences. It was the victim of nature. Its condition was in the hands of kings, administrators, and philosophes. Those with power could determine whether the people was to be miserable or content (but still poor); whether the people would be educated; what the people would believe in the future; what machines it should use; what its standard of living was to be; how it would achieve health.

This eighteenth-century sense of responsibility—both in its neutral sense of "control" and its humanitarian sense of "duty"—recast the traditional notion of Christian stewardship. In his charity sermon "on the eminent dignity of the poor in the Church," Bossuet invited his aristocratic audience to compare two forms of perception. "Those who look at [the poor] with corporal eyes see only baseness and despise them. Those who open upon them the interior eye, that is, intelligence guided by faith, see in them Jesus Christ; they see the images of his poverty, the citizens of his kingdom, the inheritors of his promises, the distributors of his grace, the true children of his Church, the first members of the mystical body."[13] More than a century later Goethe noted briefly, "The class we call the lower is in God's eyes the higher."[14] This form of magical inversion of perception could both nurture charity and invite inaction. The double nature of the people was reflected in the ambiguity of clerical attitudes toward popular credulity; the people's willingness to believe was both admired as the gateway to faith and feared as the path to superstition and heresy.[15] The *hôpitaux* of seventeenth-century France represent the best and the worst of that form of perception—large investment in care for the wretched of the earth, cruel lack of discrimination in the treatment.[16]

The traditional notion of *noblesse oblige* also masked similar ambiguities. No doubt part of the mark of privileged honor had always been some lip-service (and often some real service) to the welfare of the poor. But within the idea of *noblesse* itself rested the assumption of a hierarchy sanctioned by blood, tradition, law, and divine will. *Noblesse* may have entailed some feeling of obligation to the lowly, but at its core it entailed exploitation and dominance by right of birth. The more secular eighteenth-century sense of division emphasized the economic sources of social difference and the consequent responsibilities incumbent on the state and the holders of economic power. Neither could claim legitimacy from traditional sources; each could be justified—in the eyes of philosophes and moralists—only by its proper use of that power. To be sure, the Enlightenment idea of *bienfaisance* owed much to older ideas of charity. It was, however, less voluntary in its spirit, emphasizing as it did the dangers of failure to exercise economic power wisely. Considerably different from older notions is the widely broadened eighteenth-century sense of the role the state could play in shaping the mind and life of the masses. To many social commentators reliance on private charity no longer seemed adequate, and the state alone seemed to have the resources and energy to intervene in the life of the people.

The broadened eighteenth-century sense of responsibility emphasized, therefore, the social, economic, cultural, and political dominance of the elite and its consequent powers over the life and mind of the masses. The terms in which this perception was voiced are, as a whole, starkly realistic. Rarely does one find Bossuet's ability to make magical leaps from low to high. In all senses the lowly seemed lowly—economically poor, culturally limited, morally deficient, politically incapable. The separation seemed inescapable and its sources very human.[17] The people represented the creation of its elite, the measure of the leadership of those with power.

Hence, if not with dignity at least with a certain important clarity the people emerged as a class apart in the perceptual world of the elite. To what can we attribute this shift? Though I would give different weight to each, the sources seem threefold: the intensification of "objective" economic and physical distance between rich and poor; the increase in contact with the people in its economic and cultural roles; a shift in the perceptual world of the elite in its standards for itself which cast those who labored in a new, clearer light. In all cases these causes had roots deep in the previous century. The eighteenth century harvested in the form of new perceptions the social and administrative changes which had been going on for at least a century.

Though our knowledge is still regrettably scanty, it appears that relations between the employer of labor and the laborer had, in the seventeenth century, changed in ways to accentuate differences. In most guilds, masterships became largely limited to a hereditary group.[18] These divisions must have been, in turn, reinforced by corresponding differences in wealth, economic power, accessibility to education (the expansion, for instance, of colleges in France), and new forms of associations (horizontal associations of workers to replace the diminished functions of the vertical guild).

During the eighteenth century, in the most advanced commercial areas, the nature of the relationship between employer and employee may also have been redefined in a way to increase a sense of separation. E. P. Thompson has argued with some cogency that in England many of the traditional face-to-face dealings of elite and worker gave way to more formal cash transactions, often through a buffer zone of middlemen.[19] Still the degree of change is unclear, and it remains a very open question whether the case can be made much beyond England.

The prosperity of the eighteenth century may also have accentuated the apparent extremes between wealth and poverty in the cities. This is the impression both of Franklin Ford for eighteenth-century Strasbourg and Carl Bridenbaugh for American cities.[20] The ironic byproduct of relative prosperity, lessening of epidemics, and increased agricultural productivity was the multiplication of the number of poor, especially in England and France. Fewer people suffered and died in the manner of the great *mortalités* of previous centuries; more barely subsisted. The poor man and the beggar became more numerous and hence a deeper object of concern, sympathy, and fear in the eyes of the elite.[21] Accentuation of extremes also seems to have been reflected in living and housing patterns, as the middle and upper-middle class began to create separate suburbs (different from the aristocratic oscillation between country and city and the isolation of the rural and urban worker). Where possible—as in London after the great fire of 1666—urban patterns seem to have shifted more on lines which would accentuate distance between laborer and nonlaborer.[22]

How much these "objective" economic factors contributed to the new sense of separation is hard to judge. Even if divisions were accentuated, they had existed long before the eighteenth century began to talk of them in such consistent terms. Even when aristocrat, merchant, artisan, and laborer lived in the same building—divided vertically—no one could have mistaken them. Until there is much harder evidence of clear-cut, economically determined division, I would give low priority to this realm of causes. No doubt the economic changes of the century did, in large measure, underwrite the growing perception of separation, but the forms of production and economic relations among classes do not seem to have changed so measurably as to explain the change in perception.

Ironically, the sense of separation, insofar as it contained a more realistic assessment of differing conditions among men, was caused more by expanding contacts than by economic cleavage. This contact took the form of what the French called *police*. The will, means, and ability to supervise the economic and social functioning of society by governments—urban and national—markedly increased after the varied crises of the mid-seventeenth century. This seems especially true in France at the national level. The absolutism of Louis XIV was symbolic, violent, and largely military; his fame rested more on his control of his nobility than on his control of the nation as a whole. Colbertian regulations often went unfulfilled; edicts regulating holidays, education, militia service, return of village lands, and the like—issues which touched the people's life—went remarkably unheeded.[23] But for all the deceptiveness of his control, he set the tone for the administrative, "enlightened absolutism" which pervaded the eighteenth century.[24] As the bureaucracy of intendants and subdelègates filled out, as the farmers-general entered into much closer contact with the general machinery of government, the amount of information about and concern for what went on in the lowest levels of society underwent a measurable and consequential change. The flow of information from the countryside and regulations to it brought many issues—never before of broad concern—into the public mind of France. The contacts with the people involved, above all, the fiscal system; the role played by the *taille, gabelle, corvée*, militia service, and such was under close scrutiny by intendants and subdelegates, often called upon to grant changes and exemptions. In addition, required militia service had been created in 1688 and was extended into the cities in 1740. Theoretically, mandatory public instruction, ordered by Louis XIV in 1698, remained a goal of the government and moved on at an increased pace under church guidance. With the expulsion of the Jesuits in 1763 the problem of education occupied a significant part of the intellectual agenda. Reform of public feast days, first ordered systematically in 1666, remained source of concern, debate, and speculation.[25] The treatment of poverty and illness, the reform of the system of *hôpitaux*, the need to discriminate among rising numbers of "able-bodied" and "true" poor, drew thousands of Frenchmen into heated debate and speculation, both cruel and humane.[26] The will and ability to govern, in a broad administrative sense, brought expanded contacts, more information, more imaginative solutions, and above all, a more sophisticated sense of the people, its life and needs. Knowledge of the people came, in part, simply from experience of the people—viewed, of course, administratively from above.

This attitude of *police* was hardly confined to France. In Germany and Austria it was called "Cameralist science" and became a formal subject of study for those entering the bureaucracies of central Europe.[27] In Great Britain the study of administration was not so formalized, but the realities of *police* were not much different. The problem of growing numbers of poor occupied the best minds—administrative and literary—of England; regulation and attempted reform of life in London grew measurably.[28] Adam Smith could thus attempt to domesticate the word *police* into English parlance with no sense of disparity.[29]

The educational offensive in France also had correlates in most areas of Europe. Public instruction in Scotland, though official policy since 1560, received its most significant impetus only after 1696.[30] Frederick II of Prussia and Maria Theresa also moved toward universal instruction in the basic three R's.[31] England was something of an anomaly, since its literacy revolution—impelled by Puritanism and economic success—had already completed its first major strides. Though that nation did not lack certain new ventures, such as the Charity Schools, the eighteenth century saw an ebbing off of enthusiasm for public instruction and even, perhaps, a retrenchment.[32] Still, she did not lack the debates—endemic on the continent—which accompanied this educational offensive: Should the people be instructed at all? If so, who has that responsibility? How much, in the end, is the people capable of learning and in what form?[33]

The administrative state, therefore, perceived the people as an identifiable economic entity in a way that it had not done before. The sense of public power (as well as private rights) broadened in the eighteenth-century discussions over the proper goals of the state. In all of the debates—from taxes to market structures, from poor law reform to education—the habit of seeing the world in relatively realistic economic and social terms brought the topic of the people and its capabilities into the open. The growth of the administrative mind and its categories can, therefore, help explain the new ways under which the people was defined; it cannot, though, fully explain the sense of distance and separation which underlies much elite talk about the people. For this sense one must look within the world of the elite and its changing definition of itself and its values.

Popular culture loomed so large in the eighteenth century because it increasingly seemed, in the mind of the elite, to stand over against a newly defined, broadly based set of values which came to be called "Enlightenment." By a process whose history has not yet fully been written, the premises of Baroque elite culture—piety, honor, privilege, blood, ritual, magic, symbolic politics—gave way to an Enlightenment culture premised on gentility, moderation, leisure, secularism, toleration, and education. No doubt, to speak of *an* elite culture as if it were shared by all those above the people is to simplify greatly. I use the phrase as shorthand to indicate that in the eighteenth century a linked family of "microaristocracies"—nobility (especially those with urban connections), urban aristocracy, *rentiers*, merchants, administrators, professionals, men of letters—moved substantially toward values strikingly different from those of a century previous.[34] As individuals and groups this elite family shared in these values in differing degrees. Few were as critical of belief as Holbach, but a substantial number adhered to a decisive moderation in the style of Reformation and Counter-Reformation religiosity. Few adhered as rigidly as Condorcet to the strict empirical view of the world, but substantial numbers participated in a broadening interest in all things scientific. Hence, though we cannot claim that there was an easily definable elite with a clear set of ideas shared by all, we can say that the center of gravity of the family of elites was moving in a direction of which the Enlightenment of the philosophes was the most radical and striking manifestation.

This elite mentality was moving toward a culture of ease presupposing wealth, leisure, and education. Its advocates, from Joseph Addison to Charles Duclos, defined the new genteel style both positively and negatively. In a positive sense the "discreet man," or *honnête homme*, represented moderation, reasonableness, worldliness, empirical common sense, sociability, taste; in a negative sense, he represented withdrawal from a style of thinking and living, often viciously stereotyped, which was perceived as "vulgar" or "popular." Moralists like Duclos commonly linked the very great and the very lowly as excluded from the new values of moderation. The great, who by their rank ought to give the example to society, have too little respect for principles to do so; the poor, he continued, have no education, hence no ability to form self-conscious principles; probity, he concluded, finds fruitful ground only in the middle orders.[35]

The transformation in manners and values depended on several converging phenomena. The suppression of overt violence was a political fact before it became a moralist's program. In the course of the previous century the state had, in large measure, succeeded in gaining that monopoly on violence necessary for its survival and coherence through outright repression (e.g., the Tudor campaign against livery and maintenance, Richelieu's plan to weaken the highest nobility), co-option (the drawing of the nobility to court, political spoils, military service, bureaucracy), and circumvention (the time-honored techniques of creation of new forms of administration and nobility). The aristocratic sense of superiority through the possibility of independent violence disappeared with realities of royal control; the political history of the sixteenth and seventeenth centuries, together with the increasing social and cultural power of those outside the high nobility, brought general discredit to the warrior ethic and old noble forms of "superiority of blood." Voltaire could honestly profess to prefer the ethic of the warrior hero to that of the timid Christian, but he was much more at home in the stock exchange, the salon, and the boudoir. The sword now became a decorative ornament at the side of the gentleman.[36] The duel—once the symbolic mark of the possession of honor and the power to avenge it—withdrew into the army as its frequency declined.[37] War itself diminished in scope and violence on the continent, displaced mainly to the colonies overseas. Even nature's more overt forms of violence—the *mortalités*—declined after the last waves of the early eighteenth century. The suppression of aristocratic violence and the felicitous easing of natural violence also allowed governments to approach popular violence with greater surety and determination. Popular violence rarely succeeded on its own and had reached threatening proportions only when accompanied by aristocratic *frondeurs*. The eighteenth-century mob, for all its frequency, did not confront government and society as had uncontrollable popular crusaders of the Middle Ages, the peasant uprisings of the Reformation, or the London mobs of the Puritan revolution.[38]

The early eighteenth century also witnessed a reaction against a mental style broadly labeled "enthusiasm." The excesses of the sixteenth and seventeenth century—symbolized in the minds of many by the failure of the Puritan regime and the violence of the Revocation of the Edict of Nantes, and kept alive by the spates of religious revival in the form of English Methodism, the convulsionaries of Saint-Médard, the followers of the Great Awakening—dictated a withdrawal from its more open forms. Religiosity did not die, but the forms of religiosity which brought passion and violence were generally frowned upon, both within and without the community of believers. Bossuet's easy and deceptive sense that the poor were the true images of Christ gave way to general distrust of popular religiosity. With a measure both of realism and wishful thinking, "enthusiasm" and "superstition" became identified with the popular mind. As an ideal type, the sociable man of the eighteenth century believed, but not too much and never in a way that might seem indecorous, intolerant, or subversive of order. The emergence and growth of Freemasonry in the eighteenth century symbolizes the change in mood. Freemasonry offered religiosity, ceremony, and mysteries without the dangers of enthusiastic piety. It presupposed a syncretism of beliefs with no unique claims to salvation. And it offered a form of religious sociability which, unlike traditional Christian dogma and ceremonies, required no symbolic or social identification with the enthusiastic "wretched of the earth."[39] Indeed, in a broader sense, deism in its many varieties presupposed social-intellectual division—an educated elite capable of appreciating a purified concept of God opposed to the masses, who required elaborate ritual, visual provocation, fiery preaching, impressive miracles, and the fear of a vengeful deity.[40]

Lastly, and perhaps of greatest importance, this new direction presupposed a broad and growing amount of educational sociability. The eighteenth-century elite harvested the fruits of two centuries of educational growth, expanding literacy, multiplying academies, widened access to books, popularizing journals, more secure travel, and greater professional demands for knowledgeability. Broadened education encouraged, especially in urban Europe, a sense of common goals and intellectual experience. Though Addison and Steele could not be exactly duplicated elsewhere, the cult of letters, travel, fashion, popular science, and genteel manners had its correlates in much of Europe west of the Elbe. Scores of journals brought both specialized scientific and economic information and generalized Addisonian moralism to readers across the Continent. In treatment of manners and values, the bonds of blood ceased to have as much meaning as the bonds of leisure and literacy. The story of Edinburgh in the early eighteenth century is a paradigm of educational sociability in the urban world of the Enlightenment: the proliferation of clubs and societies uniting men who had in common their literacy and their being above the laborer in status; the reorganization of the College into a secular, practical educational instrument for the middle classes; the spread in popularity of the *Tatler, Spectator, Spectator of the North,* and other tone-setting journals.[41] These kinds of institutions nurtured that sense of common bonds in a secular intellectual world that underwrote the culture we call the Enlightenment.

Broadened literacy acted as a sealant between elite and popular minds. Urban literacy had spread in such a way that, by the late eighteenth century, it appears to have reached the boundary between laborer and master. One tends to assume that changes such as the spread of literacy work gradually and surely from top to bottom. But it appears that by the late eighteenth century, literacy was reaching a structural blockage in the society of the old regime. Those with the leisure to master sophisticated literacy had, by that time, the institutions and materials to do so. Those whose labor limited time for schooling and access to printed materials had mastered the very rudimentary skills of which they were capable. Though the line was by no means neat, literacy of the sophistication that would allow one to read the *Spectator* or the *Encyclopédie* with some ease seems to have been denied those who depended on labor.[42] Those who argued that to open literacy to the working orders might make them unfit for labor wasted their energy, since mass literacy beyond existing levels probably was impossible without the technological change of industrialism. The division between literate elite and illiterate (or semiliterate) people seems inevitable in the confines of the early-modern commercial, but preindustrial economy.

Everywhere the sense of this division is apparent. In the design of educational systems virtually everyone, from the ministers of Maria Theresa to Herder to Charity School Reformers, assumed the need for a two-class structure—elementary instruction in the three R's for the people, with few further outlets; secondary education with numerous further outlets for the elite.[43] Voltaire could speak of the difference between the prosperous urban master artisan who had access to *lumières* as opposed to the worker whose culture would "always" remain confined to the mass and the tavern as a matter of course which everyone would understand. He worried a great deal about what one could *say* in front of the servants but did not hesitate to *write* about forbidden things; he knew they would not read what he wrote. Almost as a matter of course men of letters insisted that the people would have to be spoken to in the language of images and emotions, as opposed to the literate, who had access to "concepts" engendered by sophisticated literacy.

The city of Strasbourg provides an interesting test of the reality of the divisions which literacy emphasized. After being taken over by the French in 1681, the city became linguistically divided, not around lines of acceptance or resistance, but around lines of class and literacy. Those of the master-artisan level and above generally adopted French; those below remained German in speech. The seizure was an accidental but telling litmus test of literacy; literacy proved, in turn, a test of class.[44]

Against this horizon of suppressed violence, opposition to enthusiasm, and broad educational sociability, the elite culture of the eighteenth century was formed. Gentility was its hallmark, withdrawal from the "vulgar" its social animus. Genteel culture attempted to isolate extremes—violent passions, susceptibility to unreason, blood sports, ignorance, superstition, enthusiasm, unquestioning allegiance to tradition, and the like—and identify them with the lower orders, what the French called *peuple*. The cult of the genteel, reasonable, discreet man presupposed his isolation from other forms of action, which now became identified with older ways consigned to the lowest orders.

The forms of amusement offered a dramatic testing ground for a deepening sense of division. Church rituals, village customs, and urban festivities had traditionally provided a regular meeting place of high and low. Seventeenth-century Puritans and mercantilists had attacked popular festivity as spiritually degrading and economically wasteful, but attempts to reform general manners proved, on the whole, unsuccessful.[45] The eighteenth century picked up these attacks, adopted many of the same arguments, but broadened them with a widening cult of gentility and a new variety of elite amusement.[46] Travel, coaching, letter-writing, Freemasonry, theater, gardening, vase-collecting, dog-breeding, museum-going, *fêtes galantes*—the forms of elite culture varied as they expanded, successfully competing with (if not entirely displacing) the more violent and lusty forms of amusement of the pregenteel age. Cockfighting and boxing survived, but even here only over the protests of many; most violent amusements were subjected to increased police and even their first rules.[47]

The people came to represent a world beyond the realm of polish, manners, and taste as well as *lumières*. The increase in accessibility of cheap liquor, coupled with rising urban population, gave some objective substance to the change in values and perceptions. The tavern loomed increasingly as the symbol of a separate, popular world of amusement.[48] Much of the sense of separation, however, was predictably self-fulfilling. The marketing of cheap liquor helped produce the popular drunkenness and "antisocial" behavior the elite then scorned. The cult of gentility required larger numbers of *decrotteurs* to wipe one's shoes, chairmen to carry one through the streets, torchbearers to light the path, servants to empty the waste, prostitutes to satisfy one's lusts discreetly. This in turn underscored the range of associations of the people as dwellers in the realm of the unrefined, the undignified, and the passive.

Follow James Boswell, a young gentleman of high birth, through the streets and society of London in the early 1760's; one finds in him associations and attitudes which, though not without precedent in various places, ranks, and times, are remarkable in their consistency and pervasiveness. As he embarks for London, feeling quite sprightly, chairmen bow and seem to say, "God prosper long our noble Boswell." He worries about his propensity toward what "the cool part of mankind" have named "superstition," though he ascribes this yen to his "genius for poetry." He reflects how a "person of small fortune who has only the common views of life" cannot appreciate London; rather, enjoyment of its sights and sounds belongs to the person of "imagination and feeling, such as the *Spectator* finely describes." Seeing Scottish soldiers reviled by the English, he scorns in turn the terrible "rudeness of the English vulgar," their "liberty of bullying and being abusive with their bullying and blackguard tongues." He analyzes with some amusement his friend's maid: "She is indeed one of the stupidest human beings that I have ever met with. She has not, as the philosophers say, the *anima rationalis* in a great degree, but she rather has a kind of instinct by which she is actuated, by which however, she goes on pretty well. She is very careful and diligent, and extremely good-natured and disposed to oblige, and, as she is ugly, her head is not taken off from her business." He discusses the merits of the poet Gray, bringing this exchange:

> BOSWELL: Well, I admire Gray prodigiously, I have read his odes till I was almost mad.
> GOLDSMITH: They are terribly obscure. We must be historians and learned men before we can understand them.
> DAVIES: And why not: He is not writing to porters and carmen. He is writing to men of knowledge.

Reflection on his hairdresser's manners leads to the conclusion that he is typical of his profession: he became "genteel" and "chatty" by associating so much with gentlemen. After a sober winter brought about by venereal disease, he enjoys "high debauchery," distinguished from "low debauchery" by its ceremonies and company. Other times he chooses to be a blackguard, dressed in the poorest clothes he can find in his wardrobe, and goes where he usually finds his sexual pleasure, among the whores of London. And throughout his acquaintance with

Johnson, they debate—sometimes naïvely, sometimes perceptively—the nature of poverty and its psychological effects, never for once doubting the great fact and necessity of subordination.[49]

Some of this is just Boswell, some just aristocratic tradition. But Boswell is typical of a society and an age which had developed a sense of separation of genteel from low mentality and had fixed a broad range of associations—ignorance, superstition, sensuality, inferiority, violence, credulity, passivity—with the mind of the people. The signs of this sensitivity and its importance to the elite's definition of itself are everywhere, though historians have never recognized it as a problem or an important structure in the eighteenth-century mind. A few instances: In answering the question asked by the *Berlinische Monatsschrift,* Moses Mendelssohn begins with a distinction. "The words *Aufklärung, Kultur, Bildung* are still newcomers to our language. They apparently belong to literary language [*Büchersprache*]. The people [*gemeine Haufe*] hardly understand them."[50] In outlining his philosophy, the aesthetician Abbé Du Bos felt compelled to make an initial distinction between *public* and *peuple,* the former being the only category of relevance in matters of taste. And in general those who sought to define taste in the eighteenth century assumed that it was, in part, a matter of class and consequent access to the kinds of literacy and travel that could make one a connoisseur.[51] (The word *connoisseur* itself is an eighteenth-century coinage.) In examining the forms of sociability in eighteenth-century Provence the modern historian Maurice Agulhon has discovered a significant shift in importance of participation from religious *confréries,* which were Roman Catholic, regional, public, and democratic, to Masonic lodges, which were deistic, cosmopolitan, private, and socially exclusive within the urban oligarchies.[52] And in his recent study of wills in eighteenth-century Marseilles and surrounding regions, Michel Vovelle has discovered a shift from gifts to symbolic poor (as a means of salvation) to provisions for the institutions designed to give full relief to increasingly urgent and perceived social problems of mendicity—proof of what Vovelle rightly considers a significant change in perceiving the poor.[53] Hence, at many levels and in widely differing contexts—the examples could be multiplied almost indefinitely—the changing perception of the people and its condition entered into the mentality of the eighteenth-century elite.

In a paradoxical way, therefore, the eighteenth-century elite created "popular culture" negatively—that is, by a process of elite withdrawal from a different mental world. The philosophes' association of *peuple-grands-église* may serve as a rough but perceptive observation of similar mentalities underlying vast social difference. These groups represented to the philosophes the intellectual "old regime"— those groups for whom blood, magic, belief, and tradition were the significant variables in social thinking. They represented a different mentality from those for whom gentility, science, innovation (even in the crass form of "fashion"), taste, and economic realism governed mental sets. The sociology of the distinction is admittedly crude but not the less real. Probably for the first time since Roman antiquity did the elite consciously define itself in cultural terms opposed to another, supposedly inferior pattern of thinking called "popular."[54] It may seem perverse to argue that perceiving a thing creates it, but surely the growing perception of difference in turn dictated forms of thinking and sociability which underscored and sealed the difference. We may argue that in its self-conscious withdrawal from patterns of belief and behavior a broad eighteenth-century elite divorced itself from the mentality of the people and created two *separate* cultures. For all their sophistication the Neo-Platonic intellectuals of the late Florentine Renaissance shared a number of fundamental assumptions with the village wizard. Louis XIV's and Bossuet's mental sets—blood, tradition, belief, miracles—were, for all their sophistication, the mental sets of the rural laborer. Such was no longer the case with the leaders of eighteenth-century culture, whose values of toleration, cosmopolitanism, innovation, criticism, and empiricism marked a decisive break with the traditional mentality.[55] As a stage in the history of elite culture, therefore, the phenomenon is not without interest and consequence and has yet to be investigated fully.

But the intellectual changes of the eighteenth century have, I think, important implications for the investigator of popular mentalities as well. First of all, one should not dismiss the Enlightenment's own version of the popular mind as pure projection and ideology. No doubt, part of the animus of the modern study of popular culture has been to give the people its historical due, to study it apart from the perceptions of the elite. Emphasis has consequently rested on those patterns of analysis—anthropological, "culture of poverty," class-consciousness—which emphasize separation *and* independence. But perceptiveness is a matter of more or less, and though there is much lacking in the haughty observations of Voltaire or the functional illustrations of the *Encyclopédie*, they are more realistic and useful than the texts of Bossuet's charity sermons of Tacitus's histories. For the most part the observations of the eighteenth-century elite suggest that we should perceive popular culture (though this elite would never have called it a "culture") in comparative and negative terms. Their perceptions suggest that in some fundamental way elite culture was leaving the popular mind behind. In this light, several areas seem worth exploring:

(1) Elite observations insist that the popular mind lacks the critical sense, a phenomenon which philosophes considered new to the period after the Renaissance as a self-conscious intellectual style.[56] The tendency in recent years has been, perhaps, overly democratic, to insist that the magical (or mythopoeic) and critical approaches to organizing the world have equivalent validity. Regardless of whether or not we accept this notion (more often argued in theory than demonstrated in behavior), if we accept that the critical and mythopoeic forms are different, and that the popular mentality of the eighteenth century inclined more toward the latter, then there is need to explore further. Here it seems that literacy and accessibility to the written word are of crucial importance.[57] Perhaps a revealing test of this disjunction might be found in the forms of religiosity: a close analysis of the religious syncretism of the people—which the century called "superstition"—and the religious syncretism of the elite—which the century called "natural religion."[58] Both represent forms of religious eclecticism, but indicate very different forms of mental action: the one random, traditional, cumulative, and unconscious; the other analytical, innovative, reductive, and self-conscious. We need not share the eighteenth-century elite's sense of the superiority of the latter to examine the different styles of thought.

(2) Elite talk about the people broadly assumed that the people had become the repository of the more overt forms of violence and passion. Here, of course, the eighteenth century defined its terms tendentiously. With the perspective of time and democratic sensibility we can choose to see that the suppression of grain riots represented violence every bit as much as the actions of the rioter, that debauch—whether "high" or "low"—is still debauch. But the desire of the upper orders to redefine, repress, ignore, and otherwise channel the common store of human "unreason" is an important juncture in the history of manners and society and could profit from fuller comparative study. The recent studies of Robert Malcolmson of changing forms of English amusement, Edward Shorter of shifts in family sentiment, and Maurice Agulhon of forms of sociability are important inroads to an immensely fruitful area.[59] Insofar as the elite succeeded in its attempted sublimations (and repressions) we may begin to speak of two "cultures" in the fullest sense of the word *culture*.

(3) The notion that the people dwells in the realm of concrete sense experience while the elite withdraws into a realm of abstraction is as old as philosophy itself and hence hard to take as a serious sociological judgment on a particular society. Still the study of linguistic patterns within and differences between social groupings might still be fruitful when measured against standards of concreteness versus abstraction, variety of vocabulary, range and type of vocabulary, types of associations within the vocabulary (scatological, sexual, religious, socially defiant, etc.). It may be of interest to find members of different classes in similar situations—for instance, trial for murder or political defiance—to gauge the differences in language and the implications.[60] The assumption of association of the people with senses and sense-words is so pervasive—from Holbach's sociology of religion to Wordsworth's plan for a new poetry—that it seems worthy of controlled investigation.

(4) Implicitly the elite of the eighteenth century assumed and argued that the mind and world of the people differed from the world of the genteel in the very sense of space and time. Travel, literacy, popularized knowledge, economic growth—all of those parts which combine to form the horizon of the Enlightenment—seem to have

given a self-conscious elite a sense of space and time quite different from its own habits of thought a century previous and from those who had not shared its experience of change, the people. There is a realm of comparison which has largely gone unexplored: the differing sense of political action and efficacy between elite and people; the cosmopolitan ideals of the genteel world versus the more closed, stranger-fearing world of the village; the elite's sense of history and posterity versus the people's sense of tradition and continuity. Such a return to basic categories may seem a bit simple-minded in an age of sophisticated statistical and ethnographic techniques. But a wide-ranging set of comparisons on this order might help clarify just how much popular mentality in the eighteenth century represented defiant rejection of the elite, a mirror at a less sophisticated level of elite values, or—as my analysis would predict—a residue of values left behind by that elite (for better or worse). We may find here significant differences in response at the popular level, in which rural and urban patterns differ markedly. Even within the urban setting, the case of servants seems separate because of continued contact with the upper-class household.

As sociologists, therefore, the elite writers of the eighteenth century offer us a set of crude but suggestive generalizations worth refining and pursuing. Here they acted as men with a new sense of separation, looking across a gulf which seemed remarkably and consequentially wide. But the history of elite perceptions of the people relates to the study of popular culture in another, paradoxical but probably more important way—separation dictated involvement. Elite attitudes did not remain confined to the passive disdain of a Boswell. The French philosophes are a case in point. No one is more quotable on distaste for the masses than Voltaire; yet he, and his fellow philosophes, were most systematic and wide-ranging in their designing of a program to benefit the people. The philosophes shared Boswell's sense of manners, gentility, and separation; but unlike him, their sense of separation moved toward a program. The reasons for their involvement—and they are symptomatic of the whole range of Enlightenment culture—are not hard to find. Their frame of mind was tough-minded and realistic. Even when justifying inequality in society, Voltaire could say merely that society had always been divided between "oppressors" and "oppressed," hardly a comforting notion to those who preferred more elegant titles.[61] More important, their experience with power and authority was fruitfully ambiguous. Most philosophes faced threats from those with political authority. Diderot went to jail; Holbach could not sign his works; Helvétius feared reprisals when he became the object of a clerical crusade. At the same time, the threat of power was muted by their connections with the powers of police and politics in the kingdom. Holbach did not go to the galleys; the peddlar who sold his books did. They were then, as a whole, well-placed to appreciate the uses and abuses of power and feel measured sympathy with others who experienced the full and abusive weight of authority. In addition, the fiscal issues which plagued France after mid-century kept the people in the public mind as an object of concern and debate. The philosophes participated in those administrative debates which made fiscal, economic, and social issues part of the continuous discussion of the elite. A glance at the topics for debate in provincial academies, as well as the topics and style of the *Encyclopédie*, shows a cultural world become increasingly aware of and involved in social issues. The people, and what to do with it, was part of the talk of elite society. The case as not quite so striking elsewhere, but no Western European nation was immune from the problems and solutions of France. From the Academy of Berlin to the Academy of Châlons-sur-Marne, from the world of Sonnenfels to that of Turgot to that of Fielding, the range of issues and solutions is remarkably similar.

The urge to systematic involvement by intellectuals, administrators, academicians, notables, and agitators had significant effect on our knowledge of and the actual substance of popular culture. If nothing else, involvement dictated gathering a wealth of information heretofore unavailable. The kinds of information and observations available to us in the studies of Parliamentary committees, the *Dictionnaire des arts et métiers*, the *Encyclopédie*, the intendants' reports, the studies of local doctors, reports of travellers, the inquiries of local academies and agricultural societies, and dozens of other types of sources are available in a wealth and variety that had not existed before. At work is not just the accident of historical preservation but the will to observe, record, and act on the basis of those observations. If taken together, the wealth of elite perceptions of the people in the eighteenth century should provide an immense and valuable record. To be sure, they are just perceptions, and we must balance them against popular perceptions (not necessarily more accurate), statistical studies, and our sense of the relative blindness and perceptiveness of the eighteenth-century observer. If nothing else, then, the sophisticated study of elite perceptions of popular culture could provide a valuable corrective device to measure the value of its record. To ignore or to distrust with undue severity the elite verbal record—and to rely solely on "quantifiable" evidence—would be to pass up a valuable set of observations. At the very least they raise questions which the historian—quantifier or not—must answer.

Perspective and involvement, however, eventually spelled change as well as observation. The conscious sense of distance from the popular mind and life invited active intervention in an unprecedented way. Again the French philosophes provide a good case in point. On perceiving the condition of the people, they began to advocate programs to change that condition—weaning the people from "superstition," providing the people with basic skills of reading and computation, giving the people psychological ease by withdrawing its harshest economic burdens and providing some income above the level of subsistence. These suggestions did not pass without debate; the problem of educating the people brought traditional mercantilist fears of an unmanageable and decreasing labor supply. Instructional programs recognized and reinforced social barriers. All proposals for economic reform—especially those involving tax privileges and market structures—faced heavy opposition. Still, the animus of society was interventionist, especially at the level of educating and indoctrinating the people. Popular almanacs evolved away from magic and astrology toward practical advice, less perhaps because of a change in demand than a change in the mind of the supplier.[62] Writers composed catechisms—religious and secular—with a special view toward the needs and mind of the people.[63] Reformers tried to teach the people new habits of amusement. A few even tried to give the people political awareness.

Though hardly without various precedents—the religious manipulation by the Roman Senate, the pamphlets of the Reformation, the preaching of itinerant friars—the consistent, wide-ranging, secularized attempt to mold the mind and actions of the masses dates from the eighteenth century. Insofar as these actions become an important part of popular culture in that and subsequent centuries, the study of elite perceptions of the masses becomes a crucial adjunct to the study of popular culture itself. If one studies those individuals who had impact, great or small, on popular culture since the eighteenth century—philosophical radicals, Owenites, Saint-Simonians, poor-law reformers, anti-Semitic agitators, Leninists—one finds they act with an image of the public mind and its limitations and a sense of the efficacy of intervention which is basically still eighteenth-century. Their perceptions were not always sophisticated or accurate, but they had a curious and important habit of coming true. Indeed, part of the tragedy of subsequent history is the capacity of certain elite perceptions of the masses to become self-fulfilling. The notion that the masses respond to what is violent, passionate, dramatic, primitive, warlike—a perception which dictated to eighteenth-century reformers a desire to tame and educate—became, in a time of increasingly democratic politics, a rationale for imperialism, Caesarism, anti-Semitism, and other forms of political violence. The study of elite perceptions of and interactions with the popular mind may, therefore, not only broaden our understanding of that difficult notion "popular culture," but also help us to understand a process vital to the quality of life in any nation and any time.

NOTES

1 There is a small but growing literature on elite perceptions of the people in the eighteenth century. I have drawn together several major themes relating to the *philosophes* in my book *The Philosophes and the People* (New Haven, 1976). Among the best discussions of the problem are Werner Bahner, "Le Mot et la notion de 'peuple' dans l'oeuvre de Rousseau," *Studies in Voltaire and the Eighteenth Century* (hereafter VS), no. 55 (1967), pp. 113–27; Keith Baker, "Scientism, Elitism, and Liberalism: The Case of Condorcet," VS, no. 55 (1967), pp. 129–65; A. W.

Coats, "Changing Attitudes to Labour in the Mid-Eighteenth Century," *Economic History Review*, 2nd ser., 11 (1958), 35–61; Irvin Ehrenpreis, "Poverty and Poetry; Representations of the Poor in Augustan Literature," *Studies in Eighteenth-Century Culture*, 1 (1971), 3–35; F. G. Healey, "The Enlightenment View of *homo faber*," *VS*, no. 25 (1963), pp. 837–59; Roland Mortier, "Diderot et la notion du 'peuple,'" *Europe*, nos. 405–6 (Jan.–Feb. 1963), pp. 78–88, and "Voltaire et le peuple" in *The Age of the Enlightenment* (London, 1967), pp. 137–51; Karl Weintraub, "Toward the History of the Common Man: Voltaire and Condorcet," in *Ideas in History*, ed. R. Herr (Durham, 1965), pp. 39–64; and the recent collection of essays entitled *Images du peuple au dix-huitième siècle* (Paris, 1973).

2 *Dissertations pour être lues; La première sur le vieux mot de patrie; La seconde, sur la nature du peuple* (The Hague, 1755), pp. 44–45.

3 Closely followed in the *Encyclopédie* (1765), *Le grand vocabulaire françois* (1772), and the *Dictionnaire universel* (1782).

4 On the decline of the jurists, and their mode of perceiving the world, see William F. Church, "The Decline of French Jurists as Political Theorists, 1660–1789," *French Historical Studies*, 5, no. 1 (1967), 1–40; on changing social language in one man's vocabulary, see Roland Mousnier, "D'Aguesseau et le tournant des ordres aux classes sociales," *Revue d'histoire économique et sociale*, 49, no. 4 (1971), 449–64.

5 I have traced these debates at some length in my book, cited in n. 1. For a sample of these types of debates, see Harvey Chisick, "Attitudes toward the Education of the *Peuple* in the French Enlightenment: 1762–1789," Diss. Johns Hopkins 1974, and the collection of prize competition essays in Werner Krauss, ed., *Est-il utile de tromper le peuple? Concours de la classe de philosophie speculative de l'Académie des Sciences et des Belles-Lettres de Berlin pour l'année 1780* (Berlin, 1966).

6 *Considérations sur les moeurs de ce siècle* (1751), in *Oeuvres complètes*, I (Paris, 1820), 109.

7 *De l'instruction publique* (Paris, 1775), pp. 23–24.

8 The best depiction of this new ideal, perhaps a bit more radical than its more common form, is to be found in the clandestine tract *Le philosophe*, the variations of which are available in Herbert Dieckmann, ed., *Le philosophe: Texts and Interpretations* (St. Louis, 1948). For the Addisonian ideal, see Edward and Lilian Bloom, *Joseph Addison's Sociable Animal* (Providence, 1971), and Lee Elioseff, *The Cultural Milieu of Addison's Literary Criticism* (Austin, n.d.). On Wieland see W H. Bruford, *Culture and Society in Classical Weimar* (Cambridge, 1962), pp. 296–97.

9 *Oeuvres complètes*, ed. B. Gagnebin et al., 4 vols. to date (Paris, 1959–), IV, 281.

10 For an excellent history of the reevaluation of the popular mind, see John Gagliardo, *From Pariah to Patroit: The Changing Image of the German Peasant, 1770–1840* (Lexington, 1969).

11 Cf. E. P. Thompson's perception of such "wisdom" in "The Moral Economy of the English Crowd in the Eighteenth Century," *Past and Present*, no. 50 (1971), pp. 76–136.

12 On this sense of passivity, see Asa Briggs, "The Language of Class in Early

13 Nineteenth-Century England," in *Essays in Labour History* (London, 1960), pp. 43-73.
13 *Oeuvres oratoires de Bossuet*, ed. Abbé J. Lébarq (Paris, 1928), III, 135.
14 As cited in Bruford, *Classical Weimar*, p. 114.
15 Bernard Groethuysen, *The Bourgeois* (New York, 1966), pp. 13-14.
16 On the ideology of the *hôpital* and its consequences see Emmanuel Chill, "Religion and Mendicity in Seventeenth-Century France," *International Review of Social History*, 7 (1962), 401-25.
17 See the various "natural histories" of inequality offered during the Enlightenment, such as Rousseau's *Discours sur l'inégalité* (1755); Voltaire's articles "Egalité" and "Maître" in his *Dictionnaire philosophique* (1764); and Turgot's "Lettre à Madame Graffigny" (1751), in *Oeuvres* (Paris, 1912), I, 241-43.
18 See Pierre Goubert, *Beauvais et le Beauvaisis de 1600 à 1730* (Paris, 1959), pp. 270-73; Pierre Deyon, *Amiens au xviiie siècle* (Paris, 1967), ch. 25; Maurice Garden, *Lyon et les Lyonnais au xviiie siècle* (Paris, n.d.), pp. 559-61; Gerald Soliday, *A Community in Conflict: Frankfurt Society in the Seventeenth and Early Eighteenth Centuries* (Hanover, N.H., 1974), pp. 149-51.
19 E. P. Thompson, "The Moral Economy of the English Crowd," pp. 94-95; idem, "Patrician Society, Plebeian Culture," *Journal of Social History*, 7, no. 4 (Summer 1974), 382-405.
20 Carl Bridenbaugh, *Cities in the Wilderness* (New York, 1938), pp. 299, 441; Franklin Ford, *Strasbourg in Transition* (Cambridge, 1958), pp. 181-82.
21 Olwen Hufton, *The Poor of Eighteenth-Century France, 1750-1789* (Oxford, 1974), pp. 14-15.
22 Ian Watt, *The Rise of the Novel* (1957; rpt. Berkeley, 1967), p. 178; on Geneva, see Michel Launay, "Qu'entend-on par 'peuple' à Genève au dix-huitième siècle," in *Images du peuple au dix-huitième siècle*, pp. 56-58.
23 For example, see E. L. Asher, *The Resistance of the Maritime Classes* (Berkeley, 1960), and Pierre de Saint Jacob, *Les Paysans de la Bourgogne du Nord au dernier siècle de l'Ancien Régime* (Paris, 1960).
24 The phrase "enlightened absolutism" is Peter Gay's (*The Enlightenment: An Interpretation*, vol. II, *The Science of Freedom* [New York, 1969], pp. 483-96). It ought to replace the misleading phrase "enlightened despotism."
25 See the article of J. Maarten Ultee, "The Suppression of *Fêtes* in France, 1666," *Catholic Historical Review*, 62 (April 1976), 181-99.
26 Hufton, *The Poor of Eighteenth-Century France*, passim. For a good sense of the general workings of *police* in the countryside, see A. Poitrineau, *La Vie rurale en Basse-Auvergne au XVIIIe siècle* (Paris, 1965), I, 696-717.
27 Albion Small, *The Cameralists* (Chicago, 1909), is still standard. See also the account on Sonnenfels in Robert A. Kann, *A Study in Austrian Intellectual History: From Late Baroque to Romanticism* (New York, 1960). See also the important recent article of Marc Raeff, "The Well-Ordered Police State and the Development of Modernity in Seventeenth- and Eighteenth-Century Europe: An Attempt at a Comparative Approach," *American Historical Review*, 80, no. 3 (Dec. 1975), 1221-43.

28 Watt, *Rise of the Novel*, p. 182; Dorothy M. George, *London Life in the Eighteenth Century* (New York, 1965), "Introduction" et passim.
29 *Lectures on Justice, Police, Revenue, and Arms* (1763), Part II: "Of Police."
30 Lawrence Stone, "Literacy and Education in England, 1640–1900," *Past and Present*, no. 42 (1969), p. 80.
31 On the various schemes for public instruction—a veritable educational offensive which requires a full-scale study—see, e.g., Frederick Hertz, *The Development of the German Public Mind: The Age of Enlightenment* (London, 1962), pp. 296–99, 339–40; Andreas Flitner, *Die politische Erziehung in Deutschland: Geschichte und Probleme, 1750–1880* (Tübingen, 1957), pp. 13–30; Gagliardo, *Pariah to Patriot*, ch. 4; R. J. Shafer, *The Economic Societies in the Spanish World* (Syracuse, 1958), pp. 37–38, 85–89, 95; Franco Venturi, *Italy and the Enlightenment* (New York, 1972), pp. 252–54; Helen Liebel, *Enlightened Bureaucracy versus Enlightened Despotism in Baden, 1750–1792*, in *Transactions of the American Philosophical Society*, 55, part 5 (Philadelphia, 1965), 20, 73–75, 90–92.
32 Stone, "Literacy and Education in England," p. 90; but, as Stone remarks (p. 85), "The genii could not be put back in the bottle."
33 The best account of the various arguments and schemes, fears and hopes, is the unpublished dissertation of Harvey Chisick, cited in n. 5.
34 The term "microaristocracies" is that of Maurice Agulhon, *Pénitents et Francs-Maçons de l'ancienne Provence: Essai sur la sociabilité méridionale* (Paris, 1968), p. 236. The best illustration of the convergence of a varied elite around certain cultural patterns is Louis Trénard, *Lyon: De l'Encyclopédie au Préromantisme*, 2 vols. (Paris, 1958). It is a model of its kind and needs imitation in other urban settings. J. H. Plumb has described the emergence of a new style and scope of genteel amusement in an important essay, "The Public, Literature, and the Arts in the Eighteenth Century," in *The Emergence of Leisure*, ed. M. R. Marrus (New York, 1974), pp. 11–37. His sense that this was a "middle-class" culture emerging between aristocratic and popular cultures, however provocative, needs significant refinement.
35 Duclos, *Oeuvres*, I, 61.
36 Thompson, "Plebeian Culture," p. 389.
37 F. Billacois, "Le Parlement de Paris et les duels au xviie siècle," in *Crimes et criminalité en France sous l'Ancien Régime: 17e–18e siècles* (Paris, 1971), pp. 33–47.
38 Thompson, "Moral Economy"; George Rudé, *Paris and London in the Eighteenth Century* (New York, 1971), passim.
39 On the Masonic ideal and its workings in thought and society see, e.g., Agulhon, *Pénitents et Francs-Maçons*, passim; Trénard, *Lyon*, I, 77–78; Bruford, *Classical Weimar*, pp. 64–65, 233.
40 The idea of a "double truth" pervaded Enlightenment discussions of the social role of religion. See Payne, *The Philosophes and the People*, ch. 5, and Ronald I. Boss, "The Development of Social Religion: A Contradiction of French Free Thought," *Journal of the History of Ideas*, 34, no. 4 (Oct.–Dec. 1973), 577–89.
41 Nicholas Philipson, "Towards a Definition of the Scottish Enlightenment," in *City and Society in the 18th Century*, ed. Paul Fritz and David Williams (Toronto, 1973), pp. 125–48.

42 The barriers of time and money to any significant literacy were great; see Watt, *Rise of the Novel*, pp. 39–43. England was most advanced, and even there, popular literacy was perceived as a political problem only in the 1790's. See R. K. Webb, *The British Working Class Reader* (London, 1955), chs. 1 and 2.
43 For various dual plans, see Payne, *The Philosophes and the People*, ch. 6.
44 Ford, *Strasbourg*, p. 192.
45 See Ultee, "Suppression of *Fêtes* in France"; R. W. Malcolmson, *Popular Recreations in English Society, 1700–1850* (Cambridge, 1973), ch. 1.
46 The picture is remarkably general over the range of European and American culture. See Plumb, "The Public, Literature, and the Arts"; Ford, *Strasbourg*, pp. 173–76; A. S. Turberville, ed., *Johnson's England*, 2 vols. (Oxford, 1933), esp. the chs. "Manners, Meals, and Domestic Pastimes," "Sports and Games," and "Taste"; Bridenbaugh, *Wilderness*, pp. 411–18, and idem, *Cities in Revolt* (New York, 1955), ch. 9; Maurice Agulhon, *La Sociabilité méridionale* (Aix-en-Provence, 1966), I, 424–34. The attack on the number of feast days without work continued strong in France into the eighteenth century among the philosophes.
47 See Turberville, *Johnson's England*, I, 376, on the first rules for prizefighting.
48 Bridenbaugh, *Wilderness*, pp. 265–74, 434–35; Albert Soboul, *La Civilisation et la révolution française*, I (Paris, 1970), 433; George, *London*, pp. 273–75, 290–305.
49 *Boswell's London Journal, 1762–1763*, ed. Frederick Pottle (New York, 1950), pp. 41–42, 68, 72, 86, 106, 198–99, 264 (and note), 272–73.
50 *Berlinische Monatsschrift*, 4 (Sept. 1884), 193, reproduced in J. Zehbe, ed., *Immanuel Kant: Was ist Aufklärung: Aufsätze zur Geschichte und Philosophie* (Gottingen, 1967), p. 129.
51 Rémy Saisselin, *The Rule of Reason and the Ruses of the Heart* (Cleveland, 1970), pp. 171–75, 194.
52 Agulhon, *Pénitents et Francs-Maçons*, p. 206.
53 Michel Vovelle, *Piété baroque et déchristianisation en Provence au XVIIIe siècle* (Paris, 1973), Part 1, ch. 6.
54 On the way classical rhetoric tended to stereotype and set apart the lower orders, see Erich Auerbach, *Mimesis* (Princeton, 1945), ch. 2. For similar reasons their inheritors, the Augustan poets, had similar difficulties; see Ehrenpreis, "Poverty and Poetry." Cf. Ian Watt's observation that the novel—a specifically eighteenth-century creation—was well suited to depict the people, in *Rise of the Novel*, pp. 102–4.
55 Cf. André Varagnac's remarks on elite withdrawal from traditional "folkways": "La nature scientifique acquise peu à peu par la culture des classes dirigeantes depuis la Renaissance a eu pour effet de restreindre progressivement au peuple des campagnes l'usage d'une culture principalement traditionelle" (*Civilisation traditionelle et genres de vie* [Paris, 1948], pp. 39–40). This viewpoint has also been advanced—after the first publication of this essay—independently by Eugen Weber, in *Peasants into Frenchmen* (Stanford, 1976), pp. 495–96.
56 On the critical mentality as the key to what was new in that era, see Gay, *Enlightenment*, vol. 1, passim. On the contribution of printing (and hence literacy) to criticism in a broader sense, see the article of Elizabeth Eisenstein, "Some

Conjectures about the Impact of Printing on Western Society and Thought: A Preliminary Report," *Journal of Modern History* (1968), pp. 1–56.

57 On literacy as a crucial instrument in this process, see Eisenstein, "Some Conjectures," and esp. the Introduction by Jack Goody and the essay "The Consequences of Literacy" by Goody and Ian Watt in Jack Goody, ed., *Literacy in Traditional Societies* (Cambridge, 1968).

58 On the religious "syncretism" of the Parisian people, see Jeffry Kaplow, *The Names of Kings* (New York, 1972), ch. 5.

59 Malcolmson, *Popular Recreations;* Edward Shorter, "Différences de classe et sentiment depuis 1750; L'Exemple de France," *Annales,* 29, no. 4 (July–Aug. 1974), 1034–57; Agulhon, *La Sociabilité mériodionale.*

60 Writers quite sympathetic to the people still notice that its vocabulary and images run in peculiar sensual-concrete patterns; e.g., Kaplow, *Names of Kings,* p. 107. Yves Castan has used such sources to examine rural and urban mentalities in "Mentalités rurales et urbaines à la fin de l'Ancien Régime dans le ressort du Parlement de Toulouse d'après les sacs à procès criminels (1730–1790)," in *Crimes et criminalité en France,* pp. 109–86.

61 "Egalité," *Dictionnaire philosophique* (1764).

62 See esp. the work of Geneviève Bollème: "Littérature populaire et littérature de colportage au 18e siècle," in *Livre et société dans la France du XVIIIe siècle* (Paris, 1965), and *Les Almanachs populaires aux XVIIe et XVIIIe siècles* (Paris, 1969). D'Alembert noted this phenomenon as early as 1751 in his article "Almanach" for the *Encyclopédie.*

63 E.g., Bollème, *Almanachs;* André Bourde, *Agronomie et agronomes en France au XVIIIe siècle,* 3 vols. (Paris, 1966), II, 985–87, 1058–59; Flitner, *Politische Erziehung,* pp. 26–28; Venturi, *Italy and the Enlightenment,* p. 253; M. G. Jones, *The Charity School Movement in the Eighteenth Century,* ch. 3. A characteristic piece, recommended very favorably by Diderot for Catherine the Great's schools, is Jacques Barbeu-Dubourg's *Petit Code de la raison humaine* (1774).

The World between the Literate and Oral Traditions in Eighteenth-Century France: Ecclesiastical Instructions and Popular Mentalities

HARVEY MITCHELL

The study of what is termed "popular religion" during the ancien régime in France, particularly in the eighteenth century, is hardly a new venture. More than one generation separates us from the work of Gabriel Le Bras and his followers, whose studies in religious sociology recognized the need to call on the assistance of investigators in many neighboring domains. Almost at the same time, the study of popular culture, under which popular religion can be subsumed, was being altered by the readiness with which historians, following Lucien Febvre, assimilated, though not uncritically, the perceptions and sometimes the models and style of anthropologists, sociologists, ethnologists, and psychologists. In turn, the latter have become more aware of the temporal dimensions of the materials they observe and study. Scholars are consequently more confident in expressing dissatisfaction with the distinctions that were made and are sometimes still made between "authentic" religious actions and belief and those that are consigned to a world in which large sectors of humanity practiced and believed in something called "magic," which by its very definition was assumed to be an inferior stage in human intelligence. Similarly, they are trying to avoid the traditional demarcations between rational and irrational modes of thought, and more subtly to differentiate between the rationality of magic and the rationality of science. They are also having some success in dealing with the coexistence of the literate, semiliterate, and oral worlds. Their questioning of the dyads of primitive/advanced, traditional/modern, and static/dynamic arises from the uneasiness stemming from models that split the world so artificially and so neatly. More consciously and deliberately than before, they are exploring the scope and nature of the links within a single society between dissimilar cultures and mentalities. They are not only insisting on the internal integrity of belief systems, but are challenging the notion that creativity in religious forms is the monopoly of one group within the totality of a complex society. Historians who are concerned with explanations for continuity and change, as well as resistance to change, are particularly sensitive to the nonreducible elements of individual and social behavior and are proving to be reliable guides in the study of religion.[1]

The definition or the problem of the definition of popular religion is far from straightforward or free from ambivalence. This is not the place, however, to undertake either an epistemological or a phenomenological analysis. The goals of the present study can be more effectively served by focusing on a few questions which occur to everyone who seeks to understand the social dynamics of dominant and subordinate groups and the nature of the belief systems and practices that to some degree help to maintain their separate existences. What are the manifestations of popular religion? What are its relationships with other domains of belief and practice? Who notes them and thereby appears to establish their contours, magnifying some of them and distorting others? The sources most accessible to us are the perceptions of those who, in describing and analyzing expressions of the popular mind, were impelled to single out those of its features considered to be resistant and threatening to themselves, the dominant and powerful groups in society. In short, we are in part reliant on the "they" to tell us of the "others." What the "they" can tell us about the "others" is, however, not to be discounted entirely, for even if this reveals much about the first, it is possible to delve beneath the assumptions of the first to the clues about the second. Apart from this particular process of definition, the nonélite groups in society define themselves, both in their material and spiritual beings, in a great variety of ways, all of which constitute the total fact of their existence. As Evans-Pritchard puts it, "We have to account for religious facts in terms of the totality of the culture and society in which they are found, to try to understand them in terms of what the *Gestalt* psychologists called the *Kulturganze*, or of what Mauss called *fait total*. They must be seen as a relation of parts to one another within a coherent system, each part making sense only in relation to other institutional systems, as part of a wider set of relations."[2] This formulation of the problem is close to that of Bernard Plongeron, who speaks of the need to root the religious fact of man's beliefs, rituals, and practices in his social setting.[3]

A recent *profession de foi*, by the French medievalist Jean-Claude Schmitt, makes many of the same points. Impatient with the lack of precision of Gabriel Le Bras and Etienne Delaruelle in their treatment and definition of popular religion, he defiantly states that he will avoid "popular religion" as an ambiguous term, since there exists no heuristic advantage in the demarcation of what is supposedly popular from what is supposedly official religion. He promises instead to pursue a rigorous and precise classification of social classes as they come into contact with one another, and in referring to the fragile and marginal nature of man's productive forces, closely linking him to nature, he defines religion "in the large sense" as a system of understanding the world and of "symbolic action upon it." To this end, he offers a general statement according to which officialdom, holding the power to determine religious forms, acts to legitimize established social forms. There is merit in eschewing the customary uses of social vocabulary—in this case, "popular religion"—since it capsulates and codifies a range of attitudes, past and present, concealing the very fact that demands explanation. The determination to give explicit form to the social classes under examination is similarly a step forward, meaning, within Schmitt's specialized area of study, the functioning of medieval society. The last point in his agenda may, unless care is shown, lead to a new or revived version of infra- and superstructures. Nevertheless, Schmitt's purpose is clear: he wishes to link his work as a historian to his theory, rather than become the victim of "unconscious presuppositions and the... hazards of [his] research."[4] There is indeed every expectation that his awareness of religion as an autonomous fact will preclude him from treating it as mere ideology.

At this point, some comments must be made about the functional approach to the history and sociology of religion, since it has a certain kinship with traditional Marxist views. Briefly, the functionalists, following Durkheim, analyze the religious experience as an expression of its power to preserve social unity.[5] Writers from the earliest times to the present have singled out religion as an incomparable force in reinforcing social order. Introducing the subject of religion in his *Traité de la Police*, La Mare ventured in the seventeenth century that political stability would be assured if there were a perfect correspondence between political and religious institutions.[6] As we move to anthropological observations of religion's role in specific communities, we become aware of how certain forms of religious experience can ease social tension and social conflict. The anthropological literature from which Keith Thomas, to cite one recent example, has borrowed and which he has applied to such remarkable effect, has been of much value. But he isolates the religious component in the magico-religious constellation, using it as a term explanatory of the central cosmology of the church.[7] He then proceeds to endow it with attributes of modern rationality and ultimate superiority in its struggle with the practice of magic, which he claims retained its efficacy for fewer and fewer people. Magic is consequently seen as performing fewer socially valid functions than religion; the first is restricting, while the second is expansive; the first is in a sense tribal, and in contrast, the second widens individual opportunity for action in a changing world.[8]

If I may borrow an example from another area of studies which at first glance is unconnected with the history of religion, the limitations of Thomas's approach may become more apparent. The eighteenth-century medical philosophy of the nonnaturals isolated such exogenous factors as nutrition, air, rest and motion, sleep and wakefulness, evacuation and retention, and the soul's passions as contributing to health or disease. They were believed to be within the control of the individual, who could manage his own health,[9] or in collaboration with the physician, who, within the general practice of bedside medicine, permitted the patient to determine the particular interrelatedness of his own psyche and soma.[10] The theory rested on a spirit of voluntarism consonant with bourgeois, individual ideals and practices, and demanded literacy and a particular concern for the body, absent among rural and urban masses. We may see that it corresponds to the notion that, with the widening of human choices, appeals to and reliance on practices deemed nonutilitarian will fall into desuetude. The trouble with this reasoning is that it supposes an increasing number of choices that serve the functions of both the individual and society with greater efficiency. In his uses of the functional approach, Thomas is giving primacy to those expressions of religious belief and ritual that seemingly assist the individual to find his place in a technologically evolving society. To be sure, he admits that magical healing and allied practices can offer remedies and suggest measures for very specific human problems, but these seem to be of a somewhat lower order. In short, Thomas's approach divides the religious experience into two categories, one serving rational, the other serving irrational, functions.

The relatively late efforts to expand a central Christian cosmology, whether in Catholic or Protestant Europe, served to single out alternative beliefs for attack much more systematically than before, either in their residual state or in their more vital forms, often unintentionally revitalizing them before submerging them forever, or at least forcing them to go underground until they were able to resurface in changed garb in answer to new sources of social conflict. Such religious forms may be said to be innovative or even revolutionary, and therefore hardly integrative. To be meaningful, a functional approach must not be limited to the exploration of how religion over time becomes a socially cohesive force according to so-called rational standards of behavior. According to such a viewpoint, the religious and social springs of behavior would be identical, locked together in an unchanging and perfect balance. Such an outlook is in addition unhistorical. To be productive, the historian who employs the functional approach must take special care to acknowledge the vitality of religious beliefs for people who do not conform to élitist views of how the material and spiritual worlds are ordered.[11]

Discrete areas of human experience can be treated sympathetically without the compulsion of mistaken sentimentality provoked by reaction against ethnocentrism; with an awareness of what was truly distinct about them and, if possible, why; and without being misled by a spurious necessity to create false equivalences between them. What the study of popular religion demands is some acknowledgment that the lines between it and its officially sanctioned variants wavered, and that these may be studied in terms of how multiple activities, however generated and by whomever, divide groups, or bring them together and energize them. We will want to avoid explanations that see one set of actors initiating actions and another set responding to them. In the area of popular religion as in related questions, it is far more realistic to think of a dynamic process of uninterrupted encounters over time among various groups in society, unequally distributed in space, in relationship to material resources, and in possession of varying solutions, including the religious, to life's problems.

The study of contacts in the eighteenth century between the literate culture of the church and its servants and the semiliterate and oral culture of the laity, without further distinction at the moment, is but one aspect of the larger problems we have been discussing up to this point. The crucial nature of this period in the history of France has never been in doubt since the Revolution. Now that it is being treated not only as the antechamber to that event, historians have been struck by the conscious impulse in all sections of the enlightened community, in private groups as well as within the administrative hierarchy of the state, in *philosophe* and *anti-philosophe* circles, and within the very precincts of the church, to distinguish themselves from the lower orders, yet at the same time to seek the means and generate the resources to manage their forms of behavior. What I shall be examining in the balance of this paper is the interaction between the professed goals of the church hierarchy, the clergy themselves, and the large masses of Frenchmen, whose responses sometimes met the expectations of their religious superiors and at other times startled them by shrewd and innovative adjustments.

Certain points require immediate clarification. Perhaps the most important is that, even within cultures that are said to be largely literate, the spoken word continued to enjoy a significant role; and in our period, speech was immeasurably more important. At the same time, the existence of the written word directly and indirectly affected the lives of people whose acquisition of literate skills was minimal or nonexistent. Although literacy was of course limited, no community, however much it lived on its own, was unaware of the existence in its own bosom and outside it of the products of a literate culture. People who are semiliterate or nonliterate are likely to approach the products of the book in an apprehensive or anticipatory manner, seeking answers to the ineffable, the mysterious, the refractory aspects of life, particularly if the possessors of the secrets are endowed with spiritual power. Their attitude is selective, rather than comprehensive, shaping what they need and desire to specific ends, often creatively transforming the elements thus absorbed.[12] In the opposite direction, the products of an oral culture are subject to a process of selection, which removes from them those elements considered to be unsuitable for refined taste. How these are then returned to their presumably original loci and how they are then dealt with is a problem that has not yet been fully solved.[13] We are in the present case therefore not dealing with two totally distinct cultures. Yet the groups that are loosely arranged along a spectrum from literate to nonliterate over time evolve perceptions of the "others," not only in relationship to the means of communicating the products of cultural inheritance, but as part of the larger demands of the material environment. Thus there is an advantage in not rejecting totally such distinctions between the literate and semi- and nonliterate cultures as will enable us to establish how the religious fact was mediated in both directions. Here I would like to note the work of Professors Goody and Watt, who have proposed that writing objectifies past human experience, enabling literate men to distinguish between "myth" and "history," in contrast with men who rely only on oral communication and are consequently more rooted in "the particularities of persons, place and time."[14] While the distinction may be valid in a global sense, it requires an important qualification within the context of the present study, as will soon be evident.

The place of religion in the literate and oral traditions demands some attention to three considerations. The first of these is the degree of intellectual attainment of the parish clergy. Next, a sampling of the ecclesiastical literature in the form of guides for the clergy will be made to ascertain what may have been a likely form of discourse between them and their parishioners. Thirdly, some consideration will be given to literacy levels in small communities, or, more precisely, to the availability of education for the *classes populaires* and the nature of the religious reading materials to which they had recourse. From these explorations, the relationship between literate and semi- and nonliterate cultures, the meaning of the religious fact for each, and the more difficult question of how the symbols and powers of clerical orthodoxy were employed to weaken or to tame competing belief systems may be brought into sharper focus.

One may question Certeau's serious underestimation of the conflicts between the clergy and the laity in pre-Reformation Europe. One may consequently also dispute the wide sweep of his contention that a dramatic reversal in the reciprocal roles of society and religious truth occurred in the seventeenth century in dramatic response to the successes of Protestantism. Presumably before this mutation, religion dictated the nature of society, while after, religion became an ideological superstructure, its chief purpose being to act as an integrative social force, determining membership and excluding deviants, religious or secular. One need not accept Certeau's implicit contrast between these two periods in the history of Christianity, however, to agree with him that post-Tridentine Catholicism moved quite consciously in the direction of establishing intellectual criteria to keep pace with the expansion of knowledge, to create, in short, a science of religion, the better to maintain its own coherence, ensure its doctrinal hegemony, and contribute to the maintenance of social order.[15] Religion, like science, became a discipline and, like science, was divided into subgroups for the study of its own history and for that of competing beliefs, religious and nonreligious.

Diocesan seminaries in which the new organization of religious studies were to constitute the principal means of instruction were fully established only at the end of the seventeenth century.[16] Whatever the scholarly ambitions and dedication of the theologians, the nature of seminary education poses another problem. In the first place, it seems that the middling sections of the bourgeoisie increasingly furnished recruits for the priesthood, though in some areas better-off peasant families sent their sons into the church.[17] Many envisioned a career in the church, not as a calling, but as one like many others in the civilian world.[18] Within and among the seminaries, the duration and quality of education varied greatly, extending from one to five years, so that neophytes gained either a rudimentary training or went on to study philosophy and theology more deeply. Nevertheless, for all seminaries, the major goal was to shape a model professional corps, self-disciplined and exemplary in its behavior. Such ancillary studies as history, archaeology, and comparative religion were subordinated to preparation in dogmatics, morals, and preaching. The religious ideals that inspired the church and the models offered it by the development of the new intellectual disciplines were not always compatible, for the task of creating a disciplined clergy took precedence over the pursuit of intellectual rigor in religious studies. Moreover, it was not until the very last years of the ancien régime, in the 1770's and 1780's, that there were attempts to make training in the seminaries more rigorous and intellectually respectable.[19] Thus in literate clerical culture, stress on the intellectual training of the clergy came late, stimulated in part by the need to answer attacks on the church more effectively. The skeptical outlook was, if taken up by the *lumières*, hardly considered suitable in a program of religious orthodoxy. Religious conformity could of course not restrain the questioning of members within the church, such as Meslier at one end of the scale and enlightened members of the hierarchy at the other, but they were judged to be aberrant and outside the mainstream.

Were the clerical and lay cultures divergent in their understanding and uses of the religious fact? The answer must be in the negative if selectivity is the sole criterion for judgment. On the other hand, the opposite was true in the view of the clergy who set themselves the task of conversion, of imposing proper forms of religion. As custodians of the mysteries and secrets imperishably recorded and available only to themselves, they transmitted portions of the sacred texts orally in set forms of the catechism, preaching, and daily prayer. Face-to-face communication remained much more important than any other. Books of devotion, catechisms, and other guides for the faithful were so written as to act as auxiliaries to the spoken word; they had no existence independent of it. They were designed to reinforce the processes of oral religious instruction. They were, moreover, only one manifestation, and not the most important, of the modes by which the faithful learned Christian truth and duty. In the words of the abbé Pluche, the church buildings themselves retraced the whole of religion before men's eyes, "even without books or pictures. . . . It is thus that the usages of the Catholic church, together with the painted figures, are a book that is always open to you." Pursuing the theme, he wrote: "Thus, before your pastors have given you an instruction, the exterior of the Catholic church has already taught you the selfsame principal truths. What the books say, the ceremonies echo in a hundred ways, and the more the whole is repeated, the more firmly the meaning is rooted."[20]

The abbé Fleury's *Les Devoirs des maistres et des domestiques*, first published in 1688 and reprinted in the eighteenth century, allowed us to see what the purposes of education were within the households of the well-to-do. All domestic servants were, "within their ability," to learn to read, write, and count, menservants being singled out to perfect the art of writing, while the pages in the homes of *les grands* were to be sent as students to the academy. In great houses, a chaplain was recommended as a permanent resident; his main qualification was not his erudition but his virtue. Catechisms and prayer books were the chief sources of instruction, to be followed by others, such as the historical catechism, François de Sales's *Introduction, The Imitation and Life of Jesus Christ,* the New Testament, and the lives of the Fathers in the wilderness and of other saints.[21] For the most part, however, the rudiments alone were sufficient. For "these sorts of people," the less conversation the better, since most were incapable of thought and education.[22] Simple folk, they recited their rosary, the seven psalms, litanies, and similar prayers without understanding one word, believing that the mere ritual promised salvation. To put an end to this, they were to be encouraged to say less, understand the meaning of their recitations, and read pious books in which the common prayers had been translated into French. Their true devotion consisted in "suffering, working, and keeping silent."[23] Neither should they display excessive piety, for it masked hypocrisy.[24] Rather they ought to approach confession in a true posture of contrition for sins thought and committed and, equally important, in a spiritual love of God from which all traces of profane love were to be erased. The love which "dilates the heart and agitates the blood" cannot be a religious feeling.[25]

Other examples of such ecclesiastical literature are the abbé Pierre Collet's *Prières à l'usage des domestiques et de personnes qui travaillent en ville, etc. Ouvrage qui peut servir aux confesseurs,* published in 1758; his *Instructions en forme d'entretiens sur les devoirs des gens de la campagne,* dated 1771; and Père Féline's *Catéchisme des gens mariés,* which appeared in 1782. The first of Collet's works was meant principally to meet the needs of urban domestic servants and other town workers, whom Fleury had ignored. Writing for confessors, Collet instructs them on the established forms of prayers for urban workers to mark their daily routine, life's rites of passage, and the holy days of the calendar. The obvious intention was to have the workers commit the prayers to memory and use devotional books as a constant reference for that purpose. There is not a great deal to distinguish Collet's guide from Fleury's, except that Collet's lays out in greater detail the prescribed form of prayer for every contingency and provides homilies taken from the Old and New Testaments. Fleury's *Abrégé de l'histoire sainte à l'usage des domestiques,* appended to Collet's book, retells in simple story form bits and pieces from the Old and New Testaments. The second of Collet's books takes the form of conversations between a *curé* and a few young women, some educated and belonging to prosperous rural families, the others, domestic servants, all of whom are about to be married except for a "fallen" woman intent on redemption. To be sure, Collet's attempt to capture the modalities of speech is clumsy and artificial, but the retention of the form is indicative of its primacy. He states that the conversational form "is, as it were, more instructive for the common people" and appeals to seigneurs and masters to make pious books available to the young.[26] Although Féline's instructions were meant for a bourgeois, literate audience, they follow the oral structure of the catechism, as the title suggests, and are an additional illustration of the persistence of the oral tradition within the literary form. Some of these books were conceived as being for the direct uses of the laity; others were meant to assist the clergy in their duties; while still others were produced as texts for specific use in the seminaries, with the added possibility that the last two categories of books were interchangeable.

One recent study of the reading habits of artisans, unskilled workers, land and transport laborers, clerks, and other domestic servants or employees in Grenoble between 1701 and 1790 reveals that 34 individuals fitting these social descriptions from among a total of 425 whose property inventories were examined after death, left books. Admittedly a poor statistical example, it nevertheless discloses some interesting information. With 4 exceptions, the remaining 30 inventories are dominated by books of a religious nature, and only 7 contain more than ten titles. They do not appear significantly different from the kinds of books recommended by Fleury: those dealing with the various sacraments, lives of saints, spiritual exercises, the Gospels, the New Testament, meditations on death, prayers, catechisms, mysteries of the faith, psalms, canticles, *Imitations of Jesus Christ*, consolations, the history of the church, the controversy with Protestants, or authors like Fénelon or Père Coton. If anything they appear to be more of the same, with the exception of works devoted to history and heresy. Moreover, the smallware dealer who also sold books in the popular quarters of the city in 1742 stocked those that were overwhelmingly religious in nature, side by side with alphabet primers, cooking and garden manuals, books in the local patois, and others akin to the titles found in the *Bibliothèque bleue*.[27]

From Bordeaux a local scholar, Pierre Bernadau, who devoted a lifetime to various literary projects, observed the reading habits of peasants in the first years of the Revolution. Their favorite books included prayer books, books of sums, handbooks on missions (*livrets de mission*), the *Sept Tempêtes*, described as "an ascetic work of a wretched kind," a Gallic translation of the Bible, lives of saints, the *Almanach des Dieux*, the diocesan catechism, and some works from the *Bibliothèque bleue*, but nothing on husbandry or domestic surgery. Although the books were not in the best condition, they were carefully stored and passed on within the family as a valuable inheritance.[28] Bernadau condemned the prevalence of superstitions passed on from generation to generation, noting that religion for peasants was simply a "hodgepodge of prejudices." He put much of the blame on the curés, who refused to lend books other than self-disciplinary guides (*ascétiques*) on the grounds that the peasants lacked the intelligence to understand more useful ones. More to the point, the curés' libraries were confined to traditional texts, such as four volumes on the Breviary, synodal ordinances, Jesuit sermons and meditations, the code on tithes, and cookery books; books on rural economy, veterinary science, and hygiene were utterly lacking.[29]

The priests Bernadau knew were, he claimed, perpetuating ignorance in the countryside. Country people actually liked to read and, lacking other reading materials, easily committed to memory nonsense (*billevesées*) from the *Almanach des Dieux* and the *Bibliothèque bleue*, which was bought every year. There was no question, he went on, that the intelligence of the peasant could be raised "up to a certain point," as was proven by the custom among the more prosperous farmers of reading from books of devotion to their workers after the evening meal. Remembering wistfully some verses from a work on rustic life, because of their fine descriptions of evening readings, he also wrote glowingly of Rétif de la Bretonne's account in his *Vie de mon père* of his father's serious attention to religious and secular readings during the *veillées*.[30]

Bernadau's observations form part of the survey which the abbé Grégoire initiated in 1790 to assess the extent and use of local dialects, patois, and idioms. The questionnaire covered a wide variety of subject matter, for its forty-three items inevitably touched on the connections between literacy, religion, and social and economic conditions.

For our immediate purposes, it is an important, though not an exhaustive, source of the levels of literacy among both the clergy and the laity.[31] A great number of the replies are rather laconic and formulistic, but indicate widespread illiteracy, the absence of even the most elementary forms of education, and the indifference and ignorance of the curés, most of whom had no books, had given up reading on leaving the seminaries, and were content to make few demands on themselves. A few correspondents, like Bernadau, provided much fuller accounts. They constituted a group much more critical of the clergy, much more willing to welcome radical change, even eager to participate in it. The curé in the district of Bergerac, the abbé Fonvielhe, had scathing words for the Lazaristes and Capuchins, to whom he attributed the feeding of prejudice injurious to true religion, and equally harsh criticism for the seminaries, where nothing useful was learned.[32] The clergy therefore had nothing valuable to pass on to the people. Both the clergy—who occasionally read their Breviaries, Pontas's *Dictionnaire des cas de conscience,* or guides for sinners—and the parishioners, who had some tattered copies of books of hours and almanacs, reinforced each other's ignorance. The clergy were to blame, of course; perhaps one in a thousand could be considered scholarly, Fonvielhe wrote. For the most part, they had no understanding of religion and confused divine, civil, and ecclesiastical law.[33]

Lorain *fils,* the mayor of Saint-Claude in the Jura, was just as outspoken. Since several of the curés, he wrote, were despotic busybodies, perhaps it was a good thing that they took no interest in supervising the schools. Their intellectual resources rested on Latin, and their impoverished bits of theology had been picked up in the seminaries. There were, to be sure, a few exceptions among them, men who cared for books, but generally they offered neither intellectual nor religious leadership.[34] In the diocese of Auche, the local Amis de la Constitution at Agen reported that as late as the 1770's a curé had customarily begun the mass by ordering sorcerers and cunning men and women to leave the church.[35] Although the subsequent career of François Chabot was to lead him to the Convention and contact with the *enragés,* this one-time teacher of mathematics at the *collège* of Rodez and former Capuchin father, who had been disciplined by his bishop for his political sermons, offered a rather muted criticism of conditions in his area. It was not radically different from some of the others we have noted—for example, in its allusions to the burdens of taxes and tithes, the thinness of instruction, and the ignorance of the *maîtres*—but he added that the more prosperous peasants were ruining themselves by sending their sons who were preparing for the priesthood to the curés for instruction in Latin and discovering too late that they were being robbed by men who needed the extra money to live.[36] Witnesses like Bernadau, Fonvielhe, and Chabot doubtless stressed the darkest side of the situation. Yet. even more moderate and conservative observers did not fail to express similar sentiments.

Popular literacy was at best nourished on a handful of books the clergy thought appropriate for the simple people. In that sense, the clergy were successful in restricting an already amputated literacy to religious and practical matters. They had no other goal in the *petites écoles* and *écoles de charité,* which, while far from being effective, were the only organized institutions for the education of the *peuple.* Indeed, the rudiments of education were held to be synonymous with the mastery of the catechism.[37] The objectives of Jean-Baptiste de La Salle, the founder of the *Frères des écoles chrétiennes* in the seventeenth century, were not often met in the eighteenth.[38] What lay behind his innovation was a vague desire to put an end to rote learning, to bring reason and judgment to the assimilation of religious truth, and, profiting from the example of Protestant success in religious education, to acknowledge that the people had some capacity to reach a deeper understanding of Christian doctrine.[39] It does not seem that this goal or belief in it had penetrated the thinking of the clergy.

Full literacy was not seen as a realizable or desirable goal for other reasons which arose from the survival until late in the nineteenth century not only of the Flemish, German, and Spanish languages, but also of the wide use of the Oc from Gascony to Provence, Breton in the west, and even more bewildering, the enormous number of dialects, idioms, and patois, which could vary greatly between contiguous regions and even between localities.[40] To overcome these barriers, catechisms were produced in some of the chief dialects, such as Breton, Basque, and Languedocian; and the clergy preached sermons and heard confessions in the tongues familiar to local peoples.[41] But more was involved than a mere clash of tongues. Language differences expressed collective attitudes. French symbolized for the more self-conscious members of the clergy, as it did for the other élites in society, a distinct and superior culture, generating beliefs that it was the carrier of civilization, since it permitted the development of more subtle, more complex, more logical forms of thought. Local languages were equated with inferior levels of development, closer to oral forms of communication and more proximate to presumed primitive patterns of life associated with the commands of nature. Whatever the interest local scholars and antiquarians had in observing and noting these languages in a number of published works during the eighteenth century, they were generally conceded to be carriers of traditions and outlooks antithetical to civilized behavior, the most convincing proof that they were intrinsically incapable of transmitting higher forms of thought. When the abbé Grégoire launched his inquiry, he was being given the support of the new state to gather materials for a project the goals of which he had expressed before the Revolution:

> In Europe and in no part of the globe which I know is any national language universally used by the nation. France has within its bosom perhaps eight million subjects, some of whom can hardly mumble a few maimed words or phrases dismembered from our idiom; the others are completely ignorant of it. It is known that in lower Brittany and in many places beyond the Loire the clergy are still compelled to preach in the local patois, under pain of not being understood if they spoke French. Governments are not sufficiently aware or conscious of how important the destruction of the patios is for the spread of enlightenment, the purified knowledge of religion, the ready execution of the laws, national happiness, and political tranquillity.[42]

Grégoire's inquiry provides the occasion for the fullest articulation of the notion that there was a dichotomy between the "they" who spoke an inferior tongue and the "we" who had command of a proper language. But the polarization already existed in fairly full form in the minds of all élites, and was thought to be permanent. At most, as far as the clergy considered the problem, the people could be led out of darkness slowly and imperfectly. They could with repeated exposure to the simplest materials written and spoken in their own patois achieve some approximation of the truths of Christianity, but not their fullness, since such knowledge could only be transmitted in a language that was synonymous with profound thought, reasoning, and sensibility. The acquisition of French was, they believed, a distant goal. As the clergy understood it, literacy at the popular level was of necessity restricted, and significantly, in a double way. This was so, first, because of the clergy's belief that it should serve chiefly to disseminate the fundamental Christian message and, secondly, because of their conviction that the nature of the people forbade the achievement of any wider aim.

How effectively was the limited goal pursued? This is one of the most vexing problems facing historians, who, inspired in part by Louis Maggiolo's nineteenth-century survey, are sedulously trying to measure the spread of literacy in the eighteenth century.[43] At the present stage of research, it is difficult to establish reliable global figures, and the complexity of intraregional variations warn against even the most tentative assessments. It is not my purpose, however, to deal directly with literacy rates, but rather to take note of the meaning of the penetration of and obstacles to religious instruction at the popular level, for it was not literacy as such, but education as the instrument for the achievement of conformity that most often moved the clergy. Indeed, for example, in those parts of Provence where Catholic-Protestant communities lived in proximity (such as on the right bank of the Durance), the Catholic clergy saw the schools as a weapon in their struggle against Protestant infiltration, while in homogeneous Catholic communities sharing identical social structures, that motive was absent and revealed itself in lower literacy levels.[44] Conversely, while the *petites écoles* in an urban center like Marseille were the literacy nurseries for a minute fraction (some 3 percent) of its total population on the eve of the Revolution, the religious environment which they furnished apparently did not exercise a lasting influence.[45] In this case, literacy and religion in time were uncoupled. But whatever the unintended consequences of education in the *petites écoles* throughout France, it is abundantly clear that the acquisition of literate skills was subordinate, at best, incidental, to the implanting of sound religious habits of mind. No particular attention was given to pedagogic techniques that would ease the transition from oral mastery of the catechism to its absorption in the written form.[46] Elementary education for the popular classes, let alone the substantial numbers of the poor who received no formal instruction at all, was even seen as demeaning by some members of the clergy—for example, among the *Pères de la doctrine chrétienne* in their *collège* at Draguignan[47]—and, as we have seen, was frequently if not uniformly unsupervised by the clergy elsewhere.

The corporate self-image of the clergy forbade them in some instances to believe that they had a responsibility to raise the educational levels of the popular classes, while in other instances, where the burden was felt to be justified, there was little or no confidence in the people's capacity to appreciate, understand, or even respond emotionally and fully to Christian mysteries and beliefs. The conditions of their apostolate in different regions, in rural or urban environments, and within specific social structures, doubtless exercised some power over the self-image, altering it in some cases, reinforcing it in others, but always in highly individual ways determined in advance by previous personal perceptions of how they fitted into the world. Given the nature of their seminary education, it is not likely that many gave much thought to the internal qualities of parish religiosity. Moreover, they saw the people of the parish as members of other élites did,[48] distinguishing their own drives, beliefs, and behavior from those of the "others," to whose lives they ascribed a lesser experiential quality. This is not to deny the presence of compassion, sympathy, assistance, and, as many clerical *cahiers* reveal, a keen sense of the material and physical burdens under which the masses labored. It is difficult to generalize, however, clerical poverty could just as often arouse pettiness and avarice. But whatever their personal conditions and motives, there were few priests who dissented from the prevailing view that the people required supervision and discipline. Strategies might differ. Overt psychological repression was not a universal preoccupation; subtler forms of persuasion, based on the conviction that peasant behavior and belief patterns were ineradicable, were the methods preferred by some. Constant intervention was more likely the predilection of Jansenist priests than of others, who walked more warily among their flocks.[49] Yet it is hard to escape the impression that the clergy tried to maintain their self-image by thinking of themselves as custodians of a Christian culture the preservation of which rested on the degree to which its negative aspects of guilt, fear, suffering, and the terrors of this life and the afterlife were internalized in the masses.[50]

The ecclesiastical instructions to which reference has already been made are doubly revealing in this respect. They were inspired by clerical anxieties that the unrestrained behavior of the people would shatter the social structure, and they assumed that popular apprehensions could be bent to deepen and consolidate Christian notions of guilt. The blending of the two is instructive, for appropriate forms of social behavior and external expressions of religious practice were seen as existing in one inseparable domain. Deviation from prescriptive social norms was identical with an erosion of, or failure to accept, religious norms, while the inculcation of self-debasement, humiliation, and guilt was the instrument by which the two would continue to reinforce one another. The ideal—need it be repeated—was, even in attenuated form, a single structure of secular and religious authority. The construct, however, was subject to internal contradictions, especially in the minds of the more reflective and critical members of the clergy. In the first place, even if they did not directly challenge in the structure of society, they nevertheless tended to question their own place in the religious hierarchy, thus implicitly casting doubts on the legitimacy of social divisions.[51] Secondly, by acknowledging that the possessors of power often abused it, they tended to bring authority into disrepute, however much they insisted on demonstrations of obedience. Thus the mechanisms by which the questioners among the clergy sought to win and hold parishioners could not be be infected with these doubts, both as to the full legitimacy of social demands and the universality of religious precepts. Yet the need for control of the laity was never lost from sight.

In an consideration, therefore, of the communal relationships bringing clergy and laity into contact, we cannot look only at the prescribed forms of behavior as set down in the ecclesiastical publications. They must be read to yield information not only on what these were, but also on what they were meant to combat. And they must in addition be set against specific instances of antagonism and/or cooperation between priest and parish. The clergy were themselves continually exhorted to practice submission and obedience in their own lives to qualify them to make the same demands on the laity. A manual for the use of confessors in the diocese of Bayeux placed the full weight for the maintenance of social order on the ability of the clergy to use the confessional properly, and while in its zeal, it surely pressed too hard, the manual pointed to the persistence of their neglect, waste, idleness, ignorance, and indifference to demonstrate how far the church was from achieving its goal.[52] These defects could be eradicated by recognizing that the art of confession was superior to the other arts. Indeed, it was a science, the principles of which could be perfected by unrelenting study, regular attendance at ecclesiastical conferences, and humility deepened by constant self-examination and purification.[53]

It was clearly the abhorrence and fear of disorder that animated the writers of these manuals and guides; and it is in their preaching of the virtues of deference to authority within the social hierarchy that it is possible to discern notions of vice and sin. From the exaction of submission by parents from children, to the sanctions given superiors to exercise power over those below them, the message was the same: disobedience was the gateway to viciousness and rebellion, and all three were manifestations of sin. Although superiors, it was noted, often failed to observe the boundaries of permissible behavior by abusing the limits of their authority, their transgressions were less reprehensible than those committed by the people. In the case of a rapacious seigneur who used his power to absorb bits of land from his less fortunate neighbor, Collet's curé advised his parishioner to air his grievance in the village assizes, but ultimately to trust to God, who would not abandon a victim of injustice. The curé was much harsher in his judgments of artisans, peasants, day laborers, and common laborers who wasted their masters' substance by faulty craftsmanship and poor cultivation and, in addition, cheated on the tithe, on seigneurial rights, and on their richer neighbors' pasture.[54] There could be no question that within the temporal and spiritual orders, the law demanded unfailing obedience. No matter how burdensome, for example, taxes might seem, they were justified by the state's needs, which ordinary folk could not possibly understand. A casual attitude towards the payment of *droits,* the taxes on consumer goods, especially by participating directly or indirectly in the sale and purchase of contraband goods, or by defrauding the *gabelle,* could not be countenanced, for authority could not be challenged at any level.[55]

Ideally, duties and responsibilities absorbed life. Death entered through windows, the Scriptures said; and since the eyes were man's windows, opening out into the world which fed the senses, the highest pleasure was the avoidance of all such pleasures.[56] Temptation must be resisted. Dancing, *veillées,* books about love, novels, improper dress, indecent postures, indecent statues, drinking in cabarets, were all condemned. The senses were by definition impure and chiefly so in the realm of sexual passion, the evils of which began with unchaste thoughts about one's body and led inevitably to sinful acts. Here perhaps was the fundamental source of disorder, manifesting itself in seemingly innocent diversions, but barely concealing really pernicious practices, such as the charivari, fêtes, and other forms of play and ceremony the church had been trying to extirpate as survivals from more riotous times. Sundays and holy days were subverted by markets, fairs, and caberets. The church building itself was not immune from casual indifference and hostile acts. People dared bring their dogs there; they spat and swore; they desecrated the holy water and bread, ridiculed the words of the Scriptures, mocked, insulted, and even struck the priest; and they used the cemeteries to pasture their animals, thresh their grain, and dry their linen. Instead of consulting their pastors, they sought out soothsayers, sorcerers, and folk healers, the very people who fed their wild imaginations and fears and undid the patient work of the clergy.[57]

The Christian litany, as sampled here and transmitted orally or in simpler books of devotion, was a sum of transgressions to be avoided. None of the popular practices held to be conducive to sin was fully extinguished, for two obvious reasons. The clergy could exercise degrees of surveillance, but could be realistically impose a régime of austerity without alienating the laity. Rigorist priests who pursued their confessional duties to the point of devoting sermons to parish laxity could expect various strategies of opposition.[58] There also existed a powerful tradition of practices and beliefs implanted in the very structure of communal relationships, older and more tenacious, hence resistant to external compulsion. The clergy were correct in singling them out as symbols of popular loyalties injurious to precepts learned in the seminaries. But the priest who complained that his parishioners did not divulge the enormity of their sexual sins was not as politic as the priest who took a lighter line. The first felt compelled to seek out and locate sin, while the second let it slip by him, understanding that the masses preferred secrecy in these matters, frequently admitting candidly that the laity did not associate sex with sin.[59] On this question we too must speculate, for what are we to do with evidence showing a coincidence to low illegitimacy rates and high levels of religious observance in Brittany and the eastern parts of the Massif Central, while in the department of the Nord, in the Pas-de-Calais, and in the two departments of Alsace, strong religious observance coincided with high illegitimacy rates?[60]

Repression in small, rather than large, doses was probably the strategy followed by most clergy in their attempts to influence the communities where they worked. In fact, indulgence and toleration seemed to inform the attitudes of the contributors to the volumes on theology in the *Encyclopédie méthodique*. Pleasure which met men's needs, tastes, and inclinations was permissible, but excesses stimulated by certain forms of play, luxurious display in the fêtes, entertainments, and so on, were to be avoided, because they led to licentiousness and idolatry.[61] The fêtes themselves were defended, however, on several grounds. They afforded the opportunities of sociability for people who would not otherwise have been able to come together. Critics of the fêtes as subersive of disciplined work habits failed to recognize that men were not mere "brutes" or "automatons." They needed periodic opportunities for diversion, and in many sparsely populated cantons the celebration of the faith and the ceremonies of the fête were indistinguishable. If there were too many, this was not due to deliberate clerical encouragement—indeed, the church had been trying to reduce their number—but to the tenacity and diversity of local needs and wishes. Where abuses and debauchery had crept into the celebrations, the clergy were trying to reduce them but were often forced to tolerate them, because the people could not be treated as a "herd of slaves." Besides, if truth were told, many of the fêtes were pre-Christian in origin and could not be easily suppressed.[62]

The same was true of the persistence of superstitious practices and beliefs which *philosophe* and Protestant critics claimed was due to the church's failure to act on its own findings, particularly those of J. -B. Thier's seventeenth-century compilation,[63] to offer proper instruction to the people. Such critics, insisting that only a "knowledge of nature" was "capable of curing this popular illness," were themselves incapable of appreciating the nature of the malady. "In general,

> those who are ignorant are stubborn; they neither listen to reason nor to the facts which contradict their errors; they blindly retain the prejudices of childhood. Popular tales, the stories heard during the *veillées*, make a greater impression on them than the lessons of their pastors, because they are more analagous to their ideas, because those who recite them do so in a posture of importance and authority, and sometimes swear that they have seen what they have dreamt, and because credulousness is ordinarily due to fear. Now fear does not reason and arguments do not heal. Several pastors have tried to use insults and a kind of persecution, because they do not want to lend themselves to the foolish ideas of their flocks. They are nonetheless obliged to instruct, exhort, and to return to the task at all times, and even when it is inconvenient.[64]

Enlightened people no longer believed in ghosts or sorcerers, but how does one explain the belief in the prodigalities of physics, animal magnetism, somnambulism? Did not the people have a right to laugh at these examples of foolishness in this century of *lumières*? Was it realistic to believe that the inhabitants of the Pyrénées, the Cévennes, the heaths of Berry, the Alps, the Vosges, and the Jura could understand naturalistic explanations any more than they could a century ago? It would be dangerous, moreover, to destroy harmless popular beliefs and superstitions, since they helped maintain order, morality, and the integrity of the faith. So long as the people felt that their fears, misfortunes, and suffering could be assuaged easily and quickly by such beliefs, they would not give them up. In time, however, true religion would change them. Most, in any case, had disappeared, in no small measure the result of clerical vigilance.[65]

External conformity was the response of both priests and laity. To know the parish and to live in harmony with it meant degrees of acceptance of practices which expressed local needs. That there were fears, terrors, and apprehensions associated with the perils of sickness and death; that there were rituals bound up with propitiating the power of nature; that there were traditions connected with the rites of passage; that there were, besides the curé, trusted figures in the community from whom advice and assistance were habitually sought; that there were erotic and play elements[66] inseparably tied to macabre events: all constituted the patterns of a culture which the clergy found trying and often offensive. But these patterns were utilized, exploited, attenuated, domesticated, rather than directly repressed. They continued to exist alongside the more acceptable practices introduced by the church, in some cases, and in others, were partially incorporated. The confraternities were, it should be noted, often intermediaries of varying effectiveness in the clergy's struggle to reduce or erase manifestations of popular practices outside their control. Dominated at first, for example, in the diocese of Vence, by community élites, the confraternities cooperated in limited ways with the church, but in time they began to draw their membership from the popular classes and thereby lost some of their reliability. What is more, most of the *menu peuple* did not always fully participate in the confraternities, preferring to continue practices far from the scrutiny of both these communal associations and of the curés. That they saw no conflict between their veneration of curative and protective saints, their devotions at chapels in the countryside outside the boundaries of the parish, their picturesque adornment of altarpieces, their attachment to relics, their uses of music and dancing, and the "respectable" practices which the curés believed were the true marks of religion, was imperfectly perceived by the church.[67] However zealous the clergy were in their attempts to impose uniformity of beliefs and in their desire to appear civilizing agents every bit as enlightened as their Protestant critics and *philosophe* opponents, an offensive *outrancière* would have been suicidal. If they did not fully understand the nature of the popular religious fact, believing that their own forms of devotion were qualitatively different and hence superior to those that were keeping the people in bondage to superstition, they reluctantly accepted the limitations imposed by strong, often unarticulated forms of resistance, possibly taking comfort in the thought that their burden was a heroic one.

It would be a distortion of the experience both of the popular and clerical understanding of religion, therefore, to insist that, because each was bounded by assumptions the other could neither fully comprehend nor accept, the two confronted one another in an acute state of overt opposition. The vague boundaries between clerically sanctioned and popular forms of religion provided each with means of pursuing a species of dialogue, each taking from the other what was required to make their historic coexistence tolerable. It was more politic to work at swelling the statistics of outward signs of conformity than to arouse opposition in a relentless attack on popular devotion. In this work, the clergy had the backing of the civil authorities, for whom the maintenance of order was closely linked to the enforcement of religious observance. Both La Mare's *Traité de la Police,* of the early part of the century, and La Poix de Fréminville's *Dictionnaire de Police,* published in 1756 and reprinted in a second edition in 1775, devoted considerable attention to religion, seeking to support the church in the execution of its responsibilities. It is quite clear that officials of state and church were concerned to complement their efforts and activities, but it is equally clear that the stress was on ensuring the external signs of conformity. What is more important, the state was intent not only on exercising control over the population but on extending it to the church itself by invigilating the clergy's activities. The possibility of civil encroachment on the clerical domain may indeed have had the unintended consequence of exacerbating relations between the two authorities. The church was not too reluctant, it even welcomed the movement to vest fiscal responsibility for education, poor relief, and the *hôpitaux généraux* in local community efforts and the state, so long as the church itself retained control over its sacerdotal functions in these institutions. But the civil authority's jurisdiction over the subject matter of sermons was less likely to be wholly acceptable.[68]

It is surely of some significance that the state should give prominence to the possibility of seditious collusion between clergy and laity. Fréminville's *Dictionnaire* reminded the clergy that the law "imposes general and absolute silence on disputes and controversies which cannot be stirred up without injuring the good of religion and the state in equal measure."[69] Was this an explicit recognition of the widespread peasant and communal revolts of the seventeenth century, those challenges to the state's attempts to seek a fuller monopoly of power at the expense of local interests, and the part which the clergy sometimes played in affirming them?[70] Or was it not so much the memory of the extended and intense revolts of the previous century, but the chronic rebelliousness of small communities, supposedly stimulated, in Fréminville's words, by the use of "scandalous words tending to excite the people to *émotion*"? *Emotion* is a word difficult to translate, but it means a social movement of short duration and restricted territorial extension and was distinguished from mere *"murmures"*—that is to say, verbal expressions of dissatisfaction—because it was translated into illegal forms of resistance: disorder, violent insults, plots, tumults, excesses, mutinies, uprisings, and so on.[71] Of 234 such *émotions populaires* in Savoy in the period between 1650 and 1792, 54 were directed against seigneurial dues; 38 against state taxes, militia duty, the royal *corvée*, and agents of the *gabelle*; 30 to protest high prices, scarcity, the monopolization or export of grain; and 35 to protect communal rights. Only 20, or 7 percent, expressed hostility against the church. From these statistics, a number of observations may be made. The figures provided in Nicolas's study indicate clear examples of cooperation between curés and parishioners against monastic establishments, seigneurial exactions, taxes, and the alienation of communal lands. Antimonastic sentiment was in fact very pronounced. Hostility against the curés mainly took the form of opposition to the tithe, and of the 16 such instances for the entire period, more than half occurred after 1789.[72]

On the evidence of these figures, as well as the evidence in some of the *cahiers*, the mutual vexations between clergy and laity were largely kept with bounds. Occasionally they erupted into more protracted defiance, either because of the accumulation of popular resentments stimulated by carping clergy. More often, mutual opposition was aroused on the question of the tithe or clerical demands for payments connected with baptism and burial. In many cases, though, the tithe was recognized by parishioners as the curé's due, since he had no other source of income and often shared his resources with the poorest of his flock.[73] In no small measure, antitithe sentiments were strongest in cases in which the curé was seen to have additional sources of income and was not using them in charitable works. Yet even then, monastic establishments were perceived as being the worst offenders in refusing to fulfill their obligations to help the poor.

We may suggest that the exigencies of community life forged links of varying strength between priest and parish, not because of the success which the first had in imposing a uniformity of belief and practice—we have seen how tentative the process was, in fact—but because of the tacit observance of boundaries beyond which neither could or would go. The authority of the clergy could not be infinitely extended, since the exercise of such power, even with civil assistance, would have turned the community against them. It is tempting to work within a model of confrontation in which the power of the clergy is seen in constant collision with the resistance of the laity. It is more realistic to propose another in which the uses of power were not fully exploited. Curés certainly demanded compliance and, ideally, would have welcomed the disappearance of religious forms they found repugnant or threatening, but they were ready to accept lesser instances of conformity to avoid disturbances and ensure tranquility. Successful priests were those who did not believe that they were betraying their vocation by making such compromises. If they were the wisest, there were others who, possessing neither a strong vocation nor an intellectual orientation, settled back, made no fuss, and prayed that there would be none.

Some members of the clergy were acutely conscious of popular grievances, while others were anxious to keep them under control in a strictly regulated order. Few were free from the conviction that they were dealing with people whose qualities decisively marked them off as a verifiably distinct body in society. Of no other group was this truer than the peasants, who were habitually said to constitute an undifferentiated group bound together by obsolete, ridiculous, and naïve beliefs bred in the very soil they worked and even mimetic of the animals with which they lived. The landscape of their minds was the image of the wild landscape they inhabited. There was little compulsion to penetrate beyond the facile assumption that there was an essential and timeless harmony uniting environment, people, beliefs, and practices. They were all of a piece, a totality, whose features fitted together as snugly as a Russian doll. Their holism the clergy saw as an entity, best expressed as the "others," a category interesting to observe and perhaps to assist. Their oral traditions were the most perfect reflection of their orality, their infancy, their primitiveness. If the clergy's vision of their rural parishioners was not wholly static, if they saw dimly or acutely their vocation within a perspective of acculturation, they asked themselves whether it lay within their power or the power of any other group in society to alter the natural indestructibility of the peasant world.[74] Did they do so in the belief that the people, not only the peasant, could be transformed from the "others" and united with the "we" of the customary discourse, or did they believe that the "others" would always be discernibly different and inferior? The answer almost overwhelmingly affirms a permanent dichotomy which no language could bridge.

NOTES

1 The ideas in this opening paragraph owe much to the following works: C. Geertz, "Religion as a Cultural System," in *Anthropological Approaches to the Study of Religion*, ed. M. Banton (London, 1968), pp. 1-46; *Literacy in Traditional Societies*, ed. J. Goody (Cambridge, 1968), esp. the introduction by Goody and "The Consequences of Literacy" by Goody and I. Watt, pp. 1-68; H. Geertz, "An Anthropology of Religion and Magic," *Journal of Interdisciplinary History*, 6 (1975), 71-89; K. Thomas, "An Anthropology of Religion and Magic," ibid., pp. 91-109; N. Z. Davis, "Some Tasks and Themes in the Study of Popular Religion," in *The Pursuit of Holiness in Late Medieval and Renaissance Religion: Papers from the University of Michigan Conference*, ed. C. Trinkaus and H. A. Oberman (Leiden, 1974), pp. 307-36; *Rationality*, ed. B. Wilson (New York, 1970); T. Settle, "The Rationality of Science *versus* the Rationality of Magic," *Philosophy of the Social Sciences*, 1 (1971), 173-94; J. Delumeau, "Ignorance religieuse et mentalité

magique sous l'ancien régime," paper presented to the 1972 meeting of the Society for French Historical Studies; E. P. Thompson, "Anthropology and the Discipline of Historical Context," *Midland History*, 1, no. 3 (1972), 41–55. A recent collection of studies of popular culture may be sampled in *The Wolf and the Lamb: Popular Culture in France from the Old Regime to the Twentieth Century*, ed. J. Beauroy, M. Bertrand, and E. T. Gargan (Saratoga, Calif., 1977).

2 E. E. Evans-Pritchard, *Theories of Primitive Religion* (Oxford, 1956), p. 112.

3 B. Plongeron, "Le Fait religieux dans l'histoire de la Révolution francaise: Objects, méthodes, voies nouvelles," *Annales historiques de la Révolution francaise*, 47 (1975), 95–133.

4 J. C. Schmitt, "'Religion populaire' et culture folklorique," *Annales: E.S.C.*, 31 (1976), 941–53, esp. 942, 945, 947, 950. Plongeron, even more explicitly than Schmitt, discusses the difficulty of defining "popular religion" and notes how shifting the term can be. See *La Religion populaire: Approaches historiques*, ed. B. Plongeron (Paris, 1976), pp. 15–25.

5 E. Durkheim, *The Elementary Forms of the Religious Life*, trans. J. W. Swain (New York, 1965), p. 432. For a cogent critique of the functional approach, see R. K. Fenn, "Towards a New Sociology of Religion," *Journal for the Scientific Study of Religion*, 11 (1972), 16–32. Cf. G. Lewy's discussion in his *Religion and Revolution* (New York, 1974), pp. 545–46.

6 La Mare, *Traité de la Police*, 4 vols. (Paris, 1705–38). In the first volume, p. 267, La Mare writes: "It is thus true to say that [were] religion alone well observed, all the other functions of the police would be achieved; that if on the contrary, it alone is disturbed, according to the thinking of a political philosopher the police would immediately experience the consequences. *Religio turbata, Politiam turbat.*"

7 K. Thomas, *Religion and the Decline of Magic: Studies in Popular Beliefs in Sixteenth and Seventeenth-Century England* (London, 1971), pp. 26–28, 151–54.

8 Ibid., pp. 76–77, 422–29, 667–68.

9 See W. Coleman, "Health and Hygiene in the Encyclopédie: A Medical Doctrine for the Bourgeoisie," *Journal of the History of Medicine and Allied Sciences*, 29 (1974), 399–421.

10 See N. D. Jewson, "The Disappearance of the Sick-Man from Medical Cosmology, 1770–1870," *Sociology*, 10 (May 1976), 225–44.

11 Plongeron, "Le Fait religieux," p. 132.

12 See particularly N. Z. Davis, *Society and Culture in Early Modern France* (Stanford, 1975).

13 See M. Soriano, *Les Contes de Perrault* (Paris, 1968); R. Mandroux, *De la culture populaire aux XVIIe et XVIIIe siècles*, new ed. (Paris, 1975); G. Bollème, *Les Almanachs populaires aux XVIIIe et XVIIIe siècles* (Paris and The Hague, 1969); and idem, *La Bibliothèque bleue: La Littérature populaire en France du XVIe au XIXe siècle* (Paris, 1970). For a lively discussion of these and other issues, see M. Soriano et al., "Débats et combats: Les Contes de Perrault," *Annales: E.S.C.*, 25 (1970), 633–53.

14 Goody and Watt, "Consequences of Literacy," p. 44.

15 M. de Certeau, "L'Histoire religieuse du XVIIe siècle: Problèmes de méthodes," *Recherches de Science Religieuse*, 57, no. 2 (1969), 231–50; idem, "Du système

religieux à l'éthique des lumières (XVIIe et XVIIIe siècles): La Formalité des pratiques," *Ricerche di storia sociale e religiosa*, no. 2 (July–Dec. 1972), pp. 31–94. Cf. P. Chaunu, "Le XVIIe siècle religieux: Réflexions Préalables," *Annales: E.S.C.*, 22 (1967), 279–302.

16 A. Degert, *Histoire des séminaires français jusqu'à la Révolution* (Paris, 1912), I, 192–347.

17 On clerical recruitment, see D. Julia, "Le Clergé paroissial dans le diocèse de Reims à la fin du XVIIe siècle," *Revue d'histoire moderne et contemporaine*, 13 (1966), 241–69; idem, "Le Clergé paroissial du diocèse de Reims à la fin du XVIIe siècle," *Etudes Ardennaises*, no. 49 (1967), pp. 19–35, no. 55 (1968), pp. 41–66; P. Loupès, "Le Clergé paroissial du diocèse de Bordeaux d'après la grande enquête de 1772," *Annales du Midi*, 83 (1971), 5–24; M. L. Fracart, "Le Recrutement du clergé séculier dans la région niortaise au XVIIIe siècle," *Revue d'histoire de l'Eglise de France*, 57 (1971), 241–65; T. Tackett, "Le Recrutement du clergé dans le diocèse de Gap au XVIIIe siècle," *Revue d'histoire moderne et contemporaine*, 20 (1973), 497–522; idem, "Le Clergé de l'archidiocèse d'Embrun à la fin de l'ancien régime," *Annales du Midi*, 88 (1976), 177–97.

18 See D. Julia, "Le Prêtre au XVIIIe siècle: La Théologie et les institutions," *Recherches de Science Religieuse*, 58 (1970), 521–34, esp. 524–27.

19 B. Plongeron, *La Vie quotidienne du clergé français au XVIIIe siècle* (Paris, 1974), pp. 68–71.

20 Abbé N. Pluche, *Le Spectacle de la nature* (Paris, 1750), VIII, part 2, 348ff., 362.

21 Abbé Claude Fleury, *Les Devoirs des maistres et des domestiques* (Paris, 1736), pp. 20, 24, 27. Fleury was a student of French and canon law, as well as of religious history and literature. He undertook missionary work in the Saintonge and Poitou in the 1680's and, because of Bossuet's influence, spent a considerable time at court.

22 Ibid., p. 101.

23 Ibid., pp. 119–20, 123.

24 Ibid., p. 29.

25 Ibid., pp. 117–18.

26 Abbé Pierre Collet, *Instructions en forme d'entretiens sur les devoirs des gens de la campagne* (1771), in Migne, *Collection intégrale et universelle des orateurs sacrés du premier ordre* (Paris, 1854), LV, cols. 1026, 1028. Collet was an eminent Jesuit theologian whose works were adopted in several seminaires as a counterweight to Jansenist influence among the Christians. He was singled out for attack by the editor of *Nouvelles ecclésiastiques*, the chief Jansenist organ.

27 J. Solé, "Lecture et classes populaires à Grenoble au dix-huitième siècle: Le Témoignage des inventaires après décès," in *Images du peuple au dix-huitième siècle*, ed. Henri Coulet (Paris, 1973), pp. 95–102.

28 Bernadau's observations are reproduced in M. de Certeau, D. Julia, and J. Revel, *Une Politique de la langue: La Révolution française et les patois* (Paris, 1975), pp. 179–94. The *livres de raison* were similarly passed on from father to son, since many of them contained in written form the oral rituals connected with secret cures. See L. Bonnaud, "Prières et formules de conjuration recueillies dans un livre de

métayage," *Bulletin de la société archéologique et historique du Limousin*, 98 (1971), 223-28.
29 Certeau, Julia, and Revel, *Une Politique de la langue*, p. 193. According to Plongeron, *La Vie Quotidienne*, pp. 210-11, the diocese of Toul in 1750 established a reading list which "faithfully enough represents the mental universe of the French clergy, before the reform of the seminaries. . . . It is clear that the ideal curé will be much more a moralist and a canonist than a theologian and biblical scholar." Plongeron notes that not until the Revolution were curés advised to obtain books on rural economy, the veterinary arts, health, and botany.
30 Certeau, Julia, and Revel, pp. 193-94. See Rétif de la Bretonne, *La Vie de mon père* (Paris, 1970), pp. 131-33, for the references to the *veillées*.
31 There were forty-nine replies, the authorship of which is known in forty-three cases; and of these nineteen came from members of the clergy. If we include replies from people associated with public administration, justice, medicine, and teaching, the number of "clercs" in the largest sense swells to thirty-one. See Certeau, Julia, and Revel, pp. 28-30.
32 Ibid., pp. 198-99.
33 Ibid., p. 208.
34 A. Gazier, *Lettres à Grégoire sur les patois de France, 1790-1794: Documents inédits sur la langue, les moeurs, et l'état des esprits dans les diverses régions de la France au début de la Révolution, suivis du rapport de Grégoire à la Convention* (Paris, 1880; rpt. Geneva: Slatkine, 1969), pp. 206-6.
35 Ibid., p. 120.
36 Ibid., p. 60.
37 For the early history of the catechism, see J. C. Dhotel, *Les Origines du catéchisme moderne: D'après les premiers manuels imprimés* (Paris, 1967).
38 On La Salle, see Y. Poutet, *Le XVIIIe siècle et les origines lasalléennes: Recherches sur la genèse de l'oeuvre scolaire et religieuse de J. B. de La Salle*, 2 vols. (Rennes, 1970).
39 See J. R. Armogathe, "Les Catéchismes et l'enseignement populaire en France au dix-huitième siècle," in *Images du peuple*, ed. Henri Coulet, pp. 102-21, esp. pp. 114-15.
40 According to the *Encyclopédie, ou Dictionnaire raisonné des sciences, des arts et des métiers*, new ed. (Geneva, 1778), XXIV, 992, *patois* was "a corrupted language such as is spoken in almost all the provinces. . . . Language is spoken only in the capital."
41 Armogathe, "Les Catéchismes," pp. 117-21.
42 H. Grégoire, *Essai sur la régeneration physique, morale et politique des Juifs* (Metz, 1789), pp. 160-61, cited in Certeau, Julia, and Revel, *Une Politique de la langue*, p. 21.
43 See L. Maggiolo, *Etat récapitulatif et comparatif indiquant le nombre de conjoints qui ont signé leur acte de mariage* (Paris, 1881). For an evaluation of Maggiolo's work, see M. Fleury and P. Valmary, "Les Progrès de l'instruction élémentaire de Louis XIV à Napoléon d'après l'enquête de Louis Maggiolo, 1877-1879," *Population*, 12 (1957), 71-92; and for an indication of recent global attempts to measure literacy,

see F. Furet and W. Sachs, "La Croissance de l'alphabétisation en France, XVIIIe–XIXe siècle," *Annales: E.S.C.*, 29 (1974), 715–39.
44 See M. Vovelle, "Y a-t-il eu une révolution culturelle au XVIIIe siècle? A propos de l'éducation populaire en Provence," *Revue d'histoire moderne et contemporaine*, 22 (1975), 135.
45 Ibid., pp. 126, 135.
46 The most recent synthesis on the subject is a joint work by R. Chartier, M. M. Compère, and D. Julia, *L'Education en France du XVIe au XVIIIe siècle* (Paris, 1976). Part I of M. Gontard's *L'Enseignement primaire en France de la Révolution à la loi Guizot (1789–1833)* (Paris, 1959) may also be consulted. Additional recent work on the subject of elementary education may be sampled in the following articles: D. Julia, "L'Enseignement primaire dans le diocèse de Reims à la fin de l'ancien régime," *Annales historiques de la Révolution française*, 42 (1970), 233–86; M. Langet, "Petites Ecoles en Languedoc au XVIIIe siècle," *Annales, E.S.C.*, 26 (1971), 1398–1418; R. Taveneaux, "Les Ecoles de campagne en Lorraine au XVIIIe siècle: A propos d'une étude récente," *Annales de l'Est*, 22 (1970), 159–71. L. Trénard alludes to the problems of the *petites écoles* in his article "Culture, alphabétisation et enseignment au 18e siècle," *Dix-huitième siècle*, no. 5 (1973), pp. 139–50. I am indebted to Dr. H. Chisick for letting me see his article, "School Attendance, Literacy, and Acculturation: *Petites Ecoles* and Popular Education in Eighteenth-Century France," which is forthcoming. In his new study, *The Philosophes and the People* (New Haven and London, 1976), pp. 100–101, H. Payne perhaps gives more credit to the church's ostensible than to its actual attitudes on popular education.
47 Vovelle, "Une révolution culturelle," p. 126.
48 See Payne, *The Philosophes and the People*, passim.
49 On the impact of Jansenism in general and in education, see P. Chaunu, "Jansénisme et frontière de catholicité (17e et 17e siècles): A propos du Jansénisme lorrain," *Revue historique*, 227 (1962), 115–38; B. Plongeron, "Une Image de l'Eglise d'après les *Nouvelles ecclésiastiques* (1728–1790)," *Revue d'histoire de l'Eglise de France*, 53 (1967), 242; D. Julia, "Le clergé paroissial du diocèse de Reims à la fin de l'ancien régime"; J. Fouilleron, "Oratoriens et Jésuites dans le diocèse d'Arras," *Dix-huitième siècle*, no. 8 (1976), pp. 67–75. Cf. H. Mitchell, "Resistance to the Revolution in Western France," *Past and Present*, no. 63 (1974), pp. 124, 129–30.
50 J. Delumeau, "Au sujet de la déchristianisation," *Revue d'histoire moderne et contemporaine*, 22 (1975), 52–60.
51 On Richerism, see M. G. Hutt, "The Curés and the Third Estate: The Ideas of Reform in the Pamphlets of the French Lower Clergy," *Journal of Ecclesiastical History*, 8 (1957), 74–92.
52 *Conduite des confesseurs dans le tribunal de la pénitence, selon les instructions de S. Charles Borromée, et la doctrine de S. François de Sales*, 2nd ed. (Paris, 1740), pp. vii–xi.
53 Ibid., pp. xi–xxxiv, 1–5.
54 Collet, *Instructions*, cols. 1058–60.

55 Ibid., cols. 1095-97.
56 Ibid., col. 1089.
57 Ibid., esp. cols. 1029, 1036, 1042, 1044.
58 Julia, "Le Prêtre au XVIIIe siècle," p. 531. On the entire range of questions relating to marriage, the place of sexuality in marriage, age of puberty, parental consent in marriage, and other problems, see *Conférences ecclésiastiques de Paris sur le mariage: Où l'on concilie la discipline de l'Eglise avec la jurisprudence du royaume de France. Etablies et imprimées par ordre de S. E. Monseigneur le Cardinal de Noailles, archevêque de Paris,* new ed., 5 vols. (Paris, 1745-48). On the ecclesiastical conferences, see J. M. Gouesse, "Assemblées et associations cléricales: Synodes et conférences ecclésiastiques dans le diocèse de Coutances aux XVIIe et XVIIIe siècles," *Annales de Normandie,* 24, no. 1 (1974), 37-72. Fleury, *Les Devoirs,* pp. 60-63, 115-17, urged masters to allow their servants to marry, on the grounds that they would otherwise sink into vice, but he reversed himself in his advice to servants, advising them to remain content in a celibate state and to save themselves from sin by following a life of work, application, and frequent confession.
59 J. L. Flandrin, "Mariage tardif et vie sexuelle: Discussions et hypothèses de recherche," *Annales: E.S.C.,* 27 (1972), 1351-78, esp. 1364-65. Flandrin pursues the question further in *Familles: Parenté, maison, sexualité dans l'ancienne société* (Paris, 1976).
60 J. Depauw, "Illicit Sexual Activity and Society in Eighteenth-Century Nantes," in *Family and Society,* ed. R. Forster and O. Ranum (Baltimore, 1976), p. 162.
61 *Encyclopédie méthodique: Théologie,* 3 vols., 6 parts (Paris, 1788-90), III, part 1, 212. The volumes of the *Encyclopédie méthodique* devoted to theology were under the direction of the Abbé Nicolas-S. Bergier. Principal of the *collège* at Besançon and associate member of the Académie de Stanislas at Nancy, he was a leading *anti-philosophe.* His *Déisme réfuté par lui-même* (1765) was a spirited attack on Rousseau. His articles in the *E.M.* were, however, criticized on points of doctrine and methodology by fellow theologians. For a discussion of his theology, see R. R. Palmer, *Catholics and Unbelievers in Eighteenth-Century France* (Princeton, 1939), esp. pp. 96-102, 189-92. See the references to the *Encyclopédie méthodique* in R. Darnton, "The *Encyclopédie* Wars of Pre-Revolutionary France," *American Historical Review,* 78 (1973), 1331-52.
62 *E.M.,* II, part 1, 19-21. On the attempt to suppress the fêtes in the seventeenth century, see J. M. Ultee, "The Suppression of *Fêtes* in France, 1666," *Catholic Historical Review,* 62 (1976), 181-99. On the manipulation of the fêtes by the authorities and on their evolution in the eighteenth century, see A. Poitrineau, "La Fête traditionnelle," *Annales historiques de la Révolution française,* 47 (1975), 339-55.
63 The reference is to J. B. Thiers, *Traité des superstitions selon l'écriture sainte, les décrets des conciles, et les sentimens des saints pères, et des théologiens,* 4 vols. (Paris, 1697-1704).
64 *E.M.,* III, part 2, 550.
65 Ibid.
66 The most important seventeenth-century work on the bounds within which play

should be maintained and controlled is J. B. Theirs, *Traité des jeux et des divertissemens, qui peuvent être permis, ou qui doivent être défendus aux Chrétiens selon les règles de l'Eglise et le sentiment des Pères* (Paris, 1686). On the theme of death and the catechisms devoted to preparation for its inevitability, see F. Lebrun, *Les Hommes et la mort en Anjou aux 17ᵉ et 18ᵉ siècles* (Paris, 1971), esp. pp. 436–58. On the parodying of death in popular literature, see G. Bollème, "Littérature populaire et littérature de colportage," in *Livre et société dans la France du XVIIIᵉ siècle* (Paris and The Hague, 1965), pp. 61–92, and her *Les Almanachs populaires*, pp. 45, 63–72.

67 M. H. Froeschlé-Chopard, "Les Dévotions populaires d'après les visites pastorales: Un Example, le diocèse de Vence au début du XVIIIᵉ siècle," *Revue d'histoire de l'Eglise de France*, 60 (1974), 85–99. Cf. G. Cholvy, "Le Legs religieux de l'ancien régime au département de l'Hérault," *Annales du Midi*, 85 (1973), 303–26.

68 See M. Perronet, "Police et religion à la fin du XVIIIᵉ siècle," *Annales historiques de la Révolution française*, 42 (1970), 375–97.

69 Cited in ibid., p. 389.

70 That the clergy were involved in the revolts is incontestable, though they were not always treated with deference by the rebels. Y. M. Bercé, *Croquants et nupieds: Les Soulèvements en France du XVIᵉ au XIXᵉ siècle* (Paris, 1974), pp. 81, 111, offers examples of the curé's role in the uprisings, summing it up this way: "The uneasy rifling of private papers found in the study especially brings to light the formidable and mysterious prestige of writing. Drafts of contracts, bundles of papers and registers are collected in bulk. They are taken to the priest so that he can decipher their contents and find references to the *gabelle*. This learned village curé possessed literate knowledge and also the art of interpreting it, of unmasking the execrable appearances of the gabelle. The papers identified as announcing the gabelle are not, like the others, thrown into the gutter..., but are carried away or burned." That the clergy participated more actively may be seen in the revolt of the *bonnets rouges* in Lower Brittany in 1675, when on July 11 the château of Kergoat was invaded by thousands of peasants led by their curés and some village notables. Y. Garlan and C. Nières, *Les Révoltes bretonnes de 1675: Papier timbré et bonnets rouges* (Paris, 1975), pp. 126–32, refer to the active part taken by some priests and the plight of others who found themselves the victims of the peasant's belief that they were about to increase their impositions.

71 J. Nicolas, "Pour une enquête sur les émotions populaires au XVIIIᵉ siècle: Le Cas de la Savoie," *Annales historiques de la Révolution française*, 45 (1973), 593–607. The terminology is discussed on p. 595. The two-part article was continued in ibid., 46 (1974), 111–53.

72 Ibid., 45 (1973), 600–603; 46 (1974), 112–43.

73 For examples, see P. Bois, *Paysans de l'Ouest* (Le Mans, 1960), p. 614; C. Tilly, *The Vendée* (Cambridge, Mass., 1964), pp. 104–6; M. Faucheux, *L'Insurrection vendéenne de 1793: Aspects économiques et sociaux* (Paris, 1964), pp. 89–91; L. Cathelineau, *Cahiers de doléances des sénéchaussées de Niort et de Saint-Maixent et des communautés et corporations de Niort et de Saint-Maixent* (Niort, 1912), p. 49; H. Couturier, *La Préparation des Etats-généraux de 1789 en Poitou* (Poitiers, 1909),

p. 312. See also A. Sarramon, *Les Paroisses du diocèse de Comminges en 1786* (Paris, 1968).

74 Some of the evidence for this is to be found in Certeau, Julia, and Revel, *Une Politique de la langue,* passim, and in Gazier, *Lettres à Grégoire,* passim. Belief in the intractability and immutability of popular behavior was generally shared by all members of the élite, nonclerical as well as clerical. For an attempt to deal with the enlightened community's response to the people, see Payne, *The Philosophes and the People.*

Pessimism Surpassed: New Colleges as Bastions against Barbarism in Colonial America

MARGARET W. MASSON

The newly founded Princeton College celebrated its first commencement in 1748 with pomp and an acute sense of circumstance:

> The President opened the publick Acts, first by an elegant Oration in the *Latin* Tongue, delivered *memoriter*, ... displaying the manifold Advantages of the liberal Arts and Sciences, in exalting and dignifying the humane Nature, enlarging the Soul, improving its Faculties, civilizing Mankind, qualifying them for the important Offices of Life, and rendering Men useful Members of Church and State: That to Learning and the Arts, was chiefly owing the vast Preheminence of the polished Nations of Europe, to the almost brutish Savages of *America*; a Sight of which last was the constant Object of Horror and Commiseration.[1]

One is struck by the ritual and rhetoric of the occasion. The president recited a litany of reasons for the importance of higher learning. And he added a cultural comparison in which the New Jersey college was enlisted on the side of Western civilization against the shocking brutishness of the American environment and its native inhabitants. Speaking in Latin, the language of the academic community, he voiced the fears and hopes of the colonial intelligentsia in the mid-eighteenth century. And he sounded a theme—the fear of barbarism in America—which united supporters of higher education, despite their many differences, and lent special significance to their work.

The period from 1745 to 1770 saw an extraordinary flurry of educational activity in America.[2] Six new colleges opened, representing a threefold increase in colonial colleges in just twenty-five years. Princeton, founded in 1746, was followed by the College of Philadelphia (now the University of Pennsylvania) in 1749 and by King's College (now Columbia) in 1754. The outbreak of war in the mid 1750's probably hampered further efforts, but three more projects were brought to fruition with Brown (1764), Rutgers (1766), and Dartmouth (1770).[3] Denominational rivalries and sectarian schism were often the immediate impulses behind a new college. Evangelicals in the Presbyterian, Baptist, and Dutch Reformed churches wished to control the education of candidates for the ministry: they were instrumental in founding Princeton, Brown, and Rutgers, respectively. Dartmouth grew out of the Indian missionary zeal of Congregationalist Eleazar Wheelock, and King's College was the brainchild of the Anglicans. Economic development and the evolution of a complex colonial society were additional reasons for educational activity. The non-sectarian College of Philadelphia was sponsored by a multidenominational group and designed to serve the needs of a thriving urban community. Local pride and intercolonial competition could also spur a college project; and so could aspirations for an American culture that would measure up to the European intellectual heritage.

Diverse motivations like these dictated that public relations literature on behalf of higher education cover a wide range of interests. Fund-raising tracts usually contained a collage of reasons for supporting the new colleges. Emphasis varied as the authors judged the predilections of the group they were approaching.[4] Appeals to England featured the effect of higher education in securing loyalty to the empire. A college education for the ministry was stressed to the clerical constituency.[5] Petitions for British support often played on humanitarian impulses to christianize the Indians, sentiments which were rarely found in America, judging by the omission of this objective in most educational propaganda published at home.[6] Financial arguments were offered too, particularly when help was requested from the colony where the college was situated. The local community was promised that the college would create new business, attract visitors from outside the province, and raise property values.[7] Parents were reminded that if higher education were available nearer home, their sons would be spared the expense and hazard of travel to distant colleges. This argument was especially appealing to the colonial Dutch, for whom ministerial training and ordination, before the founding of Rutgers, meant a round trip to Holland.[8]

While practical inducements were offered whenever possible to win public support, they were invariably interspersed with another kind of rationale. This was a reference to the intangible benefits of higher education, to its symbolic meaning in mid-eighteenth-century America. Promotional literature abounded with declaratory statements about learning. For example, New Yorkers were assured that "it will greatly tend to the welfare and reputation of the Colony that a proper and ample foundation be laid for the regular education of youth."[9] No further explanation was offered in this mandate for a lottery for the projected King's College. Similarly, the supporters of Brown pledged money in the belief "that Nothing hath a greater Tendency to adorn human Nature and to promote the true Interest and Happiness of Mankind than useful Literature."[10] Rather than dismissing such statements as bombastic rhetoric, this paper attempts to discover what they meant to the colonial intelligentsia. It investigates the symbolic importance of higher education and the college movement that it inspired. Let me hasten to add that I do not intend to examine here the multiple causes of the college movement. Nor does this paper discuss the specific objectives of undergraduate education, like training secular and religious leaders or preparing creditable citizens. Instead, it seeks to understand the premises that made higher education seem so important to this generation of colonial intellectuals.

According to these premises, higher education was valuable for conjectural as much as for tangible reasons. Denominational and personal differences notwithstanding, sponsors of the colleges shared a vision of the future in which the colonies might very easily be overwhelmed by the American environment and reduced to some sort of barbaric state. Consequently, they viewed the college movement as part of an epic confrontation between civilization and barbarism. New colleges represented the triumph of civilization and heralded a new era of cultural achievement. The metaphor was extended to cover the individual mind, which was a battleground between virtue and vice. Again the colleges were important. Colonial intellectuals hoped that higher education would influence the youthful personality, helping to motivate virtuous behavior. These premises functioned to lend significance to the activities of college founders and enabled them to overcome their initial pessimism.

The idea that the college movement was part of a confrontation between civilization and barbarism was vividly expressed in a fund-raising tract from Princeton, first published in 1752 and destined to become something of a prototype. It described "the thickest Darkness of *Ignorance* and *Barbarism*" that prevailed in America before European colonists brought the light of Christianity and learning.[11] This dreadful darkness was dissipated in New England and Virginia, where the earliest colleges were established, but remained impenetrable in other settlements. As number one in the battery of colleges founded in the mid-eighteenth century, Princeton was therefore in the vanguard of a continuing assault on barbarism. Opening the first commencement in 1748, President Burr referred to the college's mission by identifying the New Jersey college with European civilization and then contrasting this with the savagery of the American Indians. The dichotomy was often repeated, though the geography varied. William Livingston of New York contrasted "the polite Nations of Europe" with "the rude Savages of Africa." For a Philadelphia student expressing appreciation to the college trustees, it was "the Barbarous Clans of Tartary" that invited invidious comparison.[12] Using language so close that it seems almost liturgical, these American intellectuals juxtaposed civilization and learning with barbarism and ignorance. They established the setting for the current confrontation in America and placed the colleges in the front line.

Supporters of the college movement pessimistically imagined a number of scenarios in which the colonies might lose in this confrontation. Trustees of Philadelphia College feared that after the death of the first Pennsylvania settlers who had been educated in Europe, subsequent generations would decline into ignorance.[13] William Smith, provost of the College, depicted the consequences through analogy with the Indians. "It was obvious," Smith claimed, "that without making a provision for cultivating wisdom and goodness in the rising generation, we would soon degenerate into a state of ignorance and barbarity, little better than that of our *Neighbour-Savages*, and be neither able to preserve nor enjoy the inestimable blessings, delivered down to us from our fathers."[14] Arguing from the same assumptions about the decadence of native culture, Eleazar Wheelock of Dartmouth proposed the education and conversion of the tribes to raise them from barbarism. Wheelock was mindful that English settlers on the frontier were becoming almost as savage as the Indians.[15]

Aside from the possibility of slipping down to the cultural nadir of the Indians, the lack of education among the colonists harbored further perils. Samuel Johnson thought that widespread ignorance prevented the colonies from conforming to British cultural patterns. King's College, with its Anglican links, would provide the tool to forge a set of highly desirable English values in America.[16] William Livingston, on the other hand, believed that education was the precise antidote for such indoctrination. Ignorance paved the way for bigotry because the mind was defenseless against religious and political propaganda. Using characteristic hyperbole, Livingston said:

> He must be a Stranger to History and the World, who has not observed, that the Prosperity, Happiness, Grandeur, and even the Strength of a People, have always been the Consequences of the Improvement and Cultivation of their Minds. And, indeed, where this has been in any considerable Degree neglected, triumphant Ignorance hath open'd its Sluices, and the Country been overflowed with Tyranny, Barbarism, ecclesiastical Domination, Superstition, Enthusiasm, corrupt Manners, and an irresistible confederate Host of Evils, to its utter Ruin and Destruction.[17]

Such was the fate of New York if the population remained untutored.

To founders and educators with strong religious affiliations, ignorance meant irreligion, which was synonymous with barbarism.[18] Furthermore, the evangelicals feared that the future of their brand of Christianity might be in jeopardy unless they were able to educate their own ministers to bring pietism to an unenlightened populace.[19] Writing in 1755 to the Amsterdam Classis of the Dutch Reformed Church, Theodore Frelinghuysen (son of the Awakener) conveyed his sense of the dramatic moment. "Our church matters here have reached an important crisis, and the only remedy that can heal our difficulties seems to be the one which we are now seeking. Should that remedy not be secured, it is likely that everything will fall into disorder and get beyond the hope of any remedy."[20] The solution was the creation of an American Classis with the power to ordain evangelical ministers who would be trained at Rutgers.

In one way or another, these men all feared that the colonies faced an imminent decline into barbarism. Some, like the Philadelphia trustees and Provost Smith, pictured decadence in cultural terms; Johnson's interpretation was intellectual, while Livingston's was political; and the evangelicals shared a vision of religious catastrophe. This belief in impending disaster obviously added to the significance of their educational efforts. And it did more. When the new colleges promised to be successful, the founders could view their work in a cosmic setting, as the triumph of civilization and Christianity in some preordained westward progress.

It was axiomatic to the evangelicals that learning should be accompanied by Christianity. Thus, they thought that their educational projects helped to fulfill the divine injunction to propagate the gospel throughout the world. This idea was manifestly clear in Wheelock's program to educate the Indians. Indeed, the Connecticut clergy had a millennial vision as they imagined the successful accomplishment of Wheelock's work.[21] A passage from one of Frelinghuysen's sermons put the divine command into the American context: "As thou Sun givest Light from East to West, so shall Man, whom I have created in the East, people the Earth still Westward on; and with him shall go polish'd Life, Arts, Science, and real Religion, by which Glory redounds to my Name, Salvation to my Creatures."[22] Educators who were not evangelicals could sometimes share this vision. When Dr. James Jay, representing King's College, and Philadelphia's Provost

Smith were jointly soliciting funds in England, they obtained a royal brief instructing the British clergy to assist the effort. Smith and Jay composed a letter to accompany the brief. After reciting the achievements of the two urban colleges, the letter claimed that the opportunity was now at hand "for the advancement of divine Knowledge, and to be found a chosen Instrument in these latter days for calling New and heretofore unexplored Countries, to the enjoyment of everything that can exalt Humanity, at a time when so many of the old have fallen again into their original Barbarity."[23] Now the pessimistic fear of barbarism was surpassed by an optimistic, even millennial dream in which the colleges would be leading participants.

No doubt this letter was deliberately worded to strike the clerical conscience at its tenderest spot. But there was also a secular version of the millennial dream. This was the idea that a splendid cultural destiny lay just ahead for America once her potentialities were manifested by a well-educated generation of colonists. Benjamin Franklin's tract "On the Need for an Academy," written in 1749, hinted at this sentiment.[24] But the most vivid picture was painted by a man who had only recently left England and did not decide to make America his home until almost two years later. William Smith's *Thoughts on Education*, which appeared in 1752, made an impressive case. Smith envisaged a time when England's power would be eclipsed; then the responsibility for preserving her civilization would fall to the American settlements. Preparations should be made at once by expanding higher education so that the colonies might assume this burden and perhaps support the mother country in her decline. Smith justified his vision through an analogy with the westward course of the sun, and by the rather more bold assertion that cultural decline was inevitable for Britain because of the corruption already distinguishable in her society.[25] President Burr utilized the sun analogy too, proclaiming at the first Princeton commencement that the New Jersey college was helping to achieve the preordained intellectual heritage of the colonies.[26]

The belief that colonial colleges would help ward off barbarism and even fulfill the divine command to propagate the gospel was not new in the mid-eighteenth century. *New England's First Fruits,* written in 1643, expressed the dread with which Massachusetts Puritans contemplated the possibility of an illiterate ministry once the founding generation should die. Harvard was therefore established to preserve a tradition of learning in the wilderness. The fear of barbarism was stated in classic terms in 1663 by Jonathan Mitchell, a Harvard tutor: "What is it but Learning," he asked rhetorically, "that hath put that vast difference between [civilized nations] & salvage Barbarians?" "Wee in this Country," he went on, "being farre removed from the more cultivated parts of the world, had need to use utmost care & diligence to keep up Learning & all Helps of Education among us, lest degeneracy, Barbarism, Ignorance and irreligion doe by degrees breake in upon us." Similarly, the statutes of William and Mary gave an account of the founding in 1693 which related it to concern about ignorance among native-born Virginians. And when Yale was established in 1701, it was expected to attract recruits for the ministry who would accomplish that "Grand errand" inherited from the first generation, the mission to propagate the gospel.[27] The continuity of these ideas over almost a hundred years suggests that colonial educators would be predisposed to view colleges in symbolic terms, rather than as ends in themselves.

There was, however, a second belief among eighteenth-century intellectuals that added significance to their educational endeavors. It was their hope that learning would profoundly influence the youthful personality, not only by shaping it environmentally but also by reaching into the adolescent mind to manipulate motivations so that behavior would more likely be ethical. Seventeenth-century educators did not share this belief because their psychological notions were derived from traditional Christian theology rather than from the Enlightenment and the writings of John Locke.

The reception of Lockean psychology by American educators involved compromise.[28] Locke's new perceptions could hardly be ignored, since they gave the process of education an entirely different meaning. But their materialistic implications were unacceptable to most eighteenth-century college founders, who were committed Christians almost to a man. The Americans therefore tried to effect an accommodation in their educational theory between Christian and Lockean ideas. Men associated with the new urban colleges—

Franklin, Richard Peters, and Smith in Philadelphia; Livingston and Johnson in New York—were all Arminians. They found it fairly easy to appropriate Locke's epistemology, with its emphasis on sensory perception and cumulative learning.[29] More difficult was the reconciliation between rationalism as a basis for ethics and the traditional idea that the mind possessed the imprint of moral law, subsequently corrupted by original sin.[30] This inconsistency seems to have been resolved by concentrating on the creation of human beings in the divine image. The moral law was a potentiality more than an innate idea, a mental mold rather than a perception. Furthermore, their belief in free will allowed them to hold people responsible for moral choices. Even though human nature had been vitiated in the fall, it could still be repaired by a good education.[31]

The evangelicals who sponsored the other four colleges rejected free will and insisted on divine intervention through regeneration to attain true virtue. They found the accommodation between old and new ethics difficult but not impossible. They generally relied on the sophisticated synthesis of predestinarian Calvinism and Lockean psychology worked out by Jonathan Edwards in the early 1740's. This had become the foundation for evangelical orthodoxy.[32] Edwards had explained the conversion experience in the language of eighteenth-century rationalism. Consequently, evangelical educators were ready to use reason to prepare the youthful mind for conversion. While there was much in the new psychology they were bound to reject, the evangelicals still saw some connection between education and the pursuit of virtue.[33]

The difference between this and the more limited conception of higher education in the seventeenth century can be illustrated by student addresses to the academy trustees in Philadelphia. In 1754 John Morris plagiarized from Jonathan Mitchell's lament about American barbarism originally proclaimed in 1663. But Morris added an explanation about how to counter barbarism. It was the mind that mattered. As he said to the trustees,

> You have done your utmost Endeavours, to implant in our tender Minds, the Principles of Virtue & Honesty, & to rescue us from the Miseries of

> Ignorance & Superstition.... What is it but Learning, that gives the polite Nations of Europe, such a Superiority over the Barbarous Clans of Tartary? In the one nothing is to be seen, but brutal Rage & Barbarity: In the other, Religion, Liberty & Good Morals, Trade, Industry & Politeness.... Learning civilizes & polishes the most barbarous Nations, it renders them more tractable & Humane, & it inspires them with more gentle Thoughts & less rugged Inclinations:... Learning teaches us our Duty, to both God & Man, it enables us to requite our Conduct by Reason, & lays down Rules, whereby, we may perform, with honour, all the Duties incumbent on Man.[34]

It was not just that the polite and learned were superior to barbarous clans, nor even that learning could actually civilize a nation. The important point was that it could change personal motivations, making an entire people more tractable, gentle, humane; and individuals more dutiful, reasonable, and well-behaved. From another student at the Philadelphia College came an "Oration on Science" which stated, predictably enough, that knowledge framed the mind in wisdom. Less predictable was the claim that it elevated the thoughts, controlled the passions, fired the youthful breast with virtue, and planted "Godlike Purpose in the Soul."[35] William Livingston described King's College as "a Scheme for ennobling our Natures, exalting our Reasons, and rectifying our Judgement." The New York Assembly was congratulated for helping the college: "You have studied to deliver us from Vice and Ignorance... [and] are resolved to make us Wise and Virtuous."[36] The earlier juxtaposition of civilization and barbarism at the level of culture was now transposed to the level of the individual, with virtue and knowledge as the alternatives to vice and ignorance.

The expectations of evangelical educators were hardly less ambitious. President Burr's commencement address assumed that learning dignified human nature and enlarged the soul, propositions that were repeated by students at Rutgers in the early 1770's.[37] Public relations literature from Princeton asserted that education adorned the mind with virtue as well as useful knowledge. And claims made for the positive effect of the college on the local community included one that it had transformed the "Genious and Dispositions" of the population.[38] A petition accompanying the charter for Brown stated the connection between educated individuals and the larger society. It declared the founders' concern "for cultivating the Moralls and improving the Knowledge of the rising Generation[,] upon which Foundation the Harmony[,] good Order and Reputation of Society depend."[39] The higher education of a handful of colonial youngsters was unlikely to have had so bountiful a social outcome in reality. In symbolic terms, however, the new colleges satisfied the fears and hopes that were premises for educational activity.

Old and new ideas were interlaced in the college-founding movement of the mid-eighteenth century. On the one hand, higher education was acquiring social functions intended in some ways to supplant the family in adolescent socialization.[40] On the other hand, the priority of moral over practical training in most new colleges perpetuated traditional pedagogical goals. The fear of barbarism was a conventional theme in colonial thought, reflecting deep-seated anxiety over the possibility that Englishmen would be acculturated by the Indians. Seventeenth-century Puritans had been both attracted and repelled by the wilderness—thrilled by its potentiality as the site of a new Zion, yet horrified by the lure of a decadent Indian lifestyle. One way to overcome this painful ambivalence was to reiterate the superiority of Western civilization and to identify firmly and persistently with its heritage.[41] If Americans would eventually come to view the frontier more benignly, the eighteenth-century elite was still inclined to legitimize its culture by imitating European models.[42] While this espousal brought the new optimism of the Enlightenment to the colonies, the assumption of a European intellectual identity failed to annihilate traditional attitudes toward the environment.

Ultimately, colonial educators achieved a synthesis of their fears and hopes in a cyclical view of history.[43] Nations, like individuals, passed through cycles of birth, maturity, and death. The rise of a state was indicated by the spread of virtue among the population, just as the cancer of corruption signaled its decline.[44] Writing in 1749 to Franklin, Cadwallader Colden disputed whether material wealth actually constituted strength. "No doubt money can do great things but I think the Power of a Nation consists in the knowledge and Virtue of its inhabitants and in proof of this," he went on, "history every where allmost shews us that the Richest Nations... have been generally conquer'd by the poor but in some sense Virtuous nations."[45] The association between virtue and knowledge was not lost on supporters of the new colleges. Edward Antill gave his opinion on this matter to the trustees of King's College:

> It is not Riches Sr: [he wrote to Leonard Lispenard] that is the Strength, the Glory, the Security of a Country, no Sr: it is Virtue, Knowledge & Wisdom that have ever been, & ever will be the great Bulwork of a Nation. It is remarkably True that into Whatever Nation the Liberal Arts & Sciences have been Introduced & heartily & prudently Cultivated, so as to establish Vertue, Temperance & the true Love of ones Country, such Nation has risen into Splendour, Greatness & Power; And no sooner have the Arts & Sciences been Neglected & laid aside, . . . But such Nation has sunk into meaness, contempt & Ruine.[46]

Here, surely, was a compelling enough reason for expanding higher education in America. Provost Smith placed the college movement in this context when his *Thoughts on Education* argued that, in the inevitable event of England's decline, the culturally ascendant colonies "gratefully may prop her Fall."[47] The cyclical view of history heightened the symbolic importance of the college movement; but it also allowed the intellectuals to retain both the pessimistic and optimistic aspects of their thought. Not yet ready to foresee the future as uninterrupted progress, they could nevertheless surpass their pessimistic appraisals by actively shaping destiny through education. Consider the rhetoric of the Princeton valedictorian in 1759: "The experience of all ages, and observation of mankind, assure us, that wherever learning hath erected her auspicious smile, kingdoms have risen from their obscurity, and flourished in august and splendid majesty; but at her departure, they have sunk again in darkness, and degenerated into their native barbarism, and all the rude deformities of unpolished nature." Warming to his theme, the student then reflected on the achievements of the college movement: "Yes—America, often an uncultivated wild of beasts, and men equally savage, can now boast of her provinces, her cities and her colleges; seminaries of learning, that never fail yearly to present her well educated children to the service of the public, and the glory of the british nation and its dependants."[48] Barbarism was still there in the cyclical image, just as it was always present in the colonial psyche, but now it was held at bay by the self-conscious efforts of the intellectuals in general and of college founders in particular.

NOTES

1 Account of the first commencement at New Jersey College, Nov. 9, 1748, in *New-York Gazette Revived in the Weekly Post-Boy*, Nov. 21, 1748.
2 On this activity, including several unsuccessful projects, see Beverly McAnear, "College Founding in the American Colonies, 1745-1775," *Mississippi Valley Historical Review*, 42 (June 1955), 24-44.
3 Accounts of the origin of each of these colleges will be found in the following books. For Princeton, Leonard J. Trinterud, *The Forming of an American Tradition: A Re-Examination of Colonial Presbyterianism* (Philadelphia: Westminster Press, 1949); Thomas J. Wertenbaker, *Princeton, 1747-1896* (Princeton: Princeton University Press, 1946); Varnum L. Collins, *Princeton* (New York: Oxford University Press, 1914); John MacLean, *History of the College of New Jersey, from its origin in 1746 to the Commencement of 1854*, 2 vols. (Philadelphia: J. P. Lippincott, 1877). On the University of Pennsylvania, Edward P. Cheyney, *History of the University of Pennsylvania, 1740-1940* (Philadelphia: University of Pennsylvania Press, 1940); Thomas H. Montgomery, *History of the University of Pennsylvania from Its Foundation to A.D. 1770* (Philadelphia: George W. Jacobs, 1900); Ann D. Gordon, "The College of Philadelphia, 1749-1779: The Impact of an Institution," Diss. Wisconsin 1975. On Columbia, David C. Humphrey, *From King's College to Columbia, 1746-1800* (New York: Columbia University Press, 1976); John Howard Van Amringe et al., *A History of Columbia University, 1754-1904* (New York: Columbia University Press, 1904). For Brown University, Walter C. Bronson, *The History of Brown University, 1764-1914* (Providence: Brown University Press, 1914). On Rutgers, William H. S. Demarest, *A History of Rutgers College, 1766-1924* (New Brunswick: Rutgers College, 1924); Richard P. McCormick, *Rutgers: A Bicentennial History* (New Brunswick: Rutgers University Press, 1966). And for Dartmouth College, Leon B. Richardson, *The History of Dartmouth College*, 2 vols. (Hanover: Dartmouth College Publications, 1932); Frederick Chase, *A History of Dartmouth College and the Town of Hanover, New Hampshire*, ed. John K. Lord, 2 vols. (Cambridge, Mass.: John Wilson, 1891). For a summary, see Margaret W. Masson, "The Premises and Purposes of Higher Education in American Society, 1745-1770," Diss. University of Washington 1971, ch. 2.
4 Good examples of these characteristics in promotional literature can be found in a series of addresses prepared by King's College trustees for raising funds in England. Entered into their minutes under the same date are nine separate supplications intended for the general public, the archbishop of Canterbury, Dr. Philip Bearcroft as secretary of the SPG, Lord Sandys of the Board of Trade, the universities,

and three learned societies. See under Nov. 16, 1762, *Minutes of the Governors of the College of the Province of New York... 1755-1768 and of the Corporation of King's College in the City of New York, 1768-1770* (New York: n.p., 1932). This lithograph edition of the original MS minutes is unpaged.

5 On loyalty see Gilbert Tennent and Samuel Davies, "To the Worthy and Generous Friends of Religion and Learning..." (London: n.p., 1754), pp. 1-2, Rare Books Division, Princeton University Library; for appeals to the clergy, "To the... General Assembly of the Church of Scotland, to meet at Edinburgh, May, 1754. The Petition of the Synod of New York...," reprinted in *Records of the Presbyterian Church of the United States of America* (Philadelphia: Presbyterian Board of Publication, 1841), pp. 256-58; "Associated Pastors in Boston, Recommendation for New Jersey College, Sept., 1752," printed with Tennent and Davies, "To the Worthy and Generous Friends."

6 Typical of these appeals to British feelings was the "Society in Scotland for Propagating Christian Knowledge, Recommendation for New Jersey College, 1750," printed with Tennent and Davies, "To the Worthy and Generous Friends." Eleazar Wheelock's appeals were, of course, an exception. But Wheelock had difficulty raising funds in America. At one collection, he noted, only a flint and a bullet were donated to his cause (Wheelock to Dr. A. Gifford, Oct. 31, 1763, MS. 763581, Papers of Eleazar Wheelock, 1728-79, Archives, Dartmouth College).

7 New Jersey Trustees' Petition to the General Assembly, May 23, 1753, Trustee Minutes, Princeton Unversity, 1748-96, I, 35, microfilm in Archives, Princeton University; Benjamin Franklin, "Paper on the Academy," July 31, 1750, in Franklin, *The Papers of Benjamin Franklin*, ed. Leonard W. Labaree et al. (New Haven: Yale University Press, 1959-), IV, 35-37; William Smith, *A General Idea of the College of Mirania* (New York: J. Parker and W. Weyman, 1753), pp. 74-75; "Copy of a Letter to Town Councils of Scituate & Gloucester about College, December 8th 1769," Miscellaneous Papers concerning Rhode Island College, 1763-1804, I, 71, Archives, Brown University.

8 The Coetus to the Classis of Amsterdam, May 30, 1755, *Ecclesiastical Records of the State of New York*, ed. Hugh Hastings (Albany: J. B. Lyon, 1901-10), V, 3553-54.

9 An Act of the General Assembly of New York, quoted in Van Amringe, *History of Columbia University*, pp. 3-4.

10 Preamble to Trustee Minutes, Sept. 1764, Corporation Records, 1764-1810, I, 16, Archives, Brown University.

11 *A General Account of the Rise of the College... of New-Jersey* (New York: James Parker, 1752), p. 4. On Sept. 25, 1751, the Princeton trustees voted a committee of six to assemble papers for Ebenezer Pemberton to take to Europe. On Sept. 27, 1752, Pemberton, William Smith of New York, and William Peartree Smith were instructed to correct a fund-raising tract before sending it to the press. The first version was published in 1752 in New York. A revised version appeared in London in 1754 under the names of Gilbert Tennent and Samuel Davies. Another edition came out in Edinburgh later that year under the same names. The Rare Books

Division of Princeton University Library has all three editions. The New York edition is the one used here and will be cited as *General Account of the College of New-Jersey*. Yet another version was published as "A short account of the rise and state of the College, in the province of New Jersey, in America," in *The New American Magazine*, 27 (March 1760), 103–4. A completely new pamphlet, probably written by Samuel Blair, under the title *An Account of the College of New Jersey*, was published in 1764 at Woodbridge, N.J. In an address delivered during the Philosophical Exercises at Philadelphia Academy on Nov. 12, 1754, one student, Josiah Martin, plagiarized from p. 4 of the *General Account*. For Martin's piece see Penn MSS., 1648–1772, VII, 165, Pennsylvania Historical Society.

12 Account of the first commencement at New Jersey College, *New-York Gazette*... *Weekly Post-Boy*, Nov. 21, 1748; Hippocrates Mithridate [William Livingston], *Some Serious Thoughts on the Design of Erecting a College in... New York* (New York: John Zenger, 1749), pp. 3–4; John Morris, "Address to Trustees," Nov. 12, 1754, Penn MSS., VII, 159.

13 Address to "All Charitable Persons, Patrons of Literature, and Friends of Useful Knowledge," quoted in Montgomery, *University of Pennsylvania*, pp. 383–84. This statement repeats several points made in 1749 by Franklin's "On the Need for an Academy," reprinted in Franklin, *Papers*, III, 385–86.

14 [Smith], "Account of the College and Academy," *The American Magazine*, Oct. 1758, pp. 630ff., reprinted in Montgomery, *University of Pennsylvania*, Appendix E, p. 519.

15 Eleazar Wheelock, *A Continuation of the Narrative of the Indian Charity-School... to... 1771* ([Hartford]: n.p., 1771), pp. 23–24; see also "Wheelock's Narrative (1762) of the Original Design, Rise, Progress and Present State of the Indian Charity-School in Lebanon, Conn.," reprinted in *Old South Leaflets* (Boston) I, no. 22 [1896], 1–20.

16 Samuel Johnson to the Bishop of London, April 5, 1732, in Johnson, *Samuel Johnson, President of King's College: His Career and Writings*, ed. Herbert Schneider and Carol Schneider (New York: Columbia University Press, 1929), I, 81–82; Johnson to Bishop George Berkeley, Aug. 12, 1752, ibid., II, 329; Johnson to Dr. Bristow, Jan. 5, 1758, ibid., IV, 45; Johnson to Archbishop of Canterbury, May 3, 1737, ibid., I, 88; *Minutes of the Governors of the College of New York*, May 12, 1761.

17 "The Advantages of Education," Nov. 8, 1753, in *The Independent Reflector, or Weekly Essays on Sundry Important Subjects*, ed. Milton M. Klein (Cambridge, Mass.: Harvard University Press, 1963), pp. 419–20. See also Richard Peters, *A Sermon on Education, Wherein Some Account is given of the Academy, Established in the City of Philadelphia* (Philadelphia: B. Franklin and D. Hall, 1751), pp. 1, 3–4; Franklin, *Proposals Relating to the Education of Youth in Pensilvania*, reprinted in Franklin, *Papers*, III, 400.

18 Governor Jonathan Belcher to Rev. Jonathan Edwards, May 31, 1748, MS. in New Jersey Historical Society, copy in Archives, Princeton University; Belcher to Mr. Prince, May 21, 1752, ibid.

19 Samuel Davies to J. F., April 1, 1755, quoted in Sadie Bell, *The Church, The State, and Education in Virginia* (Philadelphia: The Science Press Printing Co., 1930), p. 142; [Blair], *Account of the College*, p. 6.
20 Theodore Frelinghuysen to the Classis of Amsterdam, Oct. 22, 1755, *Ecclesiastical Records of New York*, V, 3610.
21 Extract from a recommendatory letter printed in David McClure and Elijah Parish, *Memoirs of the Rev. Eleazar Wheelock* (Newberryport, R. I.: Edward Little, 1811), p. 179.
22 Theodore Frelinghuysen, *A Sermon Preached on Occasion of the late Treaty Held in Albany* (New York: Parker and Weyman, 1754), p. 14.
23 Reprinted in William Smith, *Life and Correspondence of the Rev. William Smith, D.D.*, ed. Horace W. Smith (Philadelphia: Ferguson, 1880), I, 309-13; see also Smith's *An Humble Representation*, addressed "To all Charitable Persons, and Patrons of Useful Knowledge" (London: n.p., 1762), Archives, University of Pennsylvania.
24 Franklin, "On the Need for an Academy," Aug. 24, 1749, Franklin, *Papers*, III, 385-86; see also "Constitutions of the Publick Academy in the City of Philadelphia," ibid., p. 422.
25 Philomathes [William Smith], *Some Thoughts on Education* (New York: J. Parker, 1752), pp. vii, 19-22. These themes were repeated in a postscript to Smith's *Mirania*, p. 83; in his preface to an English edition of Samuel Johnson's *Elementa Philosophica* (1754) (Johnson, *Writings*, II, 346); and in a fund-raising tract prepared for the West Indies, *To the Friends of Religion and Patrons of Liberty and Useful Knowledge* (Charleston, S.C.: n.p., 1772), Archives, University of Pennsylvania.
26 Account of the first commencement at New Jersey College, *New-York Gazette... Weekly Post-Boy*, Nov. 21, 1748.
27 *New England's First Fruits* (1643), reprinted in *American Higher Education: A Documentary History*, ed. Richard Hofstadter and Wilson Smith (Chicago: University of Chicago Press, 1961), I, 6-7; Jonathan Mitchell, "A Modell for Maintaining of students and fellows of Choise Abilities at the College in Cambridge," *Publications of the Colonial Society of Massachusetts*, 31 (1935), 309, 311; "Statutes of William and Mary, 1727," printed in Hofstader and Smith, *American Higher Education*, I, 39-49; "The Charter of The Collegiate School," in *Documentary History of Yale University under the Original Charter of the Collegiate School of Connecticut, 1707-1745*, ed. Franklin B. Dexter (New Haven: Yale University Press, 1916), p. 20; "Proceedings of the Trustees, Nov. 11, 1701," ibid., pp. 27-28.
28 See Lawrence A. Cremin, *American Education: The Colonial Experience, 1607-1783* (New York: Harper and Row, 1970), pp. 278-302; Henry F. May, *The Enlightenment in America* (New York: Oxford University Press, 1976), pp. 42-65; Douglas Sloan, *The Scottish Enlightenment and the American College Ideal* ([New York]: Teachers College Press, 1971). Sloan stresses the impact of the Scottish Enlightenment on American education well before the arrival of John Witherspoon at Princeton in 1768.
29 Peters, *Sermon*, pp. 4-5; Smith, *Mirania*, pp. 38, 40; Smith, "Concerning the Conversion of the Heathen Americans," *Discourses on Public Occasions in*

America, 2nd ed. (London: A. Millar, 1762), p. 153; Franklin to Johnson, Aug. 23, 1750, Franklin, *Papers*, IV, 41; [William Livingston], "Remarks on our Intended College," March 22, 1753, Klein, *Independent Reflector*, p. 173; [William Livingston], "Of Human Nature," Nov. 1, 1753, ibid., p. 416.

30 William Smith, "Some Reflexions on Education," *The Scots Magazine*, Oct. 1750, p. 488; Peters, *Sermon*, p. 32; "Of Human Nature," Klein, *Independent Reflector*, p. 413.
31 Smith, "Reflexions on Education," p. 488.
32 Perry Miller, *Jonathan Edwards* (Cleveland: Meridian Books, 1949), pp. 52–68; Alan Heimert, *Religion and the American Mind, From the Great Awakening to the Revolution* (Cambridge, Mass.: Harvard University Press, 1966), pp. 41–42; Sloan, *Scottish Enlightenment*, p. 44.
33 See Howard Miller, *The Revolutionary College: American Presbyterian Higher Education, 1707–1837* (New York: New York University Press, 1976), esp. pp. 79–102.
34 John Morris, "Address to Trustees," Nov. 12, 1754, Penn MSS., VII, 159; see also "Prologue To the Philosophical Exercises at Philadelphia, Nov. 12th 1754, Spoken by Mr. Jacob Duchè," ibid.
35 [Nathaniel Evans], "Oration on Science," MS. in University Papers Unbound, Archives, University of Pennsylvania.
36 Hippocrates Mithridate [Livingston], *Some Serious Thoughts*, dedication.
37 Account of the first commencement at New Jersey College, *New-York Gazette... Weekly Post-Boy*, Nov. 21, 1748; "Preamble to the Constitution of the Athenian Society, 1773," quoted in McCormick, *Rutgers*, p. 14.
38 *General Account of the College of New-Jersey*, pp. 1, 7; see also Commission of Rev. Theodore Frelinghuysen, by the Coetus, May 30, 1755, *Ecclesiastical Records of New York*, V, 3551.
39 The petition of 1763, reprinted in Bronson, *History of Brown*, Appendix A, I, 493.
40 Phyllis Vine, "The Social Function of Eighteenth-Century Higher Education," *History of Education Quarterly*, 16 (Winter 1976), 409–24.
41 Richard Slotkin, *Regeneration through Violence: The Mythology of the American Frontier, 1600–1860* (Middletown, Conn.: Wesleyan University Press, 1973), esp. pp. 15–23, 57–115, 143, 191–94.
42 Jack P. Greene, "Search for Identity: An Interpretation of the Meaning of Selected Patterns of Social Response in Eighteenth-Century America," *Journal of Social History*, 3 (Spring 1969–70), 205–18.
43 See Stow Persons, "The Cyclical Theory of History in Eighteenth-Century America," *American Quarterly*, 6 (1954), 147–63.
44 For the political implications of these ideas, see Bernard Bailyn, *The Ideological Origins of the American Revolution* (Cambridge, Mass.: Harvard University Press, 1967); Gordon S. Wood, *The Creation of the American Republic, 1776–1787* (Chapel Hill: University of North Carolina Press, 1969), pp. 3–45.
45 Cadwallader Colden to Benjamin Franklin, Nov. 1749, Franklin, *Papers*, III, 431–32.

46 Edward Antill to Leonard Lispenard, Feb. 19, 1761, College Papers, Columbia University Library. Punctuation supplied.
47 Philomathes [Smith], *Some Thoughts on Education*, pp. vii, 19-20. Students at Philadelphia College repeated these themes; see Martin's "Oration," Nov. 12, 1754, Penn MSS., VII, 165; Morris, "Address to Trustees," ibid., p. 159. Morris's fantasy that Philadelphia might become a "Protection to its Mother Country" angered the proprietor, who thought the idea imprudent; see Smith to Peters and Franklin [Feb. 1754], Franklin, *Papers*, V, 213. Franklin himself had speculated about a time when the colonies might inherit England's responsibilities by providing a haven for virtue (Franklin to Peter Collinson, May 9, 1753, Franklin, *Papers*, IV, 486).
48 *A Valedictory Oration, Pronounced at the Commencement, held in Nassau-Hall, in New Jersey; September 26, 1759* (New York: Gaine, 1759), pp. 6-7, 10.

Elihu Palmer, Radical Deist, Radical Republican: A Reconsideration of American Free Thought

RODERICK S. FRENCH

On July 4, 1793, Elihu Palmer addressed a sympathetic following gathered at Federal Point near Philadelphia. Palmer spoke first to those who were not in his immediate audience. "Beware, ye American aristocrats! Your principles and efforts are leading you to a precipice, from which the just resentment and indignation of an injured people will hurl you into eternal infamy." He then reminded his listeners that a double victory had been won for them. "King-craft and priest-craft, those mighty enemies to reason and liberty, were struck with death by the genius of 1776." But although mortally wounded, those demons apparently retained residual powers. All who wished to complete the Revolution according to true American principles must therefore work on *two* fronts. "The philosophy of this age, teaches the most pure and unadulterated morality; and stripping religion of its mysteries and external trappings, will present it to the view of the human mind in more beautiful and attractive charms, so that in every point of view, these great political events [the American and French Revolutions] will serve to ameliorate the conditions of the human race."[1]

There was of course no invariable correlation between radical religious views and radical political convictions either before or after 1776.² Henry May has concluded that while "real conservatives in religion and politics" were rare, "real radicals in both" were "still rarer."³ There was nonetheless a small group of people among whom the *combined* program of rationalism in religion and republicanism in politics came to be regarded as essential to the fulfillment of the promise of the Revolution. These radical deists–militant republicans represent an important transitional phase in the history of free thought.⁴ The outstanding indigenous exponent of this double radicalism was Elihu Palmer (1764–1806).

Adolph Koch is representative of previous scholars in that he assumed the dissolution of this correlation as his starting point. "The American liberal, while a republican in politics, was unable to accept republican religion. Consequently the religious implications of Revolutionary thought were quickly submerged and freethought became an isolated and irresponsible element in nineteenth-century America."⁵ Koch's research had the great merit of making eighteenth-century "infidelity" the subject of scholarly attention, and his thesis as to the *conservative* significance of the rise of Unitarianism is certainly correct. As his preface to the 1968 edition makes clear, however, he did not appreciate the progressive secularity of free thought. Contrary to Koch's suggestion, Palmer would *not* see his heroic career as vindicated in the consensual authority of the amalgam known as "civil religion." Palmer, rather, would insist that insofar as the nation has failed to fulfill the republican social ideals of the Revolution it is due to our failure to purge the national mind of the vestigial influences of the Christian religion. So convinced was Palmer that progressive knowledge and Christianity "are incompatible with each other" that he declared: "It may be confidently maintained that the world must either retrograde to a state of darkness, or . . . the belief of the Christian religion must become wholly extinct."⁶

It is telling that Koch's interpretation winds up in self-contradiction. The "religious implications of Revolutionary thought" which at first were said to have become an "isolated and irresponsible element" in American life are finally said to be widely "accepted as self-evident truths" precisely because of the failure "to establish deism as an institutionalized religion."[7] Virtually all studies dealing with this subject in any way during the last half century have relied on Koch's portrait of Palmer. A broader and more reliable presentation of Palmer's career and philosophy is to be found in Herbert Morais's study of eighteenth-century deism, also published in the 1930's.[8] Morais had a good grasp of the divisions within the deistic movement and their changing relationships to class differences. It has become a convention to cite the works of Koch and Morais in the same footnote with not so much as a hint that the two analyses are quite differently conceived. The major shortcoming in Morais's analysis was his failure to perceive the evolution of Palmer's thought beyond the critique of revealed religion to philosophical naturalism.

The radical freethinkers were those who, in Donald Meyer's terms, saw quite clearly that the "assumptions" of the "hidden logic" of the scientific philosophy of the Enlightment implied a thoroughgoing secular philosophy of naturalism. What is being challenged in this paper is Meyer's verdict that "writers like Allen and Palmer, and Paine, were stirred more by a resentment of religious authority... than by the intellectual urge to think out their personal faith" and that their position was "expressive more of anger than of curiosity, resolute inquiry, or even mischievous irreverence."[9]

Koch's focus was primarily on "the movement to establish deism as a religious cult," and the studies by Meyer and others confirm how difficult it would be to exaggerate the failure of that facet of the enterprise of enlightenment. But the implications of that failure are more limited if one's interest is a reevaluation of the defeated freethinkers from the perspective of either the continuity of political radicalism in early America or the emergence of philosophical naturalism in the history of American thought. Those who persisted in free thought have been neglected or misinterpreted in the scholarship dealing with both themes.

Although the interest of this paper centers on questions of political and intellectual history, it may be useful to introduce a brief, corrected biographical sketch of the principal figure in this movement. Elihu Palmer's life was not dominated by the public reserve characteristic of most deists, and a hostile press frequently took note of his activities.

Nonetheless, there is surprisingly little information available concerning his career, and that which does survive has become garbled as a result of generations of antagonistic or indifferent scholarship. The only contemporary source of any significance is a memoir which his friend John Fellows wrote and included in a letter to the radical London publisher Richard Carlile. In 1824 Carlile published the memoir along with three chapters of Palmer's unfinished work on politics and some other short writings under the collective title *Posthumous Pieces*. The memoir was reprinted several times by the next generation of radical free thought editors in this country.[10]

Palmer was born in 1764 on his father's farm in Canterbury, Connecticut. He entered Dartmouth at an age somewhat older than was usual for his time; did notably well, especially in literature; was elected to Phi Beta Kappa; and graduated in 1787. Whether from conviction or in the absence of other career opportunities, Palmer went to read theology under the Reverend John Foster in Pittsfield, Massachusetts. This apprenticeship of a few months was terminated by his acceptance of a call in 1788 from a Presbyterian congregation in Newtown, Queens County, Long Island. He did not wait to reach Long Island to make the first disclosure of his heterodoxy. In a Thanksgiving Day sermon delivered in Sheffield, Massachusetts, he explained to a no doubt startled congregation that instead of sitting there beating their spiritual breasts for the presumed misdeeds of Adam and his wife, they should be out celebrating the innocent delights of nature.

It took six months for him to lose his pulpit in Newtown. He then signed on with the Baptists in Philadelphia; they dismissed him for heresy in March 1791. This freed him to locate a more compatible audience. John Fitch and his associate in the steamboat enterprise, Henry Voight, were also the organizers of a deist group which met in Church Alley under the name of the Universal Society. Palmer's first appearance there was so well received that he advertised in a local paper that "on the succeeding Sunday he would deliver a discourse against the divinity of Jesus Christ." Fellows informs us that "an immense mob assembled at an early hour" and prevented Palmer from entering the building. More than that, Bishop William White, remembered as a model latitudinarian and friend of democracy, succeeded in having the society's lease revoked. Palmer, in Fellows's words, "was induced to quit the city" for his own safety.

Palmer drew both intellectual and professional conclusions from his abortive adventures as a clergyman. He left the ranks of Christianity as "a duty which he owed to the integrity of his own mind, and what was deemed the best interests of human society, to . . . assume a higher and better ground—that of Nature, and the immutability of her laws."[11] Palmer and his wife spent the next two years in western Pennsylvania, where he read law with his brother.

Palmer was admitted to the bar upon his return to Philadelphia in 1793, but before he could establish himself in a new career, yellow fever struck the city. Mrs. Palmer died; he survived but was blinded by the disease. Palmer sent his children to live with relatives in Connecticut. He moved to Augusta, Georgia, where he first devoted himself totally to the propagation of deism. When he passed through New York late in 1794 on the way to visit his children, a group of radical enthusiasts in the local Democratic Society invited him to lecture. This led eventually to the organization of a deistic society which, with the exception of a few periods of grave financial insufficiency, provided Palmer with an operational base for the remainder of his life. He frequently returned to Philadelphia to lecture; he died there while on a speaking tour in 1806.

II

In terms of political history, as the "ideological" interpretation of the sources of the American Revolution becomes more firmly established and its categories of analysis extended further into the life of the new nation, the little bands of radical deistic democrats look less and less like a fugitive fringe.[12] The militants appear, rather, to be distinguished mainly by their uncompromising insistence on drawing the full consequences of both the egalitarianism and the naturalism implicit in the eclectic ideology of popular republicanism. The standard assessment of the leading figure in this wing of the movement, Elihu Palmer, must be reconsidered accordingly.

In the eyes of the militant freethinkers, the American Revolution had opened the door to a new future for mankind, but they were apprehensive that the new nation would not cross the threshold. Moreover, they perceived certain of their contemporaries, Federalists in particular, as actively obstructing entrance into the new era. "When the justice and political utility of revolutions were first asserted, their abettors were considered, in the view of monarchy, as beings whose existence ought to be immediately sacrificed to the preservation of *order and good government*. This opinion, so fatal to the improvement of the human race, is still advocated in our own country."[13] If the Revolutionary ideology was becoming "dogma" by the end of the eighteenth century, as Bernard Bailyn suggests, it had not become praxis, and the freethinkers were very much concerned about the latter.[14]

They did not see the new federal and several state constitutions as consummate embodiments of the Revolution. "The American Constitutions are, undoubtedly, more perfect than any others that ever were formed, the effects of which have been fully experienced. But will anyone dare to say that there is no room left for improvement?"[15] Palmer for one did not regard official disestablishment as a sufficient safeguard against the inherently antidemocratic tendencies of the Christian religion. Man must recognize that "this system of religion" is "so incompatible with the dignity and happiness of his nature" that it "must be forever annihilated and destroyed."[16]

The militants were not content with a franchise open only to males. Palmer called for the "total annihilation of the prejudices which have established between the sexes an inequality of rights, fatal even to the party which it favours. In vain might we search for motives by which to justify this principle, in differences of physical organization, of intellect, or of moral sensibility. It had at first no other origin but abuse of strength, and all the attempts which have since been made to support it are idle sophisms."[17] (Palmer acknowledged parenthetically that this line of analysis had been advanced most forcibly by Condorcet.)

Neither did they regard slavery as an unfortunate but tolerable blemish on the fabric of the new republic. "We celebrate this day,"

Palmer said on July 4, 1800, "our emancipation from the British monarchy—it is well, it is vastly useful and important; but have we made thorough work of the change? . . . have we not declared that all men are born free and equal; and is there a single state in the union, in which this important, this immutable principle of justice is reduced to practice?"[18]

Finally the republican deists most certainly did not denounce the French Revolution as evidence of the dire consequences of radicalism in religion and politics. Palmer chastized his fellow Americans who had revised their democratic opinions because of the "cruel excesses which are attached to great and important revolutions." More than that he detected an old conspiracy behind this revisionism:

> It is not difficult to discover the motives of action in the profligate despots of the Old World; but it is lamentable and astonishing to observe a similar spirit actuating the minds and influencing the wishes of some of our American citizens. Whence this political apostasy, this dereliction of good principles in our own country?
>
> . . . .
>
> It is not an uncharitable conjecture to suppose that those who indulge such violent resentments against the French nation, on account of the EXCESSES of the revolution, are influenced by other sentiments than those which are purely humane and benevolent; and that some secret attachment to the British system of government has united itself with their political opinions.[19]

This cluster of principles and passions led the radical deists to associations (of friendship, when not membership) with the Democratic-Republican Societies which emerged in the 1790's. As a rule the deistic societies in each urban center were formed only slightly later than the Democratic-Republican clubs. There was always an overlap but never an identity of membership. Elihu Palmer, for example, after his arrival in the city in 1794, "joined the Democratic Society of New York. But all the members by no means went along with their deist colleagues such as Palmer, David Denniston, and John Sideall, when those formed a Deistical Society. The same was true in Philadelphia, where certain democratic society members favored and others opposed the formation of a deistical club."[20]

The situation in New York requires special clarification. The New York Democratic Society was organized in February 1794 and had a fairly wide overlap in membership with the older Tammany Society. The group which coalesced around Palmer and later (in 1796) formed the Deistical Society of New York no doubt drew from the same constituencies, but it had an orientation and program distinct from both. This corrects the impression left by Schneider: "In several cities [Palmer] helped to organize 'temples of reason' or 'theistic societies' (among them Tammany in New York)."[21] Philip Freneau was one of those who belonged to all three organizations, after moving up from Philadelphia.[22]

Alfred Young minimizes the role of Palmer and "the numerically small deists" in shaping New York Republicanism by comparison with the influence of liberal ministers of the orthodox denominations. Young's analysis does not reflect a direct knowledge of Palmer's writings. Moreover, he observed that "ideology as well as political necessity pushed Republicans toward ridding society of its 'glaring deformities.'"[23] Palmer was a voice from within the left wing of the movement trying to accelerate the reform tendency.

Allowing for the fact that they were minority voices to the left of the generality of republicans, it is nonetheless interesting to see the terms in which the militants formulated their call for the *double* fulfillment of the American experiment. Tunis Wortman, a brilliant lawyer and leading figure in the New York Democratic Society, was one of the most emphatic exponents of this radical correlation. "Why," he asked, "should we read history without profiting by it? Ambition and tyranny have always been fond of assuming the mask of religion and making instruments of judges and divines." Wortman most probably drafted the broadside circulated by the New York Democratic Society which expressed the same sentiment, more strongly phrased. "Superstition in religious creeds, and Despotism in civil institutions, bear a relation to each other.... The same principle which supports the one, tends to strengthen and invigorate the other."[24]

Another example of a militant New York deist who insisted on drawing the implications of republican ideology for social justice was the eccentric and sometimes notorious lawyer William Keteltas. He was a member of the Democratic Society in the 1790's and said to be a deist. Because of his record of opposition to "imprisonment for debt, unfair punishments, and corrupt politics, he was a popular hero whom the crowds followed, shouting 'The Spirit of '76.' "25

Dennis Driscol, immigrant Irish ex-priest, was editor of the New York Deistical Society's paper, *The Temple of Reason*. Driscol's editorial following Jefferson's victory over Adams reflected the bipolar view of national affairs held by the deistic groups in New York, Philadelphia, Baltimore, and elsewhere. Driscol interpreted the election as "the triumph of Democracy... which promises the most fortunate consequences. The Liberties of the People are placed under the safeguard of the Laws, and in the hands of men, who have given early and repeated proofs of their devotion to the Freedom and Independence of their Country. The genuine principles of the American Revolution, will be again acted upon, and Aristocracy must sink into her original insignificance." Driscol reminded his readers that *The Temple* represented a minority point of view precisely because it "combines Politics with Pure Religion.... Contrary to the opinion of most men, we hold, that Deism and Liberty should go hand in hand; and as mankind get enlightened, we are happy to find, that our opinion is verefied [*sic*]. It would appear to be a contradiction in terms, to find men renounce King-craft and still remain *enchanted* by Superstition and Priest-craft."26

On the previous Fourth of July, in an oration delivered in New York, Elihu Palmer had looked forward to the national election in exactly the same frame of reference. "In seventeen hundred and seventy-six, the people of the United States declared in the most spirited manner against all foreign tyranny or despotism whatever; in the year eighteen hundred, they are about to exercise the same holy right, and perform the same duty against their domestic oppressors."27 Such passages once would have been dismissed as eccentric and extravagant, if not purely rhetorical. More recent scholarship indicates that Palmer was not exceptional in continuing to use the language of the old opposition ideology to interpret partisan domestic issues. "Jeffersonian Republicanism was much more systematically ideological than has been seen.... To Republicans the nation was in the hands of liberticides, and the danger was serious and real."28

Palmer was distinguished only by the intense sincerity with which he held to this view of public affairs *and* his insistence on combining it with his philosophy of religion. The unity of his views was supplied by the anthropology of his confident humanism. He never tired of asserting "that the powers of man are competent to all the great purposes of human existence."[29] And of those powers of course reason was the chief. "The hopes of man all center in the power and activity of intellect."[30]

It was a central assumption of the militants that their views on society and on religion were simply correlative deductions from a rigorously *modern* philosophy of nature. Natural man is by divine design competent to manage *all* his own affairs. Their democracy and their deism had the same root. And the momentum of their thoughts ultimately carried their rationalism beyond deism to the point that they became the first tentative voices of philosophical naturalism in America.

III

This brings our inquiry to the second aspect of cultural and intellectual history in which the militant freethinkers deserve reconsideration. The misunderstanding and/or neglect of the philosophical reasonings of Palmer and his friends relates to a larger problem in the historiography of American philosophy. Historians of philosophy have tended to give only passing attention to the first and second generations of freethinkers in this country, perhaps because of their rude rhetoric or their sometimes indecorous behavior.[31] This oversight contributes to the improbable impression that there were no real precedents for the emergence of a naturalistic perspective in American thought.[32]

Harold Larrabee recognized this problem in an excellent essay published thirty years ago. "There were naturalistic forces at work in this country long before their overt manifestations in the philosophy of the closing decades of the nineteenth century, and to ignore them is to make the present vigor of that point of view unintelligible."[33] In Larrabee's own discussion of the Revolutionary period, however, he simply bracketed Palmer with Thomas Paine, Ethan Allen, and other "militants" and made no analysis of his writings. (It seems to be Palmer's fate always to be one in a list. The close personal and philosophical association of Palmer and Paine in particular has discouraged independent investigation of Palmer's writings.)

The militant deists are missing from consideration even in those studies where their role would seem most evidently relevant. A key line from an essay by Perry Miller in which he is discussing the place of Chauncy Wright in American intellectual history is illustrative: "He [Wright] is among the first, if not the very first, in our culture to assert that agnostics and naturalists can be as devoted to the aims of civilization as the righteous."[34] Yet Elihu Palmer was his most eloquent precisely on the point of the superiority, not merely the possibility, of autonomous, secular, humanist ethics.

Palmer was exceptional not only in challenging the priority of Jesus as moralist but in proposing that the soundest system of ethics would be one developed on strictly naturalistic presuppositions. In the first edition of his *Principles of Nature; or, A Development of the Moral Causes of Happiness and Misery among the Human Species* (1801), Palmer only raised the issue: "It has been a great question, how far the principle of theology affects the principle and practice of virtue." In a new chapter added to the second edition, which appeared the following year, he answered his own question in direct language. "If a thousand Gods existed, or if nature existed independent of any—the moral relation between man and man would remain exactly the same in either case. Moral principle is the result of this relation, it is founded in the properties of our nature and it is as indestructible as the basis on which it rests."[35]

Herbert Schneider did devote a few pages in his widely used history of American philosophy to the freethinkers at the close of the eighteenth century. He characterized them as "prophets of the growth of natural philosophy," but he discounted their contribution by a comparison with the work of David Rittenhouse, Benjamin Rush, and other far less radical but more technically scientific intellectuals. Professor Schneider is normally so inclusive in his consideration of possible sources that it is difficult to account for his failure to discuss the substance of Palmer's *Principles* and his passing over it as "an expression of free thought as an organized movement."[36] The *Principles* was a compilation of the lectures which Palmer delivered regularly in many cities, but it was far more than an organizational manual. Furthermore, I suspect the book may hold one key to his limited success as an organizer: he was expounding views too sharp and too advanced even for many of his deistic, freethinking friends. A passage from John Fellows's memoir supports this suspicion.

> Mr. Palmer, as a public speaker, was equalled by few.... Had he, however, been more indulgent to weak inquirers after truth, he probably would have gained more proselytes. The bold and positive manner in which he attacked popular prejudices wounded the self-pride of some, who could not bear to hear their darling scheme of revelation so roughly handled, and frightened others, who, like invalids, required to be nursed with food more tender, and better adapted to their digestive faculties.[37]

The cliché which praises Palmer the organizer (at which function he was ultimately a failure) and discounts Palmer the thinker (in which role he was truly exceptional) has given rise to some very misleading comparisons. For example, "Ethan Allen's *Reason the Only Oracle of Man* (1784) was the earliest of the major deistic books and demonstrates the deistic reaction to traditional Calvinism. Allen went further than many deists, vigorously defending anticlericalism which was its most radical expression. Elihu Palmer's *Principles of Nature* (1801 or 1802) was an excellent later expression of a similar viewpoint."[38]

When Merle Curti wrote his classic study of American thought, he had a more detailed grasp of deism in the post-Revolutionary generation. He not only knew about Palmer's book but knew what it was about. Yet, he repeated the standard stereotype: "Palmer's contribution lay less in his written exposition of deism, which after all rethreshed old straw, than in the force that he gave to a bold and, in its appeals to the masses, engaging movement."[39] That estimate simply cannot stand in view of the fact that Palmer arrived at positions distinctively novel in American thought up to his time, while he failed to win or hold "the masses" for his program of continuing radicalism.

The justification for claiming significant intellectual originality for Elihu Palmer will have to be elaborated in another context.[40] The more narrow aim of the present article has been to survey the evidence which justifies a reexamination of the militant freethinkers. The main headings of that originality, however, can be summarized by way of a very swift comparison of Palmer's views on two issues with those held by better-known American deists.

The status of Jesus was one of the most sensitive points in the eighteenth-century criticism of Christianity. Most deists stressed his humanity and tried to use his teachings as recorded in the New Testament to set him apart from the institution which bore his name. Even after the performance of the heirarchy in the French Revolution had provoked Paine to his most outspoken attacks on Christianity, he did not qualify his regard for its founder. "He was a virtuous and an amiable man. The morality that he preached and practiced has not been exceeded by any."[41] Similar sentiments are scattered throughout the writings and correspondence of Franklin and Jefferson.

Palmer would have none of this balanced view. "Christians and Deists have sometimes coincided in their opinion, that Jesus was a good character. This opinion, so far as it was acceded to by some of the first unbelievers, was either the result of ignorance, or an effect of fear." "In every moral point of view, the world is infinitely worse" as a result of the life and teachings of Jesus.[42] He insisted that moral maxims are "clearly deducible from the powers and character of man," and criticized those who, like Priestley and Godwin (and by implication, Jefferson), confused matters by trying to accommodate rational morality to "Scripture doctrines."[43] A true democracy required a univocal source of moral insight accessible to all sincere men. The Bible, including the New Testament, is "at war with moral virtue, the peace of society, and the best interests of man."[44]

Not only did Palmer challenge the priority of Jesus as a moralist and dismiss the teachings of the New Testament as dehumanizing, but, as noted above, he also took the decisive step toward secularism by asserting that the soundest system of ethics would be one developed without any theistic presuppositions. This placed him in advance of all the major American intellectuals of his period.

A second test question for the transition from natural theology to philosophical naturalism was that of immortality. Deistic rationalists generally regarded traditional notions of heaven and hell as grotesque fantasies, but they retained an unargued and dispassionate belief in a continuity of personal existence beyond death. Of even more significance in the present context, they were fully persuaded of the utility of such a belief for the sanctioning of social morality. The conventional expressions of Jefferson and Franklin on this point are, again, well known.

Palmer outlined a reinterpretation of the meaning of death which was much closer to that of the left-wing, materialist *philosophes*. The fact that death is "the inevitable portion of every living creature" could not be mitigated by any body-soul dualism. Man is a unity, "a being whose composition is purely physical, and moral properties or intellect are the necessary results of organic construction."[45] Not surprisingly, this view of human mortality reinforced Palmer's republicanism. Man "must be reconciled to that kind of immortality which nature prepares for her children, and which diffuses through the intelligent world a sentiment of equality, terrifying to every species of spiritual or political aristocracy."[46]

Palmer's most interesting passages often reflect an enthusiastic assimilation of the dynamic, organic "materialism" of d'Holbach. He both cites and paraphrases frequently from the 1797 London edition of "Mirabaud's" *System of Nature* and the 1795 New York edition of "Boulanger's" *Christianity Unveiled*. (Palmer apparently gave credence to the pseudonymous authorship of both works.) Palmer also uses long extracts from Volney's *Ruins* to reinforce his critique of Christianity from the standpoint of the new comparative study of religions. If Lumberg and May are correct that "Americans were exposed to all the major currents of the eighteenth-century French and British Enlightenment except perhaps for the extremes of French materialism," the exceptional role of Palmer receives added confirmation.[47]

Even from the condensed citations given in this paper, it should be clear that Palmer was struggling to articulate the themes which would become prominent in the classic works of American pragmatic naturalism: the continuity of human experience; intelligence as a purposeful, organic activity; the utility of experimental knowledge; and the promise inherent in the extension of scientific inquiry to all fields of study. To take one title for comparison, recall Dewey's *Quest for Certainty*, in which he seeks to overcome the history of dualism in philosophy and develops his concepts of "the naturalization of intelligence" and of "knowing as a means of secular control." Perhaps the greatest point of difference between Palmer and later Pragmatists is in the concept of natural law. As was the case with all Newtonians, Palmer was convinced of the immutability of all laws. The most significant influence accounting for the transformation of American naturalism between the beginning and the close of the nineteenth century was the work of Charles Darwin. Palmer did as well as one might using d'Holbach's chemistry and physics, but he could not explore the creative implications for philosophy of evolutionary biology. If Palmer's naturalism sometimes seemed to be little more than a critique of supernaturalism, that, too, was important in order to combat the remarkable power of the Western religious tradition to inhibit constructive secular thought.

At the same time, it must be acknowledged that Palmer is in part responsible for his neglect at the hands of scholars. Whether because of his blindness or because of a certain weakness of systematic powers, his writings are uneven and not always internally coherent. In his own book, he collected essays written at different periods without any concern for harmonizing earlier and later views. It is also important to remember that his career as a mature freethinker covered little more than a decade. Moreover, not only does his use of conventions of eighteenth-century philosophical expression give the impression of a lack of originality, but their repeated use actually obscures the originality of the ideas which he is seeking to express.

IV

Precisely in those opening years of the nineteenth century when Palmer was trying to think his way onto new ground, American popular sentiment grew hostile toward men who placed their confidence in reason. Palmer tried to challenge the motivation of those, like Timothy Dwight, who sought to discredit critical rationalism. He said, "The plain truth of the case is, that those who oppose philosophy and bestow upon it harsh and malignant epithets, are interested in keeping up a privileged system of plunder and robbery, which makes nine-tenths of the human race absolute slaves to support the other tenth in indolence, extravagance, pride, and luxury."[48] But Palmer was speaking into the wind. He and his few collaborators were no match for the trends of accommodation in politics and revivalism in religion.

It is an error, however, to suppose that free thought was extinguished. It went under a heavy eclipse for a long decade. But it is partly an ideological judgment which asserts that free thought became an "isolated and irresponsible" element in American life. The fact was that coincident with the new wave of democratic agitation in the Jacksonian period, free thought reappeared with an intellectual vigor and a breadth of following which far exceeded anything enjoyed by the earlier deists. What is more, freethinkers of this new generation were quite aware of their domestic predecessors. They began in the 1820's to republish the works of Paine and Palmer in cheap editions and to serialize them in all the radical papers.[49]

Beginning in the 1820's freethinkers in small towns and major cities regrouped and began holding celebrations on January 29 each year in observance of Tom Paine's birthday.[50] (The first recorded observance was in London in 1818.) At the New York City celebration in 1827, one toast proposed and drunk was to "the memory of Elihu Palmer, Voltaire, Hume and all those deceased philosophers who, by their writings, contributed to subvert superstition, and vindicate the rights of humanity."[51]

Palmer would have smiled at this partisan, provincial overestimation of his stature. He might, however, have accepted the judgment of an English court delivered a few years before. Widespread discontent in England had provoked a government campaign of repression, facilitated by the suspension of habeas corpus in 1817. One of the government's principal targets was Richard Carlile, "a tinplate worker turned newsvendor by the post-Waterloo distress" whose deconversion had been effected in 1817 through a reading of the *Age of Reason*. By the following year he had begun a periodical, *The Deist,* and soon republished "Elihu Palmer's *Principles of Nature,* a work of American 'infidelity' only second in influence to Paine's." Brought to trial in October 1819 as an example to other radical publishers, Carlile "was sentenced to two years' imprisonment and a £1000 fine for publishing the *Age of Reason,* one year's imprisonment and a £500 fine for republishing the *Principles of Nature.*"[52] Palmer believed Paine to have been "probably the most useful man that ever existed upon the face of the earth."[53] It would have been sufficient reward for his own labors to have been deemed even half as subversive by the enemies of liberty and reason.

NOTES

1 Elihu Palmer, *Extracts from an Oration, delivered by Elihu Palmer, the 4th of July, 1793,* in *Political Miscellany* (New York: G. Forman, 1793), pp. 23, 22, 26. Philip Freneau gave parts of the front and second pages of his paper, *The National Gazette,* of July 23, 1793, to extracts from this oration. Freneau was a deist and also active in the Democratic Society of Philadelphia, which had been formed on July 3 of that year with David Rittenhouse as president.

2 Quite similar configurations of enlightened views in religion and politics were present in France and England. Ronald I. Boss, "The Development of Social Religion: A Contradiction of French Free Thought," *Journal of the History of Ideas,* 34 (1973), 577–89, presents a careful analysis of the "contradiction" which arose because of the failure of French social theory to keep pace with the secularization of other spheres of thought beginning in the seventeenth century. D'Holbach, whose writings had a large influence on Palmer, was exceptional in advocating a rigorous consistency of views. Stromberg carries the point much too far in claiming that none "of the English deists" were "really political radicals" (Roland N. Stromberg, "Lovejoy's 'Parallel' Reconsidered," *Eighteenth-Century Studies,* 1 [March 1968], 392). To cite just one early exception, Charles Blount "admirably demonstrated all those connections conservative contemporaries most feared: the connections between near atheist views, and the political causes of liberty for the press, toleration, skepticism, and cynicism" (J. S. Redwood, "Charles Blount (1654–93), Deism, and English Free Thought," *Journal of the History of Ideas,* 35 [1974], 490). One of those who espoused both republicanism and deism in this country was Thomas Young. See the very interesting interpretation of the influence of Enlightenment science on his radicalism in Pauline Maier, "Reason and Revolution: The Radicalism of Dr. Thomas Young," *American Quarterly,* 28 (Summer 1976), 229–49.

3 Henry F. May, "The Problem of the American Enlightenment," *New Literary History*, 1 (Winter 1970), 209. May has been most impressed by the fact that in the American Enlightenment "what flourished were ideas susceptible of compromise" (p. 207). This emphasis on the "taming" of the Enlightenment has been influential on a wide range of scholarship over the last decade and tends naturally to limit interest in radical ideas and persons. See Donald H. Meyer, *The Democratic Enlightenment* (New York: Capricorn Books, 1975), esp. ch. 11. Meyer sees the outcome of the clash of the 1790's as "the containment and appropriation of Enlightenment thought" (p. 171). He recognizes that one consequence of the Americanization of the Enlightenment on those terms was the loss of the "critical spirit" from our social and political life (p. xxvii). Since this paper was written, May has published *The Enlightenment in America* (New York: Oxford University Press, 1976). Although a large body of material is reviewed, there is no fundamental change in the perspective of interpretation developed in his 1970 article. It is perhaps most significant that May's extended study culminates in an equivocation; he remains uncertain as to whether the Englightenment was defeated or assimilated.

4 The question of terminology raises a host of fascinating problems. Free thought, Skepticism, Deism, Pantheism, Infidelity—all belong to the idiom of the Age of Reason. All were controversial terms because they were used polemically in the debate as to whether Christianity could still be regarded as, first, consistent with and, later, necessary to the moral, intellectual, and political principles of an enlightened man. Probably the most significant point is that the radicals often did not know what to call themselves. For an extended discussion of terminology and related philosophical issues, see my dissertation, "The Trials of Abner Kneeland," George Washington 1971, pp. 331–45.

5 Adolph Koch, *Republican Religion, The American Revolution and the Cult of Reason* (New York: Columbia University Press, 1933), p. xii. Reprinted as *Religion of the American Enlightenment* (New York: Thomas Y. Crowell, 1968).

6 Elihu Palmer, *Principles of Nature; or, A Development of the Moral Causes of Happiness and Misery among the Human Species*, 2nd ed. (New York, 1802), p. 80.

7 Koch, *Religion of the American Enlightenment*, p. xviii. Koch also wrote the entry on Palmer in the *DAB* (IV, 177–79).

8 Herbert M. Morais, *Deism in Eighteenth-Century America* (1934; rpt. New York: Russell & Russell, 1960). See esp. ch. 5.

9 Meyer, *Democratic Enlightenment*, pp. xv, 174–75. Meyer would find more than a little "mischievous irreverence" in Palmer's "Original Sin, Atonement, Faith, etc. A Christmas Discourse delivered in New York, December, 1796." This sarcastic homily circulated as a pamphlet for at least a decade and was also printed as ch. 5 of *Principles of Nature*.

10 *The Beacon*, Nov. 5, 1836, pp. 32–34.

11 Palmer, *Principles of Nature*, p. iv.

12 In addition to the extensive journal literature which develops the arguments of Caroline Robbins, Bernard Bailyn, and Gordon Wood, see Richard Buel, Jr., *Securing the Revolution: Ideology in American Politics, 1789–1815* (Ithaca: Cornell University Press, 1972).

13 Elihu Palmer, *The Political Happiness of Nations; an Oration* (New York, 1800), pp. 7-8.
14 Bernard Bailyn, *The Ideological Origins of the American Revolution* (Cambridge, Mass.: Harvard University Press, 1967), p. 21.
15 Elihu Palmer, *An Enquiry Relative to the Moral and Political Improvement of the Human Species. An Oration Delivered in the City of New York on the Fourth of July* (New York, 1797), p. 16.
16 Palmer, *Principles of Nature*, p. 81. This is but one of countless citations which would suggest how inadequate it is to subsume Palmer's polemic under the rubric of anticlericalism.
17 Palmer, *An Enquiry*, p. 32.
18 Palmer, *Political Happiness*, pp. 19-20. As Alfred Young has demonstrated, the New York Republicans solidly supported abolition, inspired not by religious motivations but by "the new egalitarianism of the mid-1790's" (Alfred F. Young, *The Democratic Republicans of New York* [Chapel Hill: University of North Carolina Press, 1967], p. 529).
19 Palmer, *An Enquiry*, p. 11. In his annual oration delivered three years later, Palmer confessed that the "genuine republican" did not have much in France to rejoice in at the moment, but "the revolution in its principle, is the object of attachment and admiration" (*Political Happiness*, p. 13).
20 Eugene Perry Link, *Democratic-Republican Societies, 1790-1800* (New York: Columbia University Press, 1942), p. 120. Link's close analysis of the membership and political activities of forty-two of these societies founded in thirteen states effectively documents the fact that this movement not only reflected a truly popular "opposition to the anti-democratic tendencies of the period," but was also a conscious revival of "the spirit of '76." On this same point, Young has concluded that for all the qualifications that must be made of Carl Becker's thesis, "Jeffersonian Republicans of New York City . . . could claim that they were heirs to the 'spirit of '76' and that the 'revolution of 1800' was indeed the consummation of the Revolution of 1776" (Alfred Young, "The Mechanics and the Jeffersonians: New York, 1789-1801," *Labor History*, 5 [Fall 1964], 276).
21 Herbert W. Schneider, *A History of American Philosophy*, 2nd ed. (New York: Columbia University Press, 1963), p. 62.
22 E. V. Blake, *History of the Tammany Society* (New York, 1901), p. 32.
23 Young, *Democratic Republicans*, pp. 404, 570, 582.
24 Quoted in Link, *Democratic-Republican Societies*, pp. 119-20. Link further states in the same passage: "As to the religious theory of the societies, it is not accurate to make a blanket statement that the clubs were 'atheistic' or even dominantly deistic. . . . [Many] were conservatives in religion and radicals in politics. . . . The intellectual leadership of the clubs was more consistent and, in general, it saw the relationship between superstition in religion and gullibility in political life."
25 Ibid., p. 153. Keteltas's erratic career is reviewed rather thoroughly in Young's book. John Fellows (1760-1844), the "Republican book dealer" who became Palmer's friend and biographer, also belongs in any inventory of deist-republicans of this period.

26 *The Temple of Reason*, April 22, 1801. Palmer is frequently cited as the editor of this paper. Driscol began it—"to combat the enemies of Deism"—with the issue for November 8, 1800. In April of 1801 he moved operations to Philadelphia, where Palmer was spending most of his time lecturing and frankly trying to make a living. Driscol moved on to Baltimore and other ventures exactly one year later, and Palmer managed the affairs of the paper until its demise for lack of paid subscribers in February of 1803. He moved again to New York, where, with the assistance of the second Mrs. Palmer (formerly the widow Mrs. Mary Powell), he shortly began his own new paper, *Prospect*. *The Temple* had at least served as a useful vehicle for the serial publication in English of works by d'Holbach, Volney, Voltaire, and Helvétius as well as extracts from Bentham, Hume, and Locke. Driscol's views are discussed systematically in Richard J. Twomey, *Jacobins and Jeffersonians: Anglo-American Radicalism in the United States, 1790–1820* (De Kalb: Northern Illinois University, 1974).

27 Palmer, *Political Happiness*, p. 11.

28 Lance Banning, "Jeffersonian Ideology and the French Revolution: A Question of Liberticide at Home," *Studies in Burke and His Time*, 17, no. 1 (1976), 8.

29 *Prospect*, Dec. 17, 1803.

30 Palmer, *An Enquiry*, p. 23.

31 I. Woodbridge Riley's *American Philosophy: The Early Schools* (1907; rpt. New York: Russell & Russell, 1969) was the major work in this field for several decades. He presented Palmer as the chief American agent of Paine's ideas and made no analysis of Palmer's own works. He dismissed without elaboration the influence of d'Holbach and seems to have thought *Prospect* was a book rather than a paper (pp. 307–8). One difficulty with the treatment of Palmer in most surveys of American thought is that too much interpretation is based on the rather conventional eleven Principles of the Deistical Society of New York State. I suspect this has happened largely because Koch reproduced them in full, whereas Palmer's other writings are not generally available. There are at least two source books which reproduce more interesting selections: Peter Gay, ed., *Deism: An Anthology* (Princeton: D. Van Nostrand, 1968), and Gerald N. Grob and Robert N. Beck, eds., *American Ideas* (New York: The Free Press of Glencoe, 1963).

32 English free thought had a different history; the Utilitarians were the real successors to the eighteenth-century deists. They also assimilated to their legacy of English radicalism much of the work of the *philosophes*. James Mill, whose thought was influenced by Helvétius, collaborated with "infidel" radicals in writings on economic reforms (Simon Maccoby, *English Radicalism, 1786–1832* [London: Allen & Unwin, 1955], p. 476). Jeremy Bentham often had to use small radical publishers for his works as his advocacy of democratic reforms became sharper and the climate more conservative (Hugh J. Luke, Jr., *Drams for the Vulgar: A Study of Some Radical Publishers and Publications of Early Nineteenth-Century London* [Austin: University of Texas, 1963], pp. 540–41). Utilitarianism did not flourish in this country. But it was as Chauncy Wright began to utilize John Stuart Mill's empiricism to draw out the philosophical implications of Darwinism that the groundwork was laid for the emergence of Pragmatism. See Philip P. Wiener, *Evolution and the Founders of Pragmatism* (Cambridge, Mass.: Harvard University Press, 1949), esp. ch. 3.

33 Harold A. Larrabee, "Naturalism in America," in *Naturalism and the Human Spirit*, ed. Yervant H. Krikorian (New York: Columbia University Press, 1944), p. 320.
34 Perry Miller, *American Thought, Civil War to World War I* (New York, 1954), p. xxii.
35 Palmer, *Principles of Nature*, 1802 ed., pp. 24, 253. The printing history of this book is difficult to reconstruct. The first edition was printed in New York in 1801. All page references in this paper are to the 1802, or second, edition. The third U.S. edition appeared in 1806; what was called the eighth edition was published in New York by George H. Evans in 1830. The several English editions are described in a later note.
36 Schneider, *History*, pp. 61-70. It is interesting that the next reference to naturalism in Schneider's book comes in his discussion of Chauncy Wright.
37 *The Beacon*, Nov. 5, 1836.
38 Paul Russell Anderson and Max Harold Fisch, *Philosophy in America from the Puritans to James, with Representative Selections* (New York, 1939), p. 155. In questioning the comparison, I mean to take nothing away from the colorful Allen. But the main thrust of his book was the traditional deist effort to rescue true religion from superstition, to present to a lay audience a persuasive, "modern," rational concept of God and of his unfailing providence in nature. Anderson and Fisch is overall the best book on early American philosophy. Their introductions to the selections from Allen, Cooper, Rush, and other intellectuals of the period are excellent.
39 Merle Curti, *The Growth of American Thought*, 3rd ed. (New York: Harper & Row, 1964), p. 154.
40 Andrew Reck, historian of American philosophy, recently reviewed the pamphlet literature of the Revolution to see "whether in the interplay of idea and event any conceptual originality occurs." Reck concluded that, contrary to Bernard Bailyn's somewhat condescending estimate, the pamphleteers, on the whole, "were correct in their interpretations of the philosophical texts they cited." More than that, they were often "highly original" in the ways they "deduced from the philosophical theories in conjunction with the new events hitherto-unconceived implications, giving rise to novel theories." Professor Reck provides numerous illustrations of what he regards as philosophical creativity in the pamphleteers. See Andrew J. Reck, "The Philosophical Background of the American Revolution," *Southwestern Journal of Philosophy*, 5 (Spring 1974), 179-200. This is the kind of review which needs to be carried on into the post-Revolutionary period.
41 Paine, *The Age of Reason*, part I, ch. 3.
42 Palmer, *Principles of Nature*, pp. 269, 46.
43 *Prospect*, Dec. 31, 1803, pp. 25-26.
44 Palmer, *Principles of Nature*, p. 143.
45 Ibid., pp. 229, 285.
46 Ibid., p. 332.
47 David Lumberg and Henry F. May, "The Enlightened Reader in America," *American Quarterly*, 28 (Summer 1976), 262-71.
48 Palmer, *Principles of Nature*, p. 187.
49 This practice continued until this wave of free thought had run its course, around 1840. In his paper, *The Boston Investigator*, Abner Kneeland regularly advertised

an edition of the *Principles of Nature* for 75 cents, as well as prints of both Palmer and Paine.

50 In 1837, as if to redeem their city's honor from the pitifully timid reception accorded Paine on his return in 1803, the freethinkers held a dinner, followed by a ball in Tammany Hall, attended by eight hundred men and women (*The Beacon*, Feb. 11, 1837). During the 1830's the columns of *The Boston Investigator* were filled every February with reports of Paine's birthday celebrations held in villages and towns throughout New England, New York, Pennsylvania, and Ohio.

51 *The Correspondent*, Feb. 3, 1827.

52 Maccoby, *English Radicalism*, pp. 456–57. J. Cahuac also published Palmer's *Principles* in London in 1819. Carlile's imprisonment had become such a scandal by 1825 that he was released unconditionally, his effectiveness as a radical agitator now greatly enhanced. Members of his family and loyal friends who kept his press going had published the *Principles* again in 1823, and Carlile released another edition in 1826.

53 Palmer, *Principles of Nature*, p. 185. It was a relationship of mutual respect, beginning with Paine's acknowledgment of receipt of the first edition of the *Principles* in a letter from Paris dated Feb. 21, 1802. "Dear Friend, I received... the excellent work you have published. I see you have thought deeply on the subject, and expressed your thoughts in a strong and clear style. The hinting and intimating manner of writing that was formerly used on subjects of this kind, produced skepticism, but not conviction. It is necessary to be bold." The full letter is quoted in Moncure D. Conway, *The Life of Thomas Paine* (New York: G. P. Putnam, 1908), II, 298–99. Elihu and Mrs. Palmer were Paine's most unfailing friends during his last bitter years. It was Mrs. Palmer who often served as maid and nurse as he moved from one lodging to another after 1806. She used part of a $100 bequest from Paine to publish his reply to Bishop Watson in 1810.

Binding and Dressing Nature's Loose Tresses: The Ideology of Augustan Landscape Design

CAROLE FABRICANT

The symbolic association of women and land has been explored in the past through a variety of Freudian and Jungian interpretations, so that by now we are quite familiar with the image of the great mother goddess earth and of the garden as the repository of female mysteries, both maternal and erotic.[1] The trouble with viewing the feminine landscape in these terms, however, is that we tend as a result to overlook the fact that it can assume very different shapes and meanings reflecting historical changes in taste, in political and epistemological assumptions, in patterns of economic distribution and ownership. Considerations like these help to determine more precisely what "the lay of the land" signifies in any given period.[2] My particular concern in this essay is with the way in which the links between women and landscape, as they were commonly perceived and treated by poets, painters, and estate planners alike, expressed certain fundamental interconnections between aesthetics and ideology in eighteenth-century England. The political terminology frequently employed in contemporary treatises on landscape gardening possesses more than metaphorical significance and comes to assume very special nuances when understood in light of the assumed sexuality of the land. It is not coincidental that Horace Walpole chose to call Capability Brown both the "second monarch of landscape" *and* "Lady Nature's second husband."[3]

The analogy could on occasion be expressed in strikingly literal terms, as evident in Richard Bradley's primarily clinical but also faintly voyeuristic descriptions of the "female parts" of plants as they lay exposed before his minute scrutiny, alternately revealing the "Several Ovaries of the Pompion or Melon," between which, he assures us, "we may very easily perceive the Vagina," and the "Postillum or Uterus of the Tulip, cut horizontal and magnified with one of Campani's Microscopes."[4] Far more often, however, this gynecological spirit of inquiry gave way to the aesthetic but no less sexual contemplation of the gentleman builder or planter dedicated to beautifying the landscape, to rearranging a terrain that could boast of such features as "Venus's-Looking-glass" and "Venus's Navel-wort."[5] The all-important sexual dimension of Augustan gardening has previously been almost totally ignored, despite the many studies—some admirably thorough in other respects—devoted to aspects of eighteenth-century landscape design.[6]

Throughout the period, Nature was variously described as a coy or seductive maiden, as a promiscuous or chaste consort, as a naked or overadorned damsel. An obvious example occurs in Pope's depiction of Windsor Forest:

> Here waving Groves a chequer'd Scene display,
> And part admit and part exclude the Day;
> As some coy Nymph her Lover's warm Address
> Nor quite indulges, nor can quite repress.
>   (17–20)[7]

The mixture of freedom and constraint, abandonment and discipline, suggested in this passage, characterized Pope's own gardens at Twickenham judging from a description of it written three years after the poet's death by a visitor, who spoke of "Banks and Hillocks; which are entirely cover'd with Thickets of Lawrel, Bay, Holly, and many other Evergreens and Shrubs . . . where Nature freely lays forth the Branches, and disports uncontroul'd; except what may be entirely prun'd away for more Decency and Convenience to the surrounding Grass-plots."[8]

This paradoxical combination was, in fact, relevant to all eighteenth-century landscapes, particularly the gardens of the major estates, which catered to the pleasures of the "unfettered eye," to what Stephen Switzer in his *Iconographia Rustica* referred to as the mind's natural desire to "rove uncontroul'd thro' the promiscuous Scenes of a Country" (GP, p. 156), even as they insisted upon man's "skillful hand in management" in order to prevent anarchic dispersion and avoid what Humphrey Repton, in discoursing upon gardens, termed "the liberty of savages."⁹ The "opening and retiring shades of Venus's Vale" at Stourhead (the words are Walpole's [GP, p. 315]) and the suggestively sinuous banks laid out in "French curves" which William Kent designed for his canal were only two of the many forms through which the landscape's feminine allurements were highlighted but also kept in check by gentlemen gardeners who felt called upon to restrain the "careless and loose Tresses of Nature," as Switzer put it (GP, p. 153), while yet enhancing her sensuous appeal for the gratification of estate owner and visiting spectators. Both women and landscape were continually being judged for their ability to titillate the imagination and satisfy the senses while at the same time remaining within carefully prescribed moral, aesthetic, and territorial limits.

The establishment of these limits was occasionally expressed in quite forceful, even militaristic terms, as when Pope observes that Lord Peterborough "tames the Genius of the stubborn Plain, / Almost as quickly, as he conquer'd Spain" (*Satire II*, i, 131–32). More often, however, the impulse to restrict and to control was conveyed more subtly. In his *History of the Modern Taste in Gardening*, Walpole described Kent's relationship to the landscape in terms primarily sexual and aesthetic, though implicitly political as well. Seen through Walpole's eyes, Kent was a frank admirer of the landscape's feminine contours, a careful arranger of her beauteous parts, and a benevolent despot who bolstered his loverlike indulgence with a forceful imposition of his own values on the countryside. Words connoting sensuous enjoyment thus alternate with words suggesting detached, calculated control. Kent could "taste the charms of landscape... and [feel] the delicious contrast of hill and valley changing imperceptibly into each other," while, as undisputed ruler of nature's realm, he was "bold and opinionative enough to dare and to dictate." He reorganized nature according to his own lights, "removing and extending the perspective by delusive comparison" and even teaching the stream to "serpentize seemingly at its pleasure." By wielding "the pencil of his imagination," he converted the countryside into his own private canvas on which he "realized the compositions of the greatest masters in painting" (GP, pp. 313–15). Kent's treatment of nature, therefore, took the form of carefully framing her parts, of *containing* her, despite the fact that to his contemporaries (as well as to subsequent scholars) he represented a new freedom and expansiveness in landscape, having been the first who—again in Walpole's words—"leaped the fence, and saw that all nature was a garden" (GP, p. 313).

The equation of gardener and painter was a commonplace during the eighteenth century, typified by Pope's assertion that "all gardening is landscape-painting."[10] Since a walk through a well-designed garden was viewed as a "journey... through a succession of pictures,"[11] the grounds of an estate were in effect a natural extension of the picture galleries constructed indoors, in the great halls and salons, where both landscapes and women were commonly framed and placed on display. We know from Walpole's testimony, for example, that the great salon at Stourhead contained "eight very large pictures," five of them depicting women in the representative female figures of Salome, Dido, Helen, Venus, and Andromeda.[12] Adorning the entrance hall was Mengs's seductively disarrayed Cleopatra, a visual emblem of submissiveness as she kneels before Augustus, her arms outstretched in supplication. She hung, significantly, next to the large equestrian portrait of Henry the Magnificent, a contrasting image of forcefulness and authority in his red and gold coat, whip in hand.

Pope too was both an outdoor painter of landscapes and a painter of women indoors. An amateur artist himself and a friend to noted artists of the day, he kept a picture gallery at Twickenham and adopted the role of painter in his epistle *To a Lady* ("Come then, the colours and the ground prepare..."). The relationship between painter and model in this poem, as I have suggested elsewhere, is essentially a power relationship, rooted in the distinction between capturer and captured, definer and defined.[13] So too is the relationship between gardener and landscape, which was often conceived of also in terms of artist and model.

Throughout eighteenth-century treatises on landscape, Nature was given her due, allowed to assert—indeed, *flaunt*—her superiority over the quaint and rigidly confining forms of art, before she was, as it were, put in her place, subordinated to the spectator's critical eye and the re-creator's shaping hand. Even Addison, for all his exaltation of the "bold and masterly [features] in the rough careless strokes of Nature," saw fit to claim that the poet frequently "seems to get the better of Nature," for "he takes the Landskip after her, but gives it more vigorous Touches [and] heightens its Beauty."[14] The poet, moreover, like Milton's God fashioning Eve out of a mere rib, "has the modelling of Nature in his own Hands, and may give her what Charms he pleases" (*Spectator*, no. 418). This notion of Nature's subordinate status and borrowed charms found its most extreme—and absurd—expression in William Whitehead's verses *On the Late Improvements at Nuneham*, where Nature and Brown clash verbally in a struggle for supremacy, with Brown gaining the clearcut victory. Triumphantly he demands to know, "Who drew o'er the surface, did you or did I, / The smooth-flowing outline, that steals from the eye, / ... Who thinn'd, and who group'd, and who scatter'd the trees? / Who bade the slopes fall with such elegant ease?"[15]

I wish to suggest that passages like these are not merely commonplaces or figures of speech (though through repeated usage they may have come to be these as well) but statements about how power was conceived and wielded during this period. There is little doubt as to who was the master, who the obedient and submissive servant—though admittedly a servant well cared for, lavishly fed, and dressed in the finest money could buy. This is apparent from the enormous sums men like Lord Cobham and Henry Hoare spent in clothing and decorating their respective landscapes at Stowe and Stourhead.[16] Pope's tailoring skills vis-à-vis the landscape were attested to by Thomson: "See! sylvan scenes, where art alone pretends / To dress her mistress, and disclose her charms— / Such as a Pope in miniature has shown..." (*Liberty*, V, 696-98).[17] Pope too spent considerable amounts to obtain appropriately elegant garb for Twickenham's anatomy, as is readily apparent from John Serle's seemingly interminable list of the valuable minerals and rocks collected in lavish quantity as adornments for his famed grotto.[18] Inevitably, Nature had to pay a price for being kept in such high style. As contemporary treatises on landscape make clear, she was expected to "yield Satisfaction to the Eye of the Beholder" and "Entertain the Sight every Moment."[19]

Consistent with this emphasis upon the visual, it was generally assumed that a major function of Nature was to "perform" as if on stage for the benefit of spectators. Words such as *scene, theatre, platform,* and *entertainment* echo throughout contemporary writings on landscape design, and while they can denote a range of meanings, they invariably suggest on some level the idea of spectacle and theatrical display. Contemporary drawings of Pope's grotto and the Queen's Theatre at Stowe tend to underscore this aspect. It is thus most appropriate that in recent years the Lady's Temple on the latter estate was used as a setting for outdoor productions of Shakespeare. In his poem "Stowe," Gilbert West conducts us through a series of both painted scenes and dramatic, primarily mythological scenarios. The amorous ritual he stages in the "cool Recess... Sacred to Love, to Mirth, and rural Play" follows from the "mysterious Orgies" depicted on the "painted Walls" of the Rustick Temple (*GP*, pp. 220–22). Sir Thomas Whately, for his part, notes that at Stowe "the views of the country are only circumstances subordinate to the scenes" and marvels how "the whole space is divided into a number of scenes, each distinguished with taste and fancy."[20] His emphasis on Stowe's carefully contrived "scenes" serves to underscore both the pictorial and the theatrical aspect of Cobham's gardens: both the way they were laid out in prospect views similar to those captured on canvas and the way they were turned into participants in the great dramatic spectacle devised by the owner-director for continuous performances on the discretely outlined "stages" (e.g., the "perfect garden scene" known as "the queen's ampitheatre," the "scene at the Temple of Bacchus," etc.) of his estate.

The profounder ideological implications of this become clearer when we consider John Berger's remarks about European art during the period as it related to what he calls "the experience of taking possession" and "the metaphorical act of appropriation": "Just as its perspective gathers all that is extended to render it to the individual eye, so its means of representation render all that is depicted into the hands of the individual owner-spectator.... By the sixteenth century it was no longer assembled or hoarded riches which the painting rendered up to the spectator-owner but, thanks to the unity that chiaroscuro could give to the most dramatic actions, whole *scenes* complete with their events and protagonists. These scenes were 'ownable' to the degree that the spectator understood that wealth could produce and control action at a distance."[21]

These remarks, I submit, have a very special relevance for eighteenth-century gardens—for the way in which they were divided up into discrete pictures or dramas readily apprehendable by the eye and "possessable" on a number of levels, both literal and figurative. Landscape theorists often recommended assembling nature's best features into small, framed spaces specifically suited to a human scale of proportions and needs. In William Shenstone's view, for example, "taste in gardening" is demonstrated by "Collecting, or collecting into a smaller compass, and then disposing without crowding [,] the several varieties of Nature," a practice he also refers to as "contracting Nature's beauties" (*GP*, pp. 244–45). Interestingly, Addison's praise of concave and convex shapes in architecture was based on the fact that they lend themselves so well to man's visual appropriation and possession: "Look upon the Outside of a Dome, your Eye half surrounds it; look up into the Inside, and at one Glance you have all the Prospect of it; the intire Concavity falls into your Eye at once, the Sight being as the Center that collects and gathers into it the Lines of the whole Circumference" (*Spectator*, no. 415). The principle of chiaroscuro mentioned by Berger was likewise stressed throughout this period in relation to both painting and landscape gardening, and often linked to the proper arrangement and unification of parts in order to produce an entire scene. A typical formulation of this aesthetic principle may be seen in the following lines:

> Yet there's a happiness that baffles Art,
> In showing Nature *great* in every part,

> Which chiefly flows from mingled lights and shades,
> In lawns, and woods, hills, rivers, rocks and glades;
> For only happy's that assemblage made,
> Where force of light contends with force of shade.
>   (GP, p. 299)

A similar intermixture of light and shade, open lawns and thickets, characterized Pope's garden and was readily visible from the "Forest Seat or Chair, that may hold three or four Persons at once" placed at the top of the mount (GP, p. 252). Here too the "rude and undigested Materials" of nature were transformed into participants in a carefully staged spectacle unfolded for the visual delectation of those chosen guests seated on the mount, "overlook[ing] the various Distribution of the Thickets, Grass plots, Alleys, Banks, &c." as though scrutinizing the walls of a picture gallery or watching a theatrical production (GP, p. 252).

Significantly, eighteenth-century descriptions of gardening procedures tended to assume the distinction between a God-like actor/creator and the passive, volitionless matter upon which he acted—what Whately termed "the objects of nature" which are the gardener's "only materials"[22]—even as they personified the landscape by making it into a sensuous and active (in the sense of "performing") female. Addison's account of the plantations at Kensington, "lying so conveniently under the Eye of the Beholder" (*Spectator*, no. 477), conveys this sense of dominance, here perceptual, over an essentially inert or docile object. It is equally significant that throughout the *Spectator* essays, women are portrayed in terms similar to the ones used for depicting gardens. They too are the seemingly animated yet finally passive objects of "Mr. Spectator's" carefully laid out prospect view. As "lovely pieces of human nature" on display for "their Male-Beholders," they too are continually judged for their ability to gratify the eye and the senses. Moreover, women, like landscapes, are converted into paintings, into framed—hence ownable and "possessable"—objects designed specifically for male scrutiny; as Addison puts it, "A virtuous Mind in a fair body is indeed a fine Picture in a good Light, and therefore it is no wonder that it makes the beautiful Sex all over Charms" (no. 243).

Again, inevitably, we must return to the concepts of ownership and possession. For Addison, correct epistemology and good aesthetics were not only sensually satisfying but lucrative as well. In this respect he was in the mainstream of contemporary opinion; Switzer repeatedly coupled the terms "pleasure" and "profit" in referring to the proper disposition of landscape (*IR*, I, i–xlv), while Batty Langley characterized a good garden as one "both profitable and delightful."[23] Addison, for his part, suggested ways in which "a whole estate [can] be thrown into a kind of Garden . . . that may turn as much to the Profit, as the Pleasure of the Owner" (no. 414) and contended that a "Man of a Polite Imagination . . . feels a greater Satisfaction in the Prospect of Fields and Meadows, than another does in the Possession. It gives him, indeed, a kind of Property in every thing he sees, and makes the most rude uncultivated Parts of Nature administer to his Pleasures" (no. 414). The choice of language here underscores the profound interconnections between aesthetic, economic, and sexual forms of possession. The relationship between spectator and prospect view, no less than that between owner and estate, reflected the desire to assert mastery over one's surroundings, to lay claims to pieces of an environment otherwise beyond one's control. Switzer made the same point in his own way by stressing the materialistic aspect of possession. Landscaped gardens, he argued, were a sound financial investment, hence a means by which "the most provident part of Men [can] heap up Wealth for their Families" (*IR*, I, 284).

This economic dimension sheds additional light on the interwoven images of boundlessness and limitation previously noted. The same duality may be seen to have characterized the movement throughout the century whereby common pasturelands were enclosed, divided up into pieces of private property, while at the same time estates increased in size through combined economic and territorial expansion.[24] Although this movement is usually associated with the second half of the century, references to it appear in both Switzer and Pope. The latter, for example, advised Bathurst to "Enclose whole Downs in Walls" (Epistle II, ii, 261)—partly to protect Pope's own financial investment in Bathurst's land improvements. And Switzer offered advice regarding "the Fencing and Enclosing [of] Large and Waste Lordships, Commons, etc." His support of this practice was unequivocal, for "'Tis by this means, of enclosing Lands, that Estates advance considerably in Value" (*IR*, I, 276). Switzer's distaste for walls and other obstructions "by which the Eye is as it were imprisoned, and the Feet fetter'd" did not prevent his advocating "an easy, unaffected manner of Fencing" in order to protect and enhance the worth of one's property (*IR*, I, xviii–xix, xxxvii). The ha-ha (or sunken fence), so characteristic a feature of the contemporary garden, undoubtedly owed its great popularity to the fact that it managed to answer these conflicting needs by contributing to a sense of expansiveness (since it in no way interfered with open prospect views) while yet establishing definite boundaries. During the eighteenth century, fences—along with, in another but related way, social institutions like marriage and moral prescriptions governing female chastity and fidelity—became increasingly necessary to ensure those supreme capitalist values, *ownership* and *privacy*, both of which entail the exclusion of "outsiders" and protect against external invasions of all sorts. Thus, under the entry for *fences* a mid-century *Gardener's Dictionary*, while expressing concern for their aesthetic drawbacks, stressed their importance for preventing that peculiarly Augustan bane, "being exposed to the View of all Passengers; which is very disagreeable."[25] Walpole, lamenting Sir William Stanhope's folly in having cut down the groves at Twickenham when he became its owner, noted that Stanhope had finally been compelled to build a wall, "for there was not a Muse could walk there but that she was spied by every country fellow that went by with a pipe in his mouth."[26] Similarly, the author of the "Epistolary Description" of Twickenham written shortly after Pope's death observed: "Near the Bounds of the Garden, the Trees unite themselves more closely together, and cover the Hedges with a thick Shade, which prevents all prying from without, and preserves the Privacy of the interior Parts" (*GP*, pp. 250–51).[27]

Pope himself exploited both the aesthetic and the ideological dimensions of this aspect of enclosure throughout his poetry. His re-creation of the ideal garden, based on Alcinous's in Homer's *Odyssey*, pictured "a spacious Garden" embodying nature's plenitude, which is nevertheless limited to "Four Acres" and "Fenc'd with a green Enclosure all around" (*The Guardian*, no. 173). The description could apply equally to the poet's own Twickenham estate, which was likewise both literally and symbolically "fenced." Its grotto became an emblem of the ideal Augustan community largely by constituting a hidden retreat closed to the public, invulnerable to the intrusion of pro-Ministry Whigs, Grub Street hacks, middle-class tradesmen, and others outside Pope's elite circle. Scorning the barbarian hordes who "fly to Twitnam," intent upon "pierc[ing its] thickets," Pope instructs his servant, "Shut, shut the door, good John!" Within the confines of his grotto he reigned supreme and could remain aloof from indiscriminate mobs and sprawling urban landscapes:

> Know, all the distant Din that World can keep
> Rolls o'er my Grotto, and but sooths my Sleep.
> There, my Retreat the best Companions grace,
> Chiefs, out of War, and Statesmen, out of Place.
> (Satire II, i, 124-27)

Henry Hoare's version of Pope's "Shut, shut the door" was the inscription taken from the Sixth Book of the *Aeneid—Procul, o procul este profani*—placed over the Temple of Flora on his Stourhead estate, warning the unhallowed to stand clear and thus protecting the Sybil's Cave from all intruders. Hoare too mythologized his habitation into a sanctified and hidden retreat which could be entered only by the initiates, the privileged few chosen by Hoare himself to follow in the footsteps of the great Aeneas.

The sense of enclosure became a virtually obligatory feature of eighteenth-century estates, almost all of which included a hermitage and a grotto, as well as other related structures, like Merlin's Cave at Richmond and the Sleeping-House at Stowe. Contemporary accounts of landscape gardens continually referred to "close winding walks," to intricate hidden paths suggesting privacy and solitude. That ardent defender of open prospects, Switzer himself, advocated the preservation of "some private Walks and Cabinets of Retirement, some select Places of Recess... where the Mind may privately exult" (IR, I, xxxvi). Admittedly these descriptions often tended to emphasize the spiritual and philosophic aspects of such retreats, and certainly the reference to *secretum iter* inscribed over the entrance to Pope's garden indicates the poet's links to the classical retirement tradition and the theme of *beatus ille*.[28] It may well also have expressed a facet of Pope's romantic sensibility, as John Dixon Hunt suggests.[29] But on another level—the one which I wish to stress here—this preoccupation with private, enclosed space represented part of an outlook particularly appropriate to the newly emergent agrarian capitalist class with which Pope had much in common. To many members of this class a private garden retreat had less to do with the spiritual delights of an Horatian retirement than with the bodily and social pleasures of a fashionable men's club transposed to rural surroundings, as the following demystifying verses suggest:

> A place—for holy meditation,
> For solitude, and contemplation;
> Yet what himself [the landowner] will rarely use,
> Unless to conn his weekly news;
> Or with some jovial friends, to sit in,
> To take his glass, and smoke, and spit in.[30]

Interestingly, statements stressing the virtues of hidden retreats, where one could be alone and unobserved, appeared side by side with assertions that the land's sensuous contours must (in Switzer's words) he "laid open to View," that the spectator-owner's eye should be free to survey the "unbounded Felicities" and the "extensive Charms of Nature" (*GP*, p. 152). Thus, as Thomson's Lord Lyttelton walks through Hagley Park in *The Seasons*, his eye "excursive roams" while "The bursting prospect spreads immense around" ("Spring," 950–62). Nature is continually described here in terms of a total visual (as well as implicitly sexual) yielding of herself, as she "spreads / Unbounded beauty to the roving eye" ("Spring," 506–7). The conclusion one draws from these examples is that while the spectator-owner was encouraged to create his own private spaces capable of protecting *him* from exposure to the view of *others,* his *own* possessions were to remain wholly exposed to *his* view.

This ability to see without being seen, coupled with the ability to see things inaccessible to others' eyes, conferred a very special power on the one possessing it and helped promote an elitist ideology equally suitable to the Tory aristocrat presiding over his inherited estate and the Whig *nouveau riche,* the city merchant or banker turned country gentleman. Both aristocratic and middle-class values help to define Addison's perspective. As one of the few men "of a Polite Imagination" who are "let into a great many Pleasures, that the Vulgar are not capable of receiving," he "discovers [in nature] a Multitude of Charms, that conceal themselves from the generality of Mankind" (*Spectator*, no. 414). In other words, those men of taste, leisure, and money, educated in how to see the world correctly, were understood to possess special privileges in relation to nature similar in many ways to a husband's conjugal rights. Like a wife—indeed, like the wives continually pictured, admonished, and instructed throughout the pages of the *Spectator*—Nature was to reveal her full charms and give of herself generously to her husbandlike viewers while remaining a discreet, modest maiden who conceals her bountiful endowments from the vulgar, prying eyes of all other suitors. We have only to compare Addison's observations on the landscape with a contemporary conduct book for wives in order to appreciate the full force of this analogy: "Not coy, nor yet profusely kind, is, therefore, my advice to all who become brides. . . . I would have the husband firmly persuaded that his wife has a great fund of tenderness in her heart; but would have no room given him to entertain a thought that she has so much in her composition as to make her able to bestow the least portion of it on any other than himself."[31] Nature, in effect, was to be at once the sensual mistress and the chaste wife of her cultivated admirers. It is of particular significance, then, that Addison continually referred to the "secret Refreshment," the "secret Delight," and the "Secret Satisfaction" he derived from his encounters with the landscape—terms which combine a sense of personal possessiveness with a suggestion of sexual stimulation and release. This private enjoyment of nature's charms became outright cohabitation for Lord Shaftesbury: "The wildness pleases; we seem to live alone with nature. We view her in her inmost recesses" (GP, p. 123). Later in the century, Sir William Chambers was to describe the landscape at Kew in terms of its "arbours of jessamine, vines and roses" haunted by "beauteous Tartarian damsels in loose transparent robes,"[32] while Sir John Clerk of Penicuik verbally painted rural bowers "Where every Goddess and their train / A clear and Secret Bathing Place may find" (GP, p. 198). In these and similar instances, the hidden retreats of a landscape became settings where one could feast the eyes and the imagination; privacy implied voyeuristic delights and sexual fantasies—assorted forms of mediated erotic experience kept at a safe remove from physical reality.

The estate owner's or privileged guest's saunterings through nature's "interior parts" and "inmost recesses," thus eroticized, lent themselves to descriptions suggestive of a sexual ritual, as we can see from Pope's depiction of himself as "the Magician appropriated to the place [Bathurst's "enchanted Forest"], without whom no mortal can penetrate into the Recesses of those sacred Shades."[33] The male owner's "penetration" into the "inner spaces" of his garden was a journey into and through a variety of enclosures and structures deliberately designed as parts of a feminine landscape: e.g., the Vale of Venus at Rousham, the Temple of Flora at Stourhead, and the Lady's Temple, the Temple of Venus, and the Queen's Valley at Stowe. Included were numerous statues of women, often in varying states of disarray or undress. There were, as might be expected, a number of representations of Venus, including the Venus Callipicia at Stourhead who, as Edward Malins notes, "twists sensually, like an apsara, in a niche at the side of the portico."[34] Stourhead's Pantheon featured a marble statue by Rysbrack of Flora and another of an antique Livia Augusta as Ceres. The sleeping, scantily draped nymph in Stourhead's grotto, associated by Walpole with Cleopatra, was commemorated in verse by Pope himself.[35] The nymph, in an appropriately quiescent and innocently seductive posture, forms a clear and telling contrast to the nearby statue of the River God, with one arm upraised in a gesture of command, who constitutes a forceful and imposing figure of authority. The inscription from Ovid's *Metamorphoses*, placed on a wooden tablet hung above him, identified him with the river god Peneus, who dispensed justice to the waves and to the nymphs inhabiting his stream.

Pope's treatment of the myth of Lodona in *Windsor-Forest* may be viewed as a poetic counterpart to the emblematic structure of Stourhead's grotto. The "rural nymph," scorning man-made boundaries and definitions, "[stray'd] Beyond the Forest's verdant Limits" (182). Her fate consisted of being "caught," frozen in space, and transformed into a piece of the landscape: "melting as in Tears she lay, / In a soft, silver Stream dissolv'd away" (203-4). She is, in short, finally contained—captured for all time—within both geographic and poetic boundaries. Presiding over and directing the now-liquefied nymph is another commanding figure embodying patriarchal control: "Old Father Thames" with "his rev'rend Head" (330), at whose words "the Winds forget to roar / And the hush'd Waves glide softly to the Shore" (353-54). On one level, Father Thames represents the poet himself, for in *Windsor-Forest,* Pope's "masculine" artistry, the potency of both his perception and his song, impregnates what is initially a "dreary Desart and a gloomy Waste" (**44**) and fathers forth a fruitful garden lubricated by "soft showers" and characterized by words like "swelling," "teeming," and "precious loads." The sexual landscape depicted here had its counterpart in actual landscapes of the period; thus Pope, envisioning the improved grounds at Bathurst's Cirencester, wrote of "the meeting of the Thames and the Severn which... are to be led into each others' embraces thro' secret caverns... till they rise and openly celebrate their marriage in the midst of an immense ampitheatre."[36] Even the translation of women into portions of the natural surroundings played a role in contemporary estate planning, so that Stourhead's lake, as Kenneth Woodbridge suggests, was probably modelled upon Lake Nemi, where the nymph Egeria, having disturbed Diana with her loud mourning for her husband, was turned into a spring.[37] Pope, interestingly, referred to his own Twickenham retreat as "th' Ægerian Grott" ("Verses on a Grotto by the River Thames...").

Pope presents us with another godlike regulator of nature in his portrait of Richard Boyle, Earl of Burlington, who in partnership with Kent constructed and landscaped his own estate at Chiswick as well as other noted structures of the period. Pope hails him as a miracleworker capable of "erect[ing] new wonders, and the old repair[ing]" (*Epistle to Burlington,* 192). The poem ends with a vision of mastery exerted over a potentially threatening but finally subduable and acquiescent landscape. It is a magnificent fantasy of power in which Burlington is shown wielding seemingly absolute control over his environment through (once again) a combination of containment and expansion:

>   Bid Harbors open, public Ways extend,
>   Bid Temples, worthier of the God, ascend;
>   Bid the broad Arch the dang'rous Flood contain,

> The Mole projected break the roaring Main;
> Back to his bounds their subject Sea command,
> And roll obedient Rivers thro' the Land....
> (197–202)

It is apt that this poem should include Pope's most striking equation of women and landscape and underscore their mutual subordination to man-made design, just as it is particularly apt that the following aesthetic guidelines should appear in an epistle addressed to the man who, from an early age on, had adopted architecture as his "mistress art":[38]

> To build, to plant, whatever you intend,
> To rear the Column, or the Arch to bend,
> To swell the Terras, or to sink the Grot;
> In all, let Nature never be forgot.
> But treat the Goddess like a modest fair,
> Nor over-dress, nor leave her wholly bare;
> Let not each beauty ev'ry where be spy'd,
> Where half the skill is decently to hide.
> (47–54)

The *Epistle to Burlington* serves to crystallize the period's quintessential attitudes toward landscape. Moreover, it helps to clarify the three interconnected aspects of eighteenth-century thought and aesthetics most relevant to this context: namely, the myth of restoration and the ideology of improvement and of use. Regarding the last, Pope asserts in this epistle that "'Tis Use alone that sanctifies Expense"; elsewhere, noting that in this new age of impermanence "Estates have wings," he consoles both himself and a skeptical Swift with the thought that "if the Use be mine, can it concern one, / Whether the Name belong to Pope or Vernon?" (*Satire II*, ii, 164–65). Pope repeatedly provides both a mythic and a pragmatic justification for laying claims to land one does not technically own but which one has *made use of* in all ways possible—land one has designed, planted, and framed if not actually bought: "If there be truth in Law, and Use can give / A Property, that's yours on which you live. / Delightful Abscourt, if its Fields afford / Their Fruits to you, confesses you its Lord" (*Epistle II*, ii, 230–33). According to this outlook, so well suited to the situation of a gentleman tenant farmer such as Pope, Nature through proper usage will "yield" herself as readily to the resident planter-landscaper as to the affluent landowner. Land which does not so yield itself is worthless in every sense; it is like the expanse of "empty Wilds and Woods" described in *Windsor-Forest.*

Women who refused to be "used" by men—by those performing in the dual roles of husband and husbandman—were apt to incur a similar fate, so that the childless Queen Catherine, characterized by Dryden as "A Soyl ungratefull to the Tiller's Care" (*Absalom and Achitophel*, 12), was likewise treated as a piece of desolate terrain. The female vagina, no less than the arid soil portrayed in William Mason's *The English Garden*, needed to be irrigated and nourished by seminal powers properly channelled: ". . . the fountain dares no more / To fling its wasted crystals through the sky, / But pours salubrious o'er the parched lawn / Rills of fertility. . . ."[39] Implicit in these lines is the contrast between masturbatory sterility—the "spilling of one's seed"—and heterosexual fruitfulness. The respective duties of both husbandman and "wife" may be deduced from this imagery. The relationship between them is one defined primarily by proper usage and an acceptable level of productivity. Clarissa's speech in *The Rape of the Lock* also exalts the value of utility. Her advice to Belinda is that women should, in effect, allow themselves to be "used" by men within the socially and morally sanctioned institution of marriage. Her words, like Pope's on estate management elsewhere, constitute what I will call here the Augustan-capitalist version of *carpe diem*. Both encourage us to seize and utilize all the resources at our disposal without delay, for "Inexorable Death shall level all"—"Trees, and Stones, and Farms" included (*Epistle II*, ii, 254)—and, in Clarissa's words, "painted, or not painted, all shall fade, / And she who scorns a Man, must die a Maid" (*Rape*, V, 27-28). The message is clear: time is running out for virgins and soil alike; both must submit to the tiller's care lest they waste away into a barren ruin.

The men we are dealing with, however, viewed themselves much more as arbiters of taste than as utilitarians. Hence we find an even greater emphasis upon the ideology of improvement, or upon what Raymond Williams calls the "morality of improvement" and associates with "a transformed and regulated land."[40] Contemporary treatises on gardening all agree that the landscape designer should not only use Nature intelligently but *make her better*. Whately stated that the gardener's aim "is to... discover and to show all the advantages of the place upon which he is employed; to supply its defects, to correct its faults, and to improve its Beauties,"[41] while John James, in his translation of D'Argenville's *La Théorie et la pratique du jardinage*, declared that "'Tis... the great Business of an Architect, or Designer of Gardens... with his utmost Art and good Œconomy to improve the natural Advantages, and to redress the Imperfections... of the Ground" (GP, p. 125). The word *redress* is particularly apt and inevitably comes to possess a double meaning, given the continual depictions of Nature as a maiden in need of the sartorial assistance of her overseers, as a goddess alternately being stripped bare and clothed in finery. Walpole's words sum up the age's attitudes in this respect: "Poetry, Painting & Gardening, or the science of Landscape, will forever by men of Taste be deemed Three Sisters, or the *Three New Graces* who dress and adorn Nature" (GP, p. 11). It need hardly be pointed out that these "sisters" remained under the constant guidance and supervision of their loving but strong-willed "fathers"—of men like Brown, "Born to grace Nature, and her works complete, / With all that's beautiful, sublime and great" (GP, p. 300). For one so consistently exalted as a divine goddess, Nature seems to have possessed a surprising number of deficiencies and blemishes in need of correction. In this respect she had much in common with eighteenth-century women. It is more than coincidence that Addison, celebrating the attractions of Kensington, praised the "fine Genius for Gardening, that could have thought of forming such an unsightly hollow into so beautiful an Area" (*Spectator*, no. 477) and, using similar terms, assured a new husband that, although he will "find many Blemishes and Imperfections in his Wife's Humour," he can act in a manner "which by degrees [will] soften those very Imperfections into Beauties" (no. 261).

The Augustan "improvement" of nature attained perhaps its ultimate expression in the cinematic technique which Pope used to design his grotto. His own description of it, contained in a letter to his friend Edward Blount, underscores the period's simultaneous embrace and rejection of empirical reality. Pope insists upon the purely natural features of the landscape but in effect accords them legitimacy only insofar as they are filtered through his specially treated artistic "glass": 'From the river Thames, you see thro' my Arch up a Walk of the Wilderness to a kind of open Temple, wholly compos'd of Shells in the Rustic Manner; and from that distance under the Temple you look down thro' a sloping Arcade of Trees, and see the Sails on the River passing suddenly and vanishing, as thro' a Perspective Glass." Pope's account of his grotto's *camera obscura* effects crystallizes the process whereby nature's charms, in all their bewildering fullness, are subsumed into a comprehensive and controlling artifice subject to human manipulation—what the contemporary epistolary writer called "a kind of Machinery, which performs the same Part in the Grotto that supernal Powers and incorporeal Beings act in the heroick Species of Poetry" (GP, p. 249):

> When you shut the Doors of this Grotto, it becomes on the instant, from a luminous Room, a *Camera obscura*; on the Walls of which all objects of the River, Hill, Woods, and Boats, are forming a moving Picture in their visible Radiations: And when you have a mind to light it up, it affords you a very different Scene: it is finished with Shells interspersed with Pieces of Looking-glass in angular forms; and in the Cieling [sic] is a Star of the same Material, at which when a Lamp... is hung in the Middle, a thousand pointed Rays glitter and are reflected over the Place.[42]

What we see here, essentially, is a process which discards nature in the raw for nature in a finer—which is to say, a more artificial and regulatable—tone.

We come, finally, to the great overriding conception which lay behind and informed these various attitudes toward nature: namely, the myth of restoration. The very act of shaping and cultivating a garden, of course, inevitably evoked associations with man's paradisal existence and his first occupation on earth. Religious and mythic sanctions were thus readily available to elevate the role of landscape designer and to suggest that he was capable not only of improvement but of *redemption* as well. Addison, for example, reminded his readers that "A Garden was the Habitation of our first Parents before the Fall," which fact made his horticultural activity "one of the most innocent Delights in humane Life" (*Spectator,* no. 477), while Switzer spoke of landscape gardening as "a kind of Divine Revelation" and as an activity related to the "beautiful Portraiture and harmonious Distribution of Paradise" (*IR,* I, iv). These notions were concretely realized in actual gardens of the day, judging by contemporary testimony. Gray, for example, spoke of Woburn Farm as "Southcote's Paradise," and Mrs. Montagu assured her correspondent that Stowe "gives the best idea of paradise that can be," while Walpole asserted that "Brown shall enjoy unsullied fame / For many a paradise regained."[43] But whatever the traditional Christian implications of gardening—and I do not mean to deny their importance here—the fact remains that the endeavor to restore Paradise possessed a far more immediate and practical—in the broadest sense, *political*—significance. For the ability to cancel out the ill effects of the Fall and bring back a green world of harmonious beauty was a mark of power in the world; in many cases it was the only kind of power that could still be exerted by various disgruntled Tories and Opposition Whigs. If the offices obtainable through Court patronage were no longer available to them, they could always console themselves with the role of God, Milton's "sov'ran Planter" and the original creator of the garden. Men like Cobham and Bathurst, alienated from the official center of political power, could retire to their country estates and emulate the superhuman feats ascribed to Capability Brown in contemporary verses like the following: "He barren tracts with every charm illumes, / At his command a new Creation blooms" (GP, p. 300).

For Henry Hoare, the re-creation of Eden was, along with his banking enterprises and art collecting, a serious business indeed.[44] He planted his green world near the River Stour as "a pattern of perfection" and used his fortune to construct a landscape which could boast of a Paradise Well, a Paradise Temple, and a Paradise Coppice, not to mention those "enchanting paths of paradise" he alluded to in a letter to his nephew. Faced with a world recalcitrant to his hopes and desires, a vindictively mutable world which claimed the lives of his wife and children in rapid succession, Hoare carved out for himself a private world impervious to all hostile forces from without and immune to the ravages of time. It was a world both familiar and friendly because his own personal creation, a land which assumed precisely the shapes he wanted and over which he could exert control since it was rooted in a nature "redeemed" and compliant to his will, like the trees in Paradise that yielded their fruit willingly to the world's first gardener. Addison offered his own variation on this theme by recommending the contrivance of a "Winter Garden," made up "of such Trees only as never cast their Leaves," thereby reproducing an eternally springlike Enna in defiance of a fallen world where Nature, for lengthy periods of time, "presents us with nothing but Bleak and Barren Prospects" (*Spectator*, no. 477). We may recall in this connection Dryden's statement that the business of artists is to "imitat[e] the Divine Maker, form to themselves... a model of the superior beauties; and... endeavor to correct and amend the common nature, and to represent it as it was at first created."[45] Although these words do not specifically refer to the art of landscape design, they possess a special relevance for the building and gardening endeavors of those eighteenth-century estate improvers whom James Lees-Milne aptly terms "the Earls of Creation."[46]

It need hardly be pointed out that man's position of dominance in the unfallen world was rooted in his supremacy over all other created beings, including woman in the form of Eve. Perhaps it is this above all which explains the significance at the heart of the Augustan feminized landscape, with its natural features transformed to adhere to man's will and to administer to his pleasures. We may recall Milton's Eve, who, like the richly laden boughs of Eden's trees, willingly delivers up her treasures in compliance to her lord's will:

> Shee as a veil down to the slender waist
> Her unadorned golden tresses wore
> Dishevell'd, but in wanton ringlets wav'd
> As the Vine curls her tendrils, which impli'd
> Subjection, but requir'd with gentle sway,
> And by her yielded, by him best receiv'd,
> Yielded with coy submission, modest pride,
> And sweet reluctant amorous delay.
> (IV, 304–11)[47]

Eve is here presented, in effect, as a living embodiment of Switzer's landscape, with its "careless loose tresses" and "extensive Charms."

Even more, in her combination of maidenly restraint and eager submission she brings to mind the "waving Groves" of *Windsor-Forest*. Both garden and woman in these instances act out a role in what may be seen on one level as a male fantasy; each caters to the desire expressed by Rochester's Valentinian to enjoy his mistress fully but at the same time "to possess her chaste and uncorrupted."[48]

This conscious association of the eighteenth-century landscape with Paradise may help to explain the curious, paradoxical impression we get that, despite the pervasive and explicit femininity of the century's gardens, they were nevertheless very much of a man's world. It may be recalled in this connection that Sir William Temple, speaking of Paradisal existence, neglected to mention woman altogether: according to him, "we must allow that God Almighty esteemed the Life of Man in a Garden the happiest he could give him, or else he would not have placed Adam in that of Eden" (GP, p. 96). Marvell also expressed a vision of "that happy garden-state, / While man there walked without a mate" (*The Garden*, 57–8), a yearning to recapture that brief moment in human time when man had Paradise all to himself so that his mastery over the created world was absolute, not yet threatened by the anarchy of sexual passion or by rebellion in the ranks.

The basic design of eighteenth-century gardens, while it may seem to embody a very different vision, actually in many ways reflects an *extension* of such attitudes. Female shapes and structures were, it is true, allowed to occupy a place in the Augustan elysiums, but generally speaking they constituted stage props and ornaments in a great symbolic drama specifically, essentially male in character. Thus, at Stourhead, the Cumaean Sybil, Venus, and Egeria were finally subordinate figures in a landscape conceived as a setting for Aeneas's journey in order to found an empire. Henry Hoare consciously saw himself in this role, as one reproducing the actions of a great epic hero and, by implication, repeating the extended male initiation rite depicted by Virgil. "I have made the passage up from the Sousterrain Serpentine & will make it easier of access facilis descensus Averno," he wrote to Lord Bruce.[49] A world of male conquest and empire was similarly commemorated by the construction of Alfred's Tower, undertaken after Hoare had read Voltaire's exaltation of Alfred the Great's heroic and patriotic exploits.

Stowe too, for all its erotic features and abundant representations of female sexuality, was a predominantly masculine world—indeed, more insistently and aggressively so than Stourhead, as present-day as well as contemporary descriptions of its design make clear.[50] Its Temple of Friendship, containing busts of Lord Cobham himself together with his distinguished friends—known variously as "the Boy Patriots" and "Cobham's Cubs"—constituted a testimonial to one particular manifestation of "male bonding" during this period as it both grew out of and reflected other types of political and personal alliances. Similarly, the Temple of British Worthies, with its sixteen busts representing a highly select group of artists, kings, and military leaders, inevitably commemorated a form of patriarchal authority even as it officially paid tribute to specific ideological and ethical values. As a counterpart (and contrast) to these, Cobham built the Lady's Temple, adorned with paintings of women occupied in traditionally feminine pursuits, such as shell work and music, in effect instructing Lady Cobham as to a wife's proper place in the world and standing as an implicit criticism of that eminently fallen woman, Queen Caroline, who had, like the willful Eve, usurped male prerogatives and violated the divinely sanctioned hierarchy by meddling in matters of state. In a quintessential way, Stowe's landscape epitomizes what the myth of restoration meant to the wealthy amenders and adorners of nature in the eighteenth century: i.e., a re-created Paradise produced through an expensive and tasteful combination of pastoral charms and elegantly civilized comforts, where woman, as embodied in both shapes of the land and figures on canvas, performed all the functions of a yet-innocent Eve by seductively displaying her "wanton ringlets" while yet remaining subject to her master's "sway."

Eighteenth-century gardens, on the whole, tell the story of a society which demanded contradictory things from its women and its landscapes alike; of men who wanted to be gratified by the full sensual and boisterous reality existing beyond the fence while yet keeping this reality within clearly defined boundaries so that it could be controlled and possessed. The gardens emblematized their desire to "leap the fence" with Kent and tear down the walls with Switzer while yet remaining secure within the "green enclosure" of Pope's Garden of Alcinous. *Enclosure* is perhaps the key word here; throughout the century it possessed multileveled significance, functioning on economic, architectural, psychological, and verbal levels at once. The almost compulsive rearrangement and containment of the landscape during this period expressed the era's rage for order in a world perceived—whether rightly or wrongly—to be on the verge of chaos, filled with threatening, irrational forces needing to be fenced out (or, alternatively, "tamed" and incorporated within).

These topographical enclosures had a verbal counterpart in what Christopher Caudwell terms "the elegant corset of the eighteenth-century heroic couplet."[51] The phrase is peculiarly apt, for all forms of natural passions, profusions, and luxuriances, whether of women or nature, were held in careful paternal check through the girdling effects of Pope's and his contemporaries' poetic structures. (It could even be argued that enjambement performed the same function as the ha-ha, creating the impression of expansiveness—of exceeding fixed limits—while yet remaining within the basic form of the couplet, so that the good poet, like the skillful gardener, was one who "pleasingly confounds,/ Surprizes, varies, and conceals the Bounds" [*Epistle to Burlington*, 55–56].) All in all, we can derive perhaps our best insight into the nature of eighteenth-century landscape gardening—indeed, into much of eighteenth-century ideology and art in general—by exploring the process whereby reality's "bulges" were contained and aesthetically converted into perfectly formed (if serpentine) curves: the process whereby what Charles Cotton termed the "boils and warts, the *pudenda* of nature" (GP, p. 93) were transformed into the purified and modestly concealed private parts of a restored Eden.

NOTES

I wish to thank the Committee on Research of the University of California, Riverside Division for a grant which provided financial support for the writing and the manuscript preparation of this essay.

1 See, for example, Paul Shepard, *Man in the Landscape* (New York: Knopf, 1967), and essays by Adrian Stokes in the following volumes: *Inside Out* (London: Faber

and Faber, 1947); *The Invitation in Art* (New York: Chilmark, 1965); *The Image in Form: Selected Writings of Adrian Stokes* (Harmondsworth, Eng.: Penguin, 1972).
2 In this connection see Annette Kolodny, *The Lay of the Land: Metaphor as Experience and History in American Life and Letters* (Chapel Hill: University of North Carolina Press, 1975).
3 See Dorothy Stroud, *Capability Brown* (1950; rev. ed. London: Country Life, 1957), p. 198.
4 *New Improvements of Planting & Gardening, both Philosophical and Practical*, 7th ed. (London: A. Bettesworth & C. Hitch, 1739), pp. 14, 20.
5 Bradley, *New Improvements*, pp. 161-62.
6 The books on eighteenth-century estates and landscape gardening which I have found most informative and useful for this study are the following: Edward Malins, *English Landscaping and Literature, 1660-1840* (London: Oxford University Press, 1966); Christopher Hussey, *English Gardens and Landscapes, 1700-1750* (New York: Funk & Wagnalls, 1967); Derek Clifford, *A History of Garden Design* (New York: Frederick A. Praeger, 1963), chs. 6-8; Kenneth Woodbridge, *Landscape and Antiquity: Aspects of English Culture at Stourhead, 1718-1838* (London: Clarendon Press, 1970); idem, *The Stourhead Landscape* (London: National Trust, 1971); Laurence Whistler, Michael Gibbon, and George Clarke, *Stowe: A Guide to the Gardens*, 3rd ed. (London: Country Life, 1974); John Dixon Hunt and Peter Willis, eds., *The Genius of the Place: The English Landscape Garden, 1620-1820* (London: Paul Elek, 1975); Ronald Paulson, *Emblem and Expression: Meaning in English Art of the Eighteenth Century* (Cambridge, Mass.: Harvard University Press, 1975), ch. 2; and John Dixon Hunt, *The Figure in the Landscape: Poetry, Painting, and Gardening during the Eighteenth Century* (Baltimore and London: The Johns Hopkins University Press, 1976).
7 All quotations from Pope's poetry are from *The Twickenham Edition of the Poems of Alexander Pope*, ed. John Butt et al. (London and New Haven: Yale University Press, 1939-61), and are cited by line number in the text.
8 "An Epistolary Description of the Late Mr. Pope's House and Gardens at Twickenham," in *Genius of the Place*, p. 251. Hereafter abbreviated as GP and cited in the text.
9 Repton, *An Enquiry into the Changes of Taste in Landscape Gardening* (London: J. Taylor, 1806).
10 Quoted in Joseph Spence, *Anecdotes*, ed. James M. Osborn (Oxford: Clarendon Press, 1966), I, 252.
11 Horace Walpole, *Anecdotes of Painting* (Strawberry Hill, 1762-71), IV, 148.
12 *Journals of Visits to Country Seats*, in *The Walpole Society*, 16 (1927-28). See also Kenneth Woodbridge, "Henry Hoare's Paradise," *Art Bulletin*, 47 (March 1965), 83-116.
13 See my article "Pope's Portraits of Women: The Tyranny of the Pictorial Eye," in *Women and Men: The Consequences of Power*, eds. Dana V. Hiller and Robin Ann Sheets (Cincinnati: University of Cincinnati Office of Women's Studies, 1977), pp. 74-91.
14 *Spectator*, no. 416. In Addison & Steele, and others, *The Spectator*, ed. Gregory Smith, 4 vols. (London and New York: Everyman's Library, 1945). All references to the *Spectator* papers are to this edition and are hereafter cited in the text.

15 Quoted in Elizabeth W. Manwaring, *Italian Landscape in Eighteenth-Century England* (New York: Russell & Russell, 1925), p. 142.
16 For a detailed account of Hoare's expenditures for building, landscaping, and purchasing assorted art objects, see Woodbridge, *Landscape and Antiquity*, pp. 19-23, 38-44, et passim.
17 References to Thomson's poetry are taken from *The Complete Poetical Works of James Thomson*, ed. J. Logie Robertson (London: Oxford University Press, 1908).
18 *A Plan of Mr. Pope's Garden* (London: R. Dodsley, 1745).
19 See, for example, Stephen Switzer, *Iconographia Rustica*, 2nd ed. (London: J. and J. Fox, 1742), III, 5. Hereafter abbreviated as *IR* and cited in the text.
20 *Observations on Modern Gardening*, 2nd ed. (London: T. Payne, 1770), pp. 213-15.
21 "Past Seen from a Possible Future," in *The Look of Things: Essays by John Berger*, ed. and intro. Nikos Stangos (New York: Viking, 1974), p. 215.
22 *Observations on Modern Gardening*, p. 1.
23 Batty Langley, *New Principles of Gardening* (London: A. Bettesworth & J. Batley, 1728), p. 193.
24 For important insights into the nature and effects of land enclosure in eighteenth-century England, see John Barrell, *The Idea of Landscape and the Sense of Place, 1730-1840: An Approach to the Poetry of John Clare* (Cambridge: Cambridge University Press, 1972); and Raymond Williams, *The Country and the City* (New York: Oxford University Press, 1973), esp. chs. 10-12.
25 Philip Miller, *The Gardener's Dictionary*, 6th ed. (London, 1752).
26 Quoted in Malins, *English Landscaping and Literature*, p. 41.
27 Jay Appleton, in *The Experience of Landscape* (London: John Wiley, 1975), interprets geographical enclosures (as well as their opposite, expansive views) in terms of fundamental biological instincts and needs—what he calls the "prospect-refuge" theory of landscape.
28 In this connection, see Maren-Sofie Røstvig, *The Happy Man: Studies in the Metamorphoses of a Classical Ideal*, 2 vols. (1954; New York: Humanities Press, 1971), esp. II, 29-86, where Røstvig explores the continuance of the Horatian and the *beatus ille* traditions into the eighteenth century and notes their specific links to Pope. Also see Maynard Mack, *The Garden and the City: Retirement and Politics in the Later Poetry of Pope, 1731-1743* (Toronto: University of Toronto Press, 1969), esp. his chapter on "Secretum Iter" (pp. 77-115).
29 *The Figure in the Landscape*, pp. 72-78.
30 Quoted by Hunt in ibid., p. 8.
31 Mira [Eliza Haywood], *The Wife* (London: T. Gardner, 1756), p. 8.
32 In *A Dissertation on Oriental Gardening* (London: W. Griffin, 1772).
33 Pope to Robert Digby, May 1722, *The Correspondence of Alexander Pope*, ed. George Sherburn, 5 vols. (Oxford: Clarendon Press, 1956), II, 115-16.
34 *English Landscaping and Literature*, p. 53.
35 This verse was a translation of an anonymous fifteenth-century inscription to a classical sculpture of a sleeping girl: "Nymph of the Grot, these sacred Springs I keep,/And to the Murmur of these Waters sleep;/Whoe'er thou art, ah gently tread the Cave,/Ah Bathe in silence, or in silence lave." For a discussion of the type of

the sleeping nymph as it was used interchangeably for Diana, Venus, and Cleopatra, see Otto Kurz, "Huius Nympha Loci," *Journal of the Warburg and Courtauld Institutes*, 16 (1953), 171–77.
36 Cited by Hussey, *English Gardens and Landscapes*, p. 81.
37 *The Stourhead Landscape*, p. 11.
38 This epithet is mentioned by Christopher Hussey in his Introduction to Margaret Jourdain, *The Work of William Kent* (London: Country Life, 1948), p. 42.
39 Quoted in Clifford, *A History of Garden Design*, p. 126 n.
40 *The City and the Country*, pp. 60–61.
41 *Observations on Modern Gardening*, p. 1.
42 Pope to Edward Blount, June 1725, in Sherburn, *Correspondence of Pope*, II, 296–97.
43 See H. F. Clark, "Eighteenth-Century Elysiums," *Journal of the Warburg and Courtauld Institutes*, 6 (1943), 165–89.
44 See Woodbridge, "Henry Hoare's Paradise," pp. 84–90.
45 This is Dryden's translation of a maxim of Bellori's which appears in A *Parallel of Poetry and Painting* (in *Essays of John Dryden*, ed. W. P. Ker, 2 vols. [New York: Russell & Russell, 1961], II, 118).
46 *The Earls of Creation: Five Great Patrons of Eighteenth-Century Art* (London: Hamish Hamilton, 1962). The five men treated here are Burlington; Henry Bathurst; Herbert, ninth Earl of Pembroke; Edward Harley, second Earl of Oxford; and Thomas Coke, first Earl of Leicester.
47 *Paradise Lost*, ed. Merritt Y. Hughes (New York: Odyssey Press, 1962), p. 93.
48 John Wilmot, Earl of Rochester, *Valentinian: A Tragedy* (London: Timothy Goodwin, 1685).
49 Quoted in Woodbridge, *Landscape and Antiquity*, p. 35.
50 See, e.g., George Clarke, "The Gardens of Stowe" and "Grecian Taste and Gothic Virtue: Lord Cobham's Gardening Programme and Its Iconography," *Apollo*, 97 (June 1973), 558–65, 566–71.
51 *Illusion and Reality: A Study of the Sources of Poetry* (London: Macmillan, 1937), p. 89.

Rochester's Sexual Politics

REBA WILCOXON

In Rochester's satire "Timon" the speaker tells the pressing bore that he "never rhymed but for my pintle's sake."[1] It is tempting to identify this speaker with Rochester himself and to think that Freud might have found here a self-confessed Don Juan who used poetry as a means of sexual conquest. This would be a mistake. For in spite of his reputation as a rake and in spite of poems saturated with sex and obscenity, Rochester reveals in his poems a sexual politics contrary to that of a power-driven Don Juan.[2]

I borrow the useful term "sexual politics" from Kate Millett. Millett refers to politics as "power-structured relationships, arrangements whereby one group of persons is controlled by another," and to sexual politics as the power-structured relationship whereby men by "birthright priority" dominate women. The ideal and rational politics would be one in which "power *over* others" (her italics) no longer exists, in sex or society.[3] This ideal is a persistent theme in Rochester's poetry, fleshed out in satire against male or female dominance in a love relationship and against sex as a means to political or social power.

Of course, one may argue that there are at least two other Rochesters: one the boastful conquistador of sex, the other the servile slave of love. I shall argue that these roles are usually ironic and that Rochester rejects enslavement of either of the sexes.

In "The Imperfect Enjoyment," "The Disabled Debauchee," and

"To the Postboy," a libertine speaker appears to play the part of a Don Juan who exults in sexual conquests for their own sake. "The Imperfect Enjoyment" shows us a lover unable to satisfy his mistress after premature ejaculation. In his frustration, he begins what at first seems a boastful account of sexual prowess, but pure sexual power is put in a context that undercuts its value.[4] A distinction is explicitly made between lewdness and love, and the weapon of conquest, the phallus, is given valor that is only "brutal." The instrument of power is also reduced at one point to an emblem of passivity rather than of passion, "a common fucking post." Thus, sexual victory, if the rules are only those of warfare, turns into defeat.

A similar kind of satire is leveled against the sexual conqueror in "The Disabled Debauchee" and "To the Postboy." The former envisions "days of impotence" when the pox and alcohol will have forced his retirement from the war of sex; in "To the Postboy" the narrator calls us to witness the "heroic scars" of his sexual victories: "Cerecloths and ulcers from top to toe." Although the speakers' self-portraits are not without ambivalence—self-mockery is mixed with self-defense—their experience with brute sexual violence is couched in terms that invite condemnation.

In all three poems the force of the language is against force itself, and the braggadocio of the speakers is punctured with irony. If the women are merely means, Rochester seems to feel they need not be women at all—any object will do. For example, the offending penis in "The Imperfect Enjoyment" in its fury has created its own sexual objects: "Where'er it pierced, a cunt it found or made." In "The Disabled Debauchee" sexual union becomes so casual that a kiss decides whether the love triangle with Chloris and the linkboy will be a heterosexual or homosexual affair. We may find a sardonic comedy in the triangle, but nonetheless it adds to my claim that the sexual politics of Rochester is not one of mere male supremacy. If the issue is body alone, it does not matter much who swives whom—or what. The same position occurs in Rochester's most antifemale poem, "Love a woman? You're an ass!" If "busy love entrenches," Rochester will just as soon settle for the "sweet, soft page" who can do the "trick worth forty wenches." "Trick" seems to be used in the contemporary sense: a physiological conjunction, nothing more. In this poem the virtues of "health, wealth, mirth, and wine" are found in a male world, unassociated with women. This is Rochester in his "errant fumbler" mood. I refer to his letter to Henry Savile in 1674, in which he says: "I have seriously considered one thinge, that of the three buisnisses of this Age, Woemen, Polliticks & drinking, the last is the only exercise att wch. you & I have nott prouv'd our selves Errant fumblers."[5] It is a curious remark for one considered the prime rake of the Restoration. What it signifies, however, is that in the business of women, Rochester rejected sex for its own sake—and, as I shall argue, yearned to meet woman on even ground, be it bed, heart, or understanding.

At the opposite extreme of the Rochester who would settle for any sexual object as a physical release is the courtly lover's posture of servitude. This posture occurs almost exclusively in poems which David Vieth labels "Prentice Work." Thus, it is most often the young lover who is able to say, "I triumph in my chain," and to call himself slave and faithful servant—or perhaps it is the young *poet* still enslaved by the language of the tradition.[6] More typically, the courtly vein is likely to be subverted by an unexpected reversal of tone or logic, especially at the end of the poem. The conclusion of a song, "What cruel pains Corinna takes," is illustrative:

> The scorn she bears so helpless proves,
>   When I plead passion to her,
> That much she fears, but more she loves,
>   Her vassal should undo her.
>   (13–16)

The conventional love game is exposed as just that, where the rules are pretense and the score is sex. Vassalage is even more overtly ridiculed in the close of "To My More Than Meritorious Wife":

> With low-made legs and sugared speeches,
> Yielding to your fair bum the breeches,
> I'll show myself, in all I can,
> Your faithful, humble servant,
>   John.
>   (7–11)

The servant is one in the grossest sense: the stud that serves a female. If Rochester will use the language of servitude and play the role, he will insist on making it double-edged. He holds himself in reservation against being mastered by sex, a state of being that is savagely denounced in the lampoon on the prostitute Mrs. Willis:

> Against the charms our ballocks have
> How weak all human skill is,
> Since they can make a man a slave
> To such a bitch as Willis.
> (1–4)

The same idea appears in the scepter lampoon on Charles II. Law and religion go by the board because "His scepter and his prick are of a length; / And she may sway the one who plays with th'other."

That Rochester satirizes males who are the slaves of women and of their own sexual appetites does not entirely make the case for a politics of sexual equality. It is possible to turn the argument around and say that the scorn of enslavement is the male chauvinist's creed. There is, however, evidence that Rochester condemns male mastery as well. Consider, for example, the happy sultan passage in "A Very Heroical Epistle in Answer to Ephelia." Although the particular victim of the satire is John Sheffield, Earl of Mulgrave, the happy sultan is the universalized portrait of arrogant and pitiless male dominance, he who "with awful pride walk'st careless by," conferring his sexual favor as a mode of power and silencing his female critics:

> No loud reproach nor fond unwelcome sound
> Of women's tongues thy sacred ear dares wound.
> If any do, a nimble mute straight ties
> The true love knot, and stops her foolish cries.
> (49–52)

There is patent distaste for the tyrant who feels the "joys of love without the pain"—that is, he who uses women as objects and forswears a mutual human obligation, however painful it might be.[7]

The Restoration analogue of the sultan and his serail appears in an incomplete poem, "What vain, unnecessary things are men!" The female narrator speaks for the same Rochester of "A Very Heroical Epistle" as she pictures male dealers in human flesh, where the beast to be bought and used is woman:

> T' th' Pall Mall, playhouse, and the drawing room,
> Their women fairs, these women-coursers come
> To chaffer, choose, and ride their bargains home.
> At the appearance of an unknown face,
> Up steps the arrogant, pretending ass,
> Pulling by th' elbow his companion Huff.
> Cries, "Look! de God, that wench is well enough:
> Fair and well-shaped, good lips and teeth, 'twill do;
> She shall be tawdry for a month or two
> At my expense, be rude and take upon her,
> Show her contempt of quality and honor,
> And, with the general fate of errant woman,
> Be very proud awhile, then very common."
> (8–20)

The women-courser takes the traditional moral stance of double standards: the errant woman gets what she deserves. Rochester may be saying the same, although I would argue that his criticism falls not on a sexual degeneration but on the conditions of the bargain. This is reflected in the female narrator's lament:

> Whence comes this mean submissiveness we find
> This ill-bred age has wrought on womankind?
> Fall'n from the rights their sex and beauties gave
> To make men wish, despair, and humbly crave,
> Now 'twill suffice if they vouchsafe to *have*.
> (3–7)

The women of "this ill-bred age" are of a pattern with the mythical sultan's harem, where the sex objects of the day are content merely to be chosen: "Then from thy bed submissive she retires,/And thankful for the grace, no more requires." Rochester also mentions other women, such as Carwell and Nell Gywnn, who sell their integrity in the marketplace of sex and are trapped in the bargain—or so we are told in the scepter lampoon.

Thus, it takes two to play the politics of dominance: one who is willing to sell and one who is willing to buy.

But there is more to the target than mere female submission for favors or for a day in the sun. Rochester's animus toward men enslaved by sexual desire is also aimed at the same propensity in women. In Rochester's poetry the ultimate of the insatiable female, amounting to a personification of nymphomania, is Phyllis in "The Mock Song," a parody of a sentimental song by Sir Carr Scroope. Rochester gives us a woman so sexually ravenous that she calls up an image of a piece of meat full of larding needles. Phyllis is the counterpart of the "fucking post" in "The Imperfect Enjoyment," because she is reduced to a mere object. As I have said, in Rochester the relationship between men and women that is no more than the use of one by the other makes *any* sexual object—or instrument—as good as another.

This position is also implicit in "Signior Dildo," which is more comic and less caustic satire of the extremes of female sexual appetite. In extolling the virtues of the dildo—"sound, safe, ready, dumb"—and arguing its popularity, Rochester can thrust his irony in two directions: women must have their sex, and men are more dispensable than they think they are.

The tone of tolerance toward the dildo suggests that its use was not a moral issue for Rochester; in fact, there is evidence that he and his good friend Henry Savile at one time trafficked in such instruments.[8] Instead, Rochester's bite is reserved for the sisters of Phyllis, the female sexmongers in his gallery of "fine" ladies of merry England. The most savage of the stanzas, which are for the most part nastily good-humored, is directed toward another of the King's mistresses, the Duchess of Cleveland:

> That pattern of virtue, Her Grace of Cleveland,
>   Has swallowed more pricks than the ocean has sand;
> But by rubbing and scrubbing so large it does grow,
>   It is fit for just nothing but Signior Dildo.
>   (37–40)

To show how women can deliberately or accidentally turn the tables on domineering males, Rochester employs not only the rollicking satire of "Signior Dildo" but also paradoxical wit and even pathos. An example of the paradoxical wit occurs in "A Dialogue Between

Strephon and Daphne." Strephon, confident that he is in control, reveals that his fancy has wandered elsewhere and argues:

> Love, like us, must fate obey,
> Since 'tis nature's law to change,
> Constancy alone is strange.
> (30–32)

With pompous rationality, he advises, "Be by my example wise: / Faith to pleasure sacrifice," only to get his comeuppance from Daphne:

> Silly swain, I'll have you know
> 'Twas my practice long ago.
> Whilst you vainly thought me true,
> I was false in scorn of you.
> By my tears, my heart's disguise,
> I thy love and thee despise.
> Womankind more joy discovers
> Making fools, than keeping lovers.
> (65–72)

Daphne does not emerge unscathed by the satire, but Rochester's wit gives her the edge over Strephon's blind egotism.

An instance of subversion of male dominance which is more pathetic than witty occurs in "Tunbridge Wells." Here we meet two wives, one barren, the other unable to produce a son and concerned about a sixteen-year-old daughter who has not yet experienced menstruation. For the teenager, Mistress Barren advises that "A back of steel will bring 'em better down," and Rochester adds about the wives: "And ten to one but they themselves will try / The same means to increase their family." True sterility lies with the husbands who ordered their wives to Tunbridge Wells so that pride in progeny might be served. These husbands will unknowingly live out the line of the female speaker in "What vain, unnecessary things are men!" when she says, "Thus tyrannies to commonwealths convert."[9]

In "A Letter from Artemisia in the Town to Chloe in the Country," Rochester pushes the extremes of male or female dominance to their logical and practical ends. In spite of the wide divergence of opinion about Artemisia's place in Rochester's scale of values, there is a certain correlation between Artemisia's definition of ideal love and other poems by Rochester. And in the introduction, it seems to me that Artemisia is a spokeswoman for the Rochester I am seeking to explicate. She levels her ironies against at least two assumptions of the typical male chauvinist. One is the ploy on poetry: a woman could do better to ride astride and fight than aspire to the "lofty flights of dangerous poetry." In the feigned posture of self-advisor, she acknowledges that a poetess is in the hell-if-you-do / hell-if-you-don't position, for she says "cursed if you fail, and scorned though you succeed." Second is Rochester's ironic pandering to the age-old myth that women are by nature irrational, unable to follow their own best reasoning, for Artemisia proceeds to write her poem (and a very successful one it is) "Pleased with the contradiction and the sin." The rhetorical effect of these introductory lines (1–31) is to establish a female narrator who beguiles us into giving her a hearing because she has admitted the faults that men will attribute to her, set in a context that repudiates their validity.

Thus, we are drawn into a vortex of sexual politics which begins with the abstract and ideal—Artemisia's unrealizable "softest refuge of love"—and then moves into the pragmatic compromise of the "fine lady," who shores up her own rationale for love and sex with the portrait of Corinna, victimized by a man of wit and in turn victimizing a poor coxcomb to serve the ends of survival and revenge. The ethical development in the poem bears out the fine lady's contention that love "rules the state." Such love is a total reversal of the starting point, but does not necessarily demolish it.

Artemisia begins with regrets for that "lost thing, love," now so debauched:

> Love, the most generous passion of the mind,
> The softest refuge innocence can find,
> The safe director of unguided youth,
> Fraught with kind wishes, and secured by truth;
> That cordial drop heaven in our cup has thrown
> To make the nauseous draught of life go down.
> (40–45)

Although Artemisia seems to take the nonsexual, or Platonic, or courtly, line by characterizing love as a "generous passion of the mind" and the refuge of innocence, we cannot dismiss the implications of the words "generous," "kind wishes," and "truth," implications for a male-female relationship that Rochester suggests in other poems as well. For example, the speaker in "A Ramble in St. James's Park" berates his sexual partner Corinna not for her lust but for her betrayal of the tender hours in which he found "security and rest." In "Absent from thee, I languish still," the mistress provides "love and peace and truth."[10] Do we not ask for, and expect, the sexual experience to be more than a transitory intensity, that it be imbedded, as Artemisia says, in a context of kind wishes, and "secured by truth"—in fact, what Freud saw as a necessary conjunction of the sensual and the affectionate?

Significantly, Artemisia deplores the women who have sold out, turned "gypsies for a meaner liberty" (the same charge made by the female speaker in "What vain, unnecessary things are men!"):

> And deaf to nature's rule, or love's advice,
> Forsake the pleasure to pursue the vice,
> To an exact perfection they have wrought
> The action, love; the passion is forgot.
> (60–63)

Here she moves closer to the Rochester we know, for nature's rule is obviously pleasure, his *summum bonum*. It becomes a vice when the sexual act is divorced from that "passion of the mind" which Artemisia has mentioned earlier. When she goes on to condemn the use of sex for fashion, whimsey, as opposed to rational choice, we are in familiar Rochester territory. I find the idea of *choice* central to his code for a sexual relationship, in contradistinction to passive submission or active exploitation. He expresses it philosophically in "A Satyr against Mankind": the reason "that bounds desires with a reforming will." It underlies his condemnation of Corinna in "A Ramble in St. James's Park" as a "whore in understanding,/A passive pot for fools to spend in" (101–2).

But Rochester was a realist. He offers, through Artemisia, the political and pragmatic way of the world, embodied in the "fine lady." She is no whore in understanding but a calculating Machiavellian defending her marriage to a fool, whom she henpecks and dismisses as a "necessary thing," on grounds that one must rule or be ruled. The alternative is to be subjected to the man of wit's intolerance of female frailty:

> Nay, take themselves for injured when we dare
> Make 'em think better of us than we are,
> And if we hide our frailties from their sights,
> Call us deceitful jilts and hypocrites,
> They little guess, who at our arts are grieved,
> The perfect joy of being well deceived.
>   (110–15)

A number of critics have pointed to the parallel argument in Swift's *Tale of a Tub*—the "sublime and refined Point of Felicity, called, *the Possession of being well deceived.*"[11] Whatever we may make of Rochester's irony here with general reference to mankind, there is a sense in which the desire to know all is the man of wit's way to dominate women. The fine lady is not herself deceived on this score. She is deliberately a woman of expedience on the assumption that tyranny and the survival of the fittest are identical in the battle of the sexes.

The fine lady builds her case on the story of Corinna, "Cozened at first by love" (perhaps an answer to Artemisia's definition of love as the "safe director of unguided youth"). Undone by a man of wit, forced into whoredom, Corinna can survive only by using the same *modus operandi* to which she has been subjected: exploitation. She ensnares a country fool—a husband and father—and acquires his estate through manipulation and murder. Although the fine lady intends to vindicate her own variety of "situation ethics," the story of Corinna carries to its logical and practical end a sexual politics based on dominance of one sex by the other. The tale ends at the opposite pole from Artemisia's vision of "kind wishes... secured by truth." Artemisia allows the fine lady "some grains of sense": love as she defines it does rule the state, which is not to say that Artemisia's cause is lost, but only that men and women whose choices are in terms of power make love the lost joy.

The antithesis of such tyranny occurs in the poignant "Song of a Young Lady to Her Ancient Lover." Whereas Artemisia is a kind of detached, Jamesian "lucid reflector," this woman is a warm and involved human being—a projection of Rochester's deepest needs in that she is a wholly sexual and deeply affectionate partner. The projection is temporal as well as psychological, for the young lady is not addressing an old man but meditating about a future condition. She speaks of him as the "Ancient person of my heart," but tells us "Long be it ere thou grow old." She tells us how she will counteract the effects of age:

> On thy withered lips and dry,
> Which like barren furrows lie,
> Brooding kisses I will pour
> Shall thy youthful [heat] restore
> (Such kind showers in autumn fall,
> And a second spring recall):
>   Nor from thee will ever part,
>   Ancient person of my heart.
>   (7–14)

Here is a kind of sequel to "The Imperfect Enjoyment"—a wish-fulfillment, the lover's dream of the sensual forever melded with the affectionate:

> All a lover's wish can reach
> For thy joy my love shall teach,
> And for thy pleasure shall improve
> All that art can add to love.
>   Yet still I love thee without art,
>   Ancient person of my heart.
>   (21–26)

    This view of Rochester may seem to overemphasize the importance of kind wishes and truth, with eyes averted from the Rochester who could dismiss women completely in a poem such as "Love a woman? You're an ass." The formula for judgment is provided by Rochester himself in a letter to his wife:

> Consider how men and woemen are compounded, that as heate and cold, soe greatness and meaness are necessary ingredients that enter both into the making up of every one that is borne, now when heate is predominant we are term'd hott, when cold is, wee are call'd cold ... now from the preheminence of either of these quallityees in us wee are termed good or bad.[12]

Thus is Rochester as poet compounded: libertine, a sometime sexist for parody or personal revenge, yet with a "preheminence" of the liberated male in the modern sense. He could envision an equality in love and sex, without fraud or the will to power. As I have argued elsewhere,[13] there is no logical contradiction in distinguishing between what *is* and what *ought* to be. The failure of Rochester or the failure of society to achieve the ideal is not a negation of that ideal; rather, it is testimony to individual perversity. As Rochester writes in "A Satyr against Reason and Mankind," man

> With voluntary pains works his distress,
> Not through necessity, but wantonness.
> (137-38)

NOTES

1 "Timon," in *The Complete Poems of John Wilmot, Earl of Rochester*, ed. David M. Vieth (New Haven: Yale University Press, 1968), p. 67. All subsequent quotations from Rochester's poems are from Vieth's edition.
2 I am mindful that the quotation, "But never rhymed but for my pintle's sake," is a perfect expression to support Freud's concept of sublimation. I consider sublimation, however, a metaphysical concept in that it is not open to empirical verification; that is, a negative instance is not possible. Therefore, it is irrelevant to the present argument.
3 Kate Millett, *Sexual Politics* (Garden City, N.Y.: Doubleday, 1970), pp. 23, 24.
4 I have defended this point in "Pornography, Obscenity, and Rochester's 'The Imperfect Enjoyment,'" *Studies in English Literature*, 15 (Summer 1975), 375-90.
5 *The Rochester-Savile Letters: 1671-1680*, ed. John Harold Wilson (Columbus: Ohio State University Press, 1941), p. 33.
6 Jeremy Treglown, in "The Satirical Inversion of Some English Sources in Rochester's Poetry," *Review of English Studies*, n.s., 24 (1973), p. 45, holds that "The Advice" employs language of courtly love to "disguise an aggressive assertion of male superiority." The would-be lover indeed praises what he has to offer as a means of persuasion, but I fail to see an assumed male superiority. Rather, the poem develops the theme of *mutual* enjoyment: "By harmony the universe does move,/And what is harmony but mutual love?" (15-16).
7 For a discussion of the complete inversion of values and the consistency of the persona as target in "A Very Heroical Epistle in Answer to Ephelia," see David M. Vieth's *Attribution in Restoration Poetry* (New Haven and London: Yale University Press, 1963), pp. 107-19.
8 *Rochester-Savile Letters*, p. 31.

9 The irony is similar to the story of the proud prince who went out to survey his kingdom-to-be when his father was near death. Meeting a peasant who resembled him markedly, the prince asked, "Was your mother ever a servant at court?" To which the peasant replied, "No, sire, but my father was."
10 Dustin Griffin has speculated that such references fit the Don Juan model; the male, according to psychoanalytic theory, searches for the mother in every woman and is impelled to deny his incestual impulses by recurring and ephemeral sexual encounters (*Satires against Man: The Poems of Rochester* [Berkeley: University of California Press, 1973], pp. 118–22). I am dubious that security, rest, truth, peace, and love, as Rochester uses the words, are psychopathological.
11 *A Tale of a Tub: With Other Early Works, 1696–1707*, ed. Herbert Davis (Oxford: Shakespeare Head Press), pp. 109–10.
12 Johannes Prinz, *John Wilmot, Earl of Rochester: His Life and Writings*, Palaestra 154 (Leipzig: Mayer & Müller, 1927), p. 270.
13 "Rochester's Philosophical Premises: A Case for Consistency," *Eighteenth-Century Studies*, 8 (Winter 1974/75), p. 197.

Mr. Locke and the Ladies:
The Indelible Words on the Tabula Rasa

SHERYL O'DONNELL

By the close of the seventeenth century, arguments about women's nature and consequent duties had shifted ground. Theological debates concerning whether or not women had souls gave way to inquiries into the nature of the "female mind," and as Locke's empiricism weakened the theory of innate ideas, religious speculations about women's inferiority were replaced by secular proposals for their education.[1] Locke's emphasis upon the connection between experience and self-knowledge, his ideas concerning the origin of knowledge, and his regard for precise language helped Restoration and eighteenth-century women recognize themselves as rational beings whose minds should be exercised and developed. Lady Damaris Cudworth Masham, Catherine Trotter Cockburn, Lady Mary Chudleigh, Lady Mary Wortley Montagu, and Hannah More were directly affected by Locke's empiricism. But they accepted patriarchal doctrines of woman's essential fitness for domestic and maternal spheres which accorded female learning no legitimacy outside the home. Rather than face public ridicule, they published anonymously, wrote in secret, burned their works, or phrased their feminism in terms of contributions to the common good. The same double bind that leads many twentieth-century women to avoid success in traditionally male-dominated areas rather than lose their "femininity" confined women thinkers of the Restoration and eighteenth century. Locke's empiricism blurred, but did not erase, patriarchal notions of women as highly venerated inferior beings.

Begun in 1671, Locke's *Essay Concerning Human Understanding* was redrafted several times and, after a long abridgement, appeared in Leclerc's Amsterdam journal, *La Bibliothèque universelle,* in 1688; it was published in England in 1690. Locke's avowed purpose, unlike that of the Scholastics or the great Continental philosophers of the seventeenth century, was practical rather than metaphysical. Written in an expansive, leisurely style, Locke's *Essay* is just that—a weighing, a trial, an experiment, or, as Locke called it, "an inquiry." Working in terms of exploration rather than declaration assures Locke an intimacy with his readers which enables him to show, lucidly, the thinking mind at work. In the "Epistle to the Reader," Locke assumes the voice of a plain, stolid man whose quest for truth is intermittent:

> If it [the *Essay*] seems too much to thee, thou must blame the Subject: for when I put Pen to Paper, I thought all I should have to say on this Matter, would have been contained in one sheet of Paper; but the farther I went, the larger Prospect I had: New Discoveries led me still on, and so it grew insensibly to the bulk it now appears in. I will not deny, but possibly it might be reduced to a narrower compass than it is; and that some Parts of it might be contracted: the way it has been writ in, by catches, and many long intervals of Interruption, being apt to cause some Repetitions. But to confess the Truth, I am now too lazie, or too busie to make it shorter.[2]

Locke's use of first person and his insistence that the reader retain an independent mind rather than remain "content to live lazily on scraps of begg'd Opinions" ("Epistle," p. 6) give his readers an active role to play. By inviting readers to set their "own Thoughts on work, to find and follow Truth" ("Epistle," p. 7), Locke abandons the rhetorical stance of authority used by many earlier philosophers. Assuring the reader that "every moment of his Pursuit, will reward his Pains with some Delight" and that "he will have Reason to think his time not ill spent, even when he cannot much boast of any great Acquisition" ("Epistle," p. 6), Locke introduces and defines the importance of thinking as experience or as *agon*.[3]

Throughout the *Essay*, Locke uses his own observations—the cassowaries in St. James Park (II, xxv; III, vi), a winter flood of the Thames (II, xxvii), a friend's story of a medical operation (II, xxxiii)—to illustrate his remarks. He reinforces the effects of these familiar examples by using the present tense, which not only renders immediacy of impression but also underscores his theory of the self as an evolving, conscious entity. Over and over again, he invites thinking readers to make themselves the subjects of their inquiries. Locke's invitation to self-consciousness is often reflected in his stylistic demonstrations of how readers can observe their own mental activities, thereby becoming their own epistemological students. For instance, to prove that reality exists outside the mind, Locke uses an immediate example:

> Thus I see, whilst I write this, I can change the Appearance of the Paper; and by designing the Letters, tell beforehand what new *Idea* it shall exhibit the very next moment, barely drawing my Pen over it: which will neither appear (let me fancy as much as I will) if my Hand stands still; or though I move my Pen, if my Eyes be shut: Nor when those Characters are at once made on the Paper, can I chuse afterwards but see them as they are; that is, have the *Ideas* of such Letters I have made. Whence it is manifest, that they are not barely the Sport and play of my own Imagination. (IV, xi, 7)

In his *Essay*, Locke often appeals to his readers' common experience, and he domesticates his arguments against the theory of innate ideas by urging his readers to observe the intellectual growth of children: "He that attentively considers the state of a *Child* at his first coming into the World, will have little reason to think him stored with plenty of *Ideas*, that are to be the matter of his future Knowledge. 'Tis by degrees he comes to be furnished with them" (II, i, 6).[4]

The immediacy, flexibility, and intimacy which characterized Locke's rhetorical style appealed to many Restoration and eighteenth-century women of thought, as did his suggestions that the mind acquaint itself with its own nature. And, given Locke's insistence upon the power of the unaided human mind, it is not surprising that opposition to his *Essay* came from high places. Many clergymen and academicians found Locke's epistemology as inimical to traditional Christianity and to conventional educational practices that they proposed, in 1703, that the *Essay* be banned from Oxford.

Six years earlier, clergyman and pamphleteer John Edwards (1637–1716) wrote *A Brief Vindication of the Fundamental Articles of Christian Faith*. In his treatise, Edwards called Locke "a lewd declaimer," a "raving tutor and reformer," a "profligate scribe," a "hater of women," and finally, "the governor of the seraglio at Oates," a scurrilous reference to Locke's lifelong friendship with Lady Damaris Cudworth Masham, at whose estate he resided from 1690 until his death in 1704. Recoiling from Locke's insistence upon the close relationship between the physical and intellectual faculties, Edwards may have especially disliked Locke's "midwifery notes" decrying the custom of confinement for pregnant gentlewomen and his theories of prenatal care and child development.[5] Edwards finds Locke inordinately obsessed by "the guts, which he very feelingly and concernedly discourses of as if they were that part of the body which he most minds." Edwards is repulsed by Locke's suggestions in *Thoughts Concerning Education* (1693) for teaching children to evacuate dexterously: "We see it [the physic] has worked, as all the filth and excrement of Mr. Locke's papers show. Dirt and ordure and dunghills are the frequent embellishments of his style." Finally, Edwards hands Locke the ultimate insult by associating him with vulgar women: "In the art of scolding," not even the fish peddlers, "the sisterhood at Billingsgate," could match Locke.

Besides presenting an obvious example of the Calvinistic mind in its most hysterical mode, Edwards's accusations indirectly suggest what is truly revolutionary in Locke's philosophy: the empirical nature of human knowledge, the interconnection between mind and body, emerges from domestic experiences available to all readers. Locke's *Essay* encouraged minds to perceive and describe themselves. In form and in content, Locke's empiricism appealed to Restoration and eighteenth-century women who struggled with problems of epistemology and personal identity.

The Lovelace Collection of Locke's personal papers contains large numbers of notes, drafts, and letters to and from over a dozen women, some of whom Locke knew during his school days at Oxford, others of whom he met through his medical practice or in the course of his remarkably full social life.⁶ Among the collection are forty letters written by Lady Damaris Cudworth Masham, daughter of Cambridge Platonist Ralph Cudworth, who was the tutor of Sir William Temple at Emmanuel College. Locke and Lady Damaris met in 1682 and exchanged *billets doux* during 1682–83, using the names of Philander and Philoclea. Locke's biographer Maurice Cranston mentions subsequent letters between Lady Damaris and Locke which trace the waning romantic aspects of their friendship, but he does not follow Locke's intellectual correspondence with Lady Damaris. Although he relies heavily on Lady Damaris's biography of Locke, Cranston fails to give a thorough account of those rational capacities which made Lady Damaris, according to Cranston, "closer to Locke than any other human being."⁷

Brought up in the Master's Lodge of Christ College, Lady Damaris was a well-educated woman who, Cranston admits, "was something of a philosopher herself."⁸ Since little evidence exists that Locke ever met Ralph Cudworth, his acquaintance with Cudworth's most important philosophical work, *The True Intellectual System of the Universe* (1678), was perhaps supplemented by talks with Lady Damaris. Like some modern scholars, Lady Damaris saw parallels between Locke and the Cambridge Platonists.⁹ But when her friend John Norris, a Platonist who published *Reflections Upon the Conduct of Human Life . . . in the form of a Letter to Lady Masham of Oates* (1690), attacked Locke in *Cursory Reflections upon a Book Called, an Essay Concerning Human Understanding* (1690), Lady Damaris published a defense of her friend. Titled *A Discourse Concerning the Love of God* (1696), the work voiced Lady Damaris's objections to the sharp distinctions Norris drew between corporeal and incorporeal sensations. She took issue with Norris's view that God causes all human sensations, and like Locke, she observed that, since we can know God only through his visible works, we question God's wisdom when we fail to use the physical powers He gave us.¹⁰

Another early defender of Locke's *Essay* was Catherine Trotter Cockburn. Although Cockburn was primarily known as a playwright—she wrote a tragedy, *Agnes de Castro* (1695), based upon Aphra Behn's novel of the same name—she wrote several philosophical essays.[11] Cockburn's anonymous *Defence of the Essay on Human Understanding* (1702) was written against Bishop Burnet's charges that Locke was a materialist, and her defense elicited a warm letter from Locke and further correspondence from Leibnitz, who frequently analyzed her theories. In her defense of Locke, Cockburn employs Lockean empiricism in noting that several people who objected to the *Essay* had "concluded it contained very dangerous Principles, and without further Examination, condemned the *Essay*, having never read, or as they own'd, very little considered it."[12]

In 1710, Lady Mary Chudleigh, in her *Essay on Knowledge,* applied Locke's epistemology to the problems of women's education: "Women should endeavor to get an insight into the useful parts of Learning, and attend more to Things than to Words. . . . Let us be solicitous only for the Substance," she urges.[13] Here, Lady Chudleigh refers to Book III of Locke's *Essay,* wherein Locke analyzes the nature and function of language. Speaking of the imperfection of words, Locke notes that although "the doubtfulness and uncertainty in the signification of some more than other Words, is the difference of *Ideas* they stand for (III, ix, 4). Locke offers several remedies for the imperfections and abuses of language, all of which concern consistent and precise usage.

Hannah More, in her *Strictures on the Modern System of Female Education* (1799), recommends Locke's *Essay* as an alternative to the usual mindless fare offered women students. Observing that young women often deal in "superlatives" and are prone to "exaggerating trifles," More notes that "precision of any kind, either moral or philological, too seldom finds its way into the education of women."[14] Because young women usually learn by superficial question-and-answer methods, they are unaccustomed to reasoning, prone to vanity and idleness, and unacquainted with their intellects, much less able to regulate or inform them.

As an educational reformer, More was convinced that women should be taught, not to be "scholastic ladies," "female dialecticians," or "authors," but to achieve religious and moral perfection.[15] Like Locke, More thought that the mind must be trained to use its God-given powers of reason. Because experience and reflection rather than innate ideas form the origin of human knowledge, the so-called innate inferiority of the "female mind" may be explained in terms of the patriarchal society which confines and distorts its development. Furthermore, adds More,

> till women shall be more reasonably educated, and till the native growth of their minds shall cease to be stinted and cramped, we have no juster ground for pronouncing that their understanding has already reached its highest attainable point, than the Chinese would have for affirming that their women have attained to the greatest possible perfection in walking, while the first care is, during their infancy, to cripple their feet.[16]

For More, the important goals of women's education included training the mind to make associations, to discern the connection between ideas, to discover causal relationships, and to sustain intellectual effort. According to More, "every kind of Knowledge which appears to be the result of observation, reflection, and natural taste, sits gracefully on a woman," but, because women were not given early intellectual training, "what knowledge they have gotten stands out as it were above the very surface of their minds, like the appliquée of the embroiderer, instead of having been interwoven with the growth of the piece, so as to have become a part of the stuff. They did not, like men, acquire what they know while the texture was forming." Lacking early intellectual experiences, a woman's mind, "which has not been given to severer exercise, loves to repose itself in a sort of creditable indolence, instead of stretching its energies in the wholesome labor of consecutive investigation."[17]

In Book II of his *Essay*, Locke warns his readers about the difficulty of attaining self-knowledge: "'Tis not easie for the Mind to put off those confused Notions and Prejudices it has imbibed from Custom, Inadvertency, and common Conversation: it requires pain and assiduity to examine its *Ideas*" (II, xiii, 27). Lady Mary Wortley Montagu echoes Locke's observation in a letter to her daughter:

> This [impartial self-examination] is the hardest of all tasks, requiring great reflection, long retirement, and is strongly repugnant to our own vanity, which very unwillingly reveals, even to ourselves, our common frailty.... Mr. Locke, who has made a more exact dissection of the human mind

than any man before him, declares he gained all his knowledge from consideration of himself.[18]

But neither Hannah More nor Lady Mary Wortley Montagu examined the dichotomy between their assumptions about the aims of women's education and their own aspirations. Despite their insistence that women were educable—since, like men, women had minds whose powers could be cultivated by proper experience and discipline—few Restoration and eighteenth-century women thought that women should aspire beyond the "natural" sphere of domesticity ordained by Providence. For instance, Hannah More flatly states that women's learning "is not often, like the learning of men, to be reproduced in some literary composition, nor ever in any learned profession; but it is to come out in conduct. . . . The great uses of study to a woman are to enable her to regulate her own mind, and to be instrumental to the good of others."[19]

The contradictions between what More says about the nature of the female mind, the uses to which she put her own mind, and the nebulously defined "practical purposes" of women's education are glaringly evident here, as well as in the writings of Lady Mary Wortley Montagu. Both women loved learning, and they embraced the cause of women's education. Yet their keen sense of social propriety and their failure to examine the patriarchal assumptions which provided theological bulwarks for sex role stereotyping imposed upon them the same difficulty which plagued Lady Damaris Cudworth decades earlier when she noted, "The Best Fate, which a Lady knowing and singular could expect" in town, would be to escape "Calumny" and become "the Jest of the *Would-be Witts*, the wonder of Fools and a Scarecrow to keep from her House many honest People." In the countryside, "her prudent conduct and Management of her Affairs would probably secure her from being thought out of her Wits by her near Neighbors; but the Country gentleman that wish'd her well could not yet chuse but be afraid for her, lest too much Learning might in Time make her Mad."[20]

Lady Mary Wortley Montagu recognizes public prejudice against learned women in a letter to her daughter, the Countess of Bute. Lady Mary cautions the Countess to warn her granddaughter that it is "absolutely necessary . . . to conceal whatever Learning she attains, with as much solicitude as she would hide crookedness or lameness."[21] Lady Mary's letters reveal a continued awareness that "there is hardly a character in the world more despicable, or more liable to universal ridicule, than that of a learned woman: those words imply, according to the received sense, a tattling, impertinent, vain, and conceited creature."[22]

As a young woman, Lady Mary had submitted her translation of Epictetus to the Bishop of Salisbury with an apologetic letter employing the usual rhetoric of female modesty. Lest the bishop misunderstand Lady Mary and think her impertinent, she hastens to explain, "I am not now arguing for an equality of the two sexes. I do not doubt God and nature have thrown us into an inferior rank; we are a lower part of creation, we owe obedience and submission to the superior sex, and any woman who suffers her vanity and folly to deny this, rebels against the law of the Creator, and indisputable order of nature."[23]

But, thirty-five years later, writing this time, not to a bishop whose own prejudices must be assuaged, but to her daughter, Lady Mary reveals deep contradictions in her attitudes toward herself, women's education, and the nature of female identity. She contends that the purpose of women's learning is to "make solitude tolerable," and mentions her own retirement to Brescia. But then she considers the "false reasoning" and "unjust customs" which prevail to "debar our sex from the advantages of learning, the men fancying the improvement of our understanding would only furnish us with more art to deceive them, which is contrary to the truth." She contradicts her earlier statements to the bishop:

> The same characters are formed by the same lessons, which inclines me to think (if I dare say it) that nature has not placed us in an inferior rank to men, no more than the females of other animals, where we see no distinction of capacity; though, I am persuaded, if there was a commonwealth of rational horses (as Doctor Swift has supposed), it would be an established maxim among them, that a mare could not be taught to pace.[24]

By this time, Lady Mary had written a critique of Addison's *Cato,* an adaptation of Virgil's bucolics, a translation of Marivaux's comedy *Le Jeu de l'amour et du hasard,* an essay for the *Spectator,* and a defense of smallpox innoculation. Her periodical, *The Nonsense of Common-Sense,* which ran for nine issues in 1738, included a feminist essay which defines women as rational beings: "Men that have not Sense enough to shew any Superiority in their Arguments, hope to be yielded to by a Faith, that, as they are Men, all the Reason that has been alloted to human kind, has fallen to their Share—I am seriously of another Opinion."[25]

Yet all of Lady Mary's works were published anonymously, or without her permission. Like other Restoration and eighteenth-century women thinkers, Lady Mary could not reconcile her passion for learning and public recognition with her deep fears of being thought unnatural. Although she could lament that "what Reason Nature has given [women] is thrown away, and a blind Obedience expected from them by all their ill-Natured Masters,"[26] she knew that society's distrust of female thinkers would deny them the public recognition they needed. In 1752, Lady Mary began to write a history of her time, but she burned the work as fast as she wrote it, explaining her actions with characteristic self-conscious cynicism: "I know Mankind too well to think they are capable of receiving the truth, much less of applauding it."[27] Earlier in her life, Lady Mary had defined female virtue as the knowledge that learning in women could be privately cultivated but would be publicly scorned:

> Mankind is too prejudiced against her woman's Sex, to give her any Degree of that Fame which is so sharp a spur to their greatest Actions. I have some Thoughts of exhibiting a Set of Pictures of such meritorious Ladies, where I shall say nothing of the Fire in their Eyes, or the Pureness of their Complexions; but give them such Priases as befits a rational sensible Being: Virtues of Choice, and not Beauties of Accident.[28]

So it seems that, although Lady Mary applauded education for women and agreed with Locke that the human mind should seek to define and discipline its own observations, the sheer weight of human prejudice would crush any attempts at reform. If Swift defined man as *rationis capax* rather than *animal rationale,* Montagu defined *femina rationis* as a contradiction in terms.

Other women thinkers of the Restoration and eighteenth century wrote about this dilemma. Mary Astell, in *A Serious Proposal to the Ladies, for the Advancement of their True and Greatest Interest* (1694), and Lady Mary Chudleigh, in *An Essay on Knowledge* (1710), mention the mean opinion women held of themselves. Astell echoes Locke when she blames mistaken education for women's ignorance. Yet, women must not presume to assert themselves too much in the world's business. Implied, if not specifically stated, is the definition of humankind as the male species.

The contradictions between women's aspirations to learn and obligations to limit their sense of personal identity to patriarchal expectations confined women thinkers of the Restoration and eighteenth century. The women who studied, defended, or applied Locke's empiricism could not afford to examine their own dependence upon the definition of woman by the Christian patriarchy.

Bertrand Russell once observed that Locke's intellectual temper was "obviously connected with religious toleration, with the success of parliamentary democracy, with laissez-faire, and with a whole system of liberal maxims."[29] Speaking of the influence of Locke's political theories, Russell mentions Locke's *Two Treatises on Government* (1689-90), the first of which attacked Sir Robert Filmer's *Patriarcha; or, The Natural Power of Kings* (1680). Filmer traces the divine right of kings to God's gift of power to Adam. Russell says, "This whole theory seems to a modern mind so fantastic that it is hard to believe it was seriously maintained. We are not accustomed to deriving our political rights from the story of Adam and Eve."[30]

But, in one sense, Russell's arch observation is inaccurate. The Christian patriarchal political and cultural system—whereby every avenue of power within society is in male hands—is ideologically rooted in the story of Adam and Eve. The birthright priority whereby males rule females, the innate distinctions presumed to fit males for domination and females for submission, is contained within the story. In the deepest sense, Adam's mastery of Eve precludes her claims to autonomous identity, while Adam's God-given power to name the creatures of the earth insures his right to define Eve with his own words. Locke's empiricism undercuts the story, not because his philosophy proves him a "hater of women," as his critics maintained, but because it insists that the human mind become aware of itself and its own powers. Ironically, the women considered in this paper agreed with Locke's notion of the *tabula rasa*, but they could not erase what patriarchal ideas of woman's innate nature had already written on their minds.

NOTES

1 See Barbara Brandon Schnorrenberg, "Education for Women in Eighteenth-Century England: An Annotated Bibliography," *Women and Literature*, 4 (1976), 49-55.
2 John Locke, *An Essay Concerning Human Understanding*, 4th ed. (1700; rpt. with Introduction, Critical Apparatus and Glossary by Peter H. Nidditch, Oxford: Clarendon Press, 1975), pp. 7-8. Subsequent references to Locke's *Essay* are from this edition and are cited in the text.
3 Rosalie Colie, "The Essayist in His *Essay*," in *John Locke: Problems and Perspectives*, ed. John Yolton (Cambridge: Cambridge University Press, 1969), shows how Locke's rhetorical stance enables him to "square himself and his readers against a restrictive and always nameless authority, against conventional men of received opinion, and against flightly followers of philosophical fashion" (p. 247).
4 Locke deliberately popularized his philosophy; he even prepared an explanation of Newtonian mechanics for Lady Damaris's twelve-year-old son, Francis (James Axtell, "Locke, Newton, and the Two Cultures," in Yolton, *John Locke*, p. 178).
5 Edward's attack on Locke is quoted in Maurice Cranston, *John Locke: A Biography* (New York: MacMillan, 1957), pp. 430-31. For Locke's notes on midwifery, written about 1695, see Kenneth Dewhurst, "Locke's Midwifery Notes," *The Lancet*, Sept. 4, 1954, pp. 490-91.
6 Cranston, *John Locke*, p. 430.
7 Ibid., p. 215. See W. von Leyden, "Notes concerning Papers of John Locke in the Lovelace Collection," *Philosophical Quarterly*, 2 (1952), 63-69, for a description of the collection.
8 Cranston, *John Locke*, p. 215. See *The Correspondence of John Locke*, ed. E. S. De Beer (Oxford: Clarendon Press, 1976), vol. 2, for the Lady Damaris-Locke correspondence, 1682-85.
9 See, for example, J. A. Passmore, *Ralph Cudworth: An Interpretation* (Cambridge: Cambridge University Press, 1951), p. 91, and Richard Aaron, *John Locke* (Oxford: Clarendon Press, 1955), p. 29.
10 Gilbert D. McEwen, ed., Introduction to *Cursory Reflections Upon a Book Call'd, An Essay Concerning Human Understanding*, by John Norris (1690; facsimile rpt. Los Angeles: Augustan Reprint Society, No. 93, 1961), p. 3. Lady Damaris's second defense of Locke, *Occasional Thoughts in Reference to a Vertuous or Christian Life*, appeared in 1705, a year after Locke's death.

11 Cockburn's treatise on moral obligation appeared in *The History of the Works of the Learned* (August 1743). In 1747, Warburton contributed a preface to Cockburn's *Remarks* on Rutherford's *Essay on the Nature and Obligations of Virtue*.
12 Preface to *A Defence of the Essay on Human Understanding, Written by Mr. Lock. Wherein its Principles with reference to Morality, Reveal'd Religion, and the Immortality of the Soul, are Consider'd and Justify'd: In Answer to Some Remarks on that Essay* [by T. Burnet], (London: Will Turner, 1702), p. [7]. Quoted in John Yolton, *John Locke and the Way of Ideas* (London: Oxford University Press, 1956), p. 17. Cockburn's subsequent defenses of Locke include *A Letter to Dr. Holdsworth* (1726–27) and *A Vindication of Mr. Locke's Christian Principles from the Injurious Imputations of Dr. Holdsworth* (1727; pub. 1751). See Robert Adams Day, ed., Introduction to *Olinda's Adventures; or, The Amours of a Young Lady*, by Catherine Cockburn (1718; facsimile rpt. Los Angeles: Augustan Reprint Society, No. 138, 1969), for a short biography of Cockburn.
13 Lady Mary Chudleigh, *Essays on Several Subjects* (1710), quoted in Dorothy Gardiner, *English Girlhood at School: A Study of Women's Education through Twelve Centuries* (London: Oxford University Press, 1929), p. 32.
14 Hannah More, *Strictures on the Modern System of Female Education* (1799), in *The Miscellaneous Works of Hannah More* (London: Thomas Tegg, 1840), I, 430–32.
15 Ibid., pp. 422–23.
16 Ibid., p. 463. More continues, using an analogy familiar to twentieth-century feminists: "At least, till the female sex are more carefully instructed, this question [women's intellectual inferiority] will always remain as undecided as to the *degree* of difference between the masculine and feminine understandings, as the question between the understandings of Blacks and Whites; for, until men and women, and until Africans and Europeans, are put more nearly on a par in the cultivation of their minds, the shades of distinction, whether they be, between their native abilities, can never be fairly ascertained" (p. 463).
17 Ibid., pp. 471, 472.
18 Lady Mary Wortley Montagu to the Countess of Bute, March 1, [1754], in *The Complete Letters of Lady Mary Wortley Montagu*, ed. Robert Halsband (Oxford: Clarendon Press, 1967), III, 48.
19 More, *Strictures*, p. 455.
20 Quoted in Gardiner, *English Girlhood at School*, pp. 380–81.
21 Lady Montagu to the Countess of Bute, Jan. 28, 1753, *Complete Letters*, III, 22.
22 Lady Montagu to the Bishop of Salisbury, July 20, 1710, ibid., I, 45.
23 Ibid.
24 Lady Montagu to the Countess of Bute, March 6, [1753], ibid., III, 25–26, 27.
25 *The Nonsense of Common-Sense*, no. 6 (1737–38), ed. Robert Halsband, Northwestern University Studies in the Humanities, No. 17 (Evanston: Northwestern University Press, 1947), p. 27.
26 *The Nonsense of Common-Sense*, p. 25.
27 Lady Montagu to the Countess of Bute, Oct. 1, [1752], *Complete Letters*, III, 19. Two fragments of the history remain: a sketch of the death of Queen Anne and an

account of George I's court in 1714. Robert Halsband, *The Life of Lady Mary Wortley Montagu* (Oxford: Clarendon Press, 1956), pp. 45-47, includes excerpts from the latter fragment.
28 *The Nonsense of Common-Sense*, p. 28.
29 Bertrand Russell, *A History of Western Philosophy* (New York: Simon and Schuster, 1945), p. 619.
30 Ibid., p. 619.

Mary Wollstonecraft's Letters Written... in Sweden: Toward Romantic Autobiography

MITZI MYERS

Curious travelogue that it is, Mary Wollstonecraft's *Letters Written during a Short Residence in Sweden, Norway, and Denmark* has pleased and perplexed readers ever since its appearance in 1796. The book was an immediate success, widely translated and enthusiastically praised by Wollstonecraft's contemporaries, who appreciated her factual record of a little-known area but delighted most in her scenery and sensibility. Eighteenth-century reviewers comment on the *Letters'* seeming lack of arrangement and richly miscellaneous content, and are touched—as well as a bit nonplused—by this suffusion of personal feeling: "She claims the traveller's privilege of speaking frequently of herself," remarks the *Monthly Review*.[1] To describe one's trip is always to reveal something of oneself, of course. Even that most reticent and decorous traveler Ann Radcliffe notes that "relating part of the history of his life... is always necessarily done by a writer of travels,"[2] but Wollstonecraft's pervasive self-emphasis goes far beyond the incidental personal references common in travel literature.

Like eighteenth-century readers, modern critics all notice this unusual confessional element in the *Letters*. For Sylva Norman, the

Werther-like passages and the "tear-salt" are embarrassing excrescences on an incisive social analysis; conversely, Carol Poston, latest editor of the work, finds that "a quality of poetic reverie" is what holds together the wide-ranging social commentary.[3] Ralph Wardle cites two discrete unifying tendencies: "Mary's remarks on the progress of society" and "her revelation of the progress of her sorrows" over the disintegration of her liaison with the American adventurer Gilbert Imlay.[4] Like Wardle, Claire Tomalin recognizes a public/private dichotomy, yet finds the book an "oddly successful" hodgepodge.[5] To grant primacy to either social criticism or personal revelation—or to see the two as disjunct—does a disservice to the organic integrity of the Letters, however.

Wollstonecraft's book is in fact a generic hybrid, a kind of subjective autobiography superimposed on a travelogue. Moreover, her theory of travel narrative (evolved in the many articles on travel she wrote for the Analytical Review) and her Advertisement to the Letters—when considered in conjunction with her general aesthetics, her personal situation, and the successive and subtly modulated versions of the self in her account of her journey—suggest that, far from being digressive or disorganized, she knew what she was about. Underlying the seeming duality of personal and social motifs in the Letters is a continuous concern with human identity and self-realization, developed in counterpoint to the related themes of society's improvement and nature's values. Wollstonecraft's autobiographical account of her journey in some ways resembles Wordsworth's later pilgrimage in search of a reintegration of self, nature, and society.[6] The Letters have long been recognized as a revelatory psychological document, but they are also a literary experiment, thematically unified and formally organized through a very personal version of associationism.

In reviewing for the Analytical, Wollstonecraft had taken travels seriously and had worked out her own set of critical standards for dealing with them. Her reviews demand significant content and emphasize the need for accurate information as a basis for moral generalization. She is interested in manners and morals, not Mrs. Piozzi's "frivolous, superficial remarks" on pictures, buildings, and social occasions.[7] Wollstonecraft also stresses the need for a unifying theme:

travelers should have "some decided point in view, a grand object of pursuit to concentre their thoughts, and connect their reflections"; she dislikes mere "detached observations, which no running interest, or prevailing bent in the mind of the writer rounds into a whole."[8] It is the reflective traveler's consciousness which most often makes connections and supplies unity; indeed, "the art of travel is only a branch of the art of thinking."[9] She favors a simple style and unpremeditated reflections made on the spot, for tours elaborated and revised after the fact falsify the record and savor of affectation.[10]

Wollstonecraft's criteria for travel literature are thus in line with her general ideology, which is based on direct observation and independent thought. Always stressing naturalness, originality, and thinking for oneself, she is a very personal writer in both theory and practice; from her first novel to her last essays, the individual vision is central to her work. Her fiction is organized around her heroines' content of consciousness, and even in her theoretical works, the ordonnance of her prose follows the movement of her mind. (She is often criticized for a lack of logical organization when she seems to be striving for something quite different.) If her prose is not everywhere as fresh and supple as her theories demand, her general aesthetics—most fully stated in the 1797 essay "On Poetry, and Our Relish for the Beauties of Nature"—is very much in the Romantic expressive mode. For all her reputation as an advocate of reason, Wollstonecraft always reveres imagination. She likes to measure the value of a work by the author's ability to permeate it with a unique personality and vision, and she enjoys discussing the creative process. When she wants to describe the way the mind of genius works, for example, she does it in terms of an instantaneous association of ideas. Unlike habitual associations, this kind of imaginative perception depends on the original "temperature" of the mind:

> The animal spirits, the individual character, give the colouring. . . . These fine intractable spirits appear to be the essence of genius, and . . . produce in the most eminent degree the happy energy of associating thoughts that surprise, delight, and instruct. These are the glowing minds that concentrate pictures for their fellow-creatures, forcing them to view with interest the objects reflected from the impassioned imagination, which they passed over in nature.

Most people cannot see or feel poetically, but "when an author lends them his eyes they can see as he saw."[11] Such passages are the rationale for Wollstonecraft's method in the *Letters*. For a writer so oriented, it is but a step from a reflective travelogue to a Romantic autobiography in which the perceiving self and its multifaceted relationships to the world are central.

Wollstonecraft took that step under the pressure of intense mental suffering. She did not set out on a romantic quest of self-discovery, but was sent off on a prosaic trip to disentangle Gilbert Imlay's Scandinavian business dealings. He wanted to dissolve their drawn-out affair; she wanted to reclaim him from the womanizing and commercial scheming which she felt were debasing his better self. Her journey was a brief breathing space for both, one which she came to realize offered her an opportunity to transmute the passive feminine suffering of a woman scorned into an active Romantic exploration of her now fully developed emotional and imaginative capacities. The *Letters* record, among other things, a passage from feminine romance to female Romanticism.

If the literary qualities and thematic preoccupations of Wollstonecraft's autobiographical experiment are clearly connected to those of the historical moment in which she is writing, they are as clearly related to her gender. Because she is a woman who is largely self-taught and not classically trained, she is probably more receptive to innovation. As a woman, she is especially alive to the constraints and fragmentation of her culture—she seeks renovation, a new wholeness. Much as her ideology strives to relate reason and imagination, to create a social environment hospitable to full human development, so she herself wants to be both successful professional writer and satisfied domestic woman. She experienced all the jugglings of roles and adjustings of selves that women writers are socially heir to, and she enacted in her own life their classic struggle to reconcile the claims of private emotional gratification with those of larger goals. Because the *Letters* were written in the midst of this profound crisis, the presence of Imlay, their unnamed recipient, and the questions the affair raises haunt the twenty-five essays. Because Wollstonecraft is trying to deal with complex problems at both the philosophical and the personal levels, the texture of the *Letters* is a complex interweave of issues and partial answers; its internal structure, an embodiment and revelation of the qualities and processes of a thinking and feeling woman's mind.

Such a form—the autobiographical *disjecta membra* of a real journey, fragments in search of a wholeness—would not, however, be considered true autobiography, according to the definitions of some modern theorists of life-writing, who stress formal completeness and finality of insight—serene retrospection beyond crisis—as criteria.[12] Letters, journals, and records of journeys will not do: they are bits and pieces of a quest for meaning, mere process itself—not achieved integrations of being. However incomplete, the discrete and unpremeditated self-revelations of these forms do occupy a large part in the canon of women's autobiographies—"autobiographies by indirection," they have been called.[13] The finished formality of, say, Gibbon's self-portrait, with its orderly definition of the self in terms of a public profession—a man is his work—contrasts strongly with eighteenth-century women's typical choice of forms not intended for public consumption.

Eighteenth-century women autobiographers, Patricia Meyer Spacks finds, are concerned mainly with private experiences rather than public goals. They tend to see themselves as passive victims of a social system in which men make the rules which women must obey. They define themselves not through external accomplishments but through personal relationships; they are usually resentful and apologetic about what mental life they achieve; and their private selves are often at odds with their public images of weakness and inadequacy.[14] Divided selves imply discontinuous structures: women's autobiographies are generally less structured and orderly than those of men. Indeed, some students of female autobiography suggest that diffusion and discontinuity are necessary concomitants of women's efforts to render their lives, which they perceive not as logical, linear progress toward a goal but as disconnected units of experience, a series of socially conditioned roles.[15]

Wollstonecraft shares with these other female autobiographers a painful awareness of female roles and problems, and she is using the discontinuous form of epistolary travel narrative for her autobiography by indirection. But her work differs in significant ways—both thematically and formally—from the manner in which most eighteenth-century women write of themselves. More comprehensive in scope and assertive enough to write publicly and openly of herself, she is both innovative and integrative. Using the circuitous, subjective movement of the mind to indicate the simultaneous multiplicity yet essential integrity of the self, she turns a discontinuous form into an agency of continuity. Moving beyond passive protest to active self-discovery, uniting masculine concerns with female needs, she transforms the objective travelogue into a novel exploration of both general human nature and her individual self.

Wollstonecraft's travels constitute a metaphoric as well as an actual journey; her readers participate in a romantic quest, a complex search for identity. Her personal experiences and reflections as she journeys and interacts with the natural and social worlds form stages in an ongoing process of self-knowledge, an evolution toward maturation. Her successive self-images are tested against changing settings; she finds at least a provisional identity: "What a long time it requires to know ourselves; and yet almost every one has more of this knowledge than he is willing to own, even to himself" (IX, p. 117). Her persona is not a congealed and completed self (this is what I am), but the protagonist of a quest still uncompleted at the book's conclusion (who am I, and where am I going?). She gives her readers not a retrospective assessment, but a convoluted and painful search for meaning in the midst of a crisis. If she arrives at no final answers in this search, she does achieve a notable serenity of tone and maturity of outlook, a serenity and maturity all the more surprising considering the context of personal misery and social upheaval—"horrors" in France (I, p. 11), "aristocracy and fanaticism" in England (IX, p. 114)—which generated the book.

The themes and images of Wollstonecraft's quest are embryonic in her earlier set of letters to Imlay, which are the purely private record of a woman's recognition of her emotional capacities and of the pain their thwarting causes. The *Letters to Imlay* (published by her widower Godwin after her death) document her initial happiness, the birth of Fanny, the beloved "little frolicker" of the *Letters* (XII, p. 143), and the harrowingly protracted dissolution of her hopes. Their plot is a tragic love story; Godwin compares them to *Werther*, and his hyperbole—"the finest examples of the language of sentiment and passion ever presented to the world.... the offspring of a glowing imagination, and a heart penetrated with the passion it essays to describe"[16]—is the exaggeration of a truth. But Wollstonecraft was not simply "in love with love" or confusing the new gratifications of sex with something grander, as some modern critics suggest.[17] Her commitment to Imlay satisfied her philosophical principles as well as her personal desires. She thought she had found in him a union of reason and feeling—someone with whom she could share the principled affection and domestic happiness she so frequently extolled[18]—but she discovered in him only the paradigmatic male shaped by an oppressive culture.

Wollstonecraft's *Letters to Imlay* define what feeling and happiness mean to her and try incessantly to convert him to her values. As he traveled around France and back to England, forever intent on "business and sensual pleasure," and as she continually rejoined him at his half-hearted invitation, she came more and more to see her life as an endless journey and herself as forever debarred from home: "Dear Imlay, am I always to be tossed about thus? shall I never find an asylum to rest *contented* in? How can you love to fly about continually, dropping down as it were, in a new world—cold and strange—every other day! Why do you not attach those tender emotions round the idea of home which even now dim my eyes? This alone is affection." "I am weary of traveling, yet seem to have no home—no resting place to look to."[19] To Imlay's masculine ethos of adventure and power, commerce and casual sex, Wollstonecraft opposes feminine and philosophical values. She wants to create with him a new home, to retire to an American farm. Concerned with the quality of life, with full human realization, she despairs over Imlay's transformation from unspoiled American to aggressive entrepreneur and comes to feel that developing the finest capacities of the female self only insures misery. The implicit theme of these letters is exploitation—sexual, emotional, commercial—versus nurture and development, but Wollstonecraft the philosopher is here largely subsumed in the suffering woman.

These private *Letters to Imlay* and the public *Letters Written... in Sweden* are closely connected, and in part, overlapping records of a tormented, yet extremely resilient and intensely reflective consciousness. Despite her desperation—discovering her lover's infidelities, planning suicide before her trip, and nearly succeeding in drowning herself after her return from Sweden—Wollstonecraft yet struggles in each set of letters with the difficulties of creating or finding some sort of identity, some way to be at home, in a contradictory culture. The published travel narrative explores the issues of the *Letters to Imlay* in a more comprehensive context and a more positive tone, while retaining the intimacy and discursive mode of the epistle.

Wollstonecraft recorded her Scandinavian journey in letters to Imlay and apparently also in a journal. Kegan Paul remarks that what she wrote to Imlay during the tour was afterwards "divested of all that was personal and private" and published,[20] but Wollstonecraft discusses the "keeping of a journal" early in the *Letters* (III, p. 32), stressing its value in focusing the traveler's inquiries and helping him to evolve a general theme, a point she had often made in her travel reviews for the *Analytical*. Certainly, too, she makes very pointed allusions to both herself and Imlay; for example:

> But you will say that I am growing bitter, perhaps, personal. Ah! shall I whisper to you—that you—yourself, are strangely altered, since you have entered deeply into commerce.... You will rouse yourself, and shake off the vile dust that obscures you, or my understanding, as well as my heart, deceives me egregiously—only tell me when? (XXIII, p. 252)

> A man ceases to love humanity, and then individuals, as he advances in the chase after wealth.... Cassandra was not the only prophetess whose warning voice has been disregarded. (XXIII, 255–56)

Eleanor Flexner, among others, has speculated on Wollstonecraft's motives in including such private material: perhaps she was publicly wooing Imlay or trying to embarrass him or cannily turning her anguish into hard cash.[21]

Wollstonecraft's motives in moving beyond private complaint to public examination are, I think, more subtle and complex. However wretchedly she began it, the journey gave her time to think as well as feel, to reconsider and test out her theories from a new vantage point, to see clearly how her personal problems replicated those of society. The journey was an opportunity for self-exploration. Indeed, Roy Pascal uses a journey metaphor throughout his suggestive *Design and Truth in Autobiography* as a way of indicating the quest inherent in writing about oneself: "The purpose of true autobiography must be 'Selbstbesinnung,' a search for one's inner standing.... The life is represented in autobiography not as something established but as a process; it is not simply the narrative of the voyage, but also the voyage itself. There must be in it a sense of discovery."[22]

The *Letters* are full of this sense of discovery; they are at once a literary and a personal experiment. Wollstonecraft's Romantic aesthetics and female situation—determinants in her search for autonomous self-expression—coalesce, shaping what might have been a more commonplace reflective travelogue into a fresher form. If she began writing to keep in touch with, in response to, Imlay, she soon turned her *Letters* to further uses. Just as she—the demonstration of the powers of her mind—holds the book together formally, so the writing of the book quite literally holds her together, as she discovers her power to overcome fragmentation, the power of the self to create unity and make sense of its multiple roles and painful experiences. To give the book its unity is at the same time to assert an identity. The work and the self exist in a reciprocal relationship, the work itself an image of what the self can achieve.

Wollstonecraft writes to orient, to affirm, to discover herself. She does not feel the need to justify or absolve herself, since she perceives herself as guiltless, "innocent and credulous as a child" (XXII, p. 248). Feeling misprized and misunderstood, she demonstrates and dramatizes herself in a wide variety of roles both private and public. Poston calls the persona in the *Letters* "the Traveller," a useful (if too limited) description, since it places Wollstonecraft in the eighteenth-century travel tradition of empirical observation and moral reflection: she ranges from salt-making and child care to the position of women and capital punishment. But there are many I's in the *Letters*, superimposed voices connected by subtle modulations of topic and tone.

Wollstonecraft presents herself as individual, a particular person; as representative of and spokeswoman for her gender's common experience; as observant member of society; as philosopher-traveler; and, perhaps most significantly, as archetypal spiritual consciousness alienated from society but alive to nature and expanding beyond it. These are multiple, yet coexistent roles; she is both one single self and a cumulative structure of selves. As Poston has noted, the hardy traveler who disdains physical hardships and can snatch sleep in the bottom of a boat does not forget she is also a lone woman journeying with a timid maid and small child. She asks *"men's questions,"* but she is also possible prey for "robberies, murders, or the other evil which instantly... runs foul of a woman's imagination" (I, pp. 13, 7).

If Imlay fails to live up to his better self and undervalues her, Wollstonecraft demonstrates that she knows her own worth and abilities. Despite her self-pity—the "effusions of a sensibility wounded almost to madness" (XIII, p. 153)—and her identification with female fellow-victims like Queen Matilda, Wollstonecraft's disillusion and anger are transmuted for the most part into strong images of a woman's competence and capacity. She takes full responsibility for her own ideas and feelings, and she reveals a firm sense of selfhood, even as she shows herself discovering or revaluating aspects of that self. She is particularly concerned with exploring emotion throughout the book, whether in admiring nature—"my very reason obliges me to permit my feelings to be my criterion. Whatever excites emotion has charms for me" (X, p. 118)—or in coming to terms with forces in her own personality she had long tried to suppress, such as "the extreme affection of my nature.... For years have I endeavoured to calm an impetuous tide—labouring to make my feelings take an orderly course.—It was striving against the stream.—I must love and admire with warmth, or I sink into sadness" (VIII, pp. 94–95).

Wollstonecraft's full recognition of her emotional and imaginative capacities—one positive result of the Imlay debacle—is the associative nexus of personal plight and social problem. The narrative voice of this recognition, one of the most arresting in the *Letters,* is the Rousseauistic "Solitary Walker"[23] or, to borrow one of Godwin's phrases, "female Werter," who is "endowed with the most exquisite and delicious sensibility... almost of too fine a texture to encounter the vicissitudes of human affairs."[24] Drawn to the solitude and harmony of nature, Wollstonecraft plays with the old myth of the Golden Age which her feelings endorse (XIV, p. 168; XXII, p. 245), though her reason tells her that "civilization is a blessing not sufficiently estimated by those who have not traced its progress" (II, p. 20) and that to live in a primitive society is to be "bastilled by nature—shut out from all that opens the understanding, or enlarges the heart" (XI, p. 133). She turns the familiar Georgian retirement myth with its polarities of city and country, the staple of so many fictional journeys, back and forth, using it freshly and complexly, to develop her need to find a place congenial to self-realization. "A metropolis, or an abode absolutely solitary, is the best calculated for the improvement of the heart, as well as the understanding" (III, p. 33), she decides at one point, though she perceives such problems in each that she returns to the question repeatedly.

Wollstonecraft's physical journey is matched by a teleological journey of the mind; her search is both material and mental as she tries to define social as well as personal happiness. In such passages as this, the circuitous journey of her mind is at once theme and form, as she strives to reconcile the dictates of reason with the claims of emotion, the needs of the self with what society has to offer:

> The world requires, I see, the hand of man to perfect it; and as this task naturally unfolds the faculties he exercises, it is physically impossible that he should have remained in Rousseau's golden age of stupidity. And, considering the question of human happiness, where, oh! where does it reside? Has it taken up its abode with unconscious ignorance, or with the high-wrought mind?... I am delighted with the romantic views I daily contemplate.... Still nothing so soon wearies out the feelings as unmarked simplicity. I am, therefore, half convinced, that I could not live very comfortably exiled from the countries where mankind are so much further advanced in knowledge, imperfect as it is, and unsatisfactory to the thinking mind.... My thoughts fly from this wilderness to the polished circles of the world, till recollecting its vices and follies, I bury myself in the woods, but find it necessary to emerge again, that I may not lose sight of the wisdom and virtue which exalts my nature.... I cannot immediately determine whether I ought to rejoice at having turned over in this solitude a new page in the history of my own heart. (IX, pp. 116–17)

Wollstonecraft's concern with locating the best environment for human and self-development and her delight in solitude and nature throughout the book suggest a possible provenance for her phrase "history of my own heart," as well as a major influence on the *Letters*. She had reviewed Rousseau's *Confessions* very favorably for the *Analytical* and cited with approbation his famous "history of my soul" passage.[25] Sylva Norman's and Godwin's comparisons of Wollstonecraft with Werther indicate, of course, an additional source for this narrative voice in the *Letters*.

Wollstonecraft must adapt male models—the philosophical man of feeling—to her purposes. She has no female literary patterns for the persona she is creating, one which can conflate a mother's and a philosopher's concern with human nurture. She worries, for example, over whether to cultivate her daughter's sensibilities "lest it should render her unfit for the world she is to inhabit" (VI, p. 66), and again and again adverts to discords between the realized self and "half civilized society" (XII, p. 142):

> It [is] a great misfortune for individuals to acquire a certain delicacy of sentiment, which often makes them weary of the common occurrences of life; yet it is this very delicacy of feeling and thinking which probably has produced most of the performances that have benefited mankind. (XX, pp. 223-24; see also XXII, p. 234)

> Nature is the nurse of sentiment... yet what misery, as well as rapture, is produced by a quick perception of the beautiful and sublime.... how dangerous is it to foster these sentiments in such an imperfect state of existence. (VI, p. 71)

But Wollstonecraft is not concerned merely with her individual disappointment in depicting the precarious situation of the developed self. She has always an unusual gift for dramatizing or mythologizing her personal difficulties into issues of larger consequence, and though this point has been recognized in regard to the two *Vindications*, her novels—and the *Letters*—have suffered from too limited a view of her use of private material. Her travel book shows the subtle fusing of the actual, particular experiences she has undergone with her general unifying theme: "My favorite subject of contemplation, the future improvement of the world" (XXII, p. 245); "I . . . note the present state of morals and manners, as I trace the progress of the world's improvement. . . . my principal object has been to take such a dispassionate view of men as will lead me to form a just idea of the nature of man" (XIX, pp. 215-16).

Wollstonecraft is the social meliorist on the side of progress, seeing national virtues in proportion to scientific improvements (XIX, p. 218) and noting the relationship between liberty and commerce (XIV, p. 170). But she is also—as in the very personal direct address to Imlay quoted earlier—like Cassandra, a prophetess warning against the perils that attend advancing civilization, both physical (she worries about overpopulation [XI, p. 132] and is disturbed by the despoiling of nature that accompanies progress [XVII, p. 191]) and moral. She deplores the threat to higher virtues of a mercantile society obsessed only with money and is constantly alive to the dangers as well as the benefits of commerce.[26] Thus the "you" to whom her letters are addressed is on one level Gilbert Imlay, philandering businessman, but he is also Wollstonecraft's epitome of a finer nature debased to the sordid level of the world, just as she makes herself a mythic image of the superior, improved consciousness homeless in, out of synch with, things as they are—but still representing the highest moral ideals of the culture from which she feels alienated. At the same time that she warns Imlay, Cassandra has a broader audience in view. She interrelates private life and public theme, raising autobiographical issues to a plane of symbolic significance. Her analysis of the relation between nature and culture is thematically integrated with both her improvement motif and her autobiographical revelations.

Though Wollstonecraft presents versions of the self limited by personal disappointment, gender restrictions, and social inadequacies, her more characteristic emphasis is on self-enlargement, the refusal of the self to be determined by anything exterior to it. Such self-enlargement sometimes appears through demonstrations of moral authority—Cassandra as dispossessed social conscience asking, "Where is truth or rather principle to be found?" (XIII, p. 153)—but it is most strikingly manifested through recurrent acts of imaginative transcendence which assert the self's essential integrity and inviolability, its immortality and unconditional freedom. Her journey is studded with images of entrapment and stasis. It begins with a becalmed vessel from which she seeks emancipation, and a fainting fit; she is plagued by smothering featherbeds and stuffy, overheated rooms; feels herself a bird "unable to mount" (XIII, p. 160) or a signpost pointing the road to others "whilst forced to stand still... amidst the mud and dust" (XXII, p. 242); sees villagers as "bastilled by nature," the world as a "vast prison" (XI, pp. 133, 132), human existence as "this waste of budding life," and God as caring only for the species, not individuals (XXII, p. 241).[27] External objects lead into metaphysical conundrums of identity; appalled by some dried mummies she is shown, she cries out: "Life, what art thou? Where goes this breath? this *I*, so much alive?... I feel a conviction that we have some perfectible principle in our present vestment, which will not be destroyed just as we begin to be sensible of improvement"; she seeks "a higher state of existence" (VII, pp. 91–92). She is a pilgrim in search of health, virtue, and identity; and these she finds through varied applications of her "open air... remedy" (XIII, p. 160) and the journeys of her own mind.

Such journeys, each a miniature Romantic excursus, punctuate Wollstonecraft's travel narrative throughout—exploring the self in relation to nature, God, and eternity, delineating the processes of memory and imagination which assure its coherence and continuity. These moments of heightened experience, while suggesting Rousseau and Wordsworth,[28] have each a distinctive individuality, a view of the writer as seen from within conveyed through an apparently artless and unpremeditated report of the workings of her mind. Wollstonecraft's renderings of nature have been described, along with those of Radcliffe, as the work of a "complete passionate traveler,"[29] but they really bear little resemblance to Radcliffe's lengthy accounts, in which the observer is all eye, incredibly sensitive, but rather impersonal. Wollstonecraft, on the contrary, criticized extravagant, sentimental depictions of scenery for its own sake in the *Analytical*,[30] and remarks in the *Letters* that she cannot find words to convey adequately the individuality of what she sees, though she can perhaps stimulate the reader's imagination as her own has been stirred (V, p. 43). She can be very evocative in description—desolate tracts seem "the bones of the world waiting to be clothed" (V, p. 49)—but she more characteristically converts landscape into emotional and spiritual sustenance. Scenes are portrayed through their effect on the participant. A night view, for example, offers calm, a sense of eternity, opportunities for reveries and recollections, foretastes of futurity (II, p. 25).

The delights of nature she now finds "even more alluring" than in youth (IV, p. 41), probably because they offer emotional gratification after the devastation of the Imlay affair. During her tour, she wrote Imlay that the imaginative, idealizing love she felt for him arose from the same emotional basis—"the sensibility of an expanded heart"—as literary taste and "exquisite relish for the beauties of nature"; these same feelings are "sure harbingers" of heavenly joy to come.[31] Through imaginative encounters with nature, the expanded self is itself validated and finds the home for which it has been seeking. Tensions between deprived individual and unsatisfactory world dissolve, and inner and outer reality are reconciled.

Nature presents Wollstonecraft with occasions for transcendence of material limitation and emotional privation: through the recovered past, through coalescence or fusion with the landscape before her, through intimations of immortality. Her manipulations of nature assert the continuity of the self: present feelings lead into past recollections—the experiences that made her what she is (VI, p. 72)—and anticipate future bliss. The associative linkages of the mind determine the shape of the mental excursions nature sets off. She moves from evocation of external nature to interior meditation, from the rest and repose of night, all that she sees appearing "at home," to herself as "this active principle," busy with memories and "the idea of home"; she contemplates her alienation—"a particle broken off from the grand mass of mankind"—only to reject it. "Involuntary sympathetic emotion" links her to the "mighty whole" which extends to futurity: there only can she expect happiness (I, pp. 14–16). Sometimes her responses to night are described in "voluptuous" erotic imagery (V, p. 61). Sometimes she is an "aeolian harp," all passive responsiveness (VI, p. 71), or melds into the landscape ("my very soul diffused itself... seeming to become all senses" [VIII, p. 94]), but these fusions of self and scene, which she relives again as she writes, typically resolve into memories and anticipations—layers of past and projections of future consciousness. Annihilation is the only thing she dreads: "I cannot bear to think of being no more—of losing myself.... nay, it appears to me impossible that I should cease to exist" (VIII, p. 97). Objects she sees are referred to and identified with the self. Aging pines link with her own death, which is "like something getting free—to expand.... this conscious being must be as unfettered, have the wings of thought, before it can be happy." Cascades become the uncontrollable torrents of her own ideas. Sublime scenes make immortality seem immediately graspable—she stretches out her hand—and far more real than the "dark speck of life to come" (XV, pp. 174-75).

To withdraw the mind from objects of sense renews the self's dignity and allows the soul to rise above its cares (XVIII, p. 198; XV, p. 175). Through mental resources, psychic need generates reassurance, obliterating time and pain. Imagination and reflection—activities of the mind precipitated by what she sees—assert the self's freedom. A strong imagination offers refuge from sorrow through its power to conceive "ideal forms of excellence" (X, p. 129), and though it may lead to earthly delusions, it also offers abundant compensation: imaginative capacities become guarantees of the self's immortality.[32] Striving to expand upward toward union with absolute freedom, unconditional love, and a perfection unattainable in this world, imaginative perception is the most extreme reach of Wollstonecraft's always intransigent individualism and urge toward self-realization. But such expansions are not escapes. Wollstonecraft returns from them a refreshed and renewed "female Werter," more capable of coping with the "vicissitudes of human affairs," readier to accept, as in the Appendix of the *Letters*, the inevitable imperfections and slow progress of this world.

Indeed, the self which spiritualizes natural experience coexists, almost in the same breath, with the wryly down-to-earth self who is nearly choked by the smell of rotten herrings (V, p. 47), who keeps one eye on her sleeping fellow-travelers ("fortunately they did not snore" [V, p. 61]), who goes from romantic flights in one sentence to coffee and milk in the next (I, p. 16). Moments of spiritual autobiography subside into objective travelogue with no transition—a method that implies I am this, but also simultaneously this. There are no rigid separations in the *Letters*: personal and social themes, rational assessments and emotional epiphanies, flow one into another joined by a use of associationism quite subtle and sophisticated. The structural principle—linkage of the narrator's ideas—so strikingly manifested in the nature passages operates throughout. Wollstonecraft frequently calls attention to her technique in the course of the narrative and makes her method explicit in the Advertisement. Stressing immediacy, artlessness, and the primacy of the self, she equates travels and memoirs: "I could not avoid being continually the first person—'the little hero of each tale.'" She gives up on revisions, determining "to let my remarks and reflections flow unrestrained. . . . I could not give a just description of what I saw, but by relating the effect different objects had produced on my mind and feelings, whilst the impression was still fresh." Wollstonecraft's very personal associationism, so fruitful in her self-exploration, has also a liberating effect on her style, which is always at its flowing best when most intimate and direct. Her approach in the *Letters* is in line with her travel reviews for the *Analytical*, but the personal rewards of this literary strategy are also clear.

Wollstonecraft transforms the conventions of the travel genre—its blend of objective facts and individual impressions—into a rationale for autobiographical revelation. Epistolary travel narrative gives her freedom of self-display while concurrently fulfilling other intentions. Its simultaneity of incident and response allows her to work out subjective patterns of association as well as to present verifiable empirical facts, and its ostensible formlessness and immediacy counter the vanity inherent in writing about oneself. But if travel literature offered her a pattern she could expand on in ordering her experience—and even a factual record necessarily involves shaping and selection—she also draws on many other models in her handling of the reflective consciousness. She demonstrates her knowledge of philosophical debate on the subject and her familiarity with Rousseau, Goethe, and Sterne, as well as a wide range of travel writers.

Wollstonecraft's tactic of artless associationism is the foundation of an artfully flexible organic form. In the *Letters*, thinking for oneself is quite literally form, theme, and style. Letters, journals, travel narratives—the book partakes of all these—are intrinsically episodic in structure, but self-contained units offer also possibilities of unity, through recurrent themes and patterns, through the impress of the author's personality. The *Letters* are composed of independent, yet interconnected units, discontinuous forms demonstrating continuities; their structure is a linear motion incorporating spirals. By conflation of perspectives, by a narrative mode that endorses reason and justifies imagination, Wollstonecraft reaches toward integrations. Through her orchestration of narrative voices, she manifests her capacity for both private self-awareness and public moral acuity, exploring herself as she explores the world, bringing together the "history of my own heart" and the "just idea of the nature of man" through her pervasive concern with human improvement. The catalytic crisis of the Imlay affair impels her into multiple expansions of awareness and acceptances of reality: into the nature of her varied selves, into the necessity of very gradual social change. The Appendix expresses the tempering of an ardent reformer's hopes: radical ideology seeks to make the world a home; failing that, the reformer must come to terms with the difficult process of living as best she can—through the act of writing about it.

NOTES

1 *Monthly Review*, N.S., 20 (1796), 252. Other reviews are cited and discussed in Ralph M. Wardle, *Mary Wollstonecraft: A Critical Biography* (1951; rpt. Lincoln: University of Nebraska Press, 1966), pp. 256-57, 354 n. 36, and Florence Boos, Review of Wollstonecraft's *Letters Written . . . in Sweden*, ed. Carol H. Poston, *Eighteenth-Century Studies*, 10 (Winter 1976-77), 280-81.
2 *A Journey Made in the Summer of 1794, through Holland and the Western Frontier of Germany* . . . (Dublin: P. Wogan, 1795), p. 104.
3 Sylva Norman, ed., *Letters Written . . . in Sweden*, by Mary Wollstonecraft (Fontwell, Sussex: Centaur Press, 1970), p. viii; Carol H. Poston, ed., *Letters . . .*, by Mary Wollstonecraft (Lincoln: University of Nebraska Press, 1976), p. xvi. Page references subsequently incorporated in the text refer to Norman's facsimile edition; roman numerals refer to letter number.
4 Wardle, *Mary Wollstonecraft*, p. 254.

5 Claire Tomalin, *The Life and Death of Mary Wollstonecraft* (New York: Harcourt Brace Jovanovich, 1974), p. 190.
6 On Wordsworth's journey motif, see M. H. Abrams, *Natural Supernaturalism: Tradition and Revolution in Romantic Literature* (New York: W. W. Norton, 1971); Georg Roppen and Richard Sommer, *Strangers and Pilgrims: An Essay on the Metaphor of Journey* (New York: Humanities Press, 1964).
7 Review of *Observations and Reflections made in the Course of a Journey through France, Italy, and Germany*, by Hester Lynch Piozzi, *Analytical Review*, 4 (June 1789), 144.
8 Review of *Observations on the River Wye . . .*, by William Gilpin, *Analytical Review*, 5 (Sept. 1789), 41.
9 Review of *Letters Concerning . . . Antrim*, by the Rev. William Hamilton, *Analytical Review*, 7 (Aug. 1790), 375.
10 Review of *Voyages . . . from China to the North-West Coast of America*, by John Meares, *Analytical Review*, 9 (Jan. 1791), 16; Review of *Letters from Barbary . . .*, by an English Officer [Alexander Jardine], *Analytical Review*, 4 (Appendix, Aug. 1789), 527.
11 Mary Wollstonecraft, *A Vindication of the Rights of Woman* (1792), ed. Charles W. Hagelman, Jr. (New York: W. W. Norton, 1967), pp. 177-78.
12 See, for example, Wayne Shumaker, *English Autobiography: Its Emergence, Materials, and Form* (Berkeley and Los Angeles: University of California Press, 1954), p. 128; Karl J. Weintraub, "Autobiography and Historical Consciousness," *Critical Inquiry*, 1 (June 1975), 824.
13 Patricia Meyer Spacks, "Reflecting Women," *Yale Review*, 63 (1973), 26.
14 Patricia Meyer Spacks, "Female Identities," in *Imagining a Self: Autobiography and Novel in Eighteenth-Century England* (Cambridge, Mass.: Harvard University Press, 1976), pp. 57-91.
15 Estelle C. Jelinek, "Discontinuity and Order: A Comparison of Women's and Men's Autobiographies," and Suzanne Juhasz, "'Some Deep Old Desk or Capacious Hold-All': Form and Women's Autobiography," papers read at MLA 1976; Lynn Z. Bloom and Orlee Holder, "Consciousness of the Self: Women's Autobiographies and Anaïs Nin's Diaries," paper read at MLA 1977.
16 Wollstonecraft's *Posthumous Works*, ed. William Godwin (Dublin: J. Rice, 1798), I, 118. Arrangement and pagination of the Dublin version differ from those of the original London edition.
17 Ellen Moers, "Vindicating Mary Wollstonecraft," *New York Review of Books*, 23 (Feb. 19, 1976), 39; Tomalin, *Mary Wollstonecraft*, p. 149.
18 See, for example, Wollstonecraft's 1794 description of Imlay in C. Kegan Paul, *William Godwin: His Friends and Contemporaries* (London: Henry S. King, 1876), I, 218.
19 *Letters to Imlay*, ed. C. Kegan Paul (1879; rpt. New York: Haskell House, 1971), pp. 186, 116-17, 174.
20 Ibid., p. xlvii; see also p. 142. Wardle discusses the relation between letters and journal (*Mary Wollstonecraft*, pp. 353-54, n. 22).
21 *Mary Wollstonecraft: A Biography* (New York: Coward McCann and Geoghegan, 1972), p. 222.

22 *Design and Truth in Autobiography* (Cambridge, Mass.: Harvard University Press, 1960), p. 182.
23 Wollstonecraft to Godwin, Aug. 17, 1796, *Godwin & Mary: Letters of William Godwin and Mary Wollstonecraft*, ed. Ralph M. Wardle (Lawrence: University of Kansas Press, 1966), p. 15. Wollstonecraft's use of the phrase here suggests that the "Solitary Walker" (the "promeneur solitaire" of Rousseau's *Rêveries*) was her persona in the aftermath of the Imlay affair. The *Confessions* and its uncompleted sequel were published together in the 1783 English translation.
24 William Godwin, *Memoirs of Mary Wollstonecraft*, ed. W. Clark Durant (1798; rpt. London: Constable, 1927), p. 73.
25 Review of *Seconde Partie des Confessions de J.-J. Rousseau* (Geneva, 1784), *Analytical Review*, 6 (April 1790), 386. Wollstonecraft notes that "a description of what has actually passed in a human mind must ever be useful." The "history of my soul" passage is in Book VII (New York: Random House, n.d.), p. 284. Despite her attack on Rousseau in *A Vindication of the Rights of Woman*, Wollstonecraft wrote to Imlay that she had always been "half in love" with him (*Letters to Imlay*, p. 58). See also G. D. Kelly, "Godwin, Wollstonecraft, and Rousseau," *Women and Literature*, 3 (Fall 1975), 21-26; Jean de Palacio, "La Quête de L'Éden: Mary Wollstonecraft entre Milton et Rousseau," *Revue de Littérature Comparée*, 49 (Avril-Juin 1975), 217-34.
26 Wollstonecraft saw an emergent aristocracy of riches in France and was troubled during her stay there by "the narrow principle of commerce which seems every where to be shoving aside *the point of honour* of the *noblesse*. . . . names, not principles, are changed, and . . . the turn of the tide has left the dregs of the old system to corrupt the new" ("Letter on the Present Character of the French Nation" [1793], *Posthumous Works*, I, 263, 265-66, partially reprinted and discussed by Eleanor L. Nicholes in *Shelley and His Circle*, ed. Kenneth Neill Cameron [Cambridge, Mass.: Harvard University Press, 1961], I, 62-63). Like her mentor Richard Price, Wollstonecraft feared that republican gains might lead to commercial domination.
27 Wollstonecraft wrote Imlay about how she "fell without any previous warning senseless on the rocks" upon arrival (*Letters to Imlay*, p. 143) and alludes frequently to her health throughout the *Letters*. The image of the world as a prison is repeated in the first chapter of Wollstonecraft's unfinished last novel, *The Wrongs of Woman*.
28 Many critics—Wardle, Poston, Boos, and others—make the comparison with Wordsworth or Romanticism; see also Christopher Salvesen, *The Landscape of Memory: A Study of Wordsworth's Poetry* (Lincoln: University of Nebraska Press, 1965), on the relationship between late-eighteenth-century approaches to nature and that of Wordsworth. Georges Poulet's survey of Rousseau's "moments of grace"—*Studies in Human Time*, trans. Elliott Coleman (1956; rpt. New York: Harper, 1959), pp. 158-84—offers illuminating bases for comparison with Wollstonecraft.
29 George B. Parks, "The Turn to the Romantic in the Travel Literature of the Eighteenth Century," *Modern Language Quarterly*, 25 (1964), 33.

30 Review of *Tour of the Isle of Wight,* by John Hassell, *Analytical Review,* 7 (Aug. 1790), 393.
31 *Letters to Imlay,* pp. 154, 120, 149–51.
32 See A *Vindication of the Rights of Woman,* p. 123, and "Hints" (for the unwritten second part of A *Vindication,*), *Posthumous Works,* II, 270–71. Wollstonecraft expresses some awareness of the defensive function of religion: she asked Godwin, "How can you blame me for taken [sic] refuge in the idea of a God, when I despair of finding sincerity on earth?" (Wollstonecraft to Godwin, July 4, 1797, *Godwin & Mary,* p. 111). In his study of the later permutations of spiritual autobiography, John N. Morris suggests the equation of self and soul; see *Versions of the Self: Studies in English Autobiography from John Bunyan to John Stuart Mill* (New York: Basic Books, 1966), p. 6.

Sir William Temple's Views on Science, Poetry, and the Imagination

CHARLES H. HINNANT

Temple's championship of the Ancients over the Moderns in the *Battle of the Books* defies exegesis; it seems, in *On Ancient and Modern Learning,* to confront the reader less with a work of argument than of opinion and assumption. Although there is general agreement among scholars that Macaulay's portrayal of Temple as a benighted reactionary was unfair,[1] few could contest Samuel Holt Monk's view that Temple displays "a remarkable indifference... to the achievements of the physical scientists of his and the preceding age."[2] Because of Temple's eagerness, moreover, to challenge the Moderns, not simply in the relatively safe precincts of *belles lettres,* but on the far more dangerous field of natural philosophy, his comments on modern thought often appear singularly credulous and ill-informed. But one can acknowledge Temple's lack of professionalism without necessarily concluding that his advocacy of the Ancients is devoid of philosophic significance. To devalue this advocacy by considering it solely as evidence of Temple's ignorance is to overlook its implications for his views on science, poetry, and the imagination.

I

To appreciate the nature of Temple's commitment to the Ancients, one must first recognize that, unlike Swift in *The Battle of the Books*, Temple refers not to the classical ages of Greece and Rome but to an earlier, preclassical era of wisdom and knowledge represented by the ancient sages Orpheus, Homer, Pythagoras, and the Sibyl. The reason why Temple's attachment to this distinctive way of viewing the Ancients has been overlooked is not hard to demonstrate. Though the cult of the Ancient Wisdom or Ancient Theology flourished in England during the Renaissance and early seventeenth century, it has generally been assumed that the rationalistic climate of the Restoration was becoming increasingly hostile to its survival, especially in science. In 1691 Temple was himself well aware that historical scholars had exploded the authenticity of most of the texts on which a belief in the existence of a great storehouse of Ancient Wisdom or Theology had rested during the Renaissance. He acknowledges in *On Ancient and Modern Learning* that the "golden verses that go under the name of Pythagoras, are generally rejected as spurious, like many other fragments of Sibyls, or old poets, and some entire poems that run with ancient names."[3] By the latter, Temple undoubtedly means the Orphic Hymns and the *Oracula Chaldaïca*. Together with the *Corpus Hermeticum*, these texts, supposedly of very remote ancestry, were shown through the researches of seventeenth-century scholars to be late-antique, if not medieval in origin.[4] Temple was likewise aware that the formulation of new concepts and methods had encouraged modern philosophers to question the underlying assumption on which such a faith was based. Why should anyone look back to an ancient body of wisdom and learning when modern thinkers had demonstrated that knowledge is discovered by means of hypothesis and experiment? Even if some ancient texts had survived, there was no reason for anyone to believe that a blind trust in their authority would do anything more than impede men from progress in science.

But Temple does not reach such a seemingly obvious conclusion. The reason is that he combines a belief in the Ancient Wisdom with an equally firm belief in a cyclical theory of history. How, in the face of the revolutions, wars, plagues, and floods that have made the different nations of the world "look like new-created regions... without any records or remembrances, beyond certain short periods of time" (p. 464), could one be certain of the superiority of the Moderns in learning? For Temple, the disappearance of such "records and remembrances" meant the destruction of the arts and sciences they sustained, and even of language itself. Temple's willingness to assume the existence of a vast body of lost wisdom seemed to give substance to his doubts. Assuming that continuity is necessary to progress, Temple sought to confound the Moderns by citing, without a trace of irony, numerous instances of the effects of historical cataclysms upon the "ancient records of the world." Of the original languages, writes Temple, "whether we have any thing of the old Chaldean, Hebrew, Arabian, that is truly genuine or more ancient than the Augustan age, I am much in doubt" (p. 465). Of the various branches of learning, Temple believes that "the science of music, so admired of the ancients, is wholly lost in the world" (p. 469) and the "ancient magic... seems, with several others" also "to be wholly lost" (p. 470).

Such passages, which appear frequently in *On Ancient and Modern Learning*, help to explain how Temple was able to maintain his belief in the Ancient Wisdom, even when the antiquity of the texts upon which this belief once depended had been demolished. Temple continued to assume that "the oldest books we have are still in their kind the best" (p. 478), and if the authenticity of a number of the oldest books had been disproved, it was not difficult for Temple to assimilate others to the Ancient Learning. The uncritical emphasis placed upon the *Epistles* of Phalaris in *On Ancient and Modern Learning* has often been cited as evidence of Temple's amateurism. Undoubtedly it is. But the *Epistles* of Phalaris, along with Aesop's *Fables*, are in effect Temple's substitute for the texts that once comprised the Ancient Wisdom. Richard Bentley implicitly acknowledges this connection when, in seeking to confute the antiquity of the *Epistles* of Phalaris, he cites as two examples of similar "Cheats" the pseudo-Sybilline Oracles and the alleged Orphic Hymns.[5] Even if we regard Bentley's judgment of Temple's opinions as essentially correct, there is no reason why we should not also recognize that both views represent typical if contrasting attitudes toward the Ancient Learning during the seventeenth century.

In one respect, however, Temple differs from earlier admirers of the Ancient Sages. He has no interest in showing that Orpheus and Pythagoras—as well as Moses—shared in the truths of Christianity. The relation of Temple's essay to this tradition was clearly perceived by the Reverend William Wotton. In the *Reflections upon Ancient and Modern Learning* (1694), Wotton opposed Temple's position by adopting the same argument which earlier critics had employed to challenge the alleged apologetic value of the ancient prophecies: far from providing Christians with arguments against heretics and atheists, they threatened to deprive the Christian religion of its unique status, to make it "an empty form of Words."[6] For Temple, however, such arguments were peripheral to the purpose of the Ancient Learning as he conceived it. He expressed the opinion in *Some Thoughts upon Reviewing the Essay on Ancient and Modern Learning* that the Ancient Wisdom had been "made too much use of" by theologians "since the restoration of learning in these western parts of the world" (p. 511), insisting that "our religion was as little known to the ancient sages and philosophers, as our language or our laws" (p. 508). Indeed, observed Temple, "human learning seems to have very little to do with true divinity" (p. 509).

The value Temple derived from the Ancient Learning was philosophical, not theological; it provided him, for instance, with a conception of science substantially different from that of most natural philosophers of the seventeenth century. Wotton, for example, maintained in *Reflections on Ancient and Modern Learning* that a prime goal of the Moderns in philosophy was to purge science of its reliance upon "Substantial Forms, Occult Qualities, Intentional Species, Idiosyncrasies, Sympathies and Antipathies of Things," not, he emphasized, "because they are Terms used by Ancient Philosophers, but because they are only empty Sounds, Words whereof no Man can form a certain and determinate Idea." According to Wotton, "Matter and Motion, with their several Qualities, are only considered in Modern Solutions of Physical Problems."[7] By contrast, Temple believed that "we do not so much know what motion is, nor how a stone moves from our hand, when we throw it cross [sic] the street" (p. 475). The scepticism of this passage points to the heart of Temple's antipathy to Modern Learning. Temple, though certainly aware of the achievements of the Moderns in science, was at the same time, drawn to a view of science that virtually identifies it with "natural magic." Such a view had, of course, been associated earlier in the century with the enthusiasm of radical sectarians. But Temple believed strongly enough in the importance of "true" natural magic to attempt to purge it of its Hermetic associations:

> By Magic, I mean some excelling knowledge of nature, and the various powers and qualities of its several productions, and the application of certain agents to certain patients, which by force of some peculiar qualities, produce effects very different from what fall under vulgar observation or comprehension. These are by ignorant People called Magic or Conjuring, and such like terms; and an account of them, much about as wise, is given by the common learned, from Sympathies, Antipathies, Idiosyncrasies, Talismans, and some scraps or terms left us by the Egyptians or Grecians, of the ancient magic. (p. 470)

Temple's explanation of magic in this passage dramatizes as clearly as anything in *On Ancient and Modern Learning* the philosophical bias underlying his opposition to the Moderns. Both Temple and the natural philosophers of the seventeenth century share a similar concern for exact terminology as well as a conviction that physical reality is quite different from the world pictured by our senses, but the exponents of a mechanical conception of nature sought to explain apparent "sympathies," "antipathies," and "idiosyncrasies" by the uniform operation of inert particles of matter in motion. On the other hand, Temple refers to the difference between physical reality and "what falls under vulgar observation" to diverse "peculiar qualities"—specific qualities which no sense perceives directly as the eye perceives color but which nevertheless act on bodies from within and manifest themselves by the outward "effects" they produce.

The vigor with which Temple defends the existence of these occult "powers and qualities" helps to explain why he subscribes to a belief in what Frances Yates terms "applied or power magic."[8] In recent times there has been a tendency to limit the meaning of magic to necromancy and to believe that their assumptions have no relevance to science properly speaking. But Temple conceives of a magic whose only main aim is practical, since it depends upon the existence of hidden sympathies and antipathies that can attract or repel bodies even when acting at a distance and without corporeal instruments. The virtues of the loadstone (which attracts iron but not copper) were thought to be one manifestation of these sympathies and antipathies. Significantly, Temple describes the loadstone as "the greatest invention that I know of, in latter ages" (p. 471). Apart from the invention of the loadstone, however, the triumphs of modern scientists obviously held little appeal for Temple. He did acknowledge an interest in the Florentine Platonist and early exponent of the Ancient Learning Pico Della Mirandola. He argued that Pico "might have proved a prodigy of learning, if his studies had lasted as long as those of the ancients" (p. 482). But Temple only glanced at such a possibility and insisted that in comparison with the "magical operations" of the Ancients, the discoveries of Copernicus and Harvey have "made no change in the conclusions of Astronomy, nor in the practise of Physic; and so have been of little use to the world" (p. 469). Indeed much of the mood of sophisticated irony, so evident, for example, in Temple's comments on the systems of Hobbes and Descartes, stems from his faith in applied magic—as supplying the only criteria of value, measured against which those claimed for the metaphysical hypotheses of modern science appear as mere shams,[9] and as providing the singular means whereby man can better his temporal estate. For Temple, the wisdom of the Ancients appears so wondrous to us precisely because the "almost magical force" at their disposal seems irretrievably lost.

Temple's willingness to appeal to magic as a way of casting doubt upon the achievements of the "New Science" may well seem to indicate a rather capricious attitude toward this kind of truth. But Temple was by no means alone in his views. Ralph Cudworth, who was Temple's tutor at Emmanuel College, Cambridge, also believed in both the Ancient Learning and natural magic, using the latter in *The True Intellectual System of the Universe* (1678) to confute the mechanistic hypothesis of Descartes.[10] Without making any extravagant claims for Temple's understanding of the new science, therefore, it may still be argued that such an understanding becomes comprehensible only if we recognize the intellectual context to which it properly belongs. If we acknowledge, moreover, the importance of natural magic in Temple's thought, the grounds of continuity between his views on science and poetry begin to emerge. Temple's sympathetic attitude toward "humour" and "humourists," for example, appears to rest directly upon the concept of natural idiosyncrasies. Its denial of uniformitarianism, which the mechanical philosophy asserted as a basic tenet, expressed a belief in the unique specificity of natural bodies implicit in the magical tradition.

II

Such interconnections help to account for the distinctive features of Temple's poetic theory. If his tastes in poetry were, as J. E. Spingarn believed, "markedly modern,"[11] they were nevertheless shaped by his belief that "the oldest books are the best." This notion encouraged him not only to rank Homer above Virgil but to trace the history of poetry backwards from the first age of prose to its earliest origins: "Homer and Hesiod lived some hundreds of years before that age; and Orpheus, Linus, Musaeus, some hundreds before them: and of the Sibyls, several were before any of those, and in times as well as places, whereof we have no clear records now remaining" (p. 419). To observe Temple's willingness to utilize "Sacred Writ" for specimens of "true Genius in Poetry" is to recognize how powerful is this conviction. He considers the Book of Job as the "most ancient" of the books of Scripture, for it "was a translation into Hebrew out of the old Chaldaean or Arabian Language" written, he believes, "before the times of Moses" (p. 420). Among the "books of Moses," he couples the songs of Moses and Deborah as poems which "may probably have been written before the rest" and which display "as true and noble strains of poetry and picture, as in any other language whatsoever" (p. 421). But this is by no means the only evidence of Temple's fascination with the remote past. Though he has often been praised for his contribution to the rise of literary history, Temple's chief interest lies not in the evolution of different national poetries but in their earliest manifestations. Preoccupied by the "true spirit or vein of ancient poetry," Temple found a framework for this preoccupation in a literary history concerned with the migrations of Ancient Poetry. Chaldean, Hebraic, Greek, Roman, and Runick poetries are seen by Temple as manifestations of a "true poetic vein" which shows itself in successive if attenuated reappearances—revolutions in the "empire of wit" as the "ancient poetry" moves through the ages. Temple's admiration for the true spirit of Ancient Poetry also demonstrates the strength of his contempt for the rules and makes even plainer why he shows so little interest in the poetic kinds. Temple's concept of natural genius, which assumes the uniqueness of individual poems, is fundamentally opposed to the notion of a uniform system of genres. By an example of "true genius in poetry," Temple makes clear, he means "not an ode or an elegy, a song or a satire . . . but . . . a just poem" which can appear in different guises in "any parts or ages of the world" (p. 415).

Temple's awareness of the parallel between Ancient Poetry and Learning prompts him to ask in *On Poetry* how one differs from the other. Temple tries to answer this question by assigning them to the separate but undefined "operations" of wit and wisdom. But he believes that for most men the outcome of both operations has been a "happy mixture" of pleasure and profit (p. 407). The sole difference is that the operations of wit have somehow gotten mixed up with the notion of supernatural inspiration. This occurred, Temple believes, because the ancient Greeks gave to poets the name of makers or creators, by analogy with "the first attribute and highest operation of Divine Power," and the ancient Romans, that of prophets, by analogy with "the greatest emanation of Divine Spirit in the world," and so made the "causes" of poetry to be "divine, and to proceed from a celestial fire, or divine inspiration" (pp. 407–8). From this explanation of its "causes," there was only a short step to the view that its "effects" were also "divine and supernatural" (p. 408). Temple thinks that in employing such terms as *creator* and *prophet*, ancient critics were merely seeking appropriate epithets with which to express their high opinion of poets, but as an unintentional consequence, they encouraged popular opinion to sink into superstition and delusion. It is this sort of superstition to which Temple refers when he opposes natural magic to supernatural inspiration. He expresses the conviction that "Divinity" might be "debased... by ascribing to it any thing that is in the compass of our action, or even comprehension, unless it be raised by an immediate influence from it self." For this reason, he is unwilling to "allow poetry to be more divine in its effects than in its causes, nor any operation produced by it to be more than purely natural, or to deserve any other sort of wonder than those of music, or of natural magic, however any of them have appeared to minds little versed in the speculations of nature, of occult qualities, and the force of numbers or of sounds" (p. 408). But if Temple opposes the view that poetry is divinely inspired, he admits no diminution of its power. For Temple, natural magic seems to produce effects in every way as wondrous as divine inspiration, while, at the same time, it is absolutely distinct from it.

Temple's attempt to formulate an analogy between poetry and natural magic plainly owes much to his views on science. But the tradition upon which he draws usually gave special emphasis to two related ideas: first, the poet is a divinely inspired teacher, possessed by a supernatural *furor;* second, the emotional and ethical effects of his poetry are attributable not merely to the arts of rhetoric, but to active powers that clearly transcend those arts.[12] Temple, even while rejecting the first of these notions, clearly accepts the second. Instead of describing poets as the recipients of a supernaturally revealed knowledge of human and divine things, he is content to characterize them as illusionists who "raise admirable frames and fabrics out of nothing, which strike with wonder and with pleasure the eyes and imaginations of those who behold them" (p. 407). Because Temple is convinced that poetry gives an almost magical satisfaction to the reader, he often displays what Macaulay described as an "absurd disregard" for the difference between "the historical and the fabulous."[13] In his survey of the threefold "powers of eloquence, of music, and of picture," for example, Temple refuses to have recourse to the fables of Orpheus and Amphion, but accepts "the charming of serpents, and the cure or allay of an evil spirit or possession" attributed to poetry in Scripture (p. 411). In another context, he cites both the "force of Cicero's eloquence" in defense of Labienus and anecdotes of two young Grecians, one who "ventured his life to be locked up all night in the temple, and satisfy his passion with the embraces and enjoyments of a statue of Venus," the other who "pined away and died for being hindred his perpetually gazing, admiring, and embracing a statue at Athens" (p. 411) Temple, we should note, is careful to temper the extravagance of these encomiums with an ironic scepticism: "How far these three natural powers together may extend, and to what effect (even such as may be mistaken for supernatural or magical), I leave it to such men to consider, whose thoughts turn to such speculations as these, or who, by their native temper and genius, are, in some degree, disposed, or receive the impressions of them" (p. 412). Nevertheless, the equivocal nature of Temple's doubt is shown in the following passage, where he cites the scientist Harvey and the scholar Casaubon as examples of those who "are, in some degree, disposed, or receive the impressions" of these natural powers.

In repudiating the divine *furor*, Temple expresses a historical attitude recognizably in keeping with the Restoration revolt against enthusiasm.[14] At the same time, by affirming the magical powers of poetry, Temple manages to avoid the rationalistic implications of some of the numerous late-seventeenth-century protests against inspiration. Perhaps the most important of these protests was Meric Casaubon's *Treatise upon Enthusiasme* (1655). Temple was certainly acquainted with Casaubon's book, for he refers to it in *On Poetry*, expressly naming Casaubon. It is undoubtedly from Casaubon that he derives the view that inspiration is a form of delusion "frequent in all regions and religions of the world, and which had so fatally spread over our country in that age in which this treatise was seasonably published" (p. 409). Temple accepts Casaubon's thesis that this delusion had once been a source of sectarian zeal; yet his poetic theory cannot accurately be described as rationalistic. It is the theory of a critic who sought to deny the quasi-mystical sources of poetic creation but who also wanted to preserve the traditional active powers of poetry. The assumption that poetry can be divested of its Hermetic sources of inspiration and yet still preserve its vital powers may of course be incompatible ideals: nonetheless, Temple's attempts to reconcile these two disparate aims engendered the distinguishing features of his poetics: the opposition to divine inspiration, the ascription to poetry of almost magical powers, the derivation of these powers from purely natural causes.

III

On Poetry also represents Temple's attempt to demonstrate the importance of a purely natural explanation to a full understanding of the poetic process. Temple discovers a "more true and natural source of poetry" in an interpretation of ancient myth; Apollo, or the Sun, is "a certain noble and vital heat of temper," released from the "mystery" of fable and allowed to disclose its true purpose (p. 413). Supernatural inspiration thus becomes natural genius, "agreed by all to be a pure and free gift of heaven or of nature," but subject to external influences like climate and culture. Through a sort of classicism—by an appeal to the *consensus gentium*—Temple raises natural genius to a level of human importance similar to its fabulous counterpart. "By the influence of this sun," he writes, "are produced those golden and inexhausted mines of invention, which has furnished the world with treasures so highly esteemed, and so universally known and used, in all the regions that have yet been discovered" (p. 413). The relation of this interpretation to Temple's scientific views is apparent; the natural genius of the poet is analogous on a human scale to the active powers and qualities by which all natural phenomena are given life and motion. Nonetheless, in keeping with the rhetorical tradition, Temple goes on to break down the poetic process into a series of separate, artistic operations. Even these operations, however, are assimilated to a model of continuous natural growth: "But, though invention be the mother of poetry, yet this child is, like all others, born naked, and must be nourished with care, clothed with exactness and elegance, educated with industry, instructed with art, improved by application, corrected with severity, and accomplished with labour and with time, before it arrives at any great perfection or growth" (p. 414).

This theory of natural genius, a theory fundamental to Temple's thought, left unmistakable traces of its influence in the aesthetics of later writers.[15] But Temple's significance for subsequent developments in critical theory goes beyond his general emphasis on the place of genius in the creation of great poetry. Temple was also preoccupied with specific questions concerning the nature of the poetic process, of the relation between fancy and judgment, and he draws from his explorations some important conclusions about the way poetry originates. His discussion of poetic creativity deserves our attention, I believe, because it illustrates the degree to which Temple's belief in natural magic led him to a perspective that runs counter to the more rationalistic psychology of his age.

A central purpose of Temple's essay was to rescue the fancy, or imagination, from the subordinate role it had come to perform to judgment in the British empiricist tradition. The two terms were first introduced in Thomas Hobbes's *Elements of Law* (1640), where *fancy* is defined as a power which discovers affinities, and *judgment*, as one which discovers differences between things. The two powers are interrelated, according to Hobbes, since they are two aspects of a single whole which he terms *wit*. John Locke's *Essay Concerning Human Understanding* (1690) testifies to the persistence of Hobbes's distinction. According to Locke, the work of the fancy resides in "the Assemblage of Ideas," while the judgment separates "one from another, Ideas, wherein can be found the least Difference." But Locke departs from Hobbes when he separates judgment from wit, implying that the fancy is of little consequence in the attainment of knowledge. The former is distinguished by its ability to "avoid being misled by similitude and by affinity to take one thing for another," whereas the latter produces only "pleasant Pictures and agreeable Visions."[16] The unfortunate effects of this view upon poetic theory are well known: it reduces imagination to the role of an entertainer, even while virtually subjugating it to the faculty of judgment.

Temple's debt to the empiricist tradition represented by Hobbes and Locke is quite apparent. Temple specifically follows Locke in separating the imagination, which he associates with wit or fancy, from judgment. The "sprightly" imagination, according to Temple, discovers "a thousand little bodies or images in the world, and similitudes among them, unseen to common eyes," while the judgment distinguishes "between things and conceptions, which, at first sight, or upon short glances, seem alike" (p. 414). But Temple's reluctance to accept the full implications of an empiricst epistemology can be seen not only in his use of such active verbs as *piercing, ranging,* and *discovering* to describe the operation of the imagination but also in his predilection for word pairs which imply alternative views of perception: "bodies or images," "things and conceptions." Moreover, Temple opposes the general empiricist model of the mind as largely passive, more acted upon than acting. The poet, as Temple views him, requires an inner source of energy in order to create: Temple finds this source of energy in natural genius—a "hidden spark" which, acting from within, kindles a "fire," imparts a "pleasing motion and agitation" to the poet's mental operations (pp. 413-14).

Temple goes on to take an even more emphatic position in defense of the imagination. *On Poetry* implies that the imagination is not subordinate to judgment; this view, which presupposes a rigid dichotomy between the two terms, is wholly alien to Temple's concept of natural genius. Hence he defines fancy and judgment as "contraries," opposing forces working interdependently as a single unit, each supporting and receiving support from the other: "Without the forces of wit, all poetry is flat and languishing; without the succours of judgment, it is wild and extravagant" (p. 414). The implicit repudiation of psychological dualism in these observations leads Temple to a much more complex view of the relationship between structure and expression in poetry. One consequence of this dichotomy was the separation of these two elements: from this assumed opposition was derived the argument that the judgment wholly determines the essential structure of a poem, while the imagination merely illustrates or decorates that structure. To bring imagination and judgment into relationship as contraries, Temple locates them within each element: "The true wit of poesy is . . . in expression both delicacy and force; and the frame or fabric of a true poem must have something both sublime and just, amazing and agreeable" (pp. 414-15). And more important, the poet, mindful of Temple's theory, discovers that structure and ornament are themselves contraries, organically related one to the other: "There must be, upon the same tree, and at the same time, both flower and fruit" (p. 415). Only when the poet acknowledges the coexistence of these elements will his vision of his poetic mission be complete; he will learn that "there must be a great agitation of mind to invent, a great calm to judge and correct" (p. 415).

On Poetry, then, is an important essay that places some of the critical issues raised by the empiricist formulation of the relation between fancy and judgment in a new light. There can be no doubt of the importance of the Lockean model of the mind's activities in early-eighteenth-century aesthetics; and yet it is equally apparent that Temple's interest in natural magic led him to alter this model in terms of an organicist rather than an empiricist or rationalist psychology. Nor should it necessarily be supposed that Temple's undertaking was simply an isolated event. One can discern the lineaments of Temple's notions about the poetic process in Coleridge's definition of the imagination as "a synthetic and magical power" which balances "a more than usual state of emotion, with more than usual order; judgment ever awake and steady self-possession, with enthusiasm and feeling profound and vehement."[17] Temple's view of fancy and judgment as "contraries" rather than dichotomies may also have a bearing upon Pope's declaration that "wit and judgment often are at strife/Though meant for each other's aid, like Man and Wife."[18] Regardless of whether Coleridge or Pope drew directly upon Temple's notions about the poetic process or responded in individual but parallel ways to similar ideas, *On Poetry* makes a fundamental contribution to poetic theory at the end of the seventeenth century. If this contribution has been overlooked in the past, it is undoubtedly because our bias against Temple's scientific attitudes has so colored our conception of his views on other subjects as to give a false picture of his thought. Thus, by showing that the same values which led Temple to challenge the Moderns in science also prompted him to oppose current trends in critical theory, we may delineate more accurately the true proportions of his intellectual achievement. In this way, moreover, we can make Temple's accomplishment more real, because we are aware of its precise place in relation to the rationalism and empiricism of its age.

NOTES

1 *Critical and Historical Essays*, ed. A. J. Grieve (London: J. M. Dent, Everyman ed., 1907), I, 266.
2 Samuel Holt Monk, ed., *Five Miscellaneous Essays by Sir William Temple* (Ann Arbor: University of Michigan Press, 1963), p. xxv. See also R. F. Jones, *Ancients and Moderns: A Study of the Background of the Battle of the Books*, Washington University Studies, n.s., Language and Literature, No. 6 (St. Louis, 1926), p. viii; Clara Marburg, *Sir William Temple: A Seventeenth-Century "Libertin"* (New Haven: Yale University Press, 1962), pp. 42, 70; and Homer E. Woodbridge, *Sir William Temple: The Man and His Work* (New York: MLA, 1940), pp. 308-10.
3 *The Works of Sir William Temple* (London: S. Hamilton, 1814), III, 450. All quotations from Temple's essays in my text are to this edition and volume.
   Temple again refers to the exploded texts that once formed the Ancient Wisdom in *Some Thoughts Upon Reviewing The Essay of Ancient and Modern Learning* when he cites "the verses of Orpheus and the Sibyls" which had been used by "the primitive fathers of the second age ... to confute the idolatrous worship of the heathens," though "they have since by the moderns been questioned, if not exploded" (p. 511).
4 The most important recent discussion of these texts and of their influence during the Renaissance and later is D. P. Walker's *The Ancient Theology: Studies in Christian Platonism from the Fifteenth to the Eighteenth Century* (Ithaca: Cornell University Press, 1972).
5 *Dissertations upon The Epistles of Phalaris, Themistocles, Socrates, Euripides, and the Fables of Aesop*, ed. Wilhelm Wagner (London, 1883), pp. 79, 82. For a discussion of the methods used by earlier scholars to question the authenticity of supposedly ancient texts, see Frances A. Yates, *Giordano Bruno and the Hermetic Tradition* (Chicago: University of Chicago Press, 1964), pp. 398-403.
6 William Wotton, *Reflections Upon Ancient and Modern Learning* (1694; facsimile rpt. Hildesheim: George Olms, 1968), Preface, n.p. See also Walker, *Ancient Theology*, pp. 122-30, on the strong opposition during the seventeenth century to the use of the Ancient Learning by Christians for apologetic purposes.
7 Wotton, p. 300. For an account of the variety of solutions that natural philosophers reached in their efforts to purge modern science of "occult" qualities, see Richard S. Westfall, *Force in Newton's Physics: The Science of Dynamics in the Seventeenth Century* (New York: American Elsevier, 1971).
8 *Giordano Bruno*, pp. 145-48. See also Edgar Wind, *Pagan Mysteries in the Renaissance* (Middlesex, Eng.: Penquin Books, 1967), pp. 108-12. In "Sir William Temple, Political Scientist," *Canadian Journal of Economic and Political Science*, 9 (1943), 39-43, C. B. Macpherson argues that Temple's attitudes toward science should be understood in the light of a commitment toward Baconian empiricism, embracing Bacon's method of induction and experiment. In my opinion, the parallels between Temple's scientific views and the Renaissance tradition of

applied or power magic are more pertinent. Even though Bacon himself may have conformed in some ways to this tradition, Temple clearly regarded Bacon's successors in the Royal Society as being opposed to it.

9 Wotton, we should note, shared Temple's scepticism concerning systems and system-building, suggesting in *Reflections on Ancient and Modern Learning* that the *"Hypotheses"* of Descartes, Gassendi and Hobbes "may only be Chimaera's and amusing Notions" (p. 244).

10 *The True Intellectual System of the Universe* (New York, 1837), I, 249–54. Cudworth's efforts to continue using the texts upon which the Ancient Theology had rested, even though he was aware of their spurious nature, is described in Walker, *Ancient Theology*, p. 241. For a discussion that shows the indebtedness of Isaac Newton to this tradition, see J. E. McGuire and P. Rattansi, "Newton and the Pipes of Pan," *Notes and Records of the Royal Society*, 21 (1966), 108–43.

11 J. E. Spingarn, ed., *Critical Essays of the Seventeenth Century* (Oxford: Clarendon Press, 1908–9), I, lxxxviii.

12 For a discussion of the specific background of this tradition, from the Orphic Hymns through the various revivals of Hermetic and Neo-Platonic thought in the Renaissance, see D. P. Walker, *Spiritual and Demonic Magic from Ficino to Campanella* (London: The Warburg Institute, 1958), pp. 25–26, 120; and idem, *Ancient Theology*, p. 23. See also Kitty Scoular's *Natural Magic: Studies in the Presentation of Nature in English Poetry from Spenser to Marvell* (Oxford: Clarendon Press, 1965) and David Woodman's *White Magic and Renaissance Drama* (Teaneck, N.J.: Fairleigh Dickinson University Press, 1973), esp. pp. 11–20, which discuss the general relations between natural magic and poetry during the Renaissance and seventeenth century.

13 *Critical and Historical Essays*, I, 266.

14 On the Restoration revolt against enthusiasm, see Paul Spencer Wood, "The Opposition to Neo-Classicism in England between 1660 and 1700," *PMLA*, 43 (1928), 182–97; George Williamson, "The Restoration Revolt against Enthusiasm," *Studies in Philology*, 30 (1930), 571–603; and Donald F. Bond, "Distrust of Imagination in English Neo-Classicism," *Philological Quarterly*, 14 (1935), 54–69.

15 See, e.g., Marburg, *Sir William Temple*, pp. 80–93; Woodbridge, *Sir William Temple*, pp. 300–301; and Meyer Abrams, *The Mirror and the Lamp* (1953; rpt. New York: Norton, 1958), p. 197.

16 *An Essay Concerning Human Understanding*, ed. Alexander Campbell Fraser (Oxford: Oxford University Press, 1895), I, 203–4. Elsewhere, I have discussed the distinction between fancy and judgment in the writings of the British empiricists of the seventeenth century ("Hobbes on Fancy and Judgment," *Criticism*, 18 [1976], 15–26).

17 *Biographia Literaria*, ed. J. Shawcross (Oxford: The Clarendon Press, 1907), II, 12.

18 *The Poems of Alexander Pope*, ed. John Butt (New Haven: Yale University Press, 1963), p. 146. Pope's opposition to Locke's view of fancy and judgment is set forth by Edward Niles Hooker, "Pope on Wit: The *Essay on Criticism*," in *Eighteenth-*

Century English Literature: Modern Essays in Criticism, ed. James L. Clifford (New York: Oxford University Press, 1959), pp. 42–61. While right in suggesting that Pope's contemporaries, following Locke, "were erecting a wall between fancy and judgment," Hooker is mistaken, in my opinion, when he assumes that Temple shared "Locke's way of thinking" (p. 52).

Friends and Enemies
in Verses on the Death of Dr. Swift

JAMES WOOLLEY

I

"I have been severall months writing near five hundred lines on a pleasant subject, onely to tell what my friends and enemyes will say on me after I am dead."[1] From Swift's descriptions of *Verses on the Death of Dr. Swift* in these or very similar words, over and over in his letters, it is evident that (however later critics may have described the poem) when he himself thought of it as a whole, he thought of it as a poem about friendship and enmity, and as a poem about what people would say of him after he died.[2] Despite abundant commentary on the poem's textual history, its structure, genre, irony, vanity, politics, religious lessons, and multiplication of identities, we still have not paid enough attention to the basic question of what it is about. Some discussions, moreover, have insisted too much upon finding Swift an exemplary poet and moralist. But Ronald Paulson, Marshall Waingrow, and David M. Vieth have spoken of friendship as a topic of the *Verses*; and I propose, without purporting to rescue the poem from the fascinated uneasiness with which we read it, or to explain away its rhetorical flaws, that a fuller recognition of Swift's strong emphasis on friendship and enmity would correspondingly benefit our understanding of the poem's intended meaning.[3] To that end, I seek to show how the poem emphasizes friendship of a particular kind; then, to illuminate a crucial context of the poem in the details of Swift's actual friendship and enmity with Queen Caroline and Mrs. Howard; and finally, to discuss some implications of this subject for the poem's most vexed critical problem, which is the interpretation of the concluding eulogy on Swift.

That the idea of friendship gives the *Verses* a loosely defined unity is suggested not only by Swift's own repeated descriptions of the poem and by its epigraph, but also by the large outlines of its structure. The first of the three main sections, the proem (1–72), states and illustrates with some comic irony La Rochefoucauld's bitter remark that "in the Adversity of our best Friends, we find something that doth not displease us."[4] (More accurately, this section demonstrates the slightly more palatable fact that we envy their good fortune.) The second section (73–298) loosely illustrates the maxim by showing how Swift's friends will "find their private Ends" in his last illness and death, just as much as his enemies will. The final section (299–484)—the troublesome one—is a monologue, a eulogy on Swift, delivered by neither a friend nor an enemy but, we are told, a neutral—"one quite indiff'rent in the Cause" (305). Swift's point is that he cannot expect the praise he deserves from a friend: the eulogy thus wittily and ironically underscores the statement about friendship made in the first two sections.

The emphasis on friendship is further visible in the sheer number of times *friend, friendship,* and related words appear. The importance of the idea, not merely in this poem but in Swift's verse as a whole, is suggested by the statistic that *friend* and related words appear more frequently in Swift's verse than any other noun—a distinction Swift's verse shares, to some degree, with Pope's. By contrast, Josephine Miles has shown, *friend* is not among even the ten most recurrent nouns in the poetry of Chaucer, Spenser, Marlowe, Shakespeare, Donne, Herbert, Milton, Collins, Gray, Burns, Cowper, Coleridge, Wordsworth, Keats, Shelley, Tennyson, Browning, Poe, Emerson, or Housman.[5]

Not all critics have observed the natural connection between friendship and the poem's other main topic, Swift's death. Swift is drawing upon a traditional expectation that a friend will speak in one's favor when one cannot with tact and propriety do so oneself, and will preserve one's memory when the time comes.[6] Friendship has indeed been seen as one of the few hedges against mutability which this life offers.[7] Moreover, death offers an analytical test of friendship: What residue of genuine regard for Swift will be left when people who know him have nothing to hope or fear from him any longer? Swift's ageing, illness, and loneliness make him seem to himself already moribund socially and politically; hence, probably, his interest in this mode of analysis. Edward Said and David M. Vieth have underscored the poem's effort to fix a certain image of Swift in the minds of posterity.[8] But while posterity has naturally seen the poem from this point of view, Swift's primary intent is to express his frustration, disappointment, and anger that, as he expects, his contemporaries will fail to show their friendship for him, when put to the test, in failing to confirm his view of himself.[9]

In recounting and judging various failures of friendship, Swift applies not the exalted *amicitia* so much praised by ancient moralists—and abused down to the present day by the greeting-card-sentiment mongers—although, as Paulson says, that is an unreached ideal constantly standing behind the poem. Rather he uses an equally ancient, more prudential notion of friendship, commonplace to Swift's readers and abundantly available in such sources as courtesy books. Aristotle usefully distinguishes in the *Nichomachean Ethics* between three kinds of friendship—an ideal and permanent kind based on virtue and lesser kinds based on pleasure and usefulness, respectively.[10] In his poem Swift emphasizes useful friendship, and though it was understood that a useful friendship might grow into a virtuous one, and that a virtuous one would of course be useful, he here touches friendship founded on virtue only through raillery (lines 207-8 perhaps excepted). For Swift, *amicitia* lends itself too readily to burlesque, as when, in the scatalogical anguish of "Cassinus and Peter," another poem of 1731, Peter "conjures" Cassinus "by Friendship's sacred Laws," assuring him, "Thy Friend would gladly share thy Fate."[11] Swift preferred to leave the subject alone rather than appear a sentimental hypocrite, just as he avoided the appearance of piety to avoid the appearance of pious hypocrisy. A more practical consideration may have been that, as Addison said, "no subject of morality

[had] been better handled and more exhausted" than that of friendship.[12] But Swift's readiness to think of even the highest kinds of friendship in terms of usefulness can be seen in his references to Stella as a "useful" and "valuable" friend.[13]

As Marshall Waingrow has noted, the idea of friendship broadens naturally in the poem to include the obligations of almost any public or private relationship not involving enmity.[14] The world is a moral battleground of foes and friends in which one is attempting to survive. And in these verses on Swift's death, survival is at issue. He complains that

>   "   ev'n his own familiar Friends
> "Intent upon their private Ends;
> "Like Renegadoes now he feels,
> "Against him lifting up their Heels.
>   (403-6)

His choice of words is telling. Here, as in Homer and Aristotle, a friend is a person on whom one may absolutely rely, and who will help one survive hostility or competition. Actions, not sentiments of altruism, are involved: friends do services for one another.[15] Friendship of this practical sort, like the higher sorts of friendship, ought to be based on merit, and the benefits friends mutually extend ought to be unrestrained by party or faction.[16] Such friendship is not a contract and is thus not enforceable at law; yet civil society is based upon a general and voluntary acceptance of its obligations, and they make possible whatever is good and honorable in social intercourse. To satirize false friendship against this pragmatic standard not only enables Swift to avoid cloying platitudes, but it also permits him to attack such false friends as Queen Caroline and Mrs. Howard for failing to meet even the lowest standards of decent behavior.

Gratitude is closely linked to useful friendship; thus the references in the poem (text and footnotes) to the vice of ingratitude. One of the most startling documents of Swift's later years is the list he made of his friends, classed as Grateful, Ungrateful, Indifferent, or Doubtful.[17] John Lyon, who tended Swift in his last years, preserved a copy and added this explanation: "He was so generous & warm in his Friendships, that he had a singular pleasure in recommending or doing kindnesses to all persons in whom he saw any degree of merit. And when he met with gratitude, he got his Reward, & expected no other. Upon a Paper he wrote down ye Names of several Persons... whom he stiles *Ungratefull, Gratefull, Indifferent*[.] Others, according to their behaviour at different times are marked *d. doubtfull,* & so forth—" The list happens to include some of those mentioned in *Verses on the Death:* Mr. Pope—grateful; Mr. Gay—grateful; Qu[een] C[aroline]—ungrateful. The association of friendship and gratitude, clear in the list and in Lyon's comments, is not uncommon in the more pragmatic ancient and contemporary ethical writings.[18]

Ingratitude is the vice which comprehends all others—a truism so trite Swift includes it in his "Tritical Essay."[19] The comprehensiveness is visible in the fact that we may speak of gratitude or ingratitude not only between two persons as equals but also between parent and child, host and guest, king and subject, and indeed between a person and the state or the public. Examples from ancient and Renaissance literature spring readily to mind. Gratitude, like friendship, is a public as well as a private virtue.[20]

The catalogues of virtues and vices which occur at various points in Swift's works—as in Book IV, Chapter 12, of *Gulliver's Travels*—usually include generosity, friendship, benevolence, fidelity, and gratitude among the virtues, and ingratitude and envy among the vices.[21] "Some of the blackest and basest [Vices] do often prove the surest Steps to Favour; such as Ingratitude," Swift says in his sermon "Of Conscience."[22] The utopian sixth chapter of "A Voyage to Lilliput" tells us that ingratitude is a capital offense in that place, for "whoever makes ill Returns to his Benefactor, must needs be a common Enemy to the rest of Mankind, from whom he hath received no Obligation; and therefore such a Man is not fit to live." And among the Houyhnhnms, "FRIENDSHIP and *Benevolence* are the two principal Virtues."[23]

Whenever friendship goes right, friendship and merit and power seem inseparable: the friends' interests conflict neither with each other nor with the public good. But when it does not go right, we see the selfishness of those concerned, and we find that partisan or self-serving alliances, ingratitude, and contempt for merit (whether personal virtue, wit, or judgment) are the motives. Thus a poem about the failures of friendship, especially political friendship, becomes a poem about courts and courtiers, flattery, betrayal, unworthy loyalty, and the perpetration of stupidity and bad taste. For much the same reason, one of the principal complaints in the final section of the *Verses* is that "Ingratitude he often found,/And pity'd those who meant the Wound" (359-60); and the reference in the footnotes to being "remember[ed] with Gratitude" (168 n.) is central, like much else in the footnotes. The conflict between friendship properly acted and friendship corrupted or ended by death or separation is simply what happens in the "Course of Nature" (74): "the Fault is in Mankind" (4), or as Swift explained to Mrs. Moore, "Life is a Tragedy" and "God, in his Wisdom, hath been pleased to load our declining Years with many Sufferings, with Diseases, and Decays of Nature, with the Death of many Friends, and the Ingratitude of more."[24] Given the imagined occasion of his death, therefore, Swift has ample opportunity to satirize those who fail as friends, who are ungrateful, and who disregard true merit, while he represents himself as a friend to the public and—with more delicate implications—to a small group of Englishmen on whose friendship his own self-esteem particularly depended: Pope, Arbuthnot, Bolingbroke, Pulteney, and Gay.

II

The poem draws a certain coherence from its ethical framework, but the illustrative particulars—the satiric indictments of enemies and treacherous friends—attract the reader's attention more immediately. And although Swift can illustrate the poem with details of his career in the ministry's service during Queen Anne's reign, the wrath visible in *Verses on the Death of Dr. Swift* was especially energized by his experiences in the period from his English visit of 1726 until he composed the poem in 1731.[25] For him the decisive event of these years (apart from Stella's death in 1728) was the failure of Walpole's government to fall when George II came to the throne in June 1727.

The disappointment of this moment, as seeming "friends" aligned themselves with Walpole and power, is interestingly revealed in a letter Pulteney wrote in September: "I own that I am grown quite out of humour with the world, and the more I grow acquainted with it, the less I like it. There is such a thing as cunning, there is falshood and there are views of self-interest that mix themselves in almost all the friendships that are contracted between man and man. These make friendship hardly worth cultivating any where [and] I am sure no where worth being at any considerable charge to preserve it."[26] For Swift, the event confirmed Walpole's hostility to him and brought him into the disfavor of Queen Caroline and Mrs. Howard.

In the poem, Queen Caroline and the Countess of Suffolk (formerly Mrs. Howard) suddenly appear among assorted anonymous people, as Swift's death is announced in London:

> KIND Lady *Suffolk* in the Spleen,
> Runs laughing up to tell the Queen.
> The Queen, so Gracious, Mild, and Good,
> Cries, "Is he gone? 'Tis time he shou'd.
> "He's dead you say; why let him rot;
> "I'm glad the Medals were forgot.
> "I promis'd them, I own; but when?
> "I only was the Princess then;
> "But now as Consort of the King,
> "You know 'tis quite a different Thing."
> (179–88)

Not simply enemies, the Queen and Lady Suffolk are friends turned enemies. This mockery, so daring that it was, with its footnotes, a sea of blanks in Faulkner's editions of 1739, is climactically placed in the middle of the poem. The passage concerns the most important recent failure of friendship in Swift's life. It occurred at court in 1727, and in order to explain fully the intensity of Swift's anger in these lines, it is necessary to examine the way his perception of this event developed, starting the previous year.

For most readers the importance of the summer of 1726 in Swift's biography is that he was then arranging the publication of *Gulliver's Travels*; potentially much more significant for him, however, were his meetings with Sir Robert Walpole and Caroline, then Princess of

Wales. To both he spoke as an Irish leader who, having recently triumphed as Drapier, was to be reckoned with. His principal effort—to persuade Walpole to adopt policies more favorable to Ireland (192 n.)—quickly failed, but at least he seemed successful in clearing John Gay from the accusation of having libelled Sir Robert: Walpole admitted his conviction that Gay was not the author. Swift later concluded, however, that Walpole irrationally continued to treat Gay as guilty.[27]

Swift's discussions with Caroline began formally enough, also on the subject of Ireland. Unlike Walpole, she assured Swift that she (when she became queen) would give particular attention to the Irish problems he laid before her.[28] And she shared his condemnation of Walpole's prejudice against Gay.[29] During the summer they established a relationship of familiar friendship: the Princess had a high regard for Swift's "witt & good Conversation," Dr. Arbuthnot reported, and as an excellent conversationalist herself, she was unquestionably attractive to Swift.[30] His poem "A Pastoral Dialogue between Richmond-Lodge and Marble-Hill" (1727) provides a glimpse of their easy informality, Swift paying a visit to the Princess "to Spunge a Breakfast once a Week," and joking about the quality of the food.[31] This friendship continued through letters after Swift returned to Ireland in 1726. He addressed the letters to Mrs. Howard, one of her Women of the Bedchamber, but as Swift realized, the Princess read them. To Horace Walpole's records of his conversations with Lady Suffolk we owe the information that the Princess "often made Lady Suffolk write to Swift to see his answers, & always kept a copy of Lady Suffolk's and the answers.... These and any other curious papers She could get, the Queen [then Princess] pasted into a book."[32]

With Princess Caroline Swift scrupulously avoided any appearance of sycophancy. He might otherwise have been liable to the charge, since he wished to increase his influence in Irish affairs; alternatively, he hoped to gain preferment in England, which would permit escape from his Irish "exile" and residence near his friends.[33] Swift waited, he tells us, for a dozen invitations (179 n.) before paying the first visit to the Princess, and preserved his integrity by speaking with great freedom to her and avoiding the usual flattery of courtiers.[34] They conversed in perfect frankness, as friends do; he

> "WITH Princes kept a due Decorum,
> "But never stood in Awe before 'em:
> "And to her Majesty, God bless her,
> "Would speak as free as to her dresser"

—that is, Mrs. Howard.[35] Any favor he found with Caroline could thus reflect only his true qualities, not cringing or flattery. Though Swift would not ask, from this relationship emerged several promises of preferment or employment for Swift and Gay. Swift requested only a gift worth ten pounds—a trifle, he rightly calls it—as a mark of her friendship.[36] The medal she promised would have symbolized his standing with her, the sincere regard for his merit out of which any recognition for him would come, if it did come. His acute disappointment that Caroline did not send the gift reveals, of course, his great desire for royal favor, but more important, his disgust that the Princess did not keep her promise about a trifle which could not have inconvenienced her. Caroline's high position magnified the offense. Before the medals were to have arrived (at Christmas 1726), Swift sent a gift of Irish silk poplin to the Princess and refused reimbursement. The present was both an effort to gain attention for the Irish cause, by dressing the Princess of Wales and her children in an exquisite example of Irish manufacture, and a further token of Swift's personal independence from the Princess, for his gift was more than three times the value of what she had promised him.[37] As he wrote, "After I had made my present shame would not suffer me to remind them of theirs"—characteristically linking the Princess and Mrs. Howard as conspirators in whatever concerned him.[38]

Because of this slight (if such it was), Swift was not entirely sure where he stood; an added complication was that his contacts with the Princess were often mediated by Mrs. Howard, and always so in correspondence.[39] Delightful letters remain as evidence of their once-friendly acquaintance. When Swift returned to Ireland in 1726, Mrs. Howard joined Pope, Gay, Bolingbroke, and Pulteney—all of them friends later mentioned in *Verses on the Death of Dr. Swift*—in the "cheddar letter" to him, of which, unfortunately, only Pope's "Receipt to Make Soup" survives.[40] But she is one of the chief villains in the

Verses, although in early states of Faulkner's first 1739 editions a footnote tells us, by way of contrast, that "Mrs *Howard* . . . professed much Favour for the Dean" in 1726; Swift soon sharpened the satire, making the note read "professed much Friendship for the Dean."

The modern view, which has the benefit of Lord Hervey's *Memoirs*, is that Swift drastically overestimated her power, but he was by no means alone in this error. Nor, given her role as mediator between him and the Princess, is it surprising that he thought Mrs. Howard's friendship for him more accurately reflected Caroline's than in fact it did. Not only was Mrs. Howard Prince George's mistress, but she was in constant and apparently very cordial attendance on his wife as her dresser.[41] This remarkable marital arrangement, whatever its true explanation, could only lead Swift to conclude that Mrs. Howard possessed extraordinary tact and discretion, and he might be excused for thinking also that a prince's mistress had great influence, even if, unlike Swift (who had "spent all his Credit for his Friends" [332]), she refused to use it. It is too easy for modern biographers and historians, knowing the outcome of events and benefitting from evidence like Hervey's, to deride Swift's failure to assess the situation properly.[42]

In his admiring but impatient "Character of Mrs. Howard," dated June 12, 1727, Swift approves her wit and political skill as a courtier but offers skepticism about her sincerity as a friend.[43] Against considerable praise for her, Swift weighs a doubt pregnantly summarized in one sentence: "If she had never seen a Court, it is not impossible that she might have been a friend." The charge that she is a courtier recurs in Swift's letters, with the implication that a courtier is one devoted to maneuvering for his own advantage, and is therefore incapable of friendship, whatever his protestations. Swift alludes in the "Character" to her "imperceptible dexterity" as a "politician," and again says that "she is very dextrous in that point of skill which the French call *tâter le pavé*" (testing her footing before making a move). Swift suspects she is *merely* a courtier; and if she is, he must suspect his own interests are jeopardized in her hands: "She abounds in good words and expressions of good wishes, and will concert a hundred schemes for the service of those whom she would be thought to favour . . . , although, at the same time, she very well knows [these schemes] to be without the least probability of succeeding. But, to do her justice, she never feeds or deceives any person with promises, where she does not at the same time intend a degree of sincerity. She is, upon the whole, an excellent companion for men of the best accomplishments, who have nothing to desire or expect."

Swift gave Mrs. Howard a copy of the "Character," presumably at the time it was dated, and it is worth noting that he subtitled this copy "Part the 1st." Whatever his purpose (he was about to depart for France), Mrs. Howard's response, then and repeatedly during the summer of 1727, was to offer stronger, more convincing protestations of her sincerity and of Caroline's intention to reward him and Gay. Only two days after the date of the "Character," news of the death of George I reached London. Mrs. Howard reacted by sending Swift a message not to leave England when the opportunity for English preferment at last lay before him.[44] Swift, at her invitation, attended the court, on "the third day" (about June 17, George having been proclaimed June 15) and kissed Their Majesties' hands.[45] On this occasion he made an offer of political friendship to the new King, and met with Their Majesties' "utmost Satisfaction"; he "was particularly distinguished by the queen."[46] But as the political situation stabilized, Walpole remained in power, contrary to all expectations, and the Opposition remained in opposition. This reversal of expectations established itself slowly.[47] By June 24, Swift was reporting a "moderating scheme" in which both Whigs and Tories would be accommodated in the new government. He had again set about to leave for France, and again "was with great Vehemence dissuaded from it by certain Persons whom I could not disobey."[48] One such person would have been Mrs. Howard, with intelligence from the Queen.

Because George I happened to die, the issues raised in the "Character of Mrs. Howard" were given a life, both for Swift and for Mrs. Howard, that they could hardly have otherwise had. Swift believed, and had said in the "Character," that the Prince of Wales's accession would mean a great increase of power for her. Her friendship was now put to the proof. Were promises made to old friends now to be honored? Swift kept this question alive in "A Pastoral Dialogue between Richmond-Lodge and Marble-Hill," composed late in June and sent to court. It is imagined that the King's former house, Richmond Lodge, speaks:

> The kingly Prophet well evinces,
> That we should put no Trust in Princes;
> My Royal Master promis'd me
> To raise me to a high Degree:
> But now He's grown a King, God wot,
> I fear I shall be soon forgot.
> You see, when Folks have got their Ends,
> How quickly they neglect their Friends;
> Yet I may say 'twixt me and you,
> Pray God they now may find as true.
> (13–22)[49]

By July 1 Swift had felt the new political currents, for he wrote to Sheridan, "Here are a thousand Schemes wherein they would have me engaged, which I embrace but coldly, because I like none of them. . . . I desire it may be told I never go to Court." He concluded: "I intend to be with you at *Michaelmas,* barr Impossibilities."[50] The uneasy ambivalence of "embrace but coldly" and the hopeless hope of "barr Impossibilities" indicate fairly well Swift's attitude at this time.

Any Leicester House plans to reward Swift when George I died had appeared to rest on the alliance between the Prince of Wales's court and the Opposition. That Walpole remained as chief minister removed any political rationale for preferring Swift. Therefore, any testimonies of court favor he then or subsequently received were stronger evidence of friendship than he had previously had and must have tended to override the doubts expressed in the "Character of Mrs. Howard." He wrote later that "a few weeks after the King's death" (presumably mid or late July), Mrs. Howard had once more advised him not to go to France. "I wrote to her for her opinion," Swift told Lady Betty Germain, "and particularly desired, that, since I had long done with Courts, I conjured her not to use me like a courtier; but give me her sincere advice; which she did, both in a letter and to some friends. It was by all means not to go: It would look singular, and perhaps disaffected; and to my friends, she enlarged upon the good intentions of the Court to me."[51] And as late as August 16, Mrs.

Howard continued to urge Swift to wait: "I . . . insist upon your taking no resolution to leave England till I see you," she said, and demanded that he obey her "orders without one question why I have given them."[52] While the precise content of Mrs. Howard's communications must remain in doubt, since most of them were oral messages, it is now evident that not just once but repeatedly during the summer of 1727, she was conveying to Swift what he read not only as promises of a settlement in England, but—as the backing for such promises—stronger assurances of Caroline's friendship than he had received before.

Against his previous doubts about Mrs. Howard, and against the facts that Walpole was in power (in itself an indictment of the new King and Queen) and that the Queen had failed to send him the medal, he balanced two other facts: that Mrs. Howard's power (as he, and possibly she, erroneously thought) was now stronger than ever, and that she was sending him stronger assurances of friendship than ever. The only explanation for Swift's subsequent disappointment is that these assurances were convincing. Otherwise, the Queen's failure to make him any offer would not have surprised him, since it was no more than his "Character" had predicted of Mrs. Howard and, implicitly, of her mistress.

His willingness at this juncture to entertain the possibility that Mrs. Howard's friendship was genuine appears to conflict with the eulogist's claim in Swift's *Verses* that he had had faith "in *David's* Lesson just, / In *Princes never put thy Trust.*" The conflict is significant. We may speculate that Swift's knowledge of courts and of human nature showed him the unlikelihood that the Queen's promises would be kept; and his dread of being disappointed led him to refuse to hope. On the other hand, he wished to believe he had finally found a friend in a prince, one so virtuous as to overcome the pressure of political expediency and selfishness. In this situation he did not so far trust Caroline that he was in any way dependent on her (the deanery of St. Patrick's remained his); at the same time, he went so far as to wait and see, though not so far as to attend the court and actually appear to solicit. The keenness of his anger when she failed to justify his hope is a measure of the extent to which he had allowed himself, against his better judgment perhaps, to trust her good faith. He both hoped and guarded himself against hope (and its consequent disappointment). The pressure of this doubleness of attitude lies behind many of the autobiographical simplifications of the poem, including the bald proclamation that David's lesson is just. Swift wishes at last to clarify what was never quite clear.

Swift received no offer, and before he left for Ireland in mid-September, he learned that the Queen proposed to offer Gay, who had long paid her his court, nothing more than the post of Gentleman Usher to Princess Louisa, not yet three years old.[53] He also heard rumors that Mrs. Howard had arranged two years before that Walpole would be continued in office when the then Prince of Wales became king.[54] This Swift would have credited, for he had already observed in his "Character" that "there is no politician who more carefully watches the motions and dispositions of things and persons at St. James's... or more early foresees what style may be proper upon any approaching juncture of affairs."[55] Gay's friends hoped that Mrs. Howard might yet arrange something better for him, but by October 13 the miserable appointment had been officially announced.[56] This was for Swift the denouement of the summer's conflict between his hopes and his fears. His fury against Mrs. Howard and the Queen only hardened thereafter.

In 1731 he wrote to Gay, "I always told you Mrs Howard was good for nothing but to be a rank Courtier, I care not whether She writes to me or no, She has cheated us all, and may go hang her Self, and so may her———[the Queen]."[57]

Swift's effort to make sense of what had happened to him, in *Verses on the Death of Dr. Swift* as well as in his letters, juggles two not entirely compatible interpretations. The first is that the two women never took him seriously and never intended to give him any preferment, but only considered him an amusement. Recounting the history of the medals is Swift's means of ventilating this theory, according to which the offer of medals was never seriously meant, and the supposed delays in preparing them only "an excuse."[58] In the phrase of Swift's scathing footnote, "she forgot them, or thought them too dear" (184 n.).[59] Thus, in the parallel couplets

> KIND Lady *Suffolk* in the Spleen,
> Runs laughing up to tell the Queen.
> The Queen, so Gracious, Mild, and Good,
> Cries, "Is he gone? 'Tis time he shou'd.

malicious acts do not match the beneficence that the cant praise (queenly virtues capitalized) would indicate.[60]

The other theory Swift explores is that the Queen and Mrs. Howard intended to do something for him and Gay, but that Walpole, with whom the Queen worked closely to govern the King, convinced them not to do so. In his letter to Mrs. Howard of November 21, 1730, Swift states two grievances in quick succession: (1) "I am angry with the Queen for sacrificing my friend Gay to the mistaken piques of Sr R. Walpole"; and (2) "I wish her Majesty would a little remember what I largely said to her about Ireland," referring to his first interview with her in 1726.[61] By bringing the second matter up in the context of the first, Swift intends to suggest that what he had said then would counter Walpole's current representations to her about Ireland (and about Swift). Despite her commitment, he implies, she has "sacrificed" him, no less than Gay, to Walpole's "mistaken piques." In his poem "To Mr. Gay," written in the same year as *Verses on the Death*, Swift attacks Mrs. Howard:

> Fain would I think, our *Female Friend* sincere,
> Till B——, the Poet's Foe, possess't her Ear.
> Did Female Virtue e'er so high ascend,
> To lose an Inch of Favour for a Friend?[62]

George II had been proclaimed on June 15, 1727. Within a month Sir Robert Walpole had confirmed himself in the royal family's favor by guiding through parliament an unheard-of grant of about £900,000 for the civil list plus an unprecedentedly large jointure for the Queen of £100,000.[63] Swift can hardly have avoided supposing that Caroline and Mrs. Howard, too ready to escape the burden of the gratitude they owed him for his friendship, had sold him out to the narrowly partisan considerations of alliance with Sir Robert and his cash.

This theory is the more complimentary to Swift, in that it does not entail his having been duped by Mrs. Howard all along. In the passage itself, the theory is reflected most clearly in the Queen's lines:

> "But now as Consort of a King,
> "You know 'tis quite a different Thing.

But it is also implicit in Swift's positioning the passage just before the one on Walpole (189-96); the two sections taken together emphatically suggest that the new government by Caroline and Walpole supports the "most infamous, vile Scoundrel," Francis Charteris (189 n.), while thwarting good men.

The significance of Queen Caroline and Mrs. Howard as examples in a poem on friendship and enmity lies not simply in their choosing political and financial advantage over a proper regard for human obligations. To be sure, they thereby defined a warm and genuine friendship as having been merely a courtier's relationship of temporary expediency, and their failure to acknowledge Swift's merit—to preserve it in their regard—and their inconstancy in neglecting their commitments to him bespeak ingratitude for his friendship. But beyond that, the fact that they as well as he were in the public eye helps Swift to heighten the general social consequences of false friendship: it is a loss to the public when men of merit and virtue are not cherished by those in power, and similarly a loss to the public to have in power those who would sacrifice merit to interest or faction.

Yet Swift is not so much concerned to establish any general thesis as to scorch those who have betrayed his friendship. Recounting the events of 1727 in his letters, he went so far as to suggest that Mrs. Howard made him ill by urging him to stay in London when she well knew he had nothing to gain by staying. The angry insinuation is not credible, but it is psychologically of a piece with the depiction in the *Verses* of the Queen and Lady Suffolk as rejoicing at his death. Moreover, Swift's grievances against Mrs. Howard seem linked to the genesis of the poem. For in a letter he accuses her of false friendship in these words: "I never knew a Lady who had so many qualityes to beget esteem, but how you act as a friend, is out of my way to judge." The same comment appears, rephrased, in a letter to Gay in which he announces the writing of *Verses on the Death:* "She has, Good qualityes enough to make her esteemed; but not one grain of truth or honour. I onely wish She were as great a fool as She is a knave. I have been severall months writing near five hundred lines on a pleasant Subject, onely to tell what my friends and enemyes will say on me after I am dead... I have brought in you and my other Friends, as well as enemyes and Detractors."[64] Cause and effect—the juxtaposition is remarkable.

III

In Swift and his true friends is manifest a literary tradition that friendship's bonds form a community of virtue, wit, and intellect.[65] The noble friendship of Swift, Pope, Gay, Arbuthnot, and Bolingbroke contributed to the esteem of each and helped define and strengthen each against enemies. To have friends is power, as Hobbes observed.[66] Swift, lonely and aware that at his age he would have no further opportunity for preferment, was eager to assure himself of the friendships he had.[67] His list of "Men of distinction and my friends who are yet alive," dated February 19, 1728/29, is alone sufficient evidence of this attitude, and it includes the friends who figure prominently in the *Verses*: Bolingbroke, Arbuthnot, Pope, and Gay.[68] Swift was also eager to regard others in his group as sharing his own position. Those more engaged in affairs than he might not get his wholehearted approval. Bolingbroke's activity in Opposition journalism, as much as his vaunted stoicism, is responsible for the crack that "ST. JOHN himself will scarce forbear, / To bite his Pen, and drop a Tear" (209–10); and in *A Libel on D[r.] D[elany]* (1730) Swift had already embarrassed Pope by depicting him in too staunch an anticourt posture.[69]

Of Swift's friends, John Gay was the one with whom he could most readily identify. When Gay refused the post of Gentleman Usher, Swift promptly construed his posture as enmity with Walpole.[70] Swift's third *Intelligencer* paper was influential in 1728 and subsequently in giving *The Beggar's Opera* a more polemical and satirical construction than, it may be argued, the text absolutely requires.[71]

Swift preferred to read Gay's failure at court as a result of the same forces that caused his own.[72] While *Verses on the Death* makes no direct reference to Gay's case, Swift considered himself instructed by it as he defined his own situation.

Swift's other closest friends are as important to the poem as Gay, yet, strictly speaking, the poem neither verifies nor refutes La Rochefoucauld's maxim that we take pleasure in the adversity of our *best* friends. The dangerous possibility that Swift will impeach even his dearest friends unquestionably rivets our attention from the first, but decorously he allows the possibility to hover over the poem without ever bringing it to pass. In the proem, raillery—praise by blame— admirably evokes the paradoxical proposition of enmity in friendship, but reaches no conclusions about it. Otherwise there is only the curiously invidious praise

> Poor POPE will grieve a Month; and GAY
> A Week; and ARBUTHNOTT a Day.
> (207–8)

Swift treats, rather, such anonymous faint friends as the Dublin chatterers who attend him in his illness and gossip about him after he is gone. They illustrate the maxim so blatantly and comically that they contribute little to any proof of its universal truth. Only ironically can they be called "my special Friends" (75), and Lady Suffolk and the Queen offer a much more interesting instance. But having stated his case against them and against enemies such as Walpole, and having quickly alluded to the grief of his best friends, he turns again to unknowns: "THE Fools, my Juniors by a Year" (219), "MY female Friends" (225), and "Some Country Squire" (253)—unidentified figures who naturally and easily lead down to the most anonymous and unknown, "one quite indiff'rent in the Cause" between those very faint friends and enemies who "toss [Swift's] name about" during "their Chat." The "indifferent" one offers Swift at least some hope of the regard friends had failed to give.

The eulogist's character is not strongly established or clearly maintained, and while the poem might be more satisfactory if it were, it is well to concede that an effort to interpret him as a sharply defined character is liable to fail for lack of evidence. At the same time, it appears necessary to posit at least some degree of distance between Swift *in propria persona* and the eulogist. Insofar as the character is established, I suggest that it is as a man-in-the-street (or in the Rose) whose knowledge of Swift is hardly complete.[73] Where the eulogist's character fades into the author's own voice, as it often does, it is a sign that Swift has found his character unable to serve as his biographer (he doesn't know enough) and inadequate to perform a friend's office—to say for Swift what he cannot with propriety say for himself.

With the eulogist or without him, the final section is very largely, I think, praise that Swift sincerely thought he deserved. Most inaccuracies or inadequacies can, on a sympathetic reading, be explained as resulting from the generic tendency of praise, eulogy, and character-writing to be reductive and hyperbolic, or else from the eulogist's rearing his somewhat uninformed head. Whatever else we might dispute, the eulogy is accurate in its assertion that Swift has the gratitude of the public, especially in Ireland, where "the grateful People stand his Friends" (426) and where, when he dies, he will be "remember[ed] with Gratitude" (168 n.). The eulogist, this member of the public, stresses Swift's public service, putting the matter as clearly as possible in the penultimate line, "That Kingdom he hath left his Debtor." Yet I daresay the eulogist's praise cannot have been wholly satisfactory to Swift. The friendship of the public, like that of posterity, is not enough. Swift can have no personal relationship with the public, cannot dine or converse with it. The public knows Swift only through his public acts or his works, and he doesn't know it at all. Further, it seems axiomatic for the interpretation of this poem that what *we* might consider undue self-praise, Swift would see as modest and restrained. For instance, the poem omits much of Swift's early accomplishment as a churchman, much about his private friendships, and—a nice irony, in a poem—almost everything about his stature as a writer.

Many readers have observed that this concluding section of the poem is less attractive than the beginning. Weak endings are not unusual in Swift's works, and they reflect, I think, a hardheaded and perhaps arrogant disregard for nice artistic proprieties. Swift will say what he has to say bluntly, and let it go. The letdown of the eulogy is also in keeping with what must have been its general unsatisfactoriness to Swift as a substitute for the recognition and esteem he expected from his friends.

Still, the self-praise makes us uneasy. Doesn't Swift overestimate himself when he supposes that queens and prime ministers ought to have set greater store by him? Isn't he too self-indulgent in leveling others down to his plane? We can at least understand why he did so: his intolerance of dependence and inferiority made him improve his status through wishful thinking if not otherwise. He was lonely and needed friendship, proud and needed esteem. He needed to believe that his friendships were perfect and that he could form important alliances based purely on merit and virtue. If this seems too pathetic a view of Swift, it is balanced by our knowledge of Swift the fiery pamphleteer and confident wit, at ease in the highest political and social circles.

We have ourselves been drawn into an attitude of friendship and sympathy toward Swift earlier in the poem. Now his unattractive self-presentation has the effect of opening us to the force of La Rochefoucauld's maxim. This parallel between the events narrated *in* the poem and the reader's experience *of* the poem must intensify and complicate our fascination or displeasure. It is possible to complain that the poem, particularly because of the eulogy, is artistically inferior, rhetorically ineffective, or even (Irvin Ehrenpreis has said) disgusting. Yet one might venture the opinion that it is very largely these same inartistic qualities which compel our attention with their truth, and allow us to confront what Maurice Johnson has called "the biographical presence" in the poem.[74] Finally what interests us is the tension between the man and his rhetoric, and the emotional pressures on the rectitude, sternness, and discipline of the satirist. The direct autobiography in *Verses on the Death of Dr. Swift* calls our attention to the satirist himself and makes us notice any flaws in his pose as *vir bonus*, though we would perhaps distrust the pose as artifice were it more consistently maintained. Swift's poem faces unresolved dilemmas and leaves them exposed to view: private friendship and public friendship conflict; two friends disagree on the value of their friendship; friendship creates both liberation and dependence; in friendship there is enmity.

NOTES

I am grateful to Richard E. Brantley, Maurice Johnson, Philip Pinkus, and David Woolley for their friendly and useful comments on the present essay.
1 *The Correspondence of Jonathan Swift*, ed. Harold Williams (Oxford: Clarendon, 1963-65), III, 506. Hereafter cited as *Corresp.*
2 *Corresp.*, III, 510; IV, 149, 151-52, 161; Swift's advertisement in Faulkner's *Dublin Journal*, May 12-15, 1733.
3 Paulson, "Swift, Stella, and Permanence," *ELH*, 27 (1960), 298-314, and reprinted in Paulson's *The Fictions of Satire* (Baltimore: The Johns Hopkins Press, 1967), pp. 185-210; Waingrow, "Verses on the Death of Dr. Swift," *Studies in English Literature*, 5 (1965), 513-18; Vieth, "The Mystery of Personal Identity: Swift's Verses on His Own Death," in *The Author in His Work: Essays on a Problem in Criticism*, ed. Louis L. Martz and Aubrey Williams (New Haven: Yale University Press, 1978), pp. 245-62; I am indebted to Professor Vieth for an advance copy.

Other previous scholarship on the poem includes Herbert Davis, "Verses on the Death of Dr. Swift," *Book-Collector's Quarterly*, no. 2 (March-May 1931), pp. 53-73; John Middleton Murry, *Jonathan Swift: A Critical Biography* (London: Jonathan Cape, 1954), pp. 454-59; Maurice Johnson, "'Verses on the Death of Dr. Swift,'" *Notes and Queries*, 199 (1954), 473-74; A. H. Scouten, "The Earliest London Printings of 'Verses on the Death of Doctor Swift,'" *Studies in Bibliography*, 15 (1962), 243-47; Barry Slepian, "The Ironic Intention of Swift's Verses on His Own Death," *Review of English Studies*, n.s., 14 (1963), 249-56; James L. Tyne, S.J., "Gulliver's Maker and Gullibility," *Criticism*, 7 (1965), 161-66; Robert C. Steensma, "Swift's Apologia: 'Verses on the Death of Dr. Swift,'" *Proceedings of the Utah Academy of Sciences, Arts, and Letters*, 42 (1965), 23-28; Herbert Davis, "Swift's Character," in *Jonathan Swift, 1667-1967: A Dublin Tercentenary Tribute*, ed. Roger McHugh and Philip Edwards (Dublin: Dolmen, 1967), pp. 1-23; Edward W. Said, "Swift's Tory Anarchy," *Eighteenth-Century Studies*, 3 (1969), 48-66; John Irwin Fischer, "How to Die: *Verses on the Death of Dr. Swift*," *Review of English Studies*, n.s., 21 (1970), 422-41; Gareth Jones, "Swift's *Cadenus and Vanessa*: A Question of 'Positives,'" *Essays in Criticism*, 20 (1970), 438-40; Maurice Johnson, "Swift's Poetry Reconsidered," in *English Writers of the Eighteenth Century*, ed. John H. Middendorf (New York: Columbia University Press, 1971), pp. 233-48; P. K. Elkin, *The Augustan Defence of Satire* (Oxford: Clarendon, 1973), pp. 111-14; Julie B. Klein, "The Art of Apology: 'An Epistle to Dr. Arbuthnot' and 'Verses on the Death of Dr. Swift,'" *Costerus*, 8 (1973), 77-87; Hugo M. Reichard, "The Self-Praise Abounding in Swift's Verses," *Tennessee Studies in Literature*, 19 (1973), 105-22; Arthur H. Scouten and

Robert D. Hume, "Pope and Swift: Text and Interpretation of Swift's Verses on His Death," *Philological Quarterly*, 52 (1973), 205-31; Robert W. Uphaus, "Swift's 'Whole Character': The Delany Poems and 'Verses on the Death of Dr. Swift,'" *Modern Language Quarterly*, 34 (1973), 406-16; Wayne C. Booth, *A Rhetoric of Irony* (Chicago: University of Chicago Press, 1974), pp. 121-22; Irvin Ehrenpreis, *Literary Meaning and Augustan Values* (Charlottesville: University Press of Virginia, 1974), pp. 33-37; Donald C. Mell, *A Poetics of Augustan Elegy* (Amsterdam: Rodopi, 1974), pp. 53-62; Peter J. Schakel, "The Politics of Opposition in 'Verses on the Death of Dr. Swift,'" *Modern Language Quarterly*, 35 (1974), 246-56.

The comparison between *Verses on the Death of Dr. Swift* and *An Epistle to Dr. Arbuthnot*, which many critics and teachers have found serviceable, is facilitated for the points raised in the present essay by P. Dixon, "The Theme of Friendship in the *Epistle to Dr. Arbuthnot*," *English Studies*, 44 (1963), 191-97, and Lawrence Lee Davidow, "Pope's Verse Epistles: Friendship and the Private Sphere of Life," *Huntington Library Quarterly*, 40 (1977), 151-70.

4 Swift's translation of the maxim "Dans l'adversité de nos meilleurs amis nous trouvons quelque chose, qui ne nous déplaist pas," which he uses as the poem's epigraph (*The Poems of Jonathan Swift*, ed. Harold Williams, 2nd ed. [Oxford: Clarendon, 1958], II, 551; hereafter cited as *Poems*). All references to Swift's poems are to the texts in this edition; line numbers of *Verses on the Death of Dr. Swift* (II, 551-72) are cited in the body of this essay.

5 See the Appendix of Michael Shinagel's *Concordance to the Poems of Jonathan Swift* (Ithaca: Cornell University Press, 1972); and Miles, "Some Major Poetic Words," in *Essays and Studies by Members of the Department of English, University of California*, University of California Publications in English, 14 (Berkeley: University of California Press, 1943), pp. 233-39. Shinagel finds (p. ix) that *wit* is the most recurrent noun in Swift's poems, but he does not group related forms of a word together.

6 Francis Bacon, *Essays*, 27 ("Of Friendship").

7 This idea of friendship provides an ironic context for Ronald Paulson's view (in *The Fictions of Satire*, pp. 192-93) that the poem dissociates friendship and permanence.

8 Said, "Swift's Tory Anarchy," pp. 61-66; Vieth, "The Mystery of Personal Identity," pp. 253-58.

9 Connections between friendship and death occur elsewhere in Swift's writing; a notable instance among the poems is the earlier, more pathetic "In Sickness" (1714), where Swift complains that he has "no obliging, tender Friend/To help at my approaching End" (*Poems*, I, 204).

10 1156 a 6-1157 b 4.

11 *Poems*, II, 596.

12 *Spectator*, no. 68 (May 18, 1711), ed. D. F. Bond (Oxford: Clarendon, 1965), I, 289.

13 *The Prose Writings of Jonathan Swift*, ed. Herbert Davis (Oxford: Basil Blackwell, 1939-68), XI, 255; V, 227. Hereafter cited as *Prose*.

14 Waingrow, "*Verses on the Death of Dr. Swift*," pp. 515-16.

15 Geoffrey Percival, Introduction, *Aristotle on Friendship: Being an Expanded Transla-*

tion of the *Nicomachean Ethics* (Cambridge: University Press, 1940); A. W. H. Adkins, "'Friendship' and 'Self-Sufficiency' in Homer and Aristotle," *Classical Quarterly*, n.s., 13 (1963), 30-45.
16 This practical view of friendship is discussed, for instance, in Xenophon, *Memorabilia*, II, 4-6; Aristotle, *Nicomachean Ethics*, VIII-IX; and Seneca, *De beneficiis*, passim.
17 This list is found in Lyon's annotated copy of John Hawkesworth, *The Life of the Revd. Jonathan Swift, D.D.* (Dublin: Cotter, 1755), now in the Victoria & Albert Museum Library (Forster 579), and quoted by courtesy of the Victoria & Albert Museum. As printed in *Corresp.*, V, 270, the list derives from a transcript of Lyon's transcript first published in John Nichols's 1808 edition of Swift's *Works*.
18 See especially E. Catherine Dunn, *The Concept of Ingratitude in Renaissance English Moral Philosophy* (Washington: Catholic University of America Press, 1946), pp. 23-42. See also Seneca, *De beneficiis*, IV, xviii, 1, and Dunn's commentary on it (p. 28); François Duc de La Rochefoucauld, Maxims 279 and 438, in *Réflexions ou sentences et maximes morales* (Paris: Garnier, 1961); Anthony Ashley Cooper, Earl of Shaftesbury, *Characteristicks* (1711), II, 230-42; Eustace Budgell, *Spectator*, no. 313 (Bond ed., III, 135); John Sheffield, Duke of Buckingham, "Of Friendship," *Works*, 3rd ed. corr. (London: Wotton, 1740), II, 273-76.
19 *Prose*, I, 248; see further *Spectator*, Bond ed., II, 449 n.
20 For Swift's comments on state ingratitude, see his *Journal to Stella*, ed. Harold Williams (Oxford: Clarendon, 1948), I, 13; and *Examiner*, no. 16, in *Prose*, III, 19-24. See also Thomas Hobbes, *Leviathan*, ed. C. B. Macpherson (Harmondsworth: Penguin, 1968), p. 209, as well as his *Tripos; in Three Discourses* and *Philosophical Rudiments Concerning Government and Society*, both in *The English Works of Thomas Hobbes*, ed. Sir William Molesworth, Bart. (1839; rpt. Aalen: Scientia Verlag, 1966), IV, 99; II, 35.
21 *Gulliver's Travels*, II, 6; IV, 4, 12; *Intelligencer*, no. 1, *Prose*, XII, 30; "Advertisement for the Honour of the Kingdom of Ireland," *Prose*, V, 346-47.
22 *Prose*, IX, 155.
23 *Prose*, XI, 268, 269, 274, 277.
24 Dec. 7, 1727, *Corresp.*, III, 254.
25 Sir Harold Williams's statement as to the date of composition (*Poems*, II, 553) may be accepted with little reservation. Since the poem was not published until 1739, it could have been revised after its completion in early 1732. However, there is very little evidence to that effect, and none which would alter my conclusions. Concerning evidence of post-1732 revision, see my unpublished dissertation, "Swift's Later Poems: Studies in Circumstances and Texts," Chicago, 1972, pp. 40-44.
26 William Pulteney to Francis Colman, Sept. 21, 1727, in *Posthumous Letters from Various Celebrated Men, Addressed to Francis Colman and George Colman the Elder* (London: Cadell & Davies, 1820), p. 11.
27 Swift to the Earl of Peterborough, April 28, 1726, *Corresp.*, III, 131-35; *Intelligencer*, no. 3, *Prose*, XII, 32-37; Swift to Lady Elizabeth Germain, Jan. 8, 1732/33, *Corresp.*, IV, 98.
28 Swift to Lady Suffolk, July 27, 1731, *Corresp.*, III, 484. For further information on Queen Caroline, see William Coxe, *Memoirs of the Life and Administration of Sir*

Robert Walpole, 3 vols. (London: Cadell & Davies, 1798), I, 274–81; W. H. Wilkins, *Caroline the Illustrious*, new ed. (London: Longmans, Green, 1904); John, Lord Hervey, *Some Materials towards Memoirs of the Reign of King George II* (London: [Eyre, Spottiswoode], 1931); and R. L. Arkell, *Caroline of Ansbach* (London: Oxford University Press, 1939).

29 Swift to Lady Elizabeth Germain, Jan. 8, 1732/33, *Corresp.*, IV, 98.

30 Arbuthnot to Swift, ca. Sept. 20, 1726, *Corresp.*, III, 166. On Caroline's conversational ability, see Coxe, *Walpole*, I, 274–75. On her conversations with Swift, see Horace Walpole, "Notes of Conversations with Lady Suffolk..., Now First Printed from the Original MS," in *Reminiscences Written by Mr. Horace Walpole in 1788 for the Amusement of Miss Mary and Miss Agnes Berry*, ed. Paget Toynbee (Oxford: Clarendon, 1924), pp. 119–20.

31 *Poems*, II, 409.

32 *Reminscences*, p. 116; see also pp. 119–20. For further information on Henrietta Howard, Countess of Suffolk, see "Walpole's Anecdotes of Lady Suffolk," in Horace Walpole, *Correspondence*, the Yale Edition, XXXI (London: Oxford University Press, 1961), 419–22; Coxe, *Walpole*, I, 274–81; *Letters to and from Henrietta, Countess of Suffolk*, ed. [John Wilson Croker], 2 vols. (London: Murray, 1824); Lewis Melville, *Lady Suffolk and Her Circle* (London: Hutchinson, 1924); and Marie P. G. Draper, *Marble Hill House and Its Owners* (London: Greater London Council, 1970).

33 Though Swift denies in his letters seeking "Promotion" to a bishopric, he did not rule out the possibility of "a change"—English preferment to a lesser benefice, which could be managed without capitulating to Walpole: see Paul V. Thompson, "An Unpublished Letter from Swift," *Library*, 5th ser., 22 (1967), 59; *Corresp.*, III, 423, IV, 99.

34 The precise number of invitations varies in Swift's retellings of the story: nine (*Corresp.*, IV, 98) and eleven (*Corresp.*, III, 422) both occur. For other possible motives for his delay in answering the Princess's commands, see *Corresp.*, IV, 98; for his freedom of speech with her, see *Corresp.*, III, 208, 238.

35 *Verses on the Death of Dr. Swift*, lines 339–40 and two lines inserted in MS in some early copies; see *Poems*, II, 566 n.

36 *Corresp.*, III, 392, 418, 423–24. "He taxed her with a Present worth Ten Pounds" (179 n.) is ironic: such a small amount could not have taxed her.

37 *Corresp.*, III, 176–77, 181, 184–85.

38 Swift to Gay, Nov. 10, 1730, *Corresp.*, III, 418; see also Swift to Pope, March 6, 1728/29, *Corresp.*, III, 315.

39 Etiquette probably discouraged direct correspondence with the Princess. See further Swift to Lady Suffolk, July 27, 1731, *Corresp.*, III, 483–84.

40 *Corresp.*, III, 168–69 and n., 174.

41 Hervey, *Memoirs*, I, 41–44.

42 See especially Murry, *Jonathan Swift: A Critical Biography*, pp. 410–16.

43 The date occurs in the copy Mrs. Howard actually received, now British Library Add. MS 22,625, fol. 4. It is printed in *Letters to and from Henrietta, Countess of Suffolk*, I, xxxviii. Herbert Davis, apparently unaware of this text, prints (and I

quote) a text derived from a draft Swift retained (*Prose*, V, 213–15, 357). Temple Scott's variants give an idea of the two versions: see Swift, *Prose Works*, XI (London: Bell, 1907), 147–50.

44 Bolingbroke to Swift, June 17, 1727, *Corresp.*, III, 215–16. It is likely that Bolingbroke was relaying a message from Mrs. Howard. Lady Suffolk's later claim that she did not know Bolingbroke at this time is dubious (Walpole, *Reminiscences*, pp. 19–20 n., 117).

45 Swift to Lady Elizabeth Germain, Jan. 8, 1732/33, *Corresp.*, IV, 99; Swift to Sheridan, June 24, 1727, *Corresp.*, III, 218–19.

46 The report of Swift's address has been generally unnoticed and is therefore worth quoting: Swift "express'd the utmost Loyalty and Affection for their Majesties Persons and Government, with an Address peculiar to himself, representing at the same Time the strict Adherence of his Majesty's faithful Subjects of Ireland to His Royal Person and Family, with their most grateful Acknowledgments for Favours granted to that Kingdom; the Continuation whereof they will endeavor to preserve by a distinguish'd Loyalty, as they have hitherto been remarkable for in the worst of Times, hoping the Participation of the benign Influence of his Majesty's shining Vertues &c: Which Declaration, their Majesties received with the utmost Satisfaction, shewing a particular Regard to the Welfare of the Kingdom of Ireland, as well as to the Merit of that truly great Man, and He had the Honour to kiss their Majesties Hand." (Faulkner's *Dublin Journal*, July 4–8, 1727). See also Swift to Lady Elizabeth Germain, Jan. 8, 1732/33, *Corresp.*, IV, 99.

47 Walpole's reestablishment began to be publicly visible by June 20 (J. H. Plumb, *Sir Robert Walpole: The King's Minister* [London: Cresset, 1960], p. 167 n.). Hervey (*Memoirs*, I, 35) says the matter was finally settled when Walpole and Compton competed in writing the King's speech dissolving parliament after the civil list bill was passed; the King's speech was July 17 (*Political State of Great Britain*, 34 [1727], 58).

48 Swift to Sheridan, *Corresp.*, III, 219.

49 *Poems*, II, 409. I conjecture the date from lines 37–38, in which Richmond-Lodge says, "My Master scarce a Fortnight since,/Was grown as wealthy as a Prince." Line 22 is perhaps Swift's veiled offer of friendship; for a similar rhetorical ploy, see the benediction in Swift's letter to Mrs. Howard, July 9, 1727, *Corresp.*, III, 224.

50 *Corresp.*, III, 221–22.

51 Whether the Queen—or Mrs. Howard—actually promised Swift a settlement in England is flatly denied by Murry, *Jonathan Swift*, p. 410. In fact it is an open question. Because Swift never saw Caroline after the third day of the new reign, he got word (usually orally) through Mrs. Howard or her intermediary. There are degrees of strength in a verbal commitment: to express the intent to do something may not be a contractual obligation to do it, but Swift's argument is that his former friends expressed their intention to place him in England, had the power to do so, and had no reasons except base ones for not doing so. In the absence of direct contact with the Queen and without anything put in writing, Swift speaks of assurances "they" offered or, in the passive, of assurances he was offered; sometimes he refers to "hints," but he puts the matter more strongly on at least two

occasions besides his Verses footnote. To Gay and the Duchess of Queensberry, he wrote, "The———, told me 5 years ago [1727] they would make me easy amongst you" (Aug. 12, 1732, Corresp., IV, 58); and writing to Lady Betty Germain, he refers to "the promises made me" of a settlement in England (Jan. 8, 1732/33, Corresp., IV, 99). Swift always thought Mrs. Howard had the power to offer him these assurances and could not believe her defense to him of September 25, 1731 (during the composition of the Verses): "If I cannot justifie the advice I gave you from the success of it; yet you know I gave you my reasons for it; and it was y^r business to have judg'd of my Capacity by the Solidity of my Arguments; if the Principle was false you ought not to have acted upon it; so you have only been the Dupe of your own ill Judgment and not to my falsehood" (Corresp., III, 499). What Swift called promises, Lady Suffolk now called reasons, implicitly shifting the blame to the Queen. Her statement is eloquent, but it may be doubted whether it accurately represents her communications to Swift in 1727, both because of Swift's own rejection of it and because she would naturally have been tempted to behave as though she had more influence than she did. Possibly, indeed, it was through her very effort to gain rewards for Swift and Gay that she first realized her impotence in the new court—though if this is so, Swift was not made aware of it. She may simply have been weak enough to tell Swift what he wanted to hear.

52 Corresp., III, 231.
53 The chronology can be inferred from Swift to Gay and the Duchess of Queensberry, Aug. 12, 1732, Corresp., IV, 59.
54 See Swift to Pope, Nov. 23, 1727, Corresp., III, 250-51, and Whitwell Elwin's notes on this letter in his edition of Pope's Works, VII (London: Murray, 1871), 106-7 n.
55 Prose, V, 213.
56 John Gay, Poetry and Prose, ed. Vinton A. Dearing (Oxford: Clarendon, 1974), I, 13.
57 Corresp., III, 471.
58 Corresp., III, 423-24.
59 Swift varies the details: at times "a Medal" (Corresp., III, 392, 423), at other times "Medals" (Corresp., IV, 58). Swift probably thought it unlikely that a single medal would be a "Present worth Ten Pounds" (179 n.; the usual value of a gold medal was about five guineas). If so, he was mistaken. The medal the Princess intended for Swift can be identified with considerable certainty as a large one commemorating the reestablishment of the Order of the Bath in 1725 (see Medallic Illustrations of the History of Great Britain and Ireland to the Death of George II, comp. Edward Hawkins and ed. Augustus W. Franks and Herbert A. Grueber [London: British Museum, 1885], II, 463). Because this medal bears the date 1725, numismatic historians have assumed it was issued that year. But Sir Isaac Newton, as Master of the Royal Mint, did not authorize the engraving of the medal until December 6, 1726, as the papers of the Mint's then Chief Engraver, John Croker, reveal (British Library Add. MS 18,757, fol. 20). The same papers contain a printed broadside evidently issued by Croker, A List of Medals, Struck Since the Latter End of the Reign of His Majesty King William the Third [London, mid-1730's], showing the

price of the Bath medal (gold version) as £10 (fol. 2). Caroline's interest lay in the fact that a full-length portrait of her favorite son, Prince William, Duke of Cumberland, appears on the reverse—he having been, at age four, installed by his grandfather as Principal Companion of the Order of the Bath: see further *Statutes of the Most Honourable Order of the Bath* (London, 1725), pp. 5, 55. To give Caroline her due, this medal matches exactly what she promised Swift as to value, and the delay in its production was genuine. Speculation about why she subsequently failed to send Swift his copy should await discovery of the date the medal was issued.

60 To attribute running and laughter to a woman languishing in the spleen seems contradictory, and happens to mirror the ambiguity Swift saw in Mrs. Howard's character, but the best explanation of these lines is probably that they imperfectly compress an idea of sequence: though Lady Suffolk had been in the spleen, the news of Swift's death set her gleefully running and laughing. Elsewhere in his poems Swift sometimes imagines women "in the spleen" for the sake of telling what would bring them out of it.
61 *Corresp.*, III, 424.
62 *Poems*, II, 531; see also *Corresp.*, III, 260, IV, 99.
63 Plumb, *Sir Robert Walpole: The King's Minister*, p. 168; Hervey, *Memoirs*, I, 34, 47, 68.
64 To Lady Suffolk, Oct. 26, 1731, *Corresp.*, III, 501; to Gay and the Duke and Duchess of Queensberry, Dec. 1, 1731, *Corresp.*, III, 506.
65 On the history of this tradition, see David Jay Latt, "The Progress of Friendship: The Topoi for Society and the Ideal Experience in the Poetry and Prose of Seventeenth-Century England," Diss. California, Los Angeles, 1971. The community of friendship is a constant theme of the correspondence between Swift and Pope; and about the *Dunciad* Pope writes, "It was my principal aim in the entire work to perpetuate the friendship between us, and to shew that the friends or the enemies of one were the friends or enemies of the other" (Swift, *Corresp.*, III, 351).
66 *Leviathan*, p. 150. Bertrand Goldgar notes, however, that the Scriblerians' friendships were not directly concerned with politics (*Walpole and the Wits: The Relation of Politics to Literature, 1722–1742* [Lincoln: University of Nebraska Press, 1976], p. 42).
67 At this time Swift's view of himself as virtually friendless is expressed in letters to a few trusted friends (e.g., *Corresp.*, III, 199); it is also known and repeated by his young admirer William Dunkin, who, in his "A Satyr Inscribed to S——," says (with doubtful tact) that people Swift earlier befriended and patronized now spurn him; Dunkin concludes that friendship is "fickle," "a painted show," etc. See *Poetical Works of the Late William Dunkin, D.D.*, II (Dublin: Powell, 1770), 244.
68 *Corresp.*, V, 271–72.
69 *Poems*, II, 482–83; Pope, *Correspondence*, ed. George Sherburn (Oxford: Clarendon, 1956), III, 85 (headnote), 90 n.
70 "I am perfectly confident you have a firm Enemy in the Ministry" (Swift to Gay and Pope, Nov. 23, 1727, *Corresp.*, III, 250; see also *Corresp.*, III, 267).

71 Though Swift's essay rehearses his own view of Gay's career, Gay's supposed libel of Walpole, etc., it is otherwise in line with less influential essays on *The Beggar's Opera* by Opposition writers: see John Loftis, *The Politics of Drama in Augustan England* (Oxford: Clarendon, 1963), p. 96.

72 See also Swift's *A Libel on D—— D——* (1730), 53–60, *Poems*, II, 481–82, and "To Mr. Gay" (1731), *Poems*, II, 530–36.

73 Peter J. Schakel's interesting article ("The Politics of Opposition," *Modern Language Quarterly*, 35 [1974], 246–56), with which I do not entirely agree, should be consulted here. I doubt that the eulogist is meant to represent the Opposition; Swift would probably claim that he is nonpartisan. The Opposition doctrine was that Walpole represented a narrow faction and was not running a popularly based government; and the Opposition maintained that the majority would side with them if given the chance. See Isaac Kramnick, *Bolingbroke and His Circle* (Cambridge: Harvard University Press, 1968), p. 25.

74 For the complaints, see Murry, *Jonathan Swift*, pp. 457–60; Paulson, *The Fictions of Satire*, pp. 190–91; and Ehrenpreis, *Literary Meaning and Augustan Values*, pp. 33–37. Johnson's view is in his essay "Swift's Poetry Reconsidered," in Middendorf, *English Writers of the Eighteenth Century*; Robert W. Uphaus warmly endorses it in "Swift's 'Whole Character,'" *Modern Language Quarterly*, 34 (1973), 406–16.

Ironist and Moralist:
The Two Readers of Tom Jones

WILLIAM PARK

Commenting on William Empson's essay "Tom Jones," C. J. Rawson remarked that "the overall effect of the essay is misleading... in so far as it suggests that the main doctrinal points are made by means of an essentially evasive irony rather than by what is often an emphatic explicitness."[1] Rawson was speaking of sexual morality, and perhaps we have all come into complete agreement on that subject. Yet on another "doctrinal" point—the relationship between the plot of the novel and a providential design—there have appeared in recent years two contradictory and opposed readings.

On the one hand we find Ian Watt, Martin Battestin, Aubrey Williams, and Henry Knight Miller, who see the well-ordered plot as being somehow related to Fielding's vision of a well-ordered universe.[2] As Watt says, the plot "reflects the general literary strategy of neoclassicism; just as the creation of a field of force makes visible the universal law of magnetism, so the supreme task of the writer was to make visible in the human scene the operations of universal order."[3] On the other hand we discover Sheridan Baker, John Preston, Leo Braudy, and David Goldknopf, who see the plot as an artifice, a kind of irony, a recognition of confusion, or a failure having no real significance in itself but possibly working as an aesthetic device that enables Fielding to achieve other ends.[4] According to Braudy, "In *Tom Jones* Fielding asserts that the most obvious and artificial structure (the plot) is also the most liberating. Because it does not claim to be necessary, it therefore allows the material the freest play and gives the truest and most relevant representation of life." Braudy further claims that since only the Man of the Hill, Partridge, and Blifil believe in Providence, "the providential view in *Tom Jones* is at best supererogatory and at worst ignorantly or meretriciously self serving."[5]

I believe this conflict may to some extent be resolved if we return to Empson's concept of "double irony" in Fielding and the two readers which that irony involves.[6] According to Empson, Fielding poses as the man of the world, the one who winks tolerantly at sexual misbehavior. This is his first irony, made at the expense of stuffy moralists. The second irony, however, trips up the worldly reader when either chastity or sexual license no longer appears to be a joke. Thus Fielding moves closer to a Richardsonian view, though one which has become highly qualified.

Now I would argue that the plot of *Tom Jones* is one double irony.[7] As narrator, Fielding on numerous occasions insists that the world is governed by accident and Fortune, that virtue is not rewarded by happiness in this world (XV, i), and that he will not intervene to help Tom (XVII, i). He appeals directly to the realist like Braudy and seems to be laughing at the theologically orthodox like Battestin. As he says, he is confined to "natural Means alone" (XVII, i).[8] At first, the hodgepodge of events seems to support this first irony, but as order and happiness begin to emerge out of the random and episodic world, as Tom's fortunes are reversed, the comic action contradicts this particular narrative viewpoint and reveals the second irony, namely that Fortune is but Providence improperly understood. At this point the realist who accepted all the statements about chance, accident, Fortune, and history as absolute has been revealed to be as literal-minded as his moralistic counterpart. By a careful counterpoint between statement about the plot and the plot itself, Fielding has by the last book reversed his initial position; and as he withdraws from direct commentary, the novel as a whole affirms an orthodoxy which becomes more interesting and acceptable than the simpleminded version preached by the prigs. Instead of talking about the plot of *Tom Jones* as an artifice, then, it might be more appropriate to notice how Fielding's pretense at being a naturalistic narrator is an even greater artifice. Obviously Fielding wanted it both ways.[9] He did indeed wish to be a natural historian, but he also believed in Providence. Double irony was one of his means of reconciling wish and belief.

That he believed more in the naturalism and less in his providential design or that he considered this design a mere comic or aesthetic device cannot be supported by a close study of the text. I suspect that any comic plot, in Frye's sense of that term, affirms a larger shaping moral order and is thus naturally aligned with religion. But we need not discuss archetypes to discern Fielding's own belief in the relationship of his plot to Providence. Rather, we can look at the specific occurrences of this word or idea in the book. Indeed, one of the most curious facts of *Tom Jones* is that Fielding, who is very generous in providing us with Christian sentiments, not only from Allworthy but from himself, restricts his use of "Providence" to only the most crucial events. Miller has already discussed several of them.[10] For instance, as Tom cries, "Let Fortune direct" (VII, ii) and then goes off on the wrong road to Bristol, Fielding quotes a line from Milton which implies the providential direction that will put him on the right road to Sophia. Partridge first uses the word when he sees light coming from the Man of the Hill's house (VIII, x); then Tom and the Man of the Hill discuss whether or not Providence sent Tom to his rescue. Next Mrs. Waters says that "Heaven" seemed to design Tom for her protection (IX, ii); then Fielding himself remarks that the "providential Appearance" of Jones "fortunately" prevented her murder (IX, vii). Miller believes that these two rescues, which flank the Man of the Hill episode, "simultaneously offer pointed comment upon the old man's story and invoke the overarching force that gives genuine meaning to any human actions."[11] Whether or not the skeptic is convinced by this argument, he should note that Fielding's statement about the providential rescue of Mrs. Waters is the only time in the entire novel in which in his own voice Fielding directly asserts a belief in Providence. Significantly, he does this when he describes the meeting of Tom and the only person in the world besides Blifil and Dowling who knows the secret of his birth.

The fact that Partridge refers to Providence does not mean that

Fielding is disagreeing with the idea, for Partridge, silly as he is, also happens to be the only character in the book who correctly divines the outcome, which may well be another example of double irony. Likewise in the Book (VIII) which severely limits the use of the "Marvellous" in literature, we meet the novel's most superstitious character, one who no more shares the "enlightened" notions of the narrator than, as we discover by the end of the novel, does the author himself.

When in Book XII Partridge tells Tom that Providence designed to bring him and Sophia together, Tom for the first time pays attention to his "superstitious Doctrines" (XII, viii). But throughout the entire adventure with Lady Bellaston we do not once hear of Providence. Only in Book XVII, chapter ii, immediately after Fielding has told the reader that he will not attempt a comic ending but will leave all to "natural Means" does Blifil say to Allworthy, "O, Sir... it is not without the secret Direction of Providence that you mention the Word Adoption. Your adopted Son, Sir, that *Jones*, that Wretch whom you nourished in your Bosom, hath proved one of the greatest Villains upon Earth." This is another moment of double irony involving Fortune and Providence. The first irony, picked up by Braudy, is that Blifil speaks the language of canting hypocrites, mere pietistic nonsense worthy to be put in the mouth of the novel's villain as though to indicate a kind of equation between a belief in Providence and villainy. But the second irony, which Braudy chooses to ignore, is that Bilfil, like Partridge, not only speaks the truth but unknown to himself becomes the agent of Providence.[12] His libel of Tom provokes Mrs. Miller's defense and furthers the machinery by which Tom is vindicated.[13] By this juxtaposition of comment and event the ideal reader should understand that the "natural means" of the historian and "the secret direction of Providence" are the same.

The clarity and resolution of the final two books are obvious. Mrs. Miller tells Allworthy that "Time will shew all Matters in their true and natural colours" (XVII, vii); Fielding speaks—and not ironically—of grave and good men who have concluded that Providence interposes in the discovery of secret villainy (XVIII, iii); when Allworthy hears of the plot against Tom, he exclaims, "Good

Heavens, by what wonderful Means is the blackest and deepest Villainy discovered" (XVIII, vii). And when Allworthy discovers Tom's true identity, he stands "a Minute silent, lifting up his Eyes" (XVIII, viii), a picture in the Baroque manner of piety and the interposition of Providence.

So far, then, I am in complete agreement with Battestin's "argument of design," particularly when he says that Pope declares but Fielding demonstrates the "god *in* the machine."[14] Most authors who reveal the higher harmony must take us up the Hill of Holiness or above the lunar sphere before we can see clearly the true relationship between Fortune and Providence. Fielding, more than any writer I know, really does this by natural means, which may in part be caused by his mid-century or "late Augustan" effort to reconcile a Christian tradition with an empirical epistemology. Yet by the time Battestin concludes his argument, I find myself in disagreement with him. Battestin's "strategy" also involves two readers. He must first argue with R. S. Crane and his theory of internal causality. Therefore he stresses Fielding's deliberate artifice. At this point he would seem to agree with Baker and Braudy, who see this artifice as either ironic or as a necessary aesthetic device. But no, says Battestin, the very artificiality would remind the Augustan reader of a higher causality. Fielding's intention, he says, is "ultimately symbolic," and we must read the book on a "figurative or analogical" level, where we will discover it to be a "comic apocalypse" whose "denouement reflects the purposeful movement of Time itself."[15]

We all agree that many eighteenth-century authors believed in a theory of art based on analogy and imitation. Just as the design of the work imitated the universal order, so the characters and events imitated nature and history. Art was neither nature nor the creation but analogous to them. But its analogy had to work on all levels. To think that Fielding expected his work, as analogy, to be taken as true on the archetypal level of comedy and not as analogy on the literal one of history puts him in the heretical position of believing that God exists in the abstract or in the afterlife but not in the concrete or in this life. Such a view is not Christian. The very point that all the divines whom Battestin quotes are making is that God and His Providence are very much active in this world and that we shall find evidence of Him not only in the comic apocalypse of our deaths but also in our daily lives.[16] The plot of *Tom Jones,* as art and as an analogue to life, makes this same point literally as well as figuratively.

Battestin claims that "Richardson's eye is on the fact; Fielding's on the abstraction which the fact implies."[17] But Fielding is much more factual and literal than Richardson. He gives us actual times and places, real historic events, hundreds of topical allusions, characters based on real people, and even real people themselves, whereas Richardson, however he may differ psychologically, works on a more generalized, timeless plane.[18] Pamela is "Virtue" every bit as much as Tom is "Human Nature," and if *Pamela* falls short of *Tom Jones* (which *Clarissa* does not), its flaws do not result from its literalism. The truth is that both Fielding and Richardson have their eyes on facts and "abstractions," which would be the conscious mode of any early-eighteenth-century Christian author.

Fielding's problem in *Tom Jones* is not how to transcend particulars or rise above the miseries of human existence into art, which at this point becomes emblematic, but how to render individuals *and* a species, how to present history *and* a comic romance, how to be worldly wise *and* moral, how to be empirical *and* Christian. Again, one of the means of accomplishing this balancing act was double irony. Let us look at the famous passage quoted both by those who see the plot as mere design and by those who see it as mere device: "There are a Set of Religious, or rather Moral Writers, who teach that Virtue is the certain Road to Happiness, and Vice to misery in this World. A very wholesome and comfortable Doctrine, and to which we have but one Objection, namely, That it is not true" (XV, i). First of all we note that Fielding makes clear that this is not a religious doctrine but a moral one. Having said that it was untrue, he immediately qualifies himself and tells us that practicing virtue "with regard to this Life" so contributes and leads to happiness that he would call such virtue wisdom, a point which he, Allworthy, and Tom make throughout the book. But a very active virtue, such as Tom's, he says, may well lead one to jail. So having wiped off a doctrine that has lain in his way (which he does not really wipe off at all but affirms), he can now proceed to show how the "Devil, or some other evil Spirit" was hard at work to ruin Sophia and make Tom completely miserable. Irony One, then, is at the expense of the Bildad-like moralists who have a simplistic view of reward and punishment in this life; but irony Two is at the expense of the Job-like sufferers who, with similar simplicity, have resigned the world to the devil—for as we all know, Sophia is saved and Tom is made happy. If there is some contradiction here between statement and demonstration, between individual suffering and universal joy, or between specific instances and general truths, then we must not blame Fielding or try to extricate him from difficulties of his own making, for the source of the dilemma is no less than the problem of evil itself, a problem neither Fielding, Milton, nor St. Augustine has been able to explain to everyone's satisfaction.

If double irony helps Fielding to maintain his complicated creation and to resolve or balance its contradictions, so too does his system of pairing wrongs, which is related to it. In Book V when he introduces us to the idea of contrast running through the works of creation, he seems to be referring to the comic and the serious, but by the end of the discussion they have become duller and dullest. Some other examples: Dr. Blifil and Captain Bilfil; Dr. X and Dr. Y; Square and Thwackum; Western and Mrs. Western; country ignorance and town learning; too cruel or too lenient; the Man of the Hill and Mrs. Fitzpatrick; the first half of the Man of the Hill's life and the second; the affectation of high life and the barbarity of low; Miss Graveairs and Miss Giddy; Alderman History and Monsieur Romance; books make pedants and plays make coxcombs; the last age being characterized by Vice, the present by Folly. All this weighing and balancing of wrongs, of false appearances, and of conflicting opinions produces what Wolfgang Iser has called the "virtual dimension" which the reader must supply himself.[19]

Given these ironic patterns, one is not surprised to find Fielding consciously concerned about two types of readers. For the most part he contrasts his sagacious, discerning, curious, learned, good, good-natured, and worthy readers with the modern critics, the pitiful critics, and the reptile critics. But the continuous use of these compliments, especially coming from Fielding, becomes a bit facetious, and at one point (VIII, i) he says that all readers are critics. So there exists in these epithets some possibility for double irony. On several occasions, however, he actually pairs two types of readers, both of them wrong. He refers to sneerers and profane wits and to graver readers (I, iii); he speaks of Dacier, for whom the impossible may be probable, and of others for whom nothing is either possible or probable unless they have seen it themselves (VIII, i). But the most important passage, and the one cited by Empson, occurs just after Partridge has begun to persuade Tom of his superstitious notions and immediately following Fielding's assertion that he is writing a history, not a system (XII, viii). Even if he could reconcile "every Matter to the received Notions concerning Truth and Nature," it might not be "prudent" for him to do so. For as matters now stand, he has pleased the "wise and good Men," who would see Jones punished, and the "silly and bad persons," who think that character is owing to accident rather than to Virtue. The simplistic literalness of the first view and the cynicism of the second are both wrong: they may in fact be considered Fielding's own prophecy of the types of misreading he will suffer, the one too grave, the other too cynical. But rather than contradict these conclusions and show how the incidents contribute to his great, useful, and uncommon Doctrine—a doctrine enigmatically not stated—he will not repeat himself. Thus he preserves his naturalism, his prudence, and his irony, all of which finally affirm the providential, exuberant, and sentimental vision of the book.

Tom Jones seems always to have had two readers. In the eighteenth century some thought it was "low" and immoral; others thought it was "nature as it is." Some, like Allworthy, looked too high and condemned the naturalism; others, like Black George, looked too low and missed the religion. On the whole, eighteenth-century readers were delighted with the plot and suspicious of the morals, while twentieth-century readers are delighted with the morals and suspicious of the plot.[20] Meanwhile Fielding and his work go on asserting that great, useful, and uncommon doctrine.

NOTES

A shorter and earlier version of the present paper appeared in *Enlightenment Essays*, 5, nos. 3-4 (Fall-Winter 1974), 43-48.

1 "Professor Empson's 'Tom Jones,'" *Notes & Queries*, n.s., 6 (1959), 400.
2 Ian Watt, *The Rise of the Novel* (London: Chatto and Windus, 1957); Martin Battestin, "Fielding: The Argument of Design," in *The Providence of Wit* (Oxford: Clarendon, 1974), pp. 141-63; Aubrey Williams, "Interpositions of Providence and the Design of Fielding's Novels," *South Atlantic Quarterly*, 70 (1971), 265-86; Henry Knight Miller, *Henry Fielding's "Tom Jones" and the Romance Tradition*, English Literary Studies, No. 6 (University of Victoria, B.C., 1976).
3 *The Rise of the Novel*, p. 271.
4 Sheridan Baker, "Fielding and the Irony of Form," *Eighteenth-Century Studies*, 2 (1968), 150; John Preston, "Plot as Irony," in *The Created Self: The Reader's Role in Eighteenth-Century Fiction* (London: Heinemann, 1970), pp. 95-132; Leo Braudy, *Narrative Form in History & Fiction* (Princeton: Princeton University Press, 1970), pp. 142-78; David Goldknopf, "The Failure of Plot in 'Tom Jones,'" *Criticism*, 11 (1969), 262-74.
5 *Narrative Form*, pp. 143, 163.
6 "Tom Jones," *Kenyon Review*, 20 (1958), 217-49.
7 Eleanor Hutchens, *Irony in Tom Jones* (University: University of Alabama Press, 1965), p. 67, speaks of how "the concomitant irony of plot turns things back upon themselves transformed.... The reversal of truth and expectation accompanies plot and theme as a sort of ironic *Doppelgänger*." E. Taiwo Palmer, "Irony in 'Tom Jones,'" *Modern Language Review*, 66 (1971), 504, calls attention to double irony as a structural device. Charles A. Knight, "Multiple Structures and the Unity of 'Tom Jones,'" *Criticism*, 14 (1972), 227-42, argues that Fielding resolves these contradictory viewpoints through "multiple structures." K. K. Ruthven, "Fielding, Square, and the Fitness of Things," *Eighteenth-Century Studies*, 5 (1971), 255, says: "The parodies and irreverences we all enjoy are so very illuminating, for they are the areas in which the novel threatens to escape the banalities of its moral postulates." F. Kaplan, "Fielding's Novel about Novels: The 'Prefaces' and the 'Plot' of *Tom Jones*," *Studies in English Literature*, 13 (1973), 535-49, discusses Fielding's methods of resolving contradictory viewpoints. Bernard Harrison, *Henry Fielding's "Tom Jones": The Novelist as Moral Philosopher* (Sussex University Press, 1975), p. 48, sees double irony as essential to Fielding's method of complication and his avoidance of sermonizing, but he sees the "triumphantly absurd complexity" of the plot (p. 11) only as a means of allowing the irony and the morals to unfold and develop (pp. 64-65).
8 Notice, however, that when he makes this secular claim, he couches it ironically in religious language: he will not "shock the Faith of our Reader." His denial of Virtue's bringing Happiness (XV, i) ends in an affirmation of his belief in immortality. In Book VIII, chapter i, he says that the writer, after limiting the "Marvellous" to ghosts and treating "Man" as "the highest Subject (unless on very

extraordinary Occasions indeed)," is "intitled to some Faith from his Reader, who is indeed guilty of critical Infidelity if he disbelieves him."

All quotes are from the Wesleyan Edition of *Tom Jones*, ed. Martin C. Battestin (Middletown, Conn.: Wesleyan University Press, 1975).

9 Melvyn New, "'The Grease of God': The Form of Eighteenth-Century English Fiction," *Publications of the Modern Language Association*, 91 (1976), 242. New believes that both Christian and secular readings of major eighteenth-century novels are somewhat mistaken. The novelists, he argues, "imaged forth" neither the declining Christian view nor the rising secular one which replaced it (pp. 235-44).

10 *Henry Fielding's "Tom Jones" and the Romance Tradition*, pp. 28, 32.

11 Ibid., p. 28.

12 In Book III, chapter iv, after describing the two hypocrites Square and Thwackum, Fielding says that "many true and just Sentiments" came from their mouths.

13 Irvin Ehrenpreis, *Fielding: Tom Jones* (London: Edward Arnold, 1964), p. 51, discusses Fortune and Providence and points out that the clues revealing Tom's true identity come as a result of his good deeds.

14 *The Providence of Wit*, pp. 150, 153.

15 Ibid., pp. 161, 148, 160-61.

16 On p. 153 Battestin says, "In a universe ultimately 'comic' and Christian, the occurrence of what William Turner called 'the Most Remarkable Providences, both of Judgement and Mercy' was both natural and probable. To write a novel—at least a comic novel—and fail to imply them would be, in effect, to misrepresent the creation, to belie 'what really exists.'" But by the end of his "argument" he has departed from this view, perhaps because he overstresses "ultimately" at the expense of "immediately," at least on "very extraordinary Occasions."

17 Ibid., p. 161.

18 One might say that the depiction of real and fictional characters together heightens the contrast between them and thus enhances the "artificiality" of the novel, but eighteenth-century readers did not see the novel in this light. Johnson, for instance, complained of the new "familiar histories" that "if the world be promiscuously described, I cannot see what use it can be to read the account" (*The Rambler*, no. 4).

19 *The Implied Reader: Patterns of Communication in Prose Fiction from Bunyan to Beckett* (Baltimore: The Johns Hopkins University Press, 1974), pp. 40-42. In *The Created Self*, John Preston never admits any reconciliation between the contradictory views he identifies. They contribute to the education of the reader, but the "pattern" of the book "does not in any direct way establish a moral sense in the novel" (p. 114). Harrison, *Henry Fielding's "Tom Jones,"* p. 131, points out how Fielding confronts two wrong views of self-sufficiency, that of Hobbes and Mandeville and that of Butler and the Benevolists.

20 Kenneth Rexroth has written that the "fairy tale plot" and the farcical relations between the characters all give the book "an air of quiet madness" ("*Tom Jones*," *Saturday Review*, July 1, 1967, p. 13, reprinted by Sheridan Baker in the Norton Critical Edition of *Tom Jones* [New York: W. W. Norton, 1973], pp. 904-5).

Sterne as Editor:
The "Abuses of Conscience" Sermon

MELVYN NEW

The sermon read by Corporal Trim in the middle of the second volume of *Tristram Shandy* was first preached by Laurence Sterne ten years earlier in the York Minster (July 29, 1750), at the close of the summer assizes in York. It appeared as a six-penny pamphlet less than two weeks later. In fitting the actual sermon to the fictional situation of the Shandy parlor, Sterne was not required to make a single significant alteration; indeed, the foremost pleasure in comparing the two versions is to observe the manner in which his wit was able to capitalize so brilliantly on such an innocuous passage in the original as "sits there invulnerable, fortified with *Cases* and *Reports* so strongly on all Sides."[1] In *Tristram Shandy*, Toby immediately breaks in: "Aye, —aye, *Trim!* quoth my uncle *Toby*, shaking his head, —these are but sorry fortifications, *Trim*," and the two are mounted and galloping on their hobby-horse.[2] Again, in the original, Sterne innocently wrote, "I know the banker I deal with, or the Physician I usually call in" (p. 17); in *Tristram*, the word "physician" awakens Dr. Slop: "There is no need, cried Dr. *Slop* (waking) to call in any physician in this case" (p. 135).

It is precisely Sterne's faithfulness to the original, however, that adds interest to the almost ninety substantive variants between the two versions. To be sure, a few new readings correct obvious errors in the 1750 version, including one long sentence fragment (pp. 113-14; see section 1 in the Appendix). Several others may be the result of compositorial error (or interference) or copyist error; from the evidence of other borrowed materials in *Tristram Shandy* I have suggested elsewhere that Sterne was not a precise copier, though in this instance, considering the length of the self-borrowing—3,700 words—he did very well indeed.[3]

When we have discounted these possible sources for the variants between the 1750 and 1760 versions, we still have remaining many interesting alterations in which the author's hand is evident. Together, they provide an indication of the subtlety of Sterne's prose, the care with which he sought the right word, the right phrase, even the right pointing. In rewriting his sermon for *Tristram Shandy*, Sterne knew that the humor of his endeavor resided in his capacity to incorporate into his comic world a sermon actually preached from England's second most important pulpit; he could not resist, however, the opportunity to polish and refine his effort ten years after composition—to act, that is, as his own editor.

The most interesting changes, perhaps, are Sterne's second thoughts about particular words. Sterne makes over thirty such changes, often for reasons not altogether apparent. In a few instances, the changes might suggest a careful modification of Sterne's theological position—or at least of his tone. These examples are listed in the Appendix under section 2. For example, "so great a Virtue, as moral Honesty" (p. 17) becomes "so amiable a virtue as moral honesty" (p. 134); *amiable* is a word we associate with the religion of sensibility. Similarly, Sterne's description of Catholicism as a "Religion without Morality" (p. 23) becomes "religion without mercy" (p. 146), a more telling word in view of the tortures just described, and perhaps an even stronger condemnation in Sterne's eyes. Again, he alters the phrase "Instrumental Duties of Religion" (p. 20) to "instrumental parts of religion" (p. 138), a phrase he apparently liked, for he uses it again in Volume 8 of *Tristram* (chapter 31) and in *A Sentimental Journey* (Stout ed., p. 101). It may be worth noting that in one of the two major excisions, Sterne removed a passage from the original which twice speaks of duties (pp. 19–20).[4] This softening of religious tone is perhaps also evident in the change of "that BEING, before whom thou art finally to give an Account" (p. 14) to "that Being, to whom thou art finally to give an account" (p. 128). The fearful idea of final judgment is slightly relaxed by the prepositional change.

It would not do, however, to build too much of a case upon these changes, for several others exist (section 3 in the Appendix) which conform to no such pattern. It is not clear, for example, why Sterne altered "'tis no Rarity to see a Man whose real moral Merit stands very low" (p. 20) to "'tis no prodigy to see a man whose real moral character stands very low" (p. 138); perhaps the alliteration of "moral Merit" disturbed him, perhaps the word "Merit" had more of Judgment Day in it than he wanted. I see no advantage in "prodigy" over "rarity," but obviously Sterne sensed a difference between the two strong enough to warrant an emendation.

Several changes in wording may be traced to the new context of the sermon. That Sterne altered "Discourse" (p. 24) to "sermon" (p. 147), and "Forfeiture incurr'd" (p. 9) to "forfeiture of goods and chattels incurred" (p. 120), may have seemed desirable if only because what Trim reads is several times identified as Yorick's "sermon" and because "goods and chattels" is a legalistic formula of the kind that Sterne enjoyed parodying throughout *Tristram Shandy*.

Yet another reason for the alteration of particular words is grammatical or stylistic nicety. Sterne is caught by the usual traps: once, by "shall" versus "will" (p. 11/p. 124), and several times by "the" versus "this" (pp. 5, 10, 19/pp. 114, 122, 137)—he chooses "the" in each instance. Somewhat more interesting, in the 1750 version he refers to the mind with the pronoun "herself" and a paragraph later with "itself" (p. 2). In *Tristram*, he uses "herself" on both occasions (pp. 108, 109). Similarly, the phrase "this unwary *Traveller*,— too apt . . . to go astray of himself,—and confidently speak Peace to his Soul . . ." (p. 11) is altered to "speak peace to himself" (p. 124). If the printer's eye did not simply jump to the line above, the change probably indicates an attempt to parallel the clauses rather than to make a theological point.[5]

Sterne also makes several changes aimed at simplification and specificity. "Wisdom of the Legislature" (p. 15) is altered to "law-makers" (p. 129), and "Give me Leave to illustrate" (p. 17) becomes "I will illustrate" (p. 135). In his accumulation of moral types, "Another shall," etc. (p. 9) is altered to "A fourth man shall," etc. (p. 122), and in the same paragraph, "in this Case" is made more precisely "in the present case." The passage "If he robs, or murders" (p. 10) is changed to "if he robs, —if he stabs" (p. 123), creating not only two parallel clauses but a more vivid image as well. The clumsy phrase "meets Death with as much Unconcernedness" (p. 7) is perhaps solved with "meets death as unconcernedly" (p. 116); the 1766 version of the sermon in the *Collected Sermons* reads "meets death with as much unconcern."[6]

For less obvious reasons Sterne changes the phrase "Prison opening its Gate" (p. 9) to "prison opening his gates" (p. 120), which strikes me as less effective, though perhaps it suggests that Sterne tried where possible to avoid the impersonal pronoun. Equally difficult to explain is his emendation of the original "as infallible as the Rule appears at first Sight, yet, when you look nearer to it... you find it liable to so much Error" (pp. 5–6) to "... you see it liable to so much error" (p. 114). The change suggests a difference, perhaps, between "discovering the inevitable" and "observing the probable." Or perhaps Sterne was merely tightening his diction by paralleling more closely "sight" and "look" in the first part of the sentence. At the end of the sermon he again deletes the word "finds" in the phrase "like a *British Judge* in this Land of Liberty, who... declares that glorious Law which he finds already written" (p. 26) and puts "knows" in its place (p. 149). At the same time he adds "good sense" as a further attribute of "this Land" and deletes "glorious." One might be tempted to suggest a movement in Sterne's mind from a religion of law discoverable outside oneself to a religion of perceptions recognized from within, but the evidence is really too slim to construct a very convincing argument.

A second major category of alterations is the result of Sterne's urge toward conciseness. To be sure, he cut fewer than 140 words from his original 3,700 and 109 of them occur in two deleted passages, one of 50 words, the other of 59 words (pp. 19–20, 24). In both instances, no additional transition was required; the sermon proceeds with its continuity unimpaired. Sterne, however, was not so concerned with shortening his sermon as with tightening his phrasing, and these major deletions are accompanied by numerous instances where Sterne drops an unnecessary word or phrase (see section 4 of the Appendix). Several categories are distinguishable: (1) the identification of a speaker is deleted, as "you will say" (p. 1), "continues he" (p. 14), and "says he" (p. 24); in the last two examples, Sterne is quoting Scripture; (2) sentences or clauses are given more firm closure, as in the examples *d*, *e*, and *f* of the Appendix; and (3) superfluous phrasal elements are eliminated, as in *g*, *h*, *i*, *j*, and *k*. A few modifiers are also deleted: "a studied System of *religious* Cruelty" (p. 22) becomes "a studied system of cruelty" (p. 143); "long Confinement" (p. 22) becomes "confinement" (p. 143); and "but cruelly not suffer'd to depart" (p. 23) is wisely altered to "but not suffered to depart" (p. 146). Interestingly enough, these alterations represent a toning down of the horrors of the Inquisition to which Trim responds so memorably. Far from having to elaborate his earlier description to produce Trim's tears, Sterne was actually able to remove a few of his more dramatic words, though he did add a second "hark!" to his original insistence that we listen to the "piteous groan" of the Inquisition's victim (p. 22/p. 143).

Sterne was particularly sensitive to the use of pairings linked by "and" or "or." Under section 5 of the Appendix I have noted the various times he altered such pairings, either by changing the conjunction or dropping one element of the pair. Of the few substantive variants between lifetime editions of *Tristram*, this hesitancy over "and" versus "or" occurs several times; Sterne seems to have weighed heavily the distinction between amplification, alternatives, and redundancy.

There remains to be discussed the several additions Sterne made in the 1760 version of the sermon (see section 6 of the Appendix). Two additions help to create the impression of an actual, involved moral figure behind the sermon. In the original Sterne writes: "I know their Success in the World depends upon the Fairness of their Characters; —that they cannot hurt me without hurting themselves more" (p. 18). In *Tristram* (p. 136), the following is inserted after "characters": "In a word, —I'm persuaded"; then the sentence continues as before.

Similarly, in the earlier version, Sterne writes: "I have nothing left to cast into the Scale to ballance this Temptation. —I must lay at the Mercy of Honour" (p. 19). In *Tristram*, a question is created out of the first sentence, and its answer is provided in a new sentence: "What have I left to cast into the opposite scale to balance this temptation? —Alas! I have nothing, —nothing but what is lighter than a bubble." And then, "I must lay at the mercy of HONOUR" (p. 137).

In a sentence that Sterne was particularly dissatisfied with, he made four slight modifications, each of which indicates his sensitivity to the problems of style. The original reads, "If any Man . . . thinks it impossible for Man to be such a Bubble to himself, —I must refer him a Moment to his Reflections, and shall then venture to trust the Appeal with his own Heart" (p. 11). In the 1760 version "for Man" becomes "for a man," "his Reflections," "his own reflections," "shall" becomes "will," and "the Appeal," "my appeal." The effect is an increase in specificity and, as in the additions just discussed, an increased awareness of the moral voice behind the sermon.

In the paragraph of the original describing the "Prisons of the Inquisition" (pp. 22–23), Sterne invites his auditors to go with him, and in a series of imperatives, instructs them to "See," "Behold," "Observe," etc. In *Tristram* this one paragraph is extended over five pages by Trim's emotional interpolations, and Sterne twice adds the imperative "See" to ensure the continuity of the description, in spite of the many interruptions.

I have not covered in this brief discussion every variant between the two versions of Sterne's sermon, but certainly some primary patterns are now evident. While Sterne's foremost concern was to copy his earlier sermon verbatim, he simply could not refrain from exercising some editorial judgments upon his earlier work. What emerges is a collection of slight tamperings which illustrate, perhaps better than wholesale rewriting would have done, Sterne's serious concern for each word and sentence he wrote. It is by observing carefully just such evidence that one becomes aware of certain elements governing Sterne's brilliant style, especially its precise diction and its sharp economy of expression. There is often obscurity in the pages of *Tristram Shandy*, but rarely is it the result of any failure on Sterne's part.

The image of Tristram writing his first word and praying to God for the second (a most religious way of writing) is clearly shown to be part of Sterne's fiction. It is a point that has been made many times, but there is value in reiterating it from the evidence of the sermon: Sterne was a precise, meticulous stylist who wrote his first word, and his second and his third—and then as often as not he returned to the first and reconsidered it.

NOTES

1 *The Abuses of Conscience* (York, 1750), p. 9. Hereafter cited in the text. Sterne added Gothic lettering to the original "*Cases*" and "*Reports*"; I have not considered typographical changes in this discussion.
2 *The Life and Opinions of Tristram Shandy* ([York], 1760), II, 121. Hereafter cited in the text.
3 Melvyn New, "*Tristram Shandy* and Heinrich van Deventer's *Observations*," *Papers of the Bibliographical Society of America*, 69 (1975), 84-90.
4 Sterne also emended a statement concerning the religious hypocrite's belief that he had "discharged faithfully his Duty to God" (p. 20) to "discharged truly his duty to God" (p. 138).
5 Cf. the emendation of "which a soft and flattering Hand" (p. 12) to "which a soft and a flattering hand" (p. 125).
6 Published as Sermon XII in vol. IV of the *Sermons of Mr. Yorick* (London, 1766). The copy-text for this version was unquestionably the 1750 version and not the one in *Tristram Shandy*.

APPENDIX: Alterations in the "Abuses of Conscience" Sermon

In the following selective comparison, I have italicized key words and ignored Sterne's italics in order to avoid confusion.
1.   1750: This is not Fact: —So that the common Consolation which some good Christian or other is hourly administring to himself, —That he thanks God, his Mind does not misgive him; and that, consequently, he has a good Conscience, because he has a quiet one. —As current as the Inference is...
       1760: This is not fact: —So that the common consolation... because he has a quiet one, —is *fallacious*; —and as current...

2. a. *1750*: tho' one is not willing even to suspect the Appearance of so *great* a Virtue, as moral Honesty
   1760: ... so *amiable* a virtue as moral honesty
   b. *1750*: This Principle that there can be Religion without *Morality*
   1760: this principle, that there can be religion without *mercy*
   c. *1750*: amuses himself with a few Instrumental *Duties* of Religion
   1760: amuses himself with a few instrumental *parts* of religion
   d. *1750*: that BEING, *before* whom thou art finally to give an Account
   1760: that Being, *to* whom thou art finally to give an account
3. a. *1750*: 'tis no *Rarity* to see a Man whose real moral *Merit* stands very low
   1760: 'tis no *prodigy* to see a man whose real moral *character* stands very low
   b. *1750*: perceives no Penalty or Forfeiture incurr'd
   1760: perceives no penalty or forfeiture *of goods and chattels* incurred
   c. *1750*: But here the Mind has all the Evidence and Facts within *herself*.... Now, —as Conscience is nothing else but the Knowledge which the Mind has within *itself*
   1760: ... the knowledge which the mind has within *herself*
   d. *1750*: this unwary Traveller, —too apt, God knows, to go astray of *himself*, —and confidently speak Peace to *his* Soul, when there is no Peace
   1760: ... and confidently speak peace to *himself* ...
   e. *1750*: at the last, meets Death *with as much Unconcernedness*, —perhaps, much more so than a much better Man
   1760: ... meets death *as unconcernedly;* —perhaps much more...
   1766: ... meets death *with as much unconcern*—perhaps, much more...
   f. *1750*: as infallible as the Rule appears at first *Sight*, yet, when you *look* nearer to it... you *find* it liable to so much Error
   1760: ... you *see* it liable to so much error
   g. *1750*: But like a British Judge in this Land of Liberty, who makes no new Law, —but faithfully declares that glorious Law which he *finds* already written
   1760: ... in this land of liberty and *good sense*, who makes no new law, but faithfully declares that law which he *knows* already written
4. a. *1750*: Surely, *you will say,* if there is any Thing in this Life
   1760: Surely if there is any thing in this life
   b. *1750*: Whether he be rich, *continues he,* or whether he be poor
   1760: whether he be rich, or whether he be poor
   c. *1750*: By their Fruits, *says he,* ye shall know them
   1760: By their fruits ye shall know them
   d. *1750*: you find it liable to so much Error, from a false Application *of it*
   1760: you see it liable to so much error from a false application
   e. *1750*: contrary to all the Workings of Humanity *within*, he shall ruin
   1760: contrary to all the workings of humanity, he shall ruin
   f. *1750*: add no farther to the Length of this Discourse than by two or three Rules, deducible from *what has been said*
   1760: ... deducible from *it*
   g. *1750*: and, at *the* last, meets Death
   1760: and at last meets death

h. *1750*: 'Tis nothing *else* but a cunning Contexture
   1760: 'tis nothing but a cunning contexture
i. *1750*: finds *perhaps* no express Law broken
   1760: finds no express law broken
j. *1750*: and indeed has so much *of* Honesty, as to pretend to none; who would *yet* take it as the bitterest Affront
   1760: and indeed has so much honesty as to pretend to none, who would take it . . .
k. *1750*: it will be found *at last* to rest upon
   1760: it will be found to rest upon
5. a. *1750*: Approbation *or* Censure
   1760: approbation *and* censure
   b. *1750*: Inclination *or* Custom
   1760: inclination *and* custom
   c. *1750*: corrupt *or* misguided
   1760: corrupt *and* misguided
   d. *1750*: Scorn *and* Contempt
   1760: scorn
   e. *1750*: *my best and* most
   1760: my most
   f. *1750*: *devout and* religious
   1760: religious
6. a. *1750*: I know their Success in the World depends upon the Fairness of their Characters; —that they cannot hurt me without hurting themselves more
   1760: . . . of their characters. —*In a word,* —*I'm persuaded* that they cannot . . .
   b. *1750*: *I have nothing left* to cast into the Scale to ballance this Temptation. —I must lay at the Mercy of Honour
   1760: *What have I left* to cast into the *opposite* scale to balance this temptation? —*Alas! I have nothing,* —*nothing but what is lighter than a bubble.* —I must lay at the mercy of HONOUR
   c. *1750*: If any Man . . . thinks it impossible *for* Man to be such a Bubble to himself, —I must refer him a Moment to *his Reflections,* and *shall* then venture to trust *the* Appeal with his own Heart
   1760: If any man . . . thinks it impossible for *a* man to be such a bubble to himself, —I must refer him a moment to *his own reflections,* and *will* then venture to trust *my* appeal with his own heart
   d. *1750*: Observe the last Movement of that horrid Engine. —What Convulsions it has thrown him into
   1760: Observe the last movement of that horrid engine! [I would rather face a cannon, quoth *Trim,* stamping.]—"*See* what convulsions . . .

Kant: Origin and Utopia

WALTER MOSER

Speaking of Kant without touching on any one of his *Critiques* may seem pretentious. For the purposes of this study, however, I made the tactical choice of dealing only with shorter texts, in order to treat the double problem of origin and utopia in its discursive and textual realization in Kant. Basically, the term 'discourse' here has the definition used in the work of Michel Foucault,[1] though, contrary to his questioning of the units as given, I propose as units the discursive fields as historically indicated by their institutional delimitations. 'Text' designates the particular, material realization of a discourse showing internal structure and functioning.

My reading of Kant centers on two of his treatises, *Conjectural Beginnings of Human History* (1786) and *Eternal Peace: A Philosophical Project* (1795), with the *Universal Natural History and Theory of the Heavens*,[2] Kant's great scientific treatise of 1755, kept in the background for purposes of comparison. I will examine particularly in the first two texts (hereafter *Conjectures* and *Project*) the face-to-face encounter of origin and utopia in terms of discursive and textual choices and constraints resulting from the specificity of this double problem. Since this conflict manifests itself in most of Kant's writings and thus touches different discursive fields—including the philosopher's physical, anthropological, and political lucubrations in the three texts proposed above—it enables the reader to analyze the connections between these fields as well as their contribution to Kant's discursive system.

While the *Conjectures* and the *Project* may be only minor works in Kant's canon, they are nonetheless complex enough to challenge anyone wishing to make them the object and locus of a process of critical reading. Of particular interest to discourse analysis is Kant's awareness of the discursive problems he faces when he is about to cross the borderlines of established fields of discourse. His explicit discussions of how a philosopher should write about origin and utopia provide decisively a focus of special interest in these two texts.

To begin on the thematic level, let us examine two terms which first appear in Kant's cosmogony as part of his mechanical world model, but which then remain constantly present in his writings between 1755 and 1795:

> We must consider the fact that creation cannot be constant, unless we oppose to the general force of attraction a force which moves in all its parts, an equally generalized opposing force which adequately resists the *propensity* [Hang] of the first to ruin and disorder unless therefore we add centrifugal forces which, combined with the *central penchant* [Zentralneigung = force of gravity] determine a systematic and general constitution: we will be obliged to posit a general centre for the whole universe. This centre will ensure the coherence of all the parts and permit us to conceive of nature as a single system. (T, I, 337; my italics)

Since "all worlds form a single edifice" (T, I, 337), Kant's world machine to be unified needs a central point of origin and two opposing forces. These elements account for the existence and functioning of the whole universe. They also determine the following chronology of the cosmogonic process of creation:

1. Out of the initial chaos, the establishment of a center and origin of the process of creation.
2. The force of gravity which makes all particles of matter fall towards this center.
3. An opposing force (repulsion of particles) which allows the heavenly bodies to come into being by slightly inclining the movement of these particles.

4. A provisional equilibrium between these two forces. Established locally, this equilibrium is synonymous with the existence of a single world.

Once the decisive inclination has been introduced, the created world is subjected to a general declivity which makes it run steadily down a slope toward a final catastrophe. *Hang* and *Neigung* thus become key terms in Kant's model of the physical world. The mechanical conceptualization they imply, however, is not restricted to the understanding of cosmic phenomena; it also applies to the moral world. These two terms are found throughout Kant's textual production, expressed in not only chronological but also discursive units. They contribute to the systematic coherence of Kant's "work,"[3] although, beyond any textual idiosyncrasy, they belong to the widespread mechanical world conception. Depending on Kant's subject, then, as well as upon the immediate contexts in which the words appear, *Hang* and *Neigung* may have many different translations—for example, 'slope', 'slant', 'penchant', 'propensity', 'inclination', 'declivity'.

Kant tends to think of the act of creation as an act of bending, of inclining like a decisive push to one side which sets off a developmental sequence governed by irrevocable laws. We know that in 1755 he conceived his cosmogony in the form of immense Newtonian mechanics, and he disagreed with the master only as to the precise point or moment when the hand of God started and then left his admirable machine.[4] It is less well known, however, that this mechanistic model persists in discourses other than that of physics, in much later texts, as recurrent thematic and metaphorical patterns.

In the *Theory of the Heavens,* the central subject, the solar system, appears as an immense ball abandoned to the ecliptic inclination of the galaxy. Likewise man, in Kant's anthropological system, finds himself involved in the slant of his inclinations, while Kant's political theory shows its subjects—whether individuals or peoples—abandoned to a natural propensity to war. The mechanical analogy, leaping discursive fences, connects cosmogony, anthropology, and political science in a general declivity which provokes the irrevocable decline contained in the most perfect laws of mechanics.

Yet these laws of movement irresistibly foresee the end of all movement and thereby the destruction of any subject who is involved in them. The slant of the cosmos leads naturally to the *end of all things*, to quote the title of another of Kant's treatises. This is the thrust of the mechanics of movement, which in turn comprises a natural tendency (*natürlicher Hang*) to decadence (*Verfall*), since "all things which have a beginning and are born carry the mark of a limited nature, and must die and come to an end" (T, I, 339), and "everything which has a beginning, can only approach its ruin, and will come closer to it as the distance is greater from its point of origin" (T, I, 371). A necessary logic relates the beginning directly to the end and postulates that neither of the two terms may be thought without the other. But what end is this which is inevitably inscribed in the nature of created things? Since it is given from the moment, and by the act of creation itself, it seems worthwhile to maintain the symmetry of origin and end by proposing a successive narrative reconstruction of the path of the universe and of man, as it is found in Kant.

In the beginning, there was generalized dispersion of matter in space. One particle of matter, heavier and more dense than the others, began to attract them, and thus constituted itself as origin and center of the universe. Order emerged from chaos; there was a generalized and permanent precipitation of particles toward the center, because of increasing gravity. Yet the force of repulsion working among the particles turned them ever so slightly from their rectilinear parallel fall and made them enter into a movement which became circular and gave rise to the formation of suns, planets, moons. The play between the two forces held the created world in equilibrium for a long time, without being able to prevent, in the long run, all matter from falling into the solar center; and this matter, following an explosion, was again dispersed in particles into space.

By the same token, man follows an analogous pattern in the Kantian system. In the beginning he was able to stand upright, to speak and to think, "in a kind of garden, in a kindly gentle climate" (C, VI, 86). He lived within the limitations of animal instinct. One day he transgressed these limits stated by the voice of God. He took his liberty upon himself and knew the desire which led him to warlike behavior. From then on, he lived in a state of war. When, to acquire more security and strength, he founded states, war was transposed from individuals to these states. They became so powerful and so implacable in their hostility that man ended by exterminating his own race, thereby creating eternal peace, the "eternal peace of the cemetery" (P, 1).

Each of these stories is at once complete and incomplete. In fact, they both relate, from beginning to end, a mechanical unfolding which comes directly to its declining term. Each posits a decisive moment manifested as an arbitrary deviation, an aleatory distance from a generalization set up as universal law: an imperceptible lateral inclination (T, I, 360) from a vertical fall,[5] or a minimal waver from instinctual obedience (C, VI, 88). In both cases this deviance is of little importance in itself, but will be capital and decisive for future developments (C, VI, 89), whether it decides the formation of worlds, or whether it launches man into his history.

And yet these narrative reconstructions do not tell the whole story—nor the history. They give only one version of the story, and take into account only one impetus among the vectors which form its context. The problem is that there is, in Kant, opposed to the force which operates in the direction of ruin, and is explained by the laws of mechanics, a counterforce which is called upon to balance the machine and to defer, if not to overthrow, the negative outcome of history.

To shift to the plane of this counterforce in natural history, we have merely to round out the cosmological narration above by adding that it simply represents the fate of one particular world among a virtual infinity of solar systems; the localized ruin of this world is compensated for by the creation of other worlds, elsewhere. Kant's cosmogony, proceeding from an origin-center toward infinite space, presents creation as a permanent and repetitive process during which the emergence of worlds from chaos and their subsequent return to that state can be thought of as occurring simultaneously in different places, or successively in the same place. This cosmogonic machine is constructed in such a way as to give free rein at once to the two opposite forces of history.

In its turn, human history does not put on so impressive a show, but is infinitely more complex. The counterforce should first of all prevent this history's ending in a final catastrophe. It should therefore carry with it a means to replace the satirical vision of tomblike eternal peace, the negative utopia to which Kant refers at the beginning of his *Project*, with the vision of positive utopia. This history of man-the-animal with his ill-fated penchants must be superseded by that of moral and reasoning man, capable of effecting a decisive overthrow. In Kant, both visions will be written into the concept of 'human nature' in its largest sense, including the physical and the moral. It thus becomes necessary to write, and to *do* in such a way—we will see how the writing will become such doing—that the course of human history may reascend the slope of destructive inclinations to approach a positive utopia. The opposing force which in cosmogonic mechanics is provided by the laws of nature (that is, the centrifugal force which suspends and deviates the fall) is, within the domain of moral man, to be defined and directed by a law that man will make for himself.

Before relegating the *Theory of the Heavens* to the background of my study, I would like to point out that both cosmological and human history begin with a fall, a fall of particles of matter and the moral fall of man.[6] These parallel processes indicate the analogical coherence of the various discursive fields in which Kant inscribes his philosophical activity. At the moment of the moral fall, the penchants which involve man on his destructive path are activated simultaneously with a possibility of reversal which would open up the perspective of infinite progress. Human history, from its first moment, manifests itself as a contradictory progression resulting from the conflict of two opposing sides whose potential for paradox is, however, deferred by the dimension of time. This double movement of human nature is summed up in Kant's philosophy of history and anthropology as the concept of 'perfectibility'. The task that Kant sets himself in these fields consists of exposing and resolving the paradoxes of perfectibility by writing a project for eternal peace which would not be that of the cemetery. In other words, he abstracts human history from the mechanistic model.

The following diagram attacks the double question of origin and

Kant: Origin and Utopia / 259

utopia more directly by showing the structural coherence of the problem as presented in Kant's two texts. In this diagram a certain number of elements and articulations are superimposed, because each of the two texts has a tripartite structure, even though one elaborates the beginnings of human history while the other is focused on its final destination. This three-part, two-hinged structure is perfectly regular. Setting aside the irreversible time vector, the whole diagram is symmetrical, with the symmetry of the original and the utopian in comparison to the present being the most striking. The present, or the historical, occupies the central position in relationship to which the two sections of nonpresent relate to each other in terms of functional equivalence. On either side, they represent the aim of a projection, and their equivalence is indicated textually by the use of the same terms ('nature', 'eternal peace') on both sides. This partial identity of

Origin	Present			Utopia
paradise (nostalgic projection)	history			eternal peace (utopian projection)
	animal tendencies instinct	in conflict with	rational progress liberty	
		perfectibility		
eternal peace dreamed of natural state without (human) laws	state of war (= human misery and indispensable means to perfection)			eternal peace legislated perfected art become nature again
	the fall (contract with God broken)	social contract among individuals	establishment of federal contract among states	
poet's discursive zone: the golden age	historiographer's discursive zone			poet's discursive zone: Crusoe-type stories
	transition-partition origin/present		transition-partition present/utopia	
		philosopher's discursive locus		

the two extreme zones indicates that temporal linearity, essential for the historic zone, becomes reversible and circular in connection with origin and utopia.

As the origin of all perspective and the meeting point for the nostalgic and utopian sides of perfectibility, the present also, and above all, constitutes the place and moment of discursive utterance. All the discourses that Kant envisages, discusses, and uses are uttered from this medium between past and future, as the diagram indicates. The poet, the historiographer, and the philosopher write in the present, but their discourses diverge according to their places of reference, their objectives, and the truth of their texts. By means of this diversification, the three discourses in play are capable of covering the whole of the tripartite field as proposed in the diagram.

Facts of historical reality, whether natural or human—that is, what I have called 'present' by opposition to that which is situated either in a virtual elsewhere or in a beyond which is past or yet to come— constitute the object of historiography. Based on documents (C, VI, 85) it refers to the real, and it is on the basis of this referentiality that its truth is established. Kant speaks of "established and accredited history as real documentation" (C, VI, 85). Further, its textual unfolding must follow the laws of narrative causality by copying the supposed structure of events outside the text, which allows for controlling its proper functioning as well as its truth value.

Poetic activity, conversely, rises out of the imaginary; its field of reference falls outside the present, the "serious," and the useful (C, VI, 101). For this reason, Kant excludes poetry from referential verification. Since it conveys only empty and vain desire, and refers to phantoms (*Schattenbilder*, C, VI, 100), it cannot speak truly. Consequently, Kant finds that it has to be rejected as an "arbitrary fiction" (T, I, 232, 243), likely to invalidate any serious discourse containing even the smallest part of it. That is why he begins by eliminating "novelistic fiction"[7] with a scornful gesture when, in a preliminary note to the *Conjectures*, he discusses his method of writing the beginnings of human history. He is even more explicit and vehement in his negative attitude toward poetry at the end of the same treatise when he denounces the authors of "Robinson Crusoes and voyages to the

South Seas" (C, VI, 101), accusing them of feeding "vain regrets," particularly in the form of the "phantom of the golden age." Thus Kant totally condemns utopian fiction, even though his examples belong to retrospective utopia rather than to prospective utopia.

In rejecting utopia, Kant rejects more generally any text on paradise or eternal peace insofar as it rises from poetic discourse and manifests itself as entirely fiction. If he thereby eliminates the poetic in utopia, he nevertheless retains utopia as a conceptual category, since the *Project* has an undeniably utopian dimension. As for its discursive manifestation, we must therefore situate it elsewhere than in the historic or the poetic.

Kant has left us no choice; among the three discourses to which he limited his discussion, only the philosophical remains. Since all three sections of the diagram are covered by poetry and historiography, philosophy must be the discourse of the hinges. In fact, Kant refers in both treatises to the two articulations which, while they are decisive and capital, figure in the diagram only as limits, as lines of transition and partition. The thematic content of these two articulations is the breaking of the contract with God, which coincides with the entry into human history in the *Conjectures*, and, in the *Project*, the establishment by contract of a global federation stipulating the definitive end of the state of war. These two texts take as their object a question of thresholds, if we determine a text by that to which it refers.

The poet cannot speak truly; the historiographer must speak truly—but where do we place the philosopher in relationship to truth? The problem goes beyond the dichotomy between referential truth and falsehood. In order to situate it more clearly, the analysis of the texts must be pursued. In the *Conjectures*, to write the origin of human history, and to introduce the concepts of 'liberty', 'rationality', and 'perfectibility', Kant says he must write as a "philosopher of nature" (C, VI, 85). The conjectural history that he tells is then halfway between the objective reality of the historiographer and the insubstantiality of novelistic fiction. Based on experience as well as "imagination accompanied by reason" (C, VI, 85), this conjectural discourse proceeds from Kant's initial and frank postulation that "our point of departure must be that which human reason cannot deduce as having any previous natural cause" (C, VI, 86). That is, it must comprise the following:

1. the existence of completely developed man;
2. a couple, for the propagation of the species;
3. a single couple, so that war will not break out immediately;
4. a sort of garden with an evenly mild climate;
5. man knowing how to stand upright and walk;
6. his knowing how to speak and think.

The constitution of this initial situation follows closely the biblical model to which Kant explicitly refers. Given the complexity of the human situation and the great many preliminary conditions that it implies, it is clear that what interests the philosopher is not the original moment of creation,[8] but rather the one in which man takes on his identity as historical and anthropological subject. Kant thus eliminates at the outset the controversial and unrewarding question of the state of nature: "I consider [man] only after he has taken a considerable step in the art of using his forces and consequently I do not start off from nature in its absolutely raw state" (C, VI, 86). As formulated by Kant, the question of origin does not aim to resolve the well-known dichotomies nature/culture, animal/man which underlie a great many eighteenth-century texts, and baffle those writers who try to separate the terms. Kant's entry into a historical perspective does not therefore posit a clean break with the concept of a state of nature, but rather indicates the threshold of a zone of conflict: the present articulated by the two sides of perfectibility. The act of transgression which launches the course of human history certainly takes man across the limits of animal instinct, but not out of the animality, which, on the contrary, will continue as an element of human nature, to determine historical reality. Between origin and present Kant understands a relationship which is at once continuous and discontinuous; that is why I use the expression "transition-partition" to describe the philosopher's discursive locus. I mean here that Kant's philosophical version of origin is part of an ambivalent discursive technique which, by pushing binary logic beyond its limits, threatens to undermine the logical foundations of representation and referentiality because it is neither false nor true.

By declaring this practice conjectural, Kant might avoid the danger of ambivalence, but then, he faces the paradox that historical truth is based, chronologically speaking, on mere conjecture.

History, the field for perfectibility, is seen as a process of conflict. When made concrete in the relationships among individuals and institutions, this conflict takes the form of war, an "incessant state" or at least a "permanent danger" (C, VI, 98), which causes "the greatest evils ever to overwhelm civilized peoples" (C, VI, 99) and determines the course of historic events. The outcome of this state of war can be either perfection or destruction, according to the two slopes mentioned previously. Although in the *Project* Kant sees the two possible ends of history as being logically equivalent, since they both lead to eternal peace, there is no doubt that he opted for perfection. He chooses teleologically and imposes his choice from the first moment: "The question of knowing whether man has won or lost in this change [the fall] is no longer asked, if we look at the destination of his race, which resides in a progressive movement toward perfection" (C, VI, 92). Man's achievement of this *telos* is so imperative to Kant that he very explicitly interprets even war as a positive agency of it. In the *Project*, he defines nature as that which carries this destination within itself and which sees to its execution. Nature's definitive end for man, her supreme creature, is of course eternal peace, but there are provisional means for reaching it:

> These are her preparatory arrangements:
> 1) She has in every climate provided for the existence of man.
> 2) She has by means of war dispersed them, in order to populate the most inhospitable regions.
> 3) She has, by the same means, compelled them to contract relations more or less legal. (P, p. 29)

In these circumstances, war becomes nature's method for populating the surface of the earth—against the otherwise contrary tendency of men—which must be seen as a stage on the road to perfection. In the historical analysis of his time that Kant gives in the *Conjectures*, he considers that war has not ceased to play this positive role: "Therefore in the degree of culture arrived at by the human race, war is an indispensable means to further its perfection; and it is only after the conclusion of this culture (God knows when) that eternal peace would be beneficial and become for that reason possible" (C, VI, 99-100). Peace through war! Or, as it is stated in the *Project*, nature's "mechanical march evidently announces the grand aim of producing, among men, against their intention, harmony from the very bosom of discord" (P, p. 27). This perspective on discord may be surprising, but its discursive operation is perfectly logical. The paradox lurking within it is not realized, thanks to the distinction between means and end, and to the dimension of time.

The question of knowing how and when the reversal from war to peace will happen remains unanswered. Kant suggests that this would be divine knowledge. However, he also does everything he can to put the philosopher in a position of divinity, since his project for eternal peace is nothing less than an attempt to determine the moment of and the means for entry into that benign state. Thus, by presenting himself as the uttering subject of a political utopian discourse, the philosopher claims a godlike position. His performance as author, therefore, gives him access to power, at least as far as power derives from knowledge and discursive practice. But he also attempts to gain access to political power by stating, by means of a secret article in his text, that the prince is bound to listen to the philosopher's advice. Between God, as the one who produces an efficient text, and the prince, as the one who makes decisions, the philosopher gives himself a privileged position through his discursive activity.

To elaborate on this power, obtained through writing, let us recall the symmetrical structure of the diagram. On the side of origin, an act of disobedience begins the course of history and becomes the object of the conjectural discourse. God has made a contract with man, in the double form of permission and prohibition; "Instinct, this voice of God [or: voice of nature (C, VI, 88)], permitted him to eat certain things, forbade him certain others" (C, VI, 87). To establish the beginnings of human history as a philosopher, Kant merely recounts and comments on man's breaking this contract. On the side of utopia, what is it that corresponds to the discursive mode of conjectural history?

The *Project* is legislative; as a text, it represents, more precisely, an act of human legislation. Kant wrote the text for a contract destined to be ratified simultaneously at the three levels of the state, the federation of states, and all citizens in all states. The symmetry between the two moments of transition-partition now begins to show a slight imperfection, because there is disjunction between breaking and establishing a contract, between divine and human legislation, and especially between a hypothetical narration and a bill of law. The question of the philosophical utopia must refer to the relationship between the writing of the law and eternal peace, and in consequence between legislation and utopia. Here is the beginning of the second section of the *Project*: "With men, the state of nature (status naturalis) is not a state of peace, but of war; though not of open war, at least, ever ready to break out. A state of peace must therefore be established" (P, p. 10). It is incumbent upon the legislative text to establish, found, and make (depending on the translation of the German *stiften*) peace. And "make" here must be read also in the sense of "do," as in Austin's work on speech acts, *How to Do Things with Words*.[9]

Legislative saying is, in fact, doing. By forbidding (*Verbot: leges prohibitivae*) that which may produce war and by prescribing (*Gebot: leges praescriptivae*) that which brings peace, the legislator makes speech acts. The illocutionary force of his discourse constitutes its decisive element, since its aim is to transform the world of war into a world of peace. In positing the world as other, it operates the transition-partition between the present and the utopian. The question of relating an event, a given world, becomes irrelevant; this new discursive mode is automatically situated beyond referentiality, and consequently beyond the true-false dichotomy on which Kant founded his classifications of historiographic and poetic discourses. The theory of speech acts applied to the question of juridical and legislative discourse[10] permits us, in the case of the *Project*, to give a precise answer to the question of utopia. Having rejected the poet's utopia-fiction, Kant, as a philosopher, has written a utopia-legislation. The utopian dimension of the text resides in the intention to change the present by forbidding that which causes wars, and also in the intention to produce a nonpresent world by prescribing that which will establish peace. In addition, the *Project* as a whole may be read as a promise of eternal peace. Thus it produces what has become the model example among speech acts.

The theory of the performative makes a distinction between the realization of a speech act and its success. Utopia lies entirely within that realization. If the promise, the prohibition, the prescription, are perceived in their intention to change the present, utopia is realized. But Kant also puts the question of success: what can be done so that a code has legal force, or, in terms of the speech act theory, perlocutionary force?

> For hitherto Grotius, Puffendorf, Wattel, and other useless and impotent defenders of the rights of nations, have been constantly cited in justification of war; though their code, purely philosophic or diplomatic, has never had the force of law, and cannot obtain it; states not being as yet subjected to any coercive power. There is no instance where their reasonings, supported by such respectable authorities, have induced a state to desist from its pretensions. (P, pp. 19-20)

The coercive force of the law, its effective control over the conduct of individuals and states, depends on more than its being written, on factors beyond whatever power the philosopher as text performer might have. It is true that Kant pursues this question explicitly by founding it ideally on an ethical imperative. He must nonetheless have had doubts about the perlocutionary force of his philosophical legislation, and in one of his long notes, he elaborated another aspect of his project, the ideal of a system of laws which would be perfect in its textual structure, a veritable machine of juridical formulae. Here the question of force and power is brought back into the writing of the text and, **therefore**, into the reach of the philosopher. The text must conform to the criteria of coherence, correspondence, and regularity; its phrasing must be as rigorous as that of mathematical formulae (P, p. 10). In this description of a utopian text as system, we rediscover the same postulates of quality that Kant had already stated in 1755 with respect to a perfect cosmogonic system. He proposed in 1795 that the universal value, the immutable quality of perfect legislation, be founded on the perfection of its textual mechanism. Again, the possibility of a godlike position arises: the philosopher, as text producer, could equal God, the world producer; both would be creators of a perfect machine which would function eternally.

Although it is relegated to a footnote, the mechanical model that should have been overthrown to realize the progression toward positive utopia reemerges. Forty years after the *Theory of the Heavens*, this model remains a central tendency, a kind of force of gravity in Kant's philosophical system. What has changed is that it no longer applies to the world, but rather to the realization of the text which attempts to change the world. Kant sets up the project for a perfect textual meshing comprising utopian legislation, an Utopia of utopias, in which the force of the text would ensure—or perhaps replace—the force of the law.

NOTES

1 Michel Foucault, *L'Archéologie du savoir* (Paris: Gallimard, 1969), Chapter II.
2 My readings are based on the German edition, edited by Wilhelm Weischedel: Immanuel Kant, *Werke in sechs Bänden*, 6 vols. (Darmstadt: Wissenschaftliche Buchgesellschaft, 1975). I have also used the following English translations: *Universal Natural History and Theory of the Heavens*, trans. W. Hastie (Ann Arbor: University of Michigan Press, 1969); *On History*, trans. L. W. Beck, P. E. Anchor, and E. L. Fackenheim (New York: Bobbs-Merrill, 1969), which includes *Conjectural Beginnings of Human History*; and *Perpetual Peace: A Philosophical Project*, introd. N. M. Butler (New York: Columbia University Press, 1939). At the time of writing, only the *Project* is available to me in English translation (reference: P, page). For the other two texts I am referring to the German edition while proposing my own translation (reference for the *Theory of the Heaven*: T, volume, page; for *Conjectural Beginnings*: C, volume, page).

I wish to thank Mary Louise Taylor for helping me to establish the English version of this paper.
3 I perfectly agree with Michel Foucault's questioning of what has traditionally been considered as naturally given units such as *auteur, oeuvre* (*L'Archéologie*, pp. 31–43).
4 In 1755 Kant adopted the widespread mechanistic argument: once god-the-clock-maker has started his perfectly arranged world machine, its autonomous functioning proves the infinite power and intelligence of the creator.
5 Having attended Michel Serres's seminar "Après Lucrèce," I do not hesitate to identify this minimal deviation with the CLINAMEN in Lucretius (*De Natura Rerum*, II, 292). Moreover, Kant is perfectly aware of this dangerous resemblance

with the materialistic tradition (T, I, 233–35). In order not to be accused of being an atheistic materialist, he states that this deviation has been purposely introduced by God.

6 "The first step, therefore, out of this state was from the moral point of view a fall; from the physical point of view many evils of life not known up to then were the consequences of this fall, therefore punishment" (C, VI, 93). The analogy is not perfect, however, because in the cosmogony, the fall represents a general movement established before the decisive deviation, whereas in human history, it coincides with the deviation itself.

7 In Herder's *Treatise on the Origin of Language* of 1771 (*Abhandlung über den Ursprung der Sprache* [Stuttgart: Reclam, 1966], p. 124) we can find exactly the same scornful gesture against what he calls "philosophischen Roman."

8 Herder, p. 82, makes the very same distinction between the problem of origins in theology and in philosophy.

9 J. L. Austin, *How to Do Things with Words* (London: Oxford University Press, 1973).

10 This question has been dealt with by Georges A. Legault in his doctoral dissertation "La Structure performative du language juridique," Université de Montréal, 1975.

Rudolf Erich Raspe:
The Geologist Captain Cook Refused

RUTH P. DAWSON

When Captain James Cook discovered the Hawaiian Islands for the Europeans in 1778, he gave the handsome people there a gift that stimulated their imaginations and contributed to the rapid transformation of their culture and society. It was the metal iron, an extremely useful material the Hawaiians had not known before. With it everything became easier, from cutting trees and making implements to carving decorations and preparing foods. Cook was not surprised to see how eagerly the islanders experimented with his novel present, for on his previous two voyages to the Pacific he had given other Polynesians the same gift, watched their fascination with it, and staved off their wily efforts to acquire more.

When he found Hawaii, Captain Cook was on his third great voyage, sent this time to discover the long-sought Northwest Passage. Unlike the other British searches, which had explored from the Atlantic side, Cook's was to begin from the Pacific coast of North America. He was accompanied by an illustrious staff of officers including George Vancouver, William Bligh, and James Burney. Another notable man had applied to go too, interested less in Cook's naval and geographical purposes than in the opportunity such a journey might offer for the advancement of geology. Rudolph Erich Raspe (1736–94)[1] was aware of the captain's earlier experiences with the iron-loving Polynesians and had told Cook about his idea of finding the metal on the volcanic islands of the South Pacific.

The zealous scholar from Germany had a remarkable variety of achievements to his credit. He had edited previously unknown manuscripts by Leibnitz, introduced *Ossian* and Percy's *Reliques* to the German public, written a report for the Royal Society in London on what were then called elephant teeth found in Ohio, published an elaborate book on new islands, and identified extinct volcanoes in the very woods of Hessia, the little principality where he lived. None of this counted for much, however, in light of two other of Raspe's deeds: embezzling from the Hessian Duke's coin and medal collection, of which Raspe was the curator, and fleeing from Hessian justice.[2] In England eleven years later the disgraced court scholar wrote an immensely popular collection of stories called *Baron Munchausen's Narrative of his Marvelous Travels and Campaigns in Russia,* in which the amazing Baron entertains his audience with tall tales that demonstrate his fabulous presence of mind in every emergency. Raspe, sensitive no doubt to parallels with himself, and in any case still a proud man with his university education and his scientific and literary interests, published the Baron's adventures anonymously. He never publicly claimed his lively masterpiece, and not until the nineteenth century was his authorship fully recognized.[3]

When the learned delinquent first came to London in the summer of 1775, scholarly colleagues, as yet unaware of his crimes, greeted him warmly. Since he chanced to arrive only days before Cook returned from the magnificent second voyage, Raspe was a fortunate guest at the dinner party at which the Royal Society Club welcomed back two members of the expedition. For Raspe it must have been a thrilling evening. He wished ardently to go on an expedition of almost any sort, antiquarian, scientific, or diplomatic. Now he was in a company where Cook himself sometimes dined and where most of the members, famous men in their own rights, knew the Captain well, particularly the two guests of honor that night, Johann Reinhold Forster, the naturalist on the expedition, and George, his son and assistant. Like Raspe, they were Germans.

When he heard in early 1776 that the Admiralty would send its famous explorer on yet a third voyage, Raspe saw an opportunity as good as the Forsters'. He applied to sail as the official scientist on the ship. On Cook's first voyage (1768–71) Sir Joseph Banks had done scientific work; the Forsters had been the naturalists on the second (1772–75); yet after some unsuccessful negotiation between the Admiralty and Dr. James Lind of Edinburgh, who had discovered that citrus fruit cures scurvy, no special scientific staff had been appointed for the third.[4] Raspe hoped to obtain the position, but by then he had no real chance. Before the third voyage was even planned, the news of his crimes had cut him off from most of the honorable men he had dined with that memorable evening in July 1775, and by December of his first half year in England, Raspe had become the only Fellow of the Royal Society "to be expelled on grounds of character."[5]

Despite his blemished record, Rudolf Erich Raspe was qualified to do serious geological work on Cook's expedition. On the way to getting his master's degree at the universities of Göttingen and Leipzig he had taken courses in geology, and when he started his career of scholarly publishing, the ambitious young man began working on the subject intensively. Even his first geological book, *Specimen Historiae Naturalis* (1763), received favorable attention, was still being complimented over fifty years later by the famous nineteenth-century geologist Charles Lyell, and was translated into English as recently as 1970.[6]

Specimen is worth examining briefly because it reveals some of Raspe's basic ideas, helps place him within the context of eighteenth-century geology, and shows how his geologic work could have been excellent preparation for sailing with Cook. Raspe's treatise is concerned chiefly with how mountains were formed and how what appeared to be marine fossils could be found at their peaks, a question intensely debated at the time. Raspe began with a premise that was gradually gaining attention, the idea now called actualism, which is that the processes that transformed the earth in the past can be observed actually working on it in the present.[7] In the geology of Raspe's time the opposing point of view, catastrophism, was more widespread; it explained changes in the earth through cataclysmic events such as comets or the Noachian flood. Raspe thought the proposals of such seventeenth-century catastrophists as Whiston, Woodward, and Burnet as well as the more recent theory of de Maillet were farfetched speculations, and he did not find it necessary, as he said, to "loosen the Gordonian knot in Alexandrian fashion." He continued: "The whole question concerning the evidence presented by us can be resolved more surely and with greater probability through forces which we know are active in nature and by phenomena which can occur daily and take place even now."[8]

To find evidence of the "forces which we know are active in nature," Raspe turned to a wide variety of sources. In the preface to *Specimen* he recalled his original ambitious plan: "I had in mind to assemble a complete natural history of the earth and of all its successive physical changes from the observations of philosophers and historians of all ages, so that it would be more ably and clearly understood how much the earth has changed from ancient times."[9] From our present view of geologic time, Raspe's grand study would have covered a scant second from among shifting hours, days, and years in the earth's history. Moreover, since he was searching for the changes seen and recorded by human observers, the slow, subtle effects of wind eroding hillsides or boulders grinding pebbles had little place. In fact, although he rejected the extreme of catastrophism, Raspe was quite interested in the violent natural disasters most likely to be noted in historical records. "I had begun," he wrote, "to sketch a geographic map on which would have been marked very carefully what had been changed on the surface of the earth as the result of earthquake, volcanoes, floods, through the breach of natural barriers and shores, the desiccation of swamps, the power of the sea and rivers, the violence of wind and rain and other phenomena of this kind from the remotest historical recollection."

This undertaking, however, was far too vast for the 27-year-old librarian, as he noted: "But since this requires more leisure, I here present only a small part of this history which is actually a very accurate history of the origin of new islands born from the sea through earthquake and volcanoes and of mountains uplifted within continents."[10] It is, in fact, the origin of new islands which Raspe used to give an actualist explanation of "mountains uplifted within continents." All this Raspe has condensed in the title of his work, translated as *An Introduction to the Natural History of the Terrestrial Sphere Principally Concerning New Islands Born from the Sea and Hooke's Hypothesis of the Earth on the Origin of Mountains and Petrified Bodies to be Further Established from Accurate Descriptions and Observations.*

Raspe was ever a responsive reader. Now he had, as his title announces, rediscovered the ideas of the brilliant seventeenth-century scientist Robert Hooke (1635–1703). In the introduction to his own famous *Principles of Geology,* Charles Lyell summarized Raspe's book and commented: "That Hooke's writings should have been neglected for more than half a century was a matter of astonishment to Raspe; but it is still more wonderful that his own luminous exposition of that theory should, for more than another half century, have excited so little interest."[11] Hooke's ideas and Raspe's dependence on them can be glimpsed in the title of the posthumously published work: *Lectures and Discourses of Earthquakes and Subterraneous Eruptions, Explicating the Causes of the Rugged and Uneven Face of the Earth; and What Reasons May Be Given for the Frequent Finding of Shells and other Sea and Land Petrified Substances Scattered over the Whole Terrestrial Superficies* (1705).

According to Raspe's presentation, mountains of primitive rocks had once been low places covered by an accumulation of sediments in horizontal strata, some containing fossils. Through a "subterranean force," which Raspe did not attempt to describe or explain but which he associated with earthquakes and volcanoes, the primitive rocks were thrust upward, along with their overlying beds. Through erosion much, though not all, of the sedimentary material would eventually be carried off. Thus he could explain mountains consisting essentially of primitive rocks but with fossils even on their highest peaks.

To support this theory, Raspe needed evidence that rocks, particularly sedimentary rocks, could in fact be uplifted. The best examples would be the dramatic appearance of new islands arising from the sea, and the second chapter of *Specimen* describes all the new islands that the landlocked geologist was able to find recorded in historical sources. He was not daunted by the fact that most of these islands were also volcanic, for he expected the lavas to be merely a superficial covering of newly exposed and lifted areas of sea floor. These regions should, he thought, also contain marine organisms trapped by the rise of the ocean floor, and beneath the dead shells and fish he hoped to find similar fossilized remains. This would be, then, a complete actualist analogy to the mechanism of uplift which Raspe postulated for the vexing question of fossil-topped mountains.

Of course Raspe's theory also has several distinct weaknesses. He underestimated the ability of volcanoes to form new islands completely of lava. He is quite vague about rock types, time spans, and the nature of his "subterranean force." And he did not fulfill his promise to supply examples from the Harz Mountains. Still, without ever having seen an ocean or an active volcano, Raspe wrote a successful book about new, mostly volcanic "islands born from the sea." He compensated for his lack of marine experience by reading some of the best books about the ocean then available, especially Count Luigi Ferdinando Marsigli's *Histoire physique de la mer* (1725), "the first book devoted entirely to marine science,"[12] chiefly marine biology. Raspe also referred to another important marine biologist of his century, Vitaliano Donati. Despite his location, "living inland as I do," Raspe wondered in *Specimen* about the variety and distribution of marine life, the existence and force of deep ocean currents, and the contours and composition of the ocean floor. He seemed less curious about volcanoes, perhaps because he still held a thoroughly conventional eighteenth-century view of them: they are burning mountains that require some undefined subterranean fuel and are actually stoked by splashes of sea water.

In *Specimen*, Raspe's first geological publication, he elucidated a particular theory, forced by circumstances to look for supporting evidence almost exclusively in written sources. His next geological book is quite different. *Beytrag zur allerältesten und natürlichen Historie von Hessen; oder, Beschreibung des Habichtswaldes and verschiedner andern Niederhessischen alten Vulcane in der Nachbarschaft von Cassel* (1774) was based on detailed knowledge of a particular area, which Raspe first described and then attempted to explain.

He had moved, in the meanwhile, from Hannover, where he had

been a librarian alert and persistent enough to publish the forgotten Leibnitz manuscripts there, to Kassel, where he held more positions but also had more time to himself. He seems to have tramped over all the hills and valleys surrounding the residential city until he knew every quarry and stream, every outcrop of sandstone, limestone, and basalt. He reached the startling conclusion that the Habichtswald hills, where one of the Duke's palaces was situated, were of volcanic origin. Raspe gleefully claimed that stable Germany was once the scene of jolting volcanic eruptions. He realized that many alarmed readers would wish to refute him, using, for example, the kind of historical evidence he himself had relied on in *Specimen*. Given the drastically foreshortened concept of geological time then prevalent, opponents could complain that since no historical reports even from ancient times record any volcanoes in Germany, it seemed incredible that such frightening and dangerous forces could ever have erupted there. With ironic reassurances Raspe calmed their fears of "the earth-shaking contests of Pluto and Neptune, of the furnaces of Vulcan, or what is worse, of the eternal combustion of hell," writing, "We live here on and near the ruins of our extinct volcanoes as quietly and securely as we should rest on the most bloody fields of ancient battles, or on the tombs of raging tyrants."[13] Nevertheless, to support his claim that the Habichtswald was volcanic, the saucy scholar mustered hard evidence gained from observation at the sites.

Raspe's explanation of the Habichtswald is connected with the insight that basalt is of volcanic origin. In *Beytrag* he summarized the pertinent characteristics of this rock: it generally has no parallel strata, anyway contains no fossils, and has a glassy nature not produced in water. These characteristics took the preliminary step of proving, Raspe thought, that basalt was not formed in water. On the other hand, its volcanic origin had to be deduced from the fact that basalt is found flowing from volcanoes. Raspe then identified several of the hills in the area as volcanic cones.

In this remarkable little book, Raspe demonstrated he was capable of careful observation in the field. His insights into geologic operations are decidedly advanced. Unlike *Specimen*, in this book he "described the erosive power of water, . . . observed weathering, recognized denudation on the slopes of the mountains, and described the phenomenon of contact metamorphosis."[14] He used the presence and absence of fossils in his reasoning, and examined rocks under the microscope. Without becoming entangled in any absolute chronology, he postulated the correct relative ages of the sandstone, limestone, and basalt strata he observed. Furthermore, he suggested a greatly extended time span to explain the Hessian volcanoes, writing: "Their remarkable elevation, their large extent of at least 20 English miles square, and their present exterior appearance, seem clearly to indicate, that subterraneous fermentation, heat, and fire, worked many centuries to raise and accumulate them by many eruptions upon a calcareous marine ground, and perhaps in the midst of an ancient sea; but that water, rain, frost, and the inclemencies of the atmosphere since time immemorial have been at work to destroy and to level them again." The ingenious author is even willing to go further in his ideas about volcanoes in Germany, saying they are "dispersed all over Hesse; and there seems to begin in Lower Hesse... a chain of volcanic-hills, running... to the Mayn and to the Rhine, nay perhaps through Thuringia and Franconia to the Saxonian and Bohemian mountains."[15]

Besides the controversy between actualism and catastrophism, another major geological dispute was developing in the last third of the eighteenth century—the conflict between neptunists and vulcanists. But at the time that Raspe was writing about geology, the ground was only being prepared for these two debates, and the differing scientific and philosophical implications of the ideas about the way geologic changes occur and about the physical forces behind these changes had not yet been fully explored. *Specimen* was written, it should be noted, twelve years before Abraham Gottlob Werner, the most famous neptunist of the period, began teaching at the Bergakademie in Freiberg (in 1775) and twenty-two years before the vulcanist James Hutton published his first privately circulated abstract of the *System of the Earth* (1785). Thus Raspe cannot and need not be categorized as either a vulcanist or a neptunist. In that first book, for example, he rejected the claim that wave action could explain the present shapes of mountains or the existence of tilted sedimentary beds, but neither did he imagine his "subterranean force" in terms anything like what Hutton later called "subterranean heat," and he did not envision volcanoes as shaping the world. Even in *Beytrag*, with the suggestion of ancient and widespread volcanic eruptions in Germany, Raspe seems to think that sandstone, a sedimentary rock, is probably "original" or primitive. Nevertheless, it was not enough to point out, as Raspe did in rather alchemical terms in the first chapter of *Specimen*, that he was omitting the question of "whether water or fire were the prime forces of nature and earth, and its only elements and moving force";[16] his later readers, themselves entangled in the debate, considered him a vulcanist. Not only did his undeniable interest in volcanoes draw their attention, but especially his claim that basalt was a volcanic rock, an idea that became a kind of touchstone in the argument between vulcanists and neptunists for the next half century.[17]

It was a French inspector of industries, Nicolas Desmarest, who first discovered, in 1768, that basalt was of volcanic origin, but unlike Raspe, who vigorously publicized his own scholarly work, Desmarest made his initial announcement in a short and inconspicuous article buried in the *Encyclopédie*. Although no one else paid the news much attention, one nimble mind recognized that the new idea would have startling implications for the geology of central Germany. Within a year Raspe had written two corroborating papers, one in English for the Royal Society in London, dated November 20, 1769, read February 8, 1770, and published in 1771, and the other for the Royal Society of Sciences at Göttingen, dated October 24, 1769, and also published in 1771.[18] Raspe's papers thus appeared in the same year as Desmarest's well-known report to the French Academy in 1771,[19] and in this way it was Raspe who brought the idea of volcanic basalt to Germany and probably also to England. Years later, in 1820, Goethe looking back on this achievement listed Raspe somewhat anachronistically as the first German vulcanist.[20]

Certainly when the fugitive arrived in London in person in 1775, he was eager to discuss volcanic rocks. From the start, he used his geological insights and theories as an entree to influential scientists in the city. He talked particularly happily with Sir Joseph Banks and examined rock samples the wealthy young man had collected around the world. Ever since going on Cook's first expedition to Tahiti, Banks had been one of London's most celebrated men of science; recently he had made another voyage of great interest to Raspe, for it had taken the enthusiastic Englishman to the very home of volcanoes, Iceland. After Raspe's dreadful ejection from the Royal Society in December 1775, however, the cozy winter afternoons at Banks's home must have ended, at least temporarily. As 1776 began, Raspe was more dependent than ever on the effective use of his special geological expertise. Always the skilled publicist, he rapidly finished translating *Beytrag* into English as *An Account of Some German Volcanoes and Their Productions with a New Hypothesis of the Prismatical Basaltes Established upon Facts.* He even had the cheek to give himself a kind of indirect endorsement from Banks by twice mentioning the young man's collections in some newly added footnotes. The book was well received. "The *Critical Review* gave it two pages in the same number as it noticed *The Wealth of Nations,* and the *Monthly Review* (which gave long extracts to 'show how far this learned foreigner has made himself master of the English language') was no less cordial. Even Sir Joseph Banks, who was sent a presentation copy, did it the compliment of a careful reading, whatever he may have heard or thought about the author's personal character, as his marginal notes to the British Museum copy show."[21]

How the poor German scholar must have envied the man who could finance his own expedition to Iceland. In each of Raspe's progressively improving geological works, his need for more field work is mentioned. At the end of *Specimen,* for example, he raised several fundamental questions that geology had not yet answered and concluded with a spirited plea for an expedition to explore the new islands. "To all those who rule the seas far and wide," he wrote, "I recommend that an expedition of this kind be undertaken, as large as possible and meeting the highest scientific standards."[22] Obviously, it would need to be "under the leadership of a man skilled in this field," even if that man—perhaps a talented librarian from an insignificant, landlocked German state—had not yet seen the ocean. When he wrote the reports on basalt and *Beytrag,* he had still never seen a volcanic eruption. In 1776, having sailed now to England, Raspe could readily imagine himself traveling much farther with Cook, cruising past smoking volcanoes, measuring coral atolls, and testing the sands of Tahiti.

The details of Raspe's effort to accompany the third voyage are not completely known. The episode is not mentioned by Cook's or Raspe's biographers and is directly recorded, as far as I can tell, only in a single unpublished letter, which the British Library has kindly allowed me to use.[23] Raspe wrote the letter to Captain Cook on April 22, 1776. Evidently his application had already been rejected, yet he could not resist outlining what he had planned to accomplish on the voyage. In fact, although he put on a resigned appearance, Raspe probably still thought he might somehow induce the Captain to take him along. After all, the poor fugitive had little left to sustain him besides hopes. In the letter he intended to impress the Captain, on the one hand, with his geological credentials and, on the other, with the practical nature of his work. He particularly disparaged wild speculation.

Raspe enclosed a book that was supposed to show his point of view and demonstrate, of course, his qualifications. Probably it was the just published *Account of Some German Volcanoes,* appropriately subtitled so as to reiterate his twin emphasis: *An Essay of Physical Geography for Philosophers and Miners.* This wording also illustrates one of the circumlocutions necessary before the introduction of the word *geology.* Here Raspe used "physical geography"; in the letter itself he referred to the "natural history of the Earth."

The opening of the letter is direct and unadorned and leads immediately to the two essential themes of science and practicality and the idea that such work needs and deserves further support.

> Chelsea. At Mr. Cheddintons
> five field Row.
> April 22, 1776

Sir

I take the liberty to present You inclosed some of my published observations which I desire You to consider as a detached part of a general natural history of the Earth, planned less for speculation than for usefull practical Science. As it is established upon facts only I am conscious that it will agree with Nature better than the many philosophical Romances, which some learned men have hatched in their closets. But some facts want still to be ascertained and some of my principles, deduced from facts, should and might be, perhaps with advantage to the undertaker, tried by fair experiment. In this and many other respects I might have sailed with You around the world; and I take the liberty to point out some objects, which will be worth Your while and which I recommend to Your occasional notice.

1., The anchoring grounds being hitherto but examined in nautical respects, deserve to be examined in a mineralogical respect, which may be easily done, as the Anchors commonly bring up some part of the ground. The moments, chiefly to be attended to, are
2., Whether it is a pure or mixed Substance?
3., Whether calcareous, argillaceous, siliceous or metallic?
4., Whether volcanic or not?
5., _____ mixed with calcined or petrified Shells or other marine bodies?
6., If it should prove to be calcareous, which appears by its effervescence with Acids and by its calcination in fire, the question is whether it be a substance produced by decomposed Shells and Corals? Some Philosophers have, too rashly I think, supposed that all the stratified limestones and limestone mountains are produced by such decompositions.
7. Submarine white marble
8. And calcareous Tophus and incrustations deserve particular notice; as
9. Every submarine petrification, whether animal or mineral.
10. If the ground should prove to be volcanic, which undoubtedly is the case in many places near the volcanic Islands, samples of those submarine Substances will be an improvement to Mineralogy. The submarine Pumice Stones are entirely different from those that are formed in the Volcanos above water. Many Submarine Lava's may be as different from those formed and cooled above the Level of the Sea, not only in respect of their form but likewise in respect to the crystallisations, which they commonly are observed to contain.
11. In the Volcanic Islands or parts of the world the prismatical or columnar Basaltes deserves notice in respect of its form
12. And its Situations, whether it be washed by the Sea? or appear to have been formerly covered by Seawater? which is the case, if marine beds should be found superincumbent on it or on a higher level.
13. The native phase of the green New Sealand Jade has not been hitherto neither examined nor described. Probably it will be found sticking as flint in Soap- or Racon-Stone. Serpentine-Stone rocks are likely to be met with in the neighbourhood.
14. The volcanic cement, puzzolana or Tarras is an usefull ballast, if You should want any or have no better.

15. The hot rocks near the Volcano's, burning or extinct, commonly deposit tartarous Sediments, which may be best examined by Samples brought to England.

16. Iron cannot fail to be found at Otaheitee, and in many other volcanic Islands of the South-Sea. It is a constituent part of the Lavas, and You are sure to find it in the form of black and magnetical Sand mixed perhaps with other Sands, and washed from the volcanic ashes and rocks either by rain or brookwater. It may be found in many other forms; and would be an acceptable discovery for the Otaheiteans, worth Your and the Admiralities benevolence to encourage.

17. Anything like flint, Chalcedony, Agathe, Porphyry, Jasper or crystallisation found in volcanic countries is instructive, especially if samples still sticking in their matrix should be brought home; and

18. Any calcareous Stone, and marble, or Granite and Slate in volcanic countries deserves notice.

19. Among the volcanic crystallizations is now and then found a species either in loose Lava or in the Ashes which is of a greenish colour, perhaps of a brownish too, semitransparent; truncated on both sides; rifled on the Surface longitudinally and of a roundish columnar form, similar to this drawing . It is scarce ever of a fingers bigness or length; and is endowed with the double Electricity. There is plenty of these Crystallisations in Brazil. They are known there perhaps under the name of Brasilian Turmalines, a name which the Dutch I fancy have given to a similar electric Stone found in Ceylon. You would greatly oblige the Curious to make some enquiries for this electric Stone in the volcanic countries You shall see, or in Brasil or in the East Indies. At Batavia these Stones go and are sold under the name of *Ashentrekker* which denotes its quality to attract and repell ashes if somewhat heated.

20. The Electricity I mentionned before causes me to desire You to observe if any remarkable Electricity, Magnetism and Heat be in the Air in the time of Water-spouts. Mr Adanson relates to have felt an uncommon heat during a Waterspout which he saw passing by his Ship in the River of Senega.

21. I am convinced that the Gold-dust is constantly found mixed with that black, crystalline, magnetical Iron-Sand, which I mentionned before. So it is in Guinea, in Brasil and to my knowledge in every place where Gold is washing. I have myself found not only this Iron Sand, but the Gold dust too, in three different places of a country, which is absolutely volcanic. For this reason and for many more I could wish to try the experiment in those unexamined parts of the world, which You are to see; And as I am sure that such experiments will be rewarded with some Gold, and perhaps with some Diamonds and finer stones too, I desire You

   a., to examine and try the Sands of as many *volcanic beds* and unexamined countries as You may have leisure to examine; and b., if the experiments should prove successfull, which I have no doubt, to let me have a share of the profit and the reward, which a gracious King and the generosity of Government will grant for the discovery. If I am in life at Your happy return let me have some account of the result of Your observations; if not, please to send that account *To Mrs. Raspe née Lange á Berlin* directed to the Royal Society at Berlin, which will take care of the letter. She and my family are equally entitled to the above reward. I have nothing to add but sincere wishes for Your happy successfull return and am with the warmest esteem

Sir   Your most obedient humble Servant
                                             RERaspe

We do not know how much direct contact Raspe and Cook had over his application, but in the wistful phrasing "might have sailed" in the first paragraph he clearly assumed Cook was informed. There is no reference—direct or indirect—in the letter to why or how Raspe was rejected. Probably his disreputable past came up embarrassingly again. Considering that he had stolen from his government employer in Germany, we can almost imagine what reception the man would get from the British Admiralty. The very act of writing to the Captain, on the other hand, suggests that Raspe still had faith in Cook, although any ambition or hope is concealed behind politeness and resignation.

Even if he himself could not go, Raspe wanted Cook to conduct investigations for him. As he said in his first sentence, his observations were "planned less for speculation"—by which he meant far-fetched theorizing—"than for usefull practical Science," and his experiments would, Raspe claimed, accrue some "advantage to the undertaker." Obviously, he had in mind, in part, the fantastic promises of gold and diamonds which come later. But if he himself could be the "undertaker," then some of the advantages would, in fact, be distinctly scientific. For Raspe urgently desired to do more extensive field work and to check some of his theories. What better way than to go with Cook to explore islands that had been born in the sea, observe erupting volcanoes, and examine fresh samples scraped from the bed of the ocean? Undoubtedly, Raspe also dreamt of another kind of reward. After all, Banks and the Forsters had become international celebrities after their travels, and Raspe surely wished for fame too. As a disappointing substitute he could only hope that the "advantage to the undertaker" might induce Cook to carry out some of the work in his stead.

The suggestions that follow represent in part an attempt to show the practical work Raspe himself would have undertaken and in part a last effort to salvage some usefulness from the voyage if he could not be present. Raspe, who was always fond of numbering his points, provided Cook with a numbered list of specific geological and mineralogical aspects he thought should be examined. Despite the appearance of order, the list is in fact a jumble. It is not even strictly a set of instructions, as at first seems. It contains instead several different kinds of items: requests for specific information, fundamental geological issues, practical suggestions, and one lone meteorological point (item 20) concerning the curious phenomenon of waterspouts.

Most of the items are requests for empirical information. In general, these require at least a minimal knowledge of geological terminology and sometimes also of methods. In several instances the meaning of these terms has changed since the eighteenth century. The word "mineralogical," for example, which occurs in the first item, had a broader meaning then; "the study of rocks as such (that is, petrology or petrography), was not developed as an independent subject during the eighteenth century"[24] but simply subsumed under the title "mineralogy." The word "fossil" also was more inclusive; it was used in its original sense of anything dug up. Raspe avoids "fossil" altogether and uses "petrification" instead, but some confusion still lingers on when in item 9 he suggests that these can be either animal or mineral. While the phrase "a pure or mixed substance" in item 2 is quite vague, in the next one Raspe does suggest a simplified classification system. "Calcareous" and "silaceous" imply an approach employed today in classifying rocks and minerals based on their chemical components. Such groupings were difficult at that time because chemistry was still relatively undeveloped. On the other hand, "argillaceous" (clayey) and "metallic" are external characteristics much used in classification systems then and now.

Most of Raspe's instructions for collecting new empirical data concern the sea. It is striking that his very first point is oceanographic. He was interested in the sea bed, influenced again perhaps by Robert

Hooke, whom the Royal Society had requested in 1666 to devise an instrument for collecting samples from the ocean floor.[25] Probably because he was attempting to make his suggestions sound simple, Raspe mentioned no special instruments. Without them he could not explore the ocean water, but he could gather at least some information about its solid boundaries.

The disgraced coin and medal curator was also interested in certain special minerals such as "the native phase of the green New Sealand [sic] jade" (item 13—he would like to know with what other rocks it occurs) and the "Brazilian Turmalines." When he said tourmaline samples would "oblige the curious," he was probably thinking more of wealthy collectors browsing through London's mineral shops than of scientific experiments (item 19).

Nevertheless, some of Raspe's points touch major geological issues. Although he omitted any intimidating explications of theory in the letter to Cook, it is evident from his other writings that no matter how vaguely the issues are brought up here, he had several of them clearly in mind. In item 4, for example, the question of submarine volcanic rocks first arises. Already in 1769 Raspe had written: "For a long time, I have been convinced . . . that volcanoes contributed to a large extent to the present aspect of the surface of the earth, and that their remains would be more evident if we had a correct and adequate knowledge of the great variety of lavas and scoriae they produce. But such a knowledge is until now completely wanting."[26] With Cook he wanted to investigate that important issue.

The letter shows that Raspe was interested in possible volcanic influence on a wide variety of rocks. Even limestone should be reevaluated, Raspe boldly declared. Unfortunately the letter gives us only a glimpse of the theory he thought might be wrong without specifying what he suggested instead. Also, although in this instance (item 6) he correctly indicated how to identify calcareous rocks, he did not say how to determine their origin. But farther on, in item 18, he hinted that limestone, as well as several other kinds of rocks, might have been affected by volcanoes, writing cryptically, "Any calcareous Stone, and marble, or Granite and Slate in volcanic countries deserves notice." In the preface to one of his translations, dated March 1776, Raspe clearly suggested that some limestones might be volcanic products.[27] In this case, Raspe is the rash philosopher, but the idea indicates how far his infatuation with volcanoes was leading him from the traditional explanation of the origin of rocks in water.

He was one of the first geologists to recognize that the shape and texture of volcanic rocks can be affected by the rate of cooling. In particular, he believed that when molten rock cooled at air temperature, it would be different from rock that cooled under water. In *Beytrag* Raspe applied this idea specifically to basalt to explain how that volcanic product could occur in huge prismatic columns. This was his proud addition to Desmarest's theory, and with it Raspe thought he could explain the famous and intriguing Giant's Causeway, located on the coast of Ireland, as well as rude columnar basalts he had identified around Cassel. When the eager supplicant wrote to Cook, he alluded to this idea more clearly than to the others. Plainly, submarine samples needed special attention because if their "form" and "crystallizations" were distinctive (item 10), they would help confirm his theories. Raspe particularly wanted evidence that columnar basalts had cooled in water; and he points out how the law of superincumbency can assist in determining this (item 12). Of course, at his introductory allusion to principles deduced from facts suggested, Raspe wished for confirmation of the specific theories he had been championing. He hoped Cook would find rock specimens in the field to support his contentions. Indeed, Raspe's general idea that cooling at different temperatures resulted in rocks of different shapes and textures was to prove very useful in the future when Hutton's associate, Sir James Hall, had the same thought and tested it experimentally.[28]

Less clear are Raspe's frequent allusions to crystallization (items 10, 17, 19, 21). Since crystallization was not then distinguished from jointing, his interest in columnar basalts may have led him to this topic. But here, other than plainly rejecting the notion that crystals are formed exclusively in aqueous solution, it is impossible to determine his ideas.

In any case, the promised "advantage to the undertaker" was not to be derived entirely from solving geological disputes. Raspe himself stressed his preference for useful observations over "philosophical Romances." Yet in one of his most boldly asserted remarks to Cook, he wishfully confounded hypothesis with fact. Although he understated his feelings, Raspe believed that almost no geological work could be more useful or beneficial to Polynesia than to discover local sources of iron, the transformer of civilizations. He states flatly that this can be done (item 16), and, not forgetting the politics of exploration, alludes smoothly to the goodwill Cook and the Admiralty would gain from such a find. Still, the main advantage to such a search for iron comes only in the final item, where Raspe wrote: "I am convinced that the Gold-dust is constantly found mixed with that black, crystalline, magnetical Iron-Sand, which I mentioned before." The notion is so fanciful, so transparently wishful, we cannot help wondering whether the creator of fabulous tales was not beginning to believe his own fabrications. Raspe was yearning for a gold rush. He even assured Cook of his utter seriousness by giving evidence from other countries, such as Brasil, and added a personal testimony that he himself had found "not only this Iron Sand, but the Gold Dust too, in three different places of a country, which is absolutely volcanic." If this personal claim is true, Raspe is as cagey as the most suspicious prospector in concealing where he found the precious dust, but considering the criminal form of self-help he had so recently resorted to, he could not have panned more than the merest gleaming specks. Still, he continued confidently to Cook: "For this reason and for many more I could wish to try the experiment in these unexamined parts of the world, which you are to see." The eager geologist was not really so resigned to his rejection after all.

To him, finding gold in Tahiti had almost become a fact, for in summarizing, he repeated the idea and hoped for more, perhaps diamonds or even, as he says, "finer stones." The idea was not quite as wild then as it sounds today. After Raspe had mentioned the discovery of gold in Brazil, he must have remembered that only a few years before alluvial diamonds had also been found there along with the precious metal. Today, in fact, diamonds are mined on beaches, although these are in South Africa, where the stones are traceable to the Kimberlite pipes, remanants, scientists believe, of ancient volcanoes. In any case, the man whose theories were "established upon facts only" seems quite dazzled by geology's promise.

Despite the rich bait he dangled, Raspe was evidently again rejected. No doubt, the attempt was doomed from the start by the fact that he was an accused and even admitted embezzler; one could hardly expect Cook to take on a thief as a scientific researcher. If that had not been enough, Cook had already experienced plenty of trouble with Johann Reinhold Forster, the cantankerous naturalist on the second voyage and also a German.

But Cook did not merely reject Raspe's application; he also seems to have ignored the list of suggestions. His journals give no hint that he scrutinized his "anchoring grounds" for geological information nor that he combed the abundant volcanic sands for gold, diamonds, or iron. Probably he already knew that for all practical purposes there was no iron on Tahiti or the other volcanic islands of the South Pacific. During the earlier voyages Cook had learned much from the scientific gentlemen accompanying him, especially about botany and zoology, fields for which Linnaeus had just devised a useful system of classification. On the third voyage Cook and certain experienced members of the crew carried out the tasks of observing and collecting flora and fauna on their own. To search for basalt in prismatic shapes, gather mineral samples, and test them in acids was entirely different, however. In geology the captain showed only minimal interest, and in mineralogy, virtually none. Perhaps this reflects the confusion and turmoil then dominant in those fields; Cook had no desire to become entangled in the geologists' endless imbroglios.

Raspe did not know that, however, when he wrote his letter. Whether he actually went on the voyage or not, he urgently wished to profit from it. By revealing his ideas to Cook, he could hope to make the captain beholden to him; the destitute letter-writer thought even this kind of indebtedness might be lucrative, as he stated quite explicitly. Ironically, although Raspe blithely assumed that Cook would return safely from the voyage, he was not so sure of his own survival, and asked that in case of his death, his wife in Berlin should receive what he discreetly called "some account of the result of your observations."

Events do not always proceed as anticipated. The widow to be provided for after the ships returned was Elizabeth Cook. Her husband had been killed in Hawaii on February 14, 1779, in a squabble with the islanders over the Europeans' precious items of iron, the metal Raspe confidently believed was available in Polynesia. Captain Cook was dead at fifty-one. In Berlin, meanwhile, Mrs. Raspe, to whom Rudolf Erich Raspe had entrusted his reward should he have died, initiated divorce proceedings against her absent spouse.

Raspe remained in England, far from German law, dreaming of an even better escape, another expedition. Once he sought help from a new patron, asking his famous acquaintance, Benjamin Franklin, to support an archeological expedition to Egypt. That project too was in vain, but at other times Raspe was more successful, making various mineralogical excursions through Cornwall and Wales to Scotland, where he met Hutton, who mentions him in the third volume of his *Theory of the Earth*,[29] and Ireland, where he finally died in 1794. By then the exile had achieved success in his new country, in the familiar areas of geology, with his translations, mineralogical surveys, and assay work; in literature with *Munchausen*; and in gem cataloguing with a *A Descriptive Catalogue of a General Collection of Ancient and Modern Engraved Gems... Cast... by J. Tassie* (1791). In this last serious work published under his own name, Raspe repeated the idea he had written of years before to Cook. He expressed himself with the same old confidence, asserting, "Otaheite, New-Zealand, and other Islands of the South-Sea... abound in lavas, basaltas, and other volcanic substance; which absolutely implies that there is plenty of iron."[30] A few paragraphs later he quarreled with the "exaggerated praises of the diamond above any other fine stone," which have "raised it to an unconscionable price," and he described an excellent, large jade ornament "in the possession of the widow of the late celebrated Captain James Cook." Perhaps when news of the circumnavigator's death reached England, Raspe had gone to visit Mrs. Cook. Maybe she would know whether any of Raspe's beloved suggestions had been carried out. But there was neither gold in Tahiti, nor diamonds in New Zealand, nor accessible iron even in the ferruginous lavas of Polynesia; and the rash philosopher who dreamt of those distant islands born from the sea and pictured ancient eruptions covering Germany never saw even the smoke of an active volcano.

NOTES

1 Raspe's year of birth is usually given as 1737, but the earlier date is documented in an excellent, much neglected article: Erich Haarmann, "Ein Münchhausen als Geologe: Rudolf Erich Raspe, 1736-1794," Geologische Rundschau, 33 (1942), 104-20.
2 A biography of Raspe in English along with a fairly accurate bibliography of his work (see n. 18, below) is available in John Carswell, The Prospector: Being the Life and Times of Rudolf Erich Raspe (1737-1794) (London: Cresset, 1950).
3 Thomas Seccombe, ed., "Introduction," The Surprising Adventures of Baron Munchausen (London: Medici, 1930), pp. x-xiii.
4 For a discussion of the scientific impulse on the third voyage, see J. C. Beaglehole, The Life of Captain James Cook (London: Adam and Charles Black, 1974), pp. 500-502.
5 Carswell, The Prospector, p. 104.
6 An Introduction to the Natural History of the Terrestrial Sphere, trans. and ed. Audrey Notvik Iversen and Albert V. Carozzi (New York: Hafner, 1970).
7 The term uniformitarianism should be reserved for the later, more dogmatic version of this idea propounded by Charles Lyell. For some comments on the problem, see R. H. Dott, Jr., "James Hutton and the Concept of a Dynamic Earth," in Toward a History of Geology, ed. Cecil J. Schneer (Cambridge, Mass.: M.I.T. Press, 1969), p. 138.
8 Introduction, p. 70.
9 Ibid., p. cxvii.
10 Ibid., p. cxvii.
11 Quoted by Iversen and Carozzi, "Editors' Introduction, Appendix," ibid., p. cix.
12 Margaret Deacon, Scientists and the Sea, 1650-1900 (New York: Academic, 1971), p. 176.
13 Quoted from Raspe's own English translation, An Account of Some German Volcanos, and their Productions (London: Lockyer Davis, 1776), pp. 114, 115.
14 Hanno Beck, "Rudolf Erich Raspes landeskundliche Leistung," Berichte zur deutschen Landeskunde, 28 (1961), p. 39. My translation.
15 Account, pp. 110, 111.
16 Introduction, p. 1.
17 For a more thorough discussion of the problems in describing the position in history of a precurser of vulcanism, see Kenneth L. Taylor, "Nicolas Desmarest

and Geology in the Eighteenth Century," in *Toward a History of Geology*, pp. 338–56. It should be noted, as Taylor points out, that some neptunists did accept the volcanic origin of basalt (pp. 353–56).

18 "A Letter Containing a Short Account of some Basalt Hills in Hassia," *Philosophical Transactions of the Royal Society of London*, 61 (1771), pp. 580–83; and "Nachricht von einigen niederhessischen Basalten, besonders aber einem Säulenbasaltstein Gebürge bei Felsberg und den Spuren eines verlöschten brennenden Berges am Habichtswalde über Weissenstein nahe bei Cassel," *Deutsche Schriften der Kgl. Societät der Wissenschaften in Göttingen*, 1 (Fall 1771), 72–83. The latter is missing from Carswell's bibliography.

19 Taylor, "Nicolas Desmarest," p. 347.

20 Johann Wolfgang Goethe, "Karl Wilhelm Nose," *Gedenkausgabe der Werke, Briefe und Gespräche*, ed. Ernst Beutler, 2nd ed. (Zürich: Artemis, 1966), p. 593.

21 Carswell, *The Prospector*, p. 116.

22 *Introduction*, p. 98.

23 British Library Additional MS. 30262, ff. 11–12. Reproduced by permission of the British Library Board. I wish here to express my thanks to the authorities of the British Library for permission to use this MS.

24 V. A. Eyles, "The Extent of Geological Knowledge in the Eighteenth Century, and the Methods by Which It Was Diffused," in *Toward a History*, p. 173.

25 Deacon, *Scientists and the Sea*, p. 84.

26 Quoted in Iversen and Carozzi, "Editors' Introduction," *Introduction*, p. xlv.

27 Ibid., p. lxiii.

28 Archibald Geikie, *The Founders of Geology*, 2nd ed. (London: Macmillan, 1905), pp. 318–22.

29 James Hutton, *Theory of the Earth with Proofs with Illustrations*, III, ed. A. Geikie (London: Geological Society, 1899), 255–57. Quoted in Iversen and Carozzi, "References," *Introduction*, p. lxxxvii.

30 *Catalogue* (London: Tassie and Murray), p. iv (Introduction).

Regnard and Collin d'Harleville on Legacies by Bachelor Uncles

PHILIP KOCH

In the eighth year of the eighteenth century, the Comédie-Française first performed a play by Jean-François Regnard, *Le Légataire universel* (January 9, 1708). The century had but eight years still to run when, in the winter months again (February 24, 1792), the same theater, under the "Revolutionary" title of Théâtre de la Nation, presented a new work by another Jean-François, surnamed Collin d'Harleville: *Le Vieux Célibataire*. Instantaneous successes, both comedies were rapidly acclaimed as masterpieces of their respective authors. Such random coincidences[1] would hardly legitimize a comparative study, were it not for yet another factor.

In the course of its initial run, *Le Vieux Célibataire* was the object of a lively journalistic debate on its originality.[2] Taking note of the accusations of imitation, in the "Avertissement" to the published play, Collin freely avowed his debts, among them the following: "Je pourrais citer aussi le commandeur du *Père de Famille* [by Diderot] . . . et surtout le Géronte du *Légataire universel,* qui a bien aussi ses collatéraux et sa gouvernante."[3] Although the reference to the *Légataire* was somewhat playful, it reveals itself, on examination, to be fundamentally true, for the two comedies display resemblances in a matter as elemental as the underlying dramatic situation. Both plays involve

291

old bachelor uncles and nephews who wish to be remembered in their wills. Indeed, one might say there could be no *légataire universel* if there were no *vieux célibataire*. Even the age of two uncles (Géronte in the *Légataire*, M. Dubriage in the *Célibataire*) is quite close—sixty-eight and sixty-five, respectively—as is, presumably, that of the nephews, Eraste and Armand. The two male leads of each play also have female roles dependent on them. The young men are in love— Eraste with Isabelle *(Légataire)*, Armand with Laure *(Célibataire)*— while the two elderly gentlemen are attended by "gouvernantes"— Géronte by Lisette and M. Dubriage by Mme Evrard. Thus, not only is the basic dramatic situation identical, but four principal characters of each play also maintain common relations.

It would be improper to push the parallels too far. Since Collin is not making a carbon copy of his predecessor's play but, rather, expressing his own artistic concerns, we must expect significant differences that are immediately apparent even in the common roles. Because Géronte is in very poor health (while M. Dubriage is of sound body), the matter of writing the last will is more urgent in the *Légataire*. Unlike Eraste, who has easy access to Uncle Géronte, Armand has been disowned unjustly by M. Dubriage and must hide his true identity, under the name of the servant Charle, in his uncle's house, from which he has been banned for some ten years. Further, while Eraste is only secretly affianced to Isabelle, it is well known that Armand and Laure are married, although most members of the Dubriage household are incapable of recognizing them on sight. As for the *gouvernantes*, their divergences should become apparent in the course of this study.

Besides the common roles, nonparallel parts can be found: in the *Légataire*, Crispin, Eraste's valet, and Isabelle's mother, Mme Argante; in the *Célibataire*, Ambroise, M. Dubriage's steward, and George, the concierge. There are, thus, in each play, six major characters, to which one should add various episodic, or bit parts. Of infinitely greater significance than these formal comparisons of roles, however, are the profound dissimilarities in the plot development and in the personality of the characters.

If, in *Le Légataire universel,* Eraste wishes to be named sole heir, he does so ostensibly because of his secret love for Isabelle. Practically interested in the material ease of her daughter, Mme Argante has made the total inheritance of Géronte's wealth a preliminary requirement of the marriage. In his pursuit of the means to wed Isabelle, Eraste meets a series of obstacles that constitute the plot development of the comedy. The first obstacle is reminiscent of Molière's *Avare*.[4] As in the conflict that pits Cléante against his father, Harpagon, Eraste quickly discovers that Géronte is his rival for the hand of Isabelle. This problem resolves itself easily when both Mme Argante and Géronte change their minds. If Mme Argante's decisions seem rather arbitrary (why reject the candidacy of Géronte after accepting it, when no new evidence is really introduced?), there is somewhat more credibility in the old man's about-face. Forced to cut short his "lover's conversation" when his most recent purgative began to operate, Géronte has apparently spent some of his time offstage reflecting on the incompatibilities of conjugal activity and the ailments attendant on physical decline.

The first danger eliminated, a new one immediately takes its place. Géronte will make Eraste his *légataire universel*, but only after leaving considerable legacies to two relatives, or *collatéraux*, "un neveu bas-normand, une nièce du Maine."[5] To thwart this peril (what would be left of Géronte's estate after these two generous gifts?), Crispin impersonates in succession the *collatéraux* so grotesquely and outrageously that Géronte vows to disinherit the two provincials and leave all to Eraste. Victory, at last! But, no, before he can dictate his will, Géronte falls into a coma and, according to Lisette, will shortly die—intestate (III, x). Once more, the inventive Crispin comes to the rescue, this time by impersonating Géronte and dictating his last will and testament to the *notaires*.

Three obstacles successfully overcome will satisfy neither Regnard nor the five acts of the classical French play; to round things out, a fourth obstacle is necessary for Act V.[6] As one might expect, the true Géronte revives (IV, viii), and he must be persuaded to accept the bogus will as his own. This is no small feat, and it takes the combined talents of Crispin, Lisette, and Eraste, together with the unwitting cooperation of Mme Argante and Isabelle, to achieve the desired end. These efforts include Crispin's presence of mind in covering his tracks as the counterfeit Géronte, and nothing less than blackmail. When the real Géronte lost consciousness, Eraste rifled all the negotiable notes he could find in his uncle's home and left them in the keeping of his fiancée and her mother. At the end of the play, these honest ladies return the notes, but Lisette seizes and will not relinquish them until Géronte agrees to the terms of the will.

Le Légataire universel clearly presents a linear structure with *successive* episodes that have no necessary relationship. They could also have been more or less numerous without affecting the outcome. If the episodic threads are, at bottom, unrelated and, in principle, limitlessly self-generative, Regnard took great pains to bring together all the strands he did use. He united the six main characters on stage at the denouement so that they could hear Géronte give public approval to the choice of *légataire universel,* as well as to the wedding plans not only of Isabelle and Eraste but also of Lisette and Crispin. In short, the author has given us a perfect example of the *pièce à tiroirs.*

Where the *Légataire* is linear and fragmented in plot movement, *Le Vieux Célibataire* is involuted. At the center is the elderly M. Dubriage, completely dominated, when the play begins, by the unscrupulous steward and the housekeeper, Ambroise and Mme Evrard. It is the latter, moreover, who, with clever falsehoods and judiciously chosen excerpts from Armand's letters, has so blackened the nephew's character in M. Dubriage's eyes that the uncle has refused to communicate with him for about ten years. With the help of a faithful ally, the concierge George, Armand, disguised as the domestic Charle, and, later, Armand's wife Laure introduce themselves into this closed society in order to unmask the evildoers and to help M. Dubriage "recognize" the true character of all those who surround him. The plot of *Le Vieux Célibataire* may be viewed as a contest between two "teams" for the prize—M. Dubriage—and the dramatic question becomes "Who will win?" The answer will come only after a progressive intensification of the conflict.

The initial exposition[7] is followed by the first "events" of the play that present the characters (minus Laure) either in their secret intentions or in their relations with Dubriage (I, v–II, v). Indeed, it would be well-nigh impossible to distinguish this "action" from the preliminary exposition of the situation, were it not that now, the characters are speaking to enemies rather than to trusted confidants or are trying to exert an influence on M. Dubriage. Tension increases in the next sequence (II, vi–xi), which sees the arrival of Laure (II, viii). Both camps are presently at full strength, but Laure's arrival is not the immediate circumstance that propels the play to its next, higher level of intensity. The catalyst is, rather, the ultimatum of Ambroise to Mme Evrard (II, vi). Long in love with the housekeeper, Ambroise also wishes to unite their ill-gotten gains through marriage, and he gives Mme Evrard one day to think it over. If she hesitates to accept the offer, it is because she secretly aspires to the hand of M. Dubriage and, thereby, to exclusive possession of the legacy.

Since Mme Evrard has only until the next day to achieve her ends, she must act quickly, and she arranges the justly famous *scène de séduction* (III, iv), in which she tries to entice M. Dubriage into proposing to her. The presence of Laure, however, acts as a counterforce, and this, the third sequence of the comedy, is, in essence, the contrasting pressures of each of the two women to allure M. Dubriage into her camp (III, iii–IV, xiii). It ends with a *coup de théâtre*, when Laure unintentionally reveals her true identity, to the initial shock and subsequent pleasure of M. Dubriage. But all is not yet lost, in the minds of the evildoers. Since they believe that Armand is still absent, with the help of Ambroise, Mme Evrard tries, in the climax of the play (Act V), to prove that the other woman is an adventuress impersonating the real Laure, who is living in Colmar with her ne'er-do-well husband, Armand. Needless to say, Armand finally proves the falsity of Mme Evrard's contention and opens his uncle's eyes to what has been going on for the past ten years, after which George, the concierge, can cry exultantly in conclusion: "Les bons l'emportent" (p. 226; V, ix).

Around the ever-tightening spiral of the main plot gravitate two seemingly extraneous sequences. The first involves five destitute but hopeful cousins from Arras (II, xii–xv) paralleling the *collatéraux* of the *Légataire*, as Collin d'Harleville suggested in his "Avertissement." There are also the interesting scenes (III, i–ii) where George's young children, Julien and Suson, prepare to give and then actually recite the story of Noah and the flood to the deeply moved M. Dubriage. Yet the cousins are not only mentioned again but are also financially enriched at the end of the comedy (p. 227; V, ix), and the two children are pawns in Mme Evrard's plans for seduction. The apparent digressions are thus either necessary (as illustration of ultimate justice) or integrated into the plot, which remains unified and limpidly simple to permit sharp emphasis on character portrayal.[8]

The very title suggests the centrality of M. Dubriage, "le vieux célibataire," and the effort to depict him psychologically reinforces that position. M. Dubriage's most striking trait is his weakness of character, a quality that prompts him always to agree with the person to whom he is presently speaking even though in so doing, he compromises a prior commitment. In addition to being weak, M. Dubriage is melancholy, for he has no one to love him genuinely, surrounded as he is by hired domestics. He was not always like this; "autrefois"—that is, in his younger days—he had, says he, "de l'énergie" (p. 227; V, ix). He has become what he is because he wrongly decided never to marry. Thus, his present character is explained as the result of old age and unnatural isolation, and M. Dubriage himself is the first to admit he is "un garçon, un vieillard isolé dans le monde" (p. 105; I, viii).

After M. Dubriage, Mme Evrard is unquestionably the most memorable character. She is not only determined (she and her late husband had been planning to bilk Dubriage for ten years) but also skillful, quick-witted, stealthy, and intelligent. Lenient's reference to her as an "Agrippine de la domesticité"[9] seems particularly apt in light of the way she uses innocent Julien and Suson to prepare the *scène de séduction* and utilizes Armand's letters to his uncle against him. The last effort of the evildoers to pass off Laure as an impostor in Act V is of her invention, too. Given her general personality, it is a bit surprising, perhaps, to find that she is morally "virtuous." Intrigued that she is taking Charle—that is, Armand—so easily into her confidence, George thinks she must find him physically attractive but immediately changes his mind: "Mais non, j'ai tort: madame Evrard! / Elle est d'une sagesse, oh mais! à toute épreuve" (p. 82; I, ii). The modern reader may also find it difficult to accept that so scheming a woman would jeopardize all she has worked so long to attain by confiding her deepest secrets to "Charle," who has been in the household for only three months (and who, in fact, uses what he learns to thwart his enemies). Collin was not writing for the skeptical twentieth-century audience, however, and Mme Evrard is the fullest picture of evil he was able to draw.

The remaining four major characters are more rapidly sketched, although they do present one or two distinguishing traits. Ambroise, the other evildoer, is self-important and constantly gruff to M. Dubriage. Like Mme Evrard, however, whose saving virtue is "virtue" itself, Ambroise is not all bad. He feels the power of love (for Mme Evrard) and the natural urge to establish a family. The three opponents of the villainous team are all characterized by one common quality: goodness.[10] Good though they may uniformly be, they do offer individualizing nuances, particularly evident in their attitude toward serving. Trained from childhood for service, George finds the condition quite normal and has nothing special to say about it, except to express his contentment. Armand is a bit uncomfortable at being a domestic in a house where he should be master but quickly dismisses his resentment. He gives pleasure to his uncle by his camouflaged presence, and this fact alone reconciles him to his subservient post— temporarily at least. Laure, who almost always appears trembling with timidity, is the least satisfied with her lot. When she presents herself to Ambroise for her initial job interview and he asks her whether she has been previously employed, she replies with proud irony and apparent indignation: "Qui? moi? . . . jamais. / Je ne servirai point ailleurs, je vous promets" (p. 129; II, viii). Her reaction would seem all the more astonishing since her parents were of the working class, or is this not, perhaps, the very reason for her irritation?

In contrast to *Le Vieux Célibataire*, where every character has his own personality, however quickly drawn, *Le Légataire universel* can boast no clearly defined portraits. Witness the case of Géronte. Although he and the others *speak* time and again of his avarice, the audience *sees*, rather, examples of his decrepitude, irascibility, and impotence. As in Molière's *Avare*, an important model for our comedy, the love rivalry of Eraste and Géronte, at least, should have offered ample opportunity to illustrate the old man's tightfistedness;

instead, in this episode, the audience is treated to Géronte's empty boasts about his virility and to his precipitate departure at the peremptory command of his latest physic.[11]

Eraste is another example of Regnard's somewhat inconsistent character portrayal. In an obvious effort by the author to gain audience sympathy for Eraste, the author has him frequently express regret at having to trick his uncle into naming him sole heir and, with equal frequency, attribute his dubious maneuvers to the demands of love. "Un dieu, dont le pouvoir sert d'excuse aux amants, / Saura me disculper de ces emportements" (p. 104; IV, v) is a typical statement by this character. Love must, then, be a powerful force on Eraste. Yet, in the entire play, there are only two brief love interludes: an abortive *dépit amoureux* begun in I, vii, that picks up again in II, i, and a duet of mutual affection consisting of seven lines by Eraste and an equal number by Isabelle (V, i). The rest of the time, Eraste appears to be thinking how "per fas et nefas" to be named *légataire universel*. In the very first scene of the play, Crispin exposes to Lisette the motives of his master:

> Si mon maître, *primo*, n'est nommé légataire,
> Le reste de ses jours il fera maigre chère.
> *Secundo*, quoiqu'il soit diablement amoureux,
> Madame Argante, avant de couronner ses feux,
> ....
> Veut qu'un bon testament, bien sûr et bien fidèle,
> Fasse ledit neveu légataire de tout.
> (P. 28)

Crispin's explanation seems not only to be complete but also to present the motives in the real order of the *deeds*, if not the *words* of Eraste.

Lisette and Crispin form a couple paralleling, in a lower social register, the love of Isabelle and Eraste. Since the two servants never insist seriously on their feelings for each other, there is no reason to dwell on the subject. In all other respects, they are totally conventional and traditional. Like any *soubrette*, Lisette is perceptive, sharp-tongued, free of speech, and not too scrupulous in attaining her goals. (She does not hesitate at blackmail, for example, to make Géronte accept the false will.) If these qualities are noticeable in Lisette, what shall we say of Crispin? After all, his alertness of mind averts the danger of the provincial *collatéraux,* makes it possible to dictate the fraudulent will, and helps enormously in the final hoodwinking of Géronte. It is therefore with deep admiration and total accuracy, that Lisette, no novice herself, can ask rhetorically of Crispin, "Qui peut en fourberie être si fort que toi?" (p. 100; IV, ii). Impressive though the servants' talents may be, however, they do not contribute to original psychological portraits.

The reader would be even more hard pressed to describe Mme Argante and her daughter Isabelle, both of whom pass quickly before his eyes. Isabelle is evidently obedient to her mother and, one would think, sincerely in love with Eraste—because she says so. As for Mme Argante, like all "experienced" people of middle age, she is realistic about the material conditions necessary for successful marriages. She is also rather reluctant to receive stolen goods (i.e., Géronte's negotiable notes). In short, Isabelle's mother is a practical, well-bred matron—like so many others. What a far cry from *Le Vieux Célibataire!* Collin's personages have a depth consonant with the involutions of his plot, while Regnard gives to his the same linear and episodic quality as the events portrayed. Each play is, therefore, justly considered a masterpiece of its author because the constitutive elements cooperate harmoniously to present a unified artistic vision.

If one were to seek a single word to describe the dominant tone of *Le Légataire universel,* it would have to be *egotism.* Instead of consideration for others, the characters pursue unbridled self-satisfaction, normally in the form of eroticism. Eraste, the model of earnest lovers, has not disdained to taste the delights of Crispin's first wife (God rest her soul!), and the valet chides his master about taking similar liberties with Lisette once they are wed. Crispin himself has not been above amorous dalliance with the wife of a former employer, perhaps, during his first marriage (why not?). Since Géronte boasts of his presently dubious virility, it should not be surprising to hear rumors circulating about rather intimate personal attentions the younger, more vigorous uncle used to require of his housekeeper Lisette. Although, in impersonating the provincial relatives, Crispin's intention is simply to estrange them from Géronte, it is symptomatic of the play's general atmosphere that the "fourberies" involve extramarital relations. The "neveu bas-normand" was born four months after the wedding vows, and the "nièce du Maine" bore her lamented husband a child two years after his demise. Even totally incidental roles cannot be introduced without some reference to sexual prowess. When Crispin is sent after two *notaires* for drawing up Géronte's will, he returns to tell Lisette where he found these dramatically marginal characters.

> Je les ai déterrés où l'on m'avait instruit,
> Dans un jardin, à table, en un petit réduit,
> Avec dames qui m'ont paru de bonne mine.
> Je crois qu'ils passaient là quelque acte à la sourdine.
> (P. 58; II, viii)

If the motto of the *Légataire* could be "Libido comes vincit," egotism does manifest itself in another important, though less universal way. Whenever possible, the characters will cheat each other without compunction. The primary example of unrepentant self-seeking is the extremely lavish gifts the pseudo-Géronte leaves in his will for Lisette and Crispin (i.e., himself) to the despair of Eraste, who is powerless to intervene (IV, vi). But there is another instance worthy of note. Lisette does not receive a salary as Géronte's *gouvernante*, but she has his solemn promise to remember her in his will. The value of the promise becomes clear in a conversation between these two characters:

> LISETTE— Souvenez-vous toujours, quand vous serez tranquille,
>   Dans votre testament de me faire du bien.
> GÉRONTE—Je t'en ferai, *(bas, à part.)* pourvu qu'il ne m'en coûte rien.
> (P. 71; II, xii)

Regnard's world, then, is a jungle inhabited by confirmed egocentrics. For these, life seems to consist in constantly renewed but unrelated challenges, of which the four "episodes" of *Le Légataire universel* serve as an artistic representation; and happiness, or success, is the ability to overcome the obstacles to gratification. In the most meaningful line of the comedy, Lisette says, "Il faut, par notre esprit, faire notre destin" (p. 50; II, iii). Response to the challenge is in terms of intelligence and cunning, and we side (i.e., laugh) with the clever victor while reserving our mockery for the vanquished.[12] Approving laughter, scornful mockery—are these not precisely the attitudes prompted respectively by Eraste, Crispin, and Lisette, on the one hand, and Géronte, on the other?

If vigilant egotism represents the dominant tone of the *Légataire*, goodness, on the contrary, pervades *Le Vieux Célibataire*. Goodness is certainly not sensuality, nor even passionate love; it is, rather, consideration, respect for others, loyalty to the institutions of marriage and family. Following these principles is not self-sacrifice, but rather, concurrence in the "natural" order which is the only path to true personal happiness—that is, moderate contentment. The natural order is one; there are many ways to behave unnaturally, and *Le Vieux Célibataire* presents two, the first in its very title. M. Dubriage erred in not marrying, and he admits his mistake—alas, too late. The other example of unnatural behavior is personified by Mme Evrard and Ambroise, whose flaw consists in choosing material wealth as their goal without examining how they would acquire it. Even in their abject state, these fallen angels yet display a touch of their former grace: chastity (Mme Evrard), a sincere desire to marry (Ambroise).

The world is thus peopled by rather uniformly good people and by easily distinguishable bad individuals. A dramatic situation arises when the two camps meet in conflict. But though they are a source of anxiety, the bad antagonists could not conceivably win. For one thing, they are unable to form a true, unified "team." As Armand aptly put it, "Le méchant peut trouver un complice; / Mais il n'est ici-bas, et le ciel l'a permis, / Que les honnêtes gens qui puissent être amis" (p. 208; V, ii).[13] What is even more significant, goodness has only to appear to win victory. Armand expresses his expectations for Laure once she has been introduced into M. Dubriage's household in the following terms: "Si mon oncle la voit, il l'aimera lui-même" (p. 87; I, iv); and future developments prove his assumption absolutely accurate. Were the results not similar in the case of Armand, who, under the name of Charle, has completely charmed his unsuspecting uncle? It was, in like manner, inescapable that Mme Evrard be duped by Armand-Charle's greater moral strength, however unreasonable her credulity appears to modern eyes. We understand, finally, why, beyond a certain point, *Le Vieux Célibataire* does not need the clever *meneurs* of *Le Légataire universel* to invent brilliant strategems. George has simply to introduce Armand, and Armand, Laure, for "le hasard" (p. 202; IV, xii), for "le ciel" (p. 206; IV, xiii)—for nature, in a word—to take command.

Once goodness has achieved its inevitable victory, it will continue unchanged even in the "tributes" it exacts from the vanquished. Mme Evrard and Ambroise depart from the new paradise of M. Dubriage's home, but there is no threat of legal action against them for financial mismanagement. In fact, they will apparently keep all the riches they have stolen from M. Dubriage. As for this aged gentleman, whose "crime" is one of omission, he will never have a true family, but he will find consolation in the presence of the "good" team, whose members will permit, by epithets such as "mon père," if not the "réalité," at least, the "image," the "douce et touchante erreur" of paternity (p. 228; V, ix). From beginning to end, therefore, *Le Vieux Célibataire* offers a highly optimistic,[14] heart-warming picture of the human condition with which the sensitized bourgeois audience is invited to identify through tears of virtue, *not* of laughter.[15]

After this detailed comparison, it should be obvious that differences far outweigh similarities in *Le Légataire universel* and *Le Vieux Célibataire*, which are, practically speaking, mirror images. The divergences are certainly explicable in terms of the personality of the authors—Regnard the "cynique mitigé qui jouit de la vie," Collin d'Harleville the "chantre de la vertu souriante"[16]—but the contrast can also be illuminated by the "spirit" of the times. The initial reference to the dates of the comedies was not idle rhetoric, for *Le Vieux Célibataire* would have been as inconceivable in 1708 as *Le Légataire universel* in 1792.

The cynicism, sardonic smile, and egotism that permeate Regnard's play are far from unique. In *Le Chevalier à la mode* (1687), Dancourt presents his hero, the chevalier, as simultaneously courting three women for their money: Mme Patin, a rich widow whose late husband "n'a pas gagné trop légitimement son bien en Normandie,"[17] Mme Patin's goose of a niece Lucile, and the *baronne*. When he loses the first two by pure chance, the totally unregenerate chevalier concludes lightly in the last speech of the play: "Allons retrouver la baronne, et continuons de la ménager jusqu'à ce qu'il me vienne quelque meilleure fortune."[18] Lesage's *Turcaret* (1709) contains a more celebrated example of cynicism. Reflecting on what is happening in the play (almost every character is exploiting someone else), Frontin observes: "J'admire le train de la vie humaine! Nous plumons une coquette, la coquette mange un homme d'affaires, l'homme d'affaires en pille d'autres." After the enumeration comes an evaluation that is anything but morally indignant: "Cela fait un ricochet de fourberies, le plus plaisant du monde."[19]

Carefree eroticism is present, too, just below the surface. All the while promising marriage, Turcaret heaps treasures on his beloved, another baroness. Since he is, in fact, already married, his intentions are clearly not matrimonial, and there must be favor off-stage to warrant Turcaret's constant, lavish gifts. Similarly, it is quite obvious that the "chevalier à la mode" receives somthing for his attentions, at least from the widow Patin and the *baronne*. The case of Dancourt, in general, so scandalized Rousseau that he was prompted to write, in his *Lettre à d'Alembert* (1758): "Je ne ferai pas à Dancourt l'honneur de parler de lui: ses pièces n'effarouchent pas par des termes obscènes, mais il faut n'avoir de chaste que les oreilles pour les pouvoir supporter."[20]

The attitudes discernible not only in Regnard but also in Dancourt and Lesage bespeak a value system in disarray, what has come to be called the "crise de la conscience européenne" that La Bruyère is already recording in his *Caractères*. The Age of Enlightenment develops in response to the smilingly cynical amorality of the turn of the century. Without the Regnards, Dancourts, Lesages, and Dufresnys, it is difficult to conceive of the *philosophes,* with their orientation toward society and its improvement, with their emphasis on the scientifico-moral lessons of Nature. It is equally difficult to explain otherwise the new sentimentality, the rediscovery of love, from Prévost on, which acquires an even greater élan at the time of Rousseau and Diderot.

Comedy follows the same evolution in its self-image from the seventeenth into the eighteenth century. "La comédie a toujours prétendu plaire en instruisant," Tissier generalizes with obvious reliance on the Horatian principle of "utile et dulce."[21] Whatever these terms mean precisely, it is incontrovertible that "plaire" ("dulce") involves the inherent esthetic effect of comedy, whereas "instruire" ("utile") refers to a certain salutary impact comic works will have on social behavior. Whether or not "instruire" and "plaire" are, in fact, both operative, the two terms appear constantly in the defenses of comedy in Molière's day, clear corroboration of Tissier's preceding remark. On the other hand, what positive social lessons do Regnard's contemporaries, successors of Molière, introduce in their plays?

Le Chevalier à la mode would suggest that you not give up hope if fate thwarts your (commendable?) efforts to marry the richest available woman. The most important word of the chevalier's and of the play's last speech is, thus, *continuons*. But is there not a greater moral lesson in *Turcaret*? After all, Turcaret is arrested at the end, fitting punishment for his shameless embezzlements. True enough, but if Turcaret is eliminated, he is replaced by Frontin, who will be followed by others when he, presumably, suffers, some time in the future, a fate similar to Turcaret's. To use Frontin's own words, the play offers as moral an endless "ricochet de fourberies, le plus plaisant [*not* "instructif"] du monde." In this light, a remark in Regnard's *Critique du Légataire* (1708) is worthy of special note. As part of his proof that, the critics notwithstanding, the *Légataire* is a good play, the Marquis observes: "Dans une comédie... il s'agit de *divertir* les gens d'esprit avec art."[22] A short poem by Palaprat, the "Rondeau sur le Légataire universel," echoes the Marquis's comment: "De notre scène il [Regnard] sait l'art enchanteur. / Il y fait rire, il badine avec grâce, / Il est aisé."[23] The social concern, implicit in "instruire," is unmentioned, nonexistent at the turn of the century,[24] and its only when when the Age of Enlightenment coalesces that Tissier's statement once again corresponds to literary ideals. Indeed, it is only then that a new, "philosophic" emphasis is placed on "instruire," as the rest of the observation brings out: "La comédie a toujours prétendu plaire en instruisant; mais au XVIIIe siècle, sous l'influence du drame naissant, 'le désir de plaire et d'amuser' est 'relégué au second plan, l'enseignement moral passe au premier.'"25 Something is happening to comedy through the eighteenth century, an evolution that is most clearly visible in the handling of the comic protagonist.

In *Le Légataire universel,* the comic protagonist Géronte is dealt with pitilessly. He is successively at the mercy of a laxative, threatened with violence by Crispin disguised as two provincial relatives, placed at death's door, and blackmailed into accepting a will he did not dictate. If these indignities are not enough, he is also the victim of paralysis. In fact, Regnard's treatment of Géronte so horrified Rousseau that he made a special point of commenting on the third episode in his letter to d'Alembert.

> C'est une chose incroyable qu'avec l'agrément de la police on joue publiquement au milieu de Paris une comédie où, dans l'appartement d'un oncle qu'on vient de voir expirer, son neveu, l'honnête homme de la pièce, s'occupe avec son digne cortège des soins que les lois payent de la corde; et qu'au lieu des larmes que la seule humanité fait verser en pareil cas aux indifférents mêmes, on égaye à l'envi de plaisanteries barbares le triste appareil de la mort. Les droits les plus sacrés, les plus touchants sentiments de la nature, sont joués, dans cette odieuse scène. Les tours les plus punissables y sont rassemblés comme à plaisir avec un enjouement qui fait passer tout cela pour des gentillesses.26

Rousseau's moral reaction, however, falls totally wide of the mark. Géronte is not an individualized character; he is decrepitude personified (note the Greek etymology of this typal name), with as little depth and unity as the other actors of the play. *Le Légataire universel* appeals to primitive human instincts, since it portrays youth ousting age, its scorned victim and ineluctably designated target, or butt. At this most fundamental level, Regnard has returned intuitively to the wellspring of comedy.

In the 1720's and 1730's, the plays of Marivaux still present a comic butt: the inauthentic lovers who, out of *mauvaise foi,* refuse to admit their true feelings. When they become honest with themselves, however, and openly confess their love *(la bonne foi),* the audience identifies with them. In a word, they elicit an ambiguous reaction, since the spectator successively laughs (smiles?) *at,* then *with* the same personage. A further step is taken when it becomes impossible to laugh *or* smile in the presence of the "comic" character. Such is the case in the *comédie larmoyante*. But Marivaux and the *comédie larmoyante* deal with the anguish of young people; age may still be amusing. Certain *drames bourgeois*—Diderot's *Père de famille* (1758), Sedaine's *Philosophe sans le savoir* (1765), for example—will take care of this possible exception. In the opinion of the waning century, people have become too complex for easy categorization into exclusively humorous, sympathetic, and serious types. Toward the end of the age, *bourrus* can be *bienfaisants*, and it is impossible to answer the question, "Est-il bon? Est-il méchant?"—as two plays, by Goldoni and Diderot, respectively, make abundantly clear.

Does this new, sobering complexity apply to M. Dubriage, the "vieux célibataire?" Tissier would seem to be of two minds. On the one hand, he writes, "Le vieux célibataire, tel qu'il a été présenté par Collin, lui aussi fait rire"; and, on the other, "Collin d'Harleville avait voulu intéresser à son vieux célibataire et non le rendre ridicule."[27] The very contradiction suggests this complexity, but before examining Dubriage as a potentially comic (i.e., mirth-provoking) character, it would be appropriate to ask whether any other parts in the play are risible. The answer is certainly negative for members of both the good and the bad teams; good and evil are not laughing matters for Collin. Other than Dubriage himself, the best humorous candidates are the "cinq cousins d'Arras," who display overwhelming simplicity in their thoughts, gestures, and language. Their spokesman, for example, produces a family "tree" that has been drawn by his brother, a "géographe" (p. 138; II, xiv)—he really means "généalogiste." Because they are potentially so good a source of merriment, even to their physical appearance, the cautionary note by Collin d'Harleville about the cousins takes on special significance: "N.B.: Il ne faut pas que leur habillement tienne de la caricature" (p. 137; II, xiv). At the most, they are intended to draw forth a gentle, nostalgic smile like the one produced by Julien and Suson reciting the story of Noah's ark. We are in the presence of pure innocence.

There is a similar note attached to the part of M. Dubriage. It occurs after Mme Evrard's *scène de séduction,* when, following the interruption of this intimate *tête-à-tête,* M. Dubriage. exits. It serves as a clarification to the stage direction, "Il [Dubriage] sort en regardant avec intérêt madame Evrard, qui feint de n'y pas prendre garde" (p. 164; III, v), and reads: "Je désire que l'acteur chargé du rôle de Dubriage se renferme exactement dans les termes de la note ci-dessus. Tout ce qui va au-delà est exagéré, et, j'ose le dire, hors de toute convenance." Molé, the great actor who first created the part, initially played the exit with "des 'gestes libidineux' et des 'regards lubriques,'"[28] and an indignant Collin d'Harleville had to set the matter straight. There is to be nothing caricatural, nothing Géronte-like, about M. Dubriage.

Even without the external supporting evidence of this anecdote, the play alone shows that M. Dubriage is not funny. Although he has a weak, eccentric character in his old age, the audience knows why he has come to this sorry state. What is more important, the victim is fully aware of his psychological decline and its cause. How, then, can we smile with, let alone at, such pathetic waste?[29] It would not be "natural." In the course of the eighteenth century, French comedy has passed from Géronte, the type, to M. Dubriage, the individual, by a process of continued refinement, increased complexity, and progressive edulcoration.[30] At the end of the time span, in the gentle hands of Collin d'Harleville, is the genre not on the verge of extinction?

NOTES

1 Another curious similarity is notable in the dates of the playwrights: Regnard, 1655–1709; Collin d'Harleville, 1755–1806.
2 For details on this literary quarrel, see Laurence Hervey Skinner, *Collin d'Harleville, Dramatist,* Publications of the Institute of French Studies (New York: Columbia University Press, 1933), pp. 128–29, and André Tissier, *Collin d'Harleville, chantre de la vertu souriante,* 2 vols. (Paris: Nizet, 1963–64), I, 173–75.
3 Jean-François Collin d'Harleville, "Avertissement," *Le Vieux Célibataire* (Paris: André, IX [1801]), p. iv. The Avertissement originally appeared in the 1794 edition of the play.

4 One element of Regnard's comic technique is the deliberate imitation of the seventeenth-century French "classics." For a general discussion of these calculated parodies, see Alexandre Calame, *Regnard: Sa Vie et son oeuvre* (Algiers: Baconnier, 1960), pp. 370–72.
5 Jean-François Regnard, *Le Légataire universel*, II, vi, in *Oeuvres complètes de Regnard* (Paris: Sautelet, 1826), IV, 56. All future references or quotations are from this edition and are identified in the text in parentheses (page number, where appropriate; then act and scene).
6 For the extremely clever way Regnard introduces, out of phase, four obstacles to fill five acts, see Calame, *Regnard*, pp. 326–27.
7 Jean-François Collin d'Harleville, *Le Vieux Célibataire*, I, i–iv, in *Oeuvres*, vol. II (Paris: Delongchamps, 1828). All future references and quotations are from this edition and are incorporated in the text in parentheses (pages, where appropriate; then act and scene).
8 Skinner speaks of "the strong character portrayal which makes *Le Vieux Célibataire* its author's most distinguished production and the best comedy of the Revolutionary epoch" (*Collin*, p. 72). In a similar vein, Tissier writes: "[*Le Vieux Célibataire*] s'élève à la peinture de caractères et même d'une condition" (*Collin*, II, 42).
9 Charles Félix Lenient, *La Comédie en France au XVIIIe siècle*, 2 vols. (Paris: Hachette, 1888), II, 341.
10 From a rapid statistical examination, Tissier is able to document Collin's significant abuse of the interjection "bon!" See his *Collin*, II, 307–8.
11 In Act II, scene iv, already hoping to break his marriage contract, Géronte reluctantly speaks to Eraste and Lisette of a present for his fiancée Isabelle. "Je voudrais inventer quelque petit cadeau / Qui coutât peu d'argent, et qui parût nouveau," he says (p. 52), and the subject continues for another eight lines. But even this brief Moliéresque imitation ends with a discussion of dancing and Géronte's former prowess in the art. We have, in other words, returned to the physical world.
12 Mockery of the victimized Géronte also takes the form of *doubles ententes*, dramatic ironies of which he is frequently the target.
13 It is curious to reflect that what Armand calls "le méchant" is the only type of character in *Le Légataire universel*, with the possible exceptions of Mme Argante and Isabelle. For this reason alone, the play could by no stretch of the imagination have been presented as a "team" effort for the possession of Géronte, or of anything else.
14 As early as the second scene, George tries to lift Armand's spirits by saying, "Laissez-là le passé, je vous prie: / Oui, voyez le présent, et surtout l'avenir" (p. 81; I, ii). This statement is as significant for *Le Vieux Célibataire* as Lisette's "Il faut, par notre esprit, faire notre destin" for the *Légataire*.
15 In a very apt synthesis, Tissier has defined the dramatic force of Collin d'Harleville's theater as "contempler la veru pour s'y retrouver" (*Collin*, II, 263).
16 Calame, *Regnard*, p. 74; Tissier, *Collin*, II, 295, and the title.
17 Florent Carton Dancourt, *Le Chevalier à la mode*, I, iii, in *Chefs-d'oeuvre des auteurs comiques* (Paris: Firmin-Didot, 1879), II, 9.

18 Dancourt, *Chevalier*, p. 92 (V, viii).
19 Alain René Lesage, *Turcaret*, I, xiii, in *Chefs-d'oeuvre des auteurs comiques* (Paris: Firmin-Didot, 1877), III, 64. Another of Lesage's plays, *Crispin rival de son maître* (1707), recounts the disloyal tricks the valet Crispin plays to replace his master Valère in Angélique's affections.
20 Jean-Jacques Rousseau, *Lettre à d'Alembert*, in *Du contrat social etc.*, (Paris: Garnier, 1962), p. 158, n. 1.
21 Tissier, *Collin*, II, 223.
22 Jean-François Regnard, *La Critique du Légataire*, sc. iv, in *Oeuvres complètes* (Paris: Sautelet, 1826), IV, 159. My italics.
23 Quoted in "Avertissement sur *le Légataire universel*," *Oeuvres complètes*, IV, 14.
24 In his brief history of French comedy immediately after Molière, Rousseau spoke first of some authors who exploited coarse language to "flatter une jeunesse débauchée et des femmes sans moeurs." In addition, "d'autres auteurs, plus réservés dans leurs saillies, laissant les premiers amuser les femmes perdues, se chargèrent d'encourager les filous. Regnard, un des moins libres, n'est pas le moins dangereux" (*Lettre à d'Alembert*, p. 158).
25 Tissier, *Collin*, II, 223.
26 Rousseau, *Lettre à d'Alembert*, p. 158.
27 Tissier, *Collin*, II, 283, 149. The opposition of the two passages is far from irreconcilable; Tissier could easily maintain that M. Dubriage provokes laughter *in spite of* Collin, that the (modern) reader is desperately looking for *something* to laugh at.
28 Tissier, *Collin*, II, 289.
29 Aside from the smile that innocence prompts, the only potentially comic element of this play are the double entendres with which Armand and Laure cleverly and "justly" deceive the evildoers.
30 Some thirty-five years before *Le Vieux Célibataire*—that is, at the time of the *drame bourgeois*—the genre had already lost its *vis comica* in the eyes of Rousseau, certainly not one of the greatest admirers of comedy; "Nos auteurs modernes, guidés par de meilleures intentions, font des pièces plus épurées, mais aussi qu'arrive-t-il? Qu'elles n'ont plus de vrai comique, et ne produisent aucun effet. Elles instruisent beaucoup, si l'on veut; mais elles ennuient encore davantage. Autant vaudrait aller au sermon" (*Lettre à d'Alembert*, p. 159). Chabanon struck a similar note in his *Epître sur la comédie* (1792) that reflects on the "beautiful" world painted by Collin's theater: "L'âge d'or, croyez-moi, n'eut point de comédie. / Retrancher d'ici-bas les méchants et les sots, / Thalie est sans modèle et brise ses pinceaux" (quoted by Tissier, *Collin*, II, 147).

Voltaire, "Lexicographer of the Enlightenment"

VIRGIL W. TOPAZIO

In a century characterized by René Pomeau as "l'âge d'or des dictionnaires" and during which "les 'lumières' rayonnaient d'énormes collections alphabétiques,"[1] Voltaire's classical predilections caused him to shun this literary format until well past middle age. Even after having devoted much time and effort to producing his *Dictionnaire philosophique*, the first edition of which appeared in June 1764, he made it quite clear in the Preface to this work that he made a distinction between "pure literature" and the ordinary dictionary article.[2] It is my contention, however, that Voltaire more than any other *philosophe*, Diderot not excluded, deserves the title of "lexicographer of the Enlightenment."

Voltaire's first serious interest in writing articles in the encyclopedic or dictionary format was provoked, his secretary Collini informs us, by Frederick II during that now-famous supper of September 28, 1752. According to Collini, the King, no doubt inspired by the appearance of the first two volumes of the *Encyclopédie* in July and October of 1751, suggested "le projet du dictionnaire philosophique" to his *philosophe* guests. Voltaire, "vif et ardent au travail, commença dès le lendemain,"[3] and worked so diligently that Frederick was moved to exclaim: "Si vous continuez du train dont vous allez, le *Dictionnaire* sera fait en peu de temps."[4] Unfortunately, the congenial and philosophic relationship between Voltaire and Frederick rapidly deteriorated. An even more important factor contributing to the discontinuation of the work on the dictionary project was his involvement with the *Encyclopédie* shortly after his unceremonious departure from Potsdam in 1753.

Although Voltaire had not been asked to contribute to the first volumes of the *Encyclopédie*,[5] d'Alembert did later actively seek Voltaire's participation and was able finally to announce in the "Avertissement des Editeurs" to the fourth volume (1754): "Nous ne pouvons trop nous hâter d'annoncer que M. de Voltaire nous a donné les articles ESPRIT, ELOQUENCE, ELEGANCE, LITTERATURE, etc. et nous en fait espérer d'autres."[6] No doubt Voltaire had been favorably impressed by the advantages, from a propagandist's point of view, offered by a work like the *Encyclopédie*, which ideally seemed to combine the philosophic and the useful. Therefore, when on March 8, 1759, the *privilège* was officially withdrawn from the *Encyclopédie* and many months passed without any indication that the privilège would be restored, Voltaire quite understandably once again turned his attention to the *Dictionnaire philosophique* that he had abandoned after his break with Frederick II. A letter to Mme du Deffand in 1760 reveals that he was in fact seriously working on this project: "Je suis absorbé," he wrote, "dans un compte que je me rends à moi-même par ordre alphabétique, de tout ce que je dois penser sur ce monde-ci et sur l'autre" (D8764, CV, 149).

Voltaire's discovery of the full potentialities of the encyclopedic form had not prevented him from noting the restrictions and limitations imposed upon Diderot and d'Alembert. Working alone, he was now free from censorship and therefore able to be more daring. And not having to contend with collaborators, he was able to rely exclusively on his own judgment as to whether or not an article deserved to be published, an independence Diderot and d'Alembert had not enjoyed. In short, because he was alone, he avoided what Raymond Naves described as "la masse disparate des collaborateurs spécialisés, à qui il manque trop souvent les véritables lumières."[7] More important to Voltaire the stylist was the unprecedented opportunity to produce a work stylistically in accord with his own high standards. Let us recall how often he had bitterly complained about the unevenness of both style and content in the articles being published in the *Encyclopédie*. In a real sense then, the forty-three articles Voltaire had written for volumes V–VIII of the *Encyclopédie* justified Raymond Naves's statement that "l'Encyclopédie soit à l'origine de ses divers *Alphabets* militants."[8]

Voltaire's decision to publish the *Dictionnaire philosophique portatif* was conceivably prompted by his new-found conviction that this would be the best possible method of informing his readers about the religious, aesthetic, moral, social, historical, and philosophical problems they faced in life. His limited articles in the *Encyclopédie* had been, after all, short ones and, with few exceptions like HISTOIRE, insignificant, despite the editors' remark at the end of Montesquieu's article, GOUT, that "l'on dira dans les siècles à venir: Voltaire et Montesquieu eurent part aussi à l'Encyclopédie" (VII, 767). The real Voltaire now had an opportunity to deploy his great erudition against the forces of evil and ignorance. Louis Moland confirms this in his "Avertissement" to the *Dictionnaire philosophique:* "Voltaire n'avait livré au christianisme que de légers combats. Avec le *Dictionnaire philosophique,*" he added, "c'est la guerre qui commence. Elle fut infatigable, acharnée; elle dura une quinzaine d'années sans trêve ni merci" (M. XVII, v–vi).

If George R. Havens was correct in asserting that *Candide* was written quickly because Voltaire in 1758 was at the height of his intellectual and stylistic development,[9] one can with even more justification claim that the articles of the *Dictionnaire philosophique* represent the culmination of Voltaire's literary skills and the full fruition of his philosophical thought. No single work seems to contain more succinctly and present more forcefully the ideas commonly associated with the Enlightenment in eighteenth-century France.

The first edition of the *Dictionnaire philosophique portatif*, containing seventy-three articles, appeared in June 1764. Its publication was duly reported in the *Correspondance littéraire* by Grimm in September of that year.[10] Two months earlier Bachaumont had announced in his *Mémoires:* "On parle depuis quelques jours d'un ouvrage qu'on attribue à

M. de Voltaire.... La liberté qui règne dans cet écrit et le nom imposant de son auteur, le font rechercher avec autant de soin qu'on en prendra sûrement pour en empêcher la distribution."[11] Several editions followed, of which the most important were the Varberg edition of 1765, containing 96 articles; the 1767 edition, with 114 articles; and the 1769 edition, in which the number of articles had increased to 119 and the title had been changed to *La Raison par Alphabet*. This 1769 edition was the first to include Voltaire's *L'A, B, C, Dix-sept Dialogues traduits de l'anglais*. Both works, incidentally, were condemned by Rome on July 11, 1776.

The 1770 edition, the "septième édition revue, corrigée et augmentée par l'Auteur," bore the title *Dictionnaire philosophique; ou, La Raison par alphabet*. This was the first edition to adopt the title *Dictionnaire philosophique*, and it coincided with the appearance of the first volumes of the more ambitious work *Questions sur l'Encyclopédie*, also in 1770. But before we turn our attention to the latter work, let me briefly comment on the contents of the articles of Voltaire's first major work in the alphabetical format. Even a cursory study should provide greater insight into the role this work played in the shift in emphasis the *philosophes* effected in eighteenth-century France from a religious culture, which had thoroughly dominated the Middle Ages and had remained powerfully pervasive throughout the seventeenth century, to a secular culture, in which the proper study of man had become man himself.

Several years ago, Yves Florenne gave the following breakdown of the articles by subject matter:

> Sur les 118 articles de ce *Dictionnaire philosophique*, dont le premier mot est Abbé, je n'en relève guère que sept ou huit qui se rapportent expressément à la philosophie (encore est-il rare qu'on n'y rencontre pas au moins un Juif ou un Jésuite); dix-neuf, parmi les plus longs, traitent spécifiquement de la Bible, —laquelle est répandue par tout cet alphabet de raison, avec Dieu, le christianisme et la religion en général. A ce chapitre, auquel se rattache la théologie, ne sont pas consacrés moins de quarante articles. Le reste traite de politique, de sociologie, de droit, de morale pratique, de littérature, amour, anthropophages, animaux, et autres faits divers.[12]

In a recent study of the polemical style of the *Dictionnaire philosophique* Jeanne Monty reported: "On note dès l'abord que les quatre cinquièmes des articles de 1769 traitent directement de questions religieuses, les sujets proprement philosophiques n'occupant qu'une quinzaine d'articles, et les matières politiques, cinq seulement.[13] And in an even more recent study by M. L. Perkins entitled "Theme and Form in Voltaire's Alphabetical Works," we find the following breakdown by category: arts and letters, 3; history, 5; laws, customs, and ethics, 19; mythology, 4; natural sciences, 5; orientalia, 3; philosophy and psychology, 23; politics, 8; religion, 48.[14]

In those articles classified as "arts and letters" Voltaire's intent was clearly to influence the reader to shed his prejudices and provincialism. In the historically oriented articles Voltaire's main concern was with problems created for man by the distortion of the human record, particularly as applied to religion, particularly Christianity. Another dominant theme, noticeably in those articles dealing specifically with mythology, is that of man as the originator of myth and the role this played in man's religious beliefs. The scientific articles understandably tend to throw doubt on the orthodox and traditional eighteenth-century notions of the universe. A few articles, in keeping with Voltaire's internationalism and universal humanism, encourage the typical European mind to break out of its narrow Western framework. About one-sixth of the articles deal to some degree with the study of human faculties and man's thinking processes, an eighteenth-century preoccupation. And of course those dealing with politics and government have as their aim the emphasis of human rights and man's proper role in government.

But Voltaire's primary preoccupation in the *Dictionnaire philosophique* was unquestionably religion and religiously oriented issues—that is, fanaticism, intolerance, and ignorance. In almost half of the articles we find Voltaire questioning the church's authority, accusing it of fomenting persecution, if not crimes, and pointing out the advantages of a religion stripped of dogmas, miracles, and revelation. Although he realistically recognized the foibles and weaknesses of human nature, he nonetheless repeatedly called upon man to place greater reliance upon reason. In the words of a recent critic, the goal of Voltaire was "to free man's mind by a deliberate broadening of his perspectives through the use of widely varying subject-matters rich in thematic content. The additions made in most of the categories between 1764 and 1769 show, too, a persisting effort to reinforce all of the aspects of this programme.[15]

Traditional opinion, supported by Georges Bengesco, had held that the *Questions sur l'Encyclopédie,* published in nine volumes between 1770 and 1772, contained articles written by Voltaire for the most part between 1769 and 1772—the implication being that the *Questions* were just an enlargement of his *Dictionnaire philosophique; ou, La Raison par alphabet.* Professor Ira O. Wade has contested this view, as well as the traditionally held view that the *Dictionnaire philosophique portatif* owed its origin to Frederick's suggestion at a dinner in Potsdam. According to Professor Wade, Voltaire had dashed off "petits chapitres" in prose form at least as far back as 1740. These *rogatons,* arranged in alphabetical order, had been kept in notebooks, and the *Dictionnaire philosophique portatif* was merely the first systematic publication of this material in 1764. Regardless of when the articles were written, the importance of these alphabetical works cannot be overemphasized, Professor Wade insisted. "The *Questions* represent the accumulated wisdom of Voltaire over a period of forty years. They represent the characteristic form of expression for that wisdom."[16]

The big difference in the number of articles manifestly makes the *Questions,* with its 438 articles, more than just an enlargement of the 118 articles of the *Dictionnaire philosophique.* And as Joseph-Marie Quérard had previously pointed out, "Voltaire n'avait reproduit dans les 'Questions' qu'un petit nombre d'articles du 'Dictionnaire'. A cela près, les deux ouvrages n'ont rien de commun que la distribution par ordre alphabétique."[17] The separate identity is supported by Samuel Taylor, who wrote: "There is ample evidence that Voltaire intended the *Questions sur l'Encyclopédie* to survive as a separate work, since he adds a succession of cross-references to this text by name.... In the final edition, of course, the *Questions* were cannibalized by the *Dictionnaire philosophique.*"[18] The Kehl edition, as we know, had included all of Voltaire's alphabetical works under the title *Dictionnaire philosophique.*[19]

A brief summary of the origin of the *Questions* may shed some light on its importance to eighteenth-century thought. This extraordinary achievement was essentially the work of Voltaire, despite the known contributions by certain collaborators and Voltaire's insistence on presenting it as the work of "quelques gens de lettres," a position proclaimed in the subtitle, which reads: "distribuées en forme de Dictionnaire par des Amateurs."

Before the end of 1768 Voltaire and Charles-Joseph Panckoucke—the founder, owner, publisher, or agent of many gazettes—were in frequent correspondence concerning the latter's ambitious plan to publish a revised edition of the *Encyclopédie*. He had found a sympathetic ear in Voltaire, whose dissatisfaction with several aspects of that undertaking is well known. By the fall of 1769 Voltaire had agreed to be responsible for the literary sections of the *Supplément de l'Encyclopédie*, and in a letter to Panckoucke dated December 6, 1769, he indicated that he not only had already revised and expanded his own articles previously published in the *Encyclopédie* but that he had more than one hundred other articles ready to contribute to this *Supplément*. And being a shrewd businessman, he proceeded to advise Panckoucke to include the article "Femme" with the propaganda material to stimulate interest among the readers. He also pointed out the necessity for speed, since he was 76 years old (D16025, CXIX, 354).

The correspondence of this period makes it clear that the project had galvanized Voltaire into action, that he was rapidly writing new articles and revising or expanding others taken from his notebooks or portfolios. It is equally clear that despite the importance he attached to these articles as propaganda pieces, he still did not ascribe much literary importance to them. Besides, he considered himself too old to undertake any serious writing, he explained in refusing Panckoucke's offer of 18,000 francs to write about 600 pages for the new edition of his *Oeuvres* being contemplated by Panckoucke and Cramer (see D15929, Oct. 1769, CXIX, 268).

Several reasons forced Panckoucke to abandon the publication of a revised *Encyclopédie:* Diderot refused to participate in the venture; the *Encyclopédie d'Yverdon* being published in Switzerland was bound to discourage possible subscribers; and most important, the Chancellor Maupeou refused to grant permission to publish the revision in Paris. Thwarted in that direction, he proceeded to republish the original *Encyclopédie* only to encounter more difficulties. The first three volumes were impounded by the government before they could be published; they were placed in the Bastille, where they remained for almost six years.

It was during this period of uncertainty that Voltaire decided to undertake his own publication of the articles he had intended for the *Supplément*. By the end of January 1770 we find Voltaire writing d'Alembert that he no longer planned to collaborate on the *Supplément*. One explanation was that he refused to have his name placed "avant le vôtre et celui de m. Diderot, dans un ouvrage qui est tout à vous deux," as the publishers no doubt had suggested capitalizing on Voltaire's name. And he continued, "si mes souffrances continuelles me permettent l'amusement du travail, je travaillerai sur un autre plan qui ne conviendra pas peut-être à la gravité d'un *Dictionnaire encyclopédique*" (D16123, 31 janv. 1770, CXIX, 448-49). To render his defection more acceptable, he added that those working on the bigger and more important *Encyclopédie* were free to use the contents of his contemplated *Questions sur l'Encyclopédie* in any way they wished.

Voltaire's efforts to mollify those involved in the Panckoucke project were not entirely successful. D'Alembert displayed some skepticism when, in a letter of February 22, 1770, he asked: "Vous faites donc *l'Encyclopédie* à vous seul?" (D16176, CXX, 51). And Panckoucke's apparent unhappiness caused Voltaire to urge d'Alembert on February 28, 1770, to reassure Panckoucke. "Il s'imagine," wrote Voltaire, "qu'on fait une petite *Encyclopédie*; il se trompe, et je vous prie de le lui dire. On fait, par ordre alphabétique, un ouvrage qui n'a rien de commun avec le *Dictionnaire encyclopédique*, et dans lequel on rend à cet ouvrage immense la justice qui lui est due. On y parle de vous comme vous méritez qu'on en parle; ce sont des médailles qu'on frappe à votre honneur" (D16186, CXX, 58). His message to Panckoucke repeated the same refrain: "Ceux qui travaillent à deux ou trois volumes de Questions sur l'Encyclopédie croient vous rendre un très grand service. Ils donnent les plus grands éloges à la première édition, ils annoncent la seconde; ils espèrent décréditer un peu les contrefaçons, et ils s'amusement" (D16173, CXX, 48).

The Introduction to the first volume in 1770 of the *Questions sur l'Encyclopédie par des amateurs* continued to minimize any sense of competition between this work and the Panckoucke project. Witness the use of "par des amateurs" in the title and the first paragraph, which reads: "Quelques gens de lettres qui ont étudié *l'Encyclopédie*, ne proposent ici que des questions, et ne demandent que des éclaircissemens; ils se déclarent douteurs et non docteurs." This was followed by praise for the *Encyclopédie*, and in the last paragraph Voltaire paid tribute to those engaged in producing the new edition: "C'est à eux que nous dédions notre essai, dont ils pourront prendre et corriger ou laisser les articles, à leur gré, dans la grande édition que les libraires de Paris préparent. Ce sont des plantes exotiques que nous offrons; elles ne mériteront d'entrer dans leur vaste collection qu'autant qu'elles seront cultivées par de telles mains; et c'est alors qu'elles pourront recevoir la vie."

Voltaire's claims that the *Questions* represented the work of several minds was not just rhetoric. Several of the articles were indeed written by others, and Voltaire's correspondence, for example, reveals him thanking Bertrand for "Droit canonique" and requesting of Servan his "Spectacles qui peuvent contribuer aux bonnes moeurs" (see D16026, CXIX, 355). What is more, he borrowed liberally from the *Encyclopédie*. Nonetheless, despite the typical freedom enjoyed by eighteenth-century writers to borrow or revise the works of others, the *Questions sur l'Encyclopédie* remains essentially the product of Voltaire. It was an important and effective weapon in his unending war on ignorance and superstition; it stands out as a monumental achievement and an indispensable contribution to the enlightenment of mankind. And it was accomplished at an age when most men are flirting with senility.

A brief mention should be made of a much less important alphabetical, the *Opinion en alphabet,* which surfaced after Voltaire's death. This collection of articles was among the materials which Panckoucke purchased from Mme Denis in September 1778 and later sold to Beaumarchais and which were subsequently incorporated in the Kehl edition. Recent scholars, among them Jeanne R. Monty and Bertram Eugene Schwarzbach, have been trying to solve the mystery surrounding the origin and purpose of this collection.[20] The consensus is that most of these articles are not original writings of Voltaire and that they constitute what remained in the notebooks or portfolios after Voltaire had extracted what he needed for the *Questions*. With many of these articles it has been possible to determine the author or source.

Exemplifying the broad interests of the *philosophes*, the encyclopedic tendency was widespread in eighteenth-century France, and Voltaire made the most extensive use of the alphabetical approach. For most writers the very breadth of the subject matter presented the danger of devitalizing the ideas, most of which had admittedly already been advanced by previous writers. Voltaire, however, was fortunate enough to possess a literary style that enabled him to surmount any such danger. It was a combination of unusual clarity and a pithiness of expression, enhanced by an unparalleled wit that was fired by a hatred of superstition and injustice. In short, his literary skills permitted him symbolically to open many well-marked doors to a freedom of mind and body that had previously remained stubbornly closed. A contemporary critic summarized Voltaire's contribution with these words: "Mais il est des portes ouvertes par où personne ne passe: il faut les enfoncer à coups répétés et à grand bruit. Tel fut le rôle de Voltaire et en particulier de son *Dictionnaire*."[21]

NOTES

1 René Pomeau, ed., Voltaire, *Dictionnaire philosophique* (Paris: Garnier-Flammarion, 1964), p. 9.
2 *Oeuvres de Voltaire*, ed. Louis Moland, 52 vols. (Paris: Garnier Frères, 1877–85), XVII, 2.
3 Côme-Alexandre Collini, *Mon Séjour auprès de Voltaire* (Paris: Collin, 1807), p. 32.
4 Voltaire's *Correspondence* (the definitive edition, consisting of vols. 85–132 [1968–76]), in *The Complete Works of Voltaire*, ed. Theodore Besterman (Geneva: Institut et Musée Voltaire, Les Délices, 1971), D5056, XCVII, 225.
5 Various reasons have been offered to explain the failure to enlist the services of the outstanding *philosophe* of the day. See Marta Rezler, "Voltaire and the Encyclopédie," in *Studies on Voltaire and the Eighteenth Century* (Geneva: Institut et Musée Voltaire, 1964), XXX, 147–87; also René Pintard, "Voltaire et l'Encyclopédie," *Annales de l'Université de Paris*, 22ᵉ année, n° 1 (Oct. 1952).
6 Reference is to the 17-volume edition: *Encyclopédie ou Dictionnaire Raisonné des Sciences, des Arts et des Métiers, par une société de Gens de Lettres* (Paris: Briasson,

David l'aîné, Le Breton, Durand, 1751-65). Future references will be noted in the text only by volume and page number.
7 Raymond Naves, *Voltaire et l'Encylcopédie* (Paris: Les Editions des Presses Modernes, 1938), p. 163.
8 Ibid., p. 96.
9 George R. Havens, ed., Voltaire, *Candide* (New York: Henry Holt, 1934), p. xxix.
10 Melchior Grimm, *Correspondance littéraire, philosophique et critique*, 16 vols. (Paris: Garnier, 1877-82), VI, 65.
11 Louis Petit de Bachaumont, *Mémoires secrets pour servir à l'histoire de la république des lettres en France*, 36 vols. (London: John Adamson, 1781-89), I-II, 74.
12 Yves Florenne, ed., Voltaire, *Dictionnaire philosophique, suivie de quarante questions sur l'Encyclopédie* (Paris: Le Club Français du livre, 1962), p. v.
13 Jeanne R. Monty, "Etude sur le style polémique de Voltaire: Le Dictionnaire philosophique," in *Studies on Voltaire and the Eighteenth Century* (Geneva: Institut et Musée Voltaire, Les Délices, 1966), XLIV, 14.
14 M. L. Perkins, "Theme and Form in Voltaire's Alphabetical Works," in *Studies on Voltaire and the Eighteenth Century* (Oxfordshire: The Voltaire Foundation, 1974), CXX, 17-28.
15 Ibid., p. 22; I am also indebted to Perkin's article for the preceding breakdown of articles by subject matter.
16 Ira O. Wade, "The Search for a New Voltaire," *Transactions of the American Philosophical Society*, n.s., 48, pt. 4 (July 1958), 86. See also p. 111.
17 Joseph-Marie Quérard, *La France littéraire*, 12 vols. (Paris: Firmin Didot, 1827-64), X, 288-89.
18 Samuel Taylor, "The Definitive Text of Voltaire's Works: The Leningrad Encadrée," in *Studies on Voltaire and the Eighteenth Century* (Oxfordshire: The Voltaire Foundation, 1974), CXXIV, 32.
19 For a thorough study of this question, see William H. Trapnell's "Survey and Analysis of Voltaire's Collective Editions, 1728-1789," in *Studies on Voltaire and the Eighteenth Century* (Geneva, 1970), LXXVII, 105-99. In the Preface to this work Professor Trapnell points out: "The reader may find it useful to remember that some works were integrated into larger, later works. Reference to the former ceases when reference to the latter begins. But the early alphabetical works, such as the *Questions sur l'Encyclopédie*, though separate and distinct, are considered from the outset as belonging to the ultimately all-inclusive *Dictionnaire philosophique*" (p. 107).
20 The two works to consult are: 1) Jeanne Monty's essay, "Voltaire's Debt to the *Encyclopédie* in the *Opinion en Alphabet*" (to be published in *The Complete Works of Voltaire*), and 2) Bertram E. Schwartzbach's article, "The Authenticity, Dates and Sources of Articles which first appeared in the Kehl edition of the *Dictionnaire philosophique*" (submitted to *Voltaire Studies*).
21 Florenne, *Dictionnaire philosophique*, p. iii.

The Physiocrats and the Encyclopedists

JEAN A. PERKINS

To their contemporaries, the juxtaposition of the Physiocrats and the Encyclopedists would not have been as shocking as it is to us. In the swirling waves of opinion which inundated Paris in the last half of the eighteenth century, the *Encyclopédistes* and the *Economistes*, as the Physiocrats were then called, were often taken to be two branches of the same tree (the image used by Linguet in 1774) or different generations of the same family (the image used by Le Gros in 1787).[1] The two groups were perceived to overlap both in time and approach. Most of the public controversy over the *Encyclopédie* dates from the 1750's. After its supposed suppression in 1759, the public lost track of the publication until the final ten volumes of text were distributed in 1765, after which there was a seven-year gap until the eleven volumes of plates were published in 1772. In view of this long history of publication, interrupted twice by official edicts condemning the enterprise, it is no wonder that critics of its content assumed that there existed a clandestine group behind the *Encyclopédie* responsible for its critical tone. There was never any clear definition of who belonged to this group, but most of the critics of the ancien régime were habitually placed within its fold. The Physiocrats moved into public view just as the *Encyclopédie* was forced to go underground. Quesnay actually published his first economic investigations in volumes 6 and 7 of the *Encyclopédie*, while Mirabeau's popular *L'Ami des hommes* dates from

1757. The Physiocrats also suffered from the tightened censorship imposed on publications in the wake of the condemnation of Helvétius's *De l'esprit* and the *Encyclopédie*. Mirabeau himself was imprisoned at Vincennes for a week before beginning a period of exile at his country estate after his *Théorie de l'impôt* had also been condemned in 1760. This sufficiently frightened the newly formed nucleus of the *économistes* so as to discourage them from any further publication until 1763, at which time Mirabeau produced his *Philosophie rurale*, written in close collaboration with Quesnay. After this the number of disciples in the group increased, as did the number of works published. To their opponents, the Encyclopedists and the Physiocrats were cut from the same cloth; they were critical of the basic structure of French society and suggested various schemes to improve the economic and political conditions of the country. As one group faded from public view, the other came forward.

When Bachaumont's *Mémoires secrets* were published for the first time in 1777, the editor noted that there had been a three-stage evolution of the philosophic spirit since the mid-fifties: first came the *philosophes encyclopédistes*, then the *philosophes économistes*, and finally the *patriotes*, the group which formed about 1770 to uphold the concept of sovereignty.[2] Writing in 1787, the abbé Le Gros carefully delineated the historical background of the remarkable success of the Physiocrats, who had come within a hairsbreadth of taking over the country. According to Le Gros, the Encyclopedists—among whom he numbers Voltaire, Diderot, d'Alembert, and Helvétius—dominated the literary and philosophical scene during the 1750's and early 1760's; their principles, however, were purely destructive, and they had come to be known as "les Riénistes":

> Ils n'en exerçoient pas moins un empire absolu sur le monde littéraire; l'élégance du style, les charmes de la poésie, les plaisanteries, les sarcasmes, les personnalités mêmes et les injures tenoient lieu de preuves et de raisons à ces hardis destructeurs; on les craignoit, et les gens de lettres gémissoient en silence sous le joug qui leur étoit imposé.[3]

Suddenly Jean-Jacques Rousseau burst upon the scene, showing the Encyclopedists up for what they really were—purveyors of a double doctrine, one public and open, the other private and secret. Thus disillusioned, the public was ready for a new approach to these matters and turned to the Physiocrats:

> Ainsi la place étoit vacante; les Economistes s'en emparèrent, ils le firent d'une manière si imposante et avec un appareil si séduisant, que, dès le premier instant, les esprits furent subjugués... les Encyclopédistes prirent le parti de se rallier sourdement sous les étandarts de l'économie.... Tous les gens, avides de nouveautés, devinrent alors disciples de l'Ecole économique.[4]

Le Gros had no time for any of these groups, dismissing them all finally as materialistic atheists, destructive of all proper modes of authority, both religious and political.

During his visit to Paris in 1765–66 Adam Smith had been in close contact with both the Encyclopedists and the Physiocrats, defining the latter by their belief in "the produce of land as the sole source of revenue and wealth of every country.[5] He goes on to note that their followers were extremely numerous:

> They have for some years past made a pretty considerable sect, distinguished in the French republic of letters by the name of Œconomists.... This sect, in their works, which are very numerous,... all follow implicitly, and without any sensible variation, the doctrine of Mr. Quesnai. There is upon this account little variety in the greater part of their works.[6]

Adam Smith's first editor, William Playfair, in the Introduction to the 1805 edition of the *Wealth of Nations* comes close to amalgamating the two groups. After stating that one of the main causes of the French Revolution was the theories of the Economists as put into practice by the abbé Sièyes, the abbé Morellet, Condorcet, and the younger Mirabeau, Playfair remarks upon the school's popularity in late-eighteenth-century France: "The philosophers who wished to alter the constitution of church and state... well aware that they were too feeble to attack openly the rights of either... sheltered themselves under the wings of the œconomists, whose end was legitimate."[7] Diderot himself appears to agree with this analysis of the relationship of the Encyclopedists and the Physiocrats when he notes in a letter to Grimm in November 1769 that the usefulness of the *Economistes* lies in their ability to say what they wish openly since they are so well protected:

> Ce qui me plaît le plus de cette nouvelle école de Quesneylistes, c'est que, très protégée, elle dit tout ce qu'il lui plaît, qu'elle parle avec une liberté que nous ne connoissions pas, et qu'à la longue la police, la cour et les magistrats s'accoutumeront à tout entendre, et les auteurs à tout dire.[8]

Even the abbé Galiani, after having published his scathing attack upon the free-trade principles of the Physiocrats, acknowledged that the two groups were closer together than he had admitted. Writing to Suard in September 1770, Galiani makes the following remark about Morellet, who frequented both circles: "L'abbé Morellet n'a qu'à jouer à croix ou pile s'il veut être des nôtres ou des économistes. C'est une affaire de goût."[9]

Public confusion over the identity of these two groups was reinforced by their interlocking social circles. Quesnay had held a kind of open house in his cramped quarters at Versailles ever since the early 1750's, and to this gathering came Diderot, d'Alembert, Duclos, Helvétius, and Buffon. Along with them were to be found such emerging *Economistes* as Turgot, Morellet, Le Mercier de La Rivière, le comte de Mirabeau, and Dupont. Mme de Pompadour, to whose household Quesnay was officially attached, often dropped in to share in the conversation. In addition to the gatherings at Versailles, the same group, or slight variations of it, often found themselves together at the regular meetings in the salons of Helvétius, d'Holbach, Necker, and Mme Geoffrin.

The publication of Le Mercier de La Rivière's *L'Ordre naturel et essentiel des sociétés politiques* in 1767 marks the beginning of the open divergence between the two groups, brought about finally by the abbé Galiani, whose anti-Physiocratic work the *Dialogues sur le commerce des blés* came out in December of 1770. Internecine strife between different closely related groups during this period was not at all unknown—witness the split between Diderot and d'Alembert in 1759 when the *Encyclopédie* was officially banned. From his retreat at Ferney, Voltaire could afford to take a relatively objective view of these quarrels, but even he was drawn into taking sides in the *affaire des Economistes.* Indeed, Voltaire's reaction is one of the better-known results of this battle; having been induced to apply Physiocratic principles of farming to his own estate and knowing how poorly they worked in his part of the world, Voltaire turned against them and published his *Homme aux 40 écus* in 1768, which, along with Galiani's *Dialogues* two years later, pretty well eliminated the Physiocrats from serious philosophic consideration. In a letter to Sartine, then Lieutenant General of Police, Galiani describes the Physiocratic fever in France during the 1760's: "Ce fut en enthousiasme, une mode, un caprice littéraire, un mississipi, un jansénisme, une Fronde, une croisade, enfin, une de ces maladies épidémiques d'esprit dont la nation française est parfois attaquée."[10] There is no doubt that for a certain period of time it looked as if Physiocracy would emerge as the dominant philosophical, political, moral, and economic theory in Paris. But this was not destined to be, especially since Physiocracy remained very much a theoretical issue which was too closely tied in the public's mind to certain specific political decisions concerning the grain trade. As a theory it was judged deficient by such serious thinkers as Diderot and Turgot; in practice it was tied to the sharply rising price of grain, which brought on numerous bread riots in the 1760's and 1770's.

Physiocracy had its roots in the speculations of Dr. François Quesnay, a self-made man, the son of a peasant farmer who became a surgeon and then, in a most unusual move for the period, studied medicine and became a regular doctor. He came to the attention of Mme de Pompadour and by the early 1750's was installed in her entourage at Versailles. The title "médecin consultant du roi" was conferred upon him by the King after Quesnay had been instrumental in helping the Dauphin recover from a case of smallpox. This cure also led to a title of nobility and appointment to the Académie des Sciences, where Quesnay came into contact with such luminaries as Buffon and d'Alembert. His first economic speculations are contained in two articles, "Fermiers" and "Grains," published under his son's name in volumes 6 and 7 of the *Encyclopédie.* A serious concern with the state of the French economy led Quesnay to investigate what he considered to be the main reason for its decline, that is, the government's concentration on manufacturing and commerce to the detriment of agriculture.

These rather nebulous speculations were codified by Quesnay in 1758 in his well-known "Tableau économique," the first attempt ever made to put an economic theory into mathematical form.[11] Of course, Quesnay did this visually in a flow chart, but his basic assumptions can be easily converted into twentieth-century economic terms by applying the following formula:

$$P = f(K, L, Ld)$$

where P stands for production, f for function, K for kapital, L for labor, and Ld for land.

Quesnay assumed a stationary economy and devised a linear flow chart of market exchange which postulates only three functional groups in society: the farmers, the proprietors, and all the others, called by Quesnay the sterile class. Each of these groups starts out the year with a certain number of units of working capital in goods or land which they exchange with each other in a fixed pattern during the course of the year. Starting with 1 unit of goods, by the end of the year those in the sterile class are right back where they started, having received 1 unit from the proprietors and 1 unit from the farmers as purchase price for manufactured goods and having paid the farmers for 2 units of food and raw materials. They have 1, receive 2, pay out 2, and are left with 1. The proprietors are also back where they started—that is, with 2 units of land value—having received 2 units in rent from the farmers and having paid the sterile class for 1 unit of manufactured goods and the farmers for 1 unit of food. They have 2, receive 2, pay out 2, and are left with 2. But the farmers have done something different; they start with 2 units of food and raw materials, receive 1 from the proprietors and 2 from the sterile class, pay out 2 units as rent to the proprietors and 1 unit for manufactured goods to the sterile class; theoretically they too should be back where they started, but the value of the farmers' units increases during the year, since agricultural commodities have a natural, inborn reproductive factor. Thus, the farmers end up the year, after having produced 5 units of food from their 2 units of working capital, with a clear surplus of 3 units of working capital. They have 2, receive 3, pay out 3, produce 3, and are left with 5 to carry over to the next year. This surplus Quesnay dubbed the *produit net*. According to this analysis the farmers are the only social group able to produce a *produit net*, and they are therefore the only productive class, the only source of real wealth in the nation. Quesnay continued to tinker with his *Tableau économique* for years, but the fundamental theory never changed, and this basic idea must be mastered to understand all the other ideological constructs which were developed by him and other adherents to the doctrine—including Mirabeau, who joined in 1757; Dupont, who was recruited in 1763; and Le Mercier de La Rivière, who came back from Martinique in 1764.

The social, moral, and political theories which these writers elaborated during the 1760's all rest upon the assumption, constantly reiterated, that all forms of human behavior are dependent upon a system of natural law, embodied in Quesnay's *Tableau*. There is a material base which represents the reality of the environment and which determines man's place therein. This material system is governed by a series of immutable and absolute laws of nature. The Physiocrats were sure that they had uncovered the scientific bases of these laws, and it is this combination of scientific materialism and natural law ethics and politics which makes their theories most closely resemble those of the Encyclopedists.

According to the Physiocrats, private property is the *sine qua non* of human society; it is the only real natural right, from which all other natural and social rights can be deduced in a completely logical and deductive way which the Physiocrats called *le système de l'évidence*. Man is merely a part of the order of nature, and his behavior not only should but actually does conform to its rules. Every living creature has an inalienable right to provide for itself in order to survive; this leads automatically and without exception to the right of each individual human being to acquire and keep various kinds of property, the main one being the land he works in order to produce his livelihood.

A corollary to this right of property is the right to do with it what one wishes: thus, the second major ethical and political principle is that of individual liberty, the right to enjoy one's own property. This principle is clearly based on a hedonist ethic, very close to that elucidated by Helvétius in *De l'esprit*. The major goal of any governmental structure should be to guarantee the property rights of the individuals who make up that society, while preserving the individual's right to do with his property what he wishes—that is, his liberty. This leads to the third major social principle, that of *sûreté*, the guaranteeing of a calm, ordered social organization in which each individual can be free to benefit from his own acquisitions. Many Physiocrats delineated what seemed to be the necessary consequence of such a principle: the establishment of a forceful central authority in a position to interpret the natural laws which would bring society into conformity with the rule of nature. To anyone properly brought up on Physiocratic principles, there could be no doubting the advisability of a single source of legislation and correction; what is termed *le despotisme légal* is a clear corollary to the fact that eternal physical laws govern all human activities.

The right to private property also has one other specific result: inequality is not only natural but just, not only because individuals' natural talents for acquiring property differ considerably but also because the conditions under which property rights were originally established varied considerably. If everyone were properly enlightened on the scientific basis of Physiocratic doctrine, social inequalities would be seen to be a necessary part of the continuing existence of humanity. Widespread public education should be undertaken by the state in order to ensure the proper understanding of these conditions. Nothing should be allowed to interfere with the market exchange system, for if allowed to function openly and freely, it would guarantee an increase in the real wealth of the nation, thus benefiting all its subjects. In specific terms, the Physiocrats upheld the already existent distribution of land holdings, but hoped to persuade the nobility, the church, and the monarchy—the major land owners—to invest at least part of their fortune in agricultural improvements. Since the agricultural factor is the only productive one, it does not make sense to restrict the flow of agricultural goods within a country or even from one country to another; here the Physiocrats joined forces with practical reformists clamoring for the removal of internal and external restrictions on the grain trade. And finally they advocated a complete revision of the taxation procedures in France, stating that any tax except that on the agricultural surplus was counterproductive, a form of double taxation.

The most obvious difference between the Physiocrats and the Encyclopedists is that the former constituted a school with a clearly defined membership, all of whom subscribed to the same basic doctrines. Grimm's vicious attack on the Physiocrats in his "sermon philosophique" of January 1, 1770, refers to them as a sect and compares them to the early Christians in terms of fanaticism and conformity of thought.[12] This is certainly not a good definition of the Physiocrats. As Alan Kors has recently pointed out, even the closely knit *côterie holbachique* had no single set of theories on which all members agreed.[13] Indeed, this particular salon was most appreciated by its members precisely for these disagreements, which led to extremely lively discussions and arguments.

On a speculative level, however, there is a certain similarity between some of the tenets of Physiocracy and those of such writers as Diderot, Helvétius, d'Holbach, and Condillac. The most obvious is the subscription to a generalized theory of natural law, based on a description of the material world. The Encyclopedists were struggling to find a clearly demonstrable proof of the existence of some kind of moral system that could be substituted for that of Christianity. Their attempts took many forms, but underlying them all was an almost desperate search for a foolproof argument in favor of such a law. The Physiocrats claimed to have found such a system, which they termed *l'évidence*, a series of deductive arguments linking the actually existing physical environment to a set of immutable laws. As Ellen Strenski has shown, this was the aspect of Physiocracy which most appealed to Diderot and which he finally outgrew as he reexamined his own theories in the light of social conditions of the 1770's.[14] Elizabeth Fox-Genovese has shown that the Physiocrats themselves had had to beat a hasty retreat from some of the logical consequences of their speculative theories, most particularly in the area of the legitimacy of the French monarchy. Quesnay and the elder Mirabeau had collaborated on a "Traité de la monarchie," never published because of its revolutionary political implications. After this initial attempt to relate their theory to the contemporary French political condition, they scrupulously avoided "any direct attack on the existing government" despite the fact that their economic principles called for "a social revolution for the realization of its 'neutral' goals."[15]

The Physiocrats' assumption that property rights constitute a basic natural right upon which all other forms of political and social relations must be based was also fairly widely accepted by the Encyclopedists. Truly egalitarian and common theories of property are few and far between in the eighteenth century. The belief in private property and its attendant rights had two major practical consequences according to the Physiocrats: freedom of the press and free trade. The concept of a free press was, of course, cherished by the Encyclopedists as well, and they found it helpful to have theoretical arguments to support their contention that the public welfare would be enhanced by the free circulation of ideas. Sartine had given an advance copy of *L'Ordre naturel* to Diderot for his opinion, and Diderot's enthusiastic recommendation to permit its publication was based at least in part on Mercier's eloquent defense of freedom of the press.[16] Diderot's enthusiasm for *L'Ordre naturel* was so great that he encouraged the young Dupont to produce a short, simplified version more easily accessible to the general reader. Dupont tells the tale as follows in an unpublished draft of a letter to Mercier, who had arrived in St. Petersbourg by November 1767: "L'ordre naturel continue ses succès sur les bonnes têtes.... Dessaint en a déjà vendu *trois mille exemplaires,* mais il s'est élevé une rude cabale contre lui." He distinguishes two groups, one which publishes its objections and which includes such figures as the abbé Yvon, Forbonnais, d'Angeville, and Fréron, and a second group which ridicules the work without publishing their remarks and which includes Grimm, the abbé de Gua and the abbé Raynal.

> Vous verrez par la brochure dont je vous envoye le manuscrit que Dessaint m'avait demandé que Diderot m'avait commandé et que vous m'aviez prié de faire vous verrez dis-je que je me conduis autant que je peux consequemment à vos principes j'ai idée que cette brochure qui ne repond à personne fera bien autant d'effet que plusieurs des reponses du cher abbé Baudeau. *Diderot* le pense de même. Il m'a beaucoup excité à la faire imprimer le plutot possible, on y travaille.... *Diderot, le baron d'Holbach, l'abbé de Condillac, le baron de Gleichen* vous défendent toujours.[17]

At this point it is clear that the Encyclopedists were divided in their opinion on the new school of thought, Diderot being the most enthusiastic supporter, Grimm the most critical opponent.[18]

The second major practical consequence drawn from the principle of private property was that of free trade, and it is on this point that the two groups finally diverged entirely. The inevitability of the principle of free trade was so obvious to the Physiocrats that at first they hardly did more than announce it as a necessary consequence of their primary commitment to a theory of natural rights based upon private property. Le Mercier de La Rivière buried his remarks about free trade in a couple of short chapters towards the end of his extremely long book. Dupont gave this part of the doctrine a much more important place in his resumé of Mercier's weighty tome. Yet free trade in general was not the political issue of the day. "La liberté du commerce des blés" became the rallying cry for all the *Economists,* most especially after the publication of Galiani's *Dialogues sur le commerce des blés* in December of 1768. Because Galiani had been back in Naples since June of that year, the publication of his book was entrusted to his good friend Diderot, who spent many hours preparing the manuscript for the printers. In the process Diderot began to question his own commitment to the principles of Physiocracy, if indeed its practical consequences could be so convincingly shown to be either ridiculous or, much worse, pernicious to society. The publication of Galiani's work occasioned a veritable flood of counterarguments, among them a fairly short work by Le Mercier de La Rivière and a much more lengthy refutation by the abbé Morellet. Sartine again called upon Diderot to assist the official censors in deciding whether Morellet's work should be published. Diderot's response of March 10, 1770, criticizes the work but concludes in favor of publication: "Comme censeur, je n'y vois rien qui puisse en empêcher l'impression.... Les économistes de profession sont bien d'une autre hardiesse, et la liberté, jointe au courage qui'ils ont de tout dire, est à mon sens un des principaux avantages de leur école."[19] Permission was not granted, however, and Morellet's work, printed in April 1770, remained unpublished until 1774, when the Turgot ministry experimented briefly with a totally free press. By that time no one was interested in Morellet's arguments, so the work fell completely flat. In the interim, Diderot had been busily supporting Galiani's anti-Physiocratic position on the grain trade. In October 1771, Diderot and Morellet were visiting Grandval at the same time, and the abbé provided his friend with a copy of his *Réfutation*, not realizing that Diderot had already reviewed it for Sartine. This gift stimulated Diderot to write a refutation of Morellet's *Réfutation*, the so-called "Apologie de Galiani." This work was never published, but Diderot did manage to arrange for the publication in the June 1771 issue of the *Mercure de France* of his "Mémoire sur Galiani," a biographical sketch of Galiani full of praise for his various works. By this time the correspondence of both Diderot and Mme d'Epinay shows that Physiocracy had become a subject of considerable ridicule to the inner circle of the *côterie holbachique*. Grimm's devastating attack in his "Sermon du jour de l'an" of 1771 follows the receipt of another work by Galiani, "La Bagarre," a satirical refutation of Mercier's *L'Ordre naturel*. Mme d'Epinay describes the effect this satire had on Grimm, Diderot, and the marquis de Croismare: "A minuit. Ils ne font que partir.... *La Bagarre* a paru un chef d'oeuvre et une critique sanglante à tous ceux qui ont présent le livre de La Rivière, et surtout à Diderot, qui en a fait des rires fous."[20]

When Turgot came to power in the summer of 1774, there was a brief reconciliation between Diderot and the younger generation of Physiocrats, including Dupont and Condorcet. Writing in December 1774 to Catherine the Great, Diderot makes the following comments about the new ministry: "Au moins ceux-cy sont justes, instruits et désintéressés; et l'expérience des choses les défera peut-être un peu de la morgue de l'école, et de la folie du sistème. L'économiste est en administration, ce qu'est le stoïcien en morale. Ils ne sont supportables que dans le moment du malheur."[21] The ministry of Turgot, who was considered by many to be a staunch Physiocrat although he had established his independence from them many years before, appeared to the *philosophes* to be a definite improvement over what had gone before. Diderot was troubled by his commitment to free trade, and when Necker published *Sur la législation et le commerce des grains* in 1775 supporting restrictions on the grain trade, Diderot wrote Necker directly questioning the possibility of ever arriving at the truth about the *Economistes:*

> Qui est-ce qui décidera la querelle des Economistes et de leurs adversaires? La raison? Et où est la raison? Dans les hommes d'Etat? assurément elle y est en puissance, mais ceux qui croient tout savoir n'ont guère la tentation de s'instruire. Dans le peuple? il n'a malheureusement pas le tems de la cultiver, de l'étendre et de s'en servir. Dans les gens du monde? Quand ils se résoudroient à vous sacrificier l'impérieuse frivolité de leurs distractions, ils ne vous entendroient pas. L'intérêt remue et déplace trop les gens d'affaires pour en espérer la lecture suivie d'un ouvrage qui demande de la tenue. A qui vous êtes-vous donc adressé? ... Qui est-ce qui en assurera le mérite et en accélèrera le fruit? C'est celui dont la fonction habituelle est de méditer; celui dont la lampe éclairoit vos pages pendant la nuit, tandis que le reste des citoyens dormoit autour de lui, épuisé par la fatigue des travaux ou des plaisirs. C'est l'homme de lettres, le littérateur, le philosophe.[22]

His own response to the question is now quite clear: the philosopher prefers the pragmatic approach of Necker to the theoretical one of the Physiocrats. Although none of the Encyclopedists would publish anything further on the Physiocrats, and although none of them would openly criticize Turgot for fear of jeopardizing his position in the government, it is quite clear that whatever sympathy they might have had for the theories of the Physiocrats had been completely undermined by their deep distrust of its practical consequences, most particularly the violent bread riots which shook Paris and other parts of France during 1775.

NOTES

1 Simon N. H. Linguet, *Théorie des loix civiles* (Paris, 1774); Jean C. F. Le Gros, *Analyse et examen du système des philosophes économistes par un solitaire* (Paris: Duchesne, 1787).
2 Louis Petit de Bachaumont, *Mémoires secrets*, ed. F. Pidansat de Mairobert and M. d'Angerville (London: Adamson, 1777-89).
3 Le Gros, *Analyse*, p. 250.
4 Ibid., pp. 252-53.
5 Adam Smith, *An Inquiry into the Nature and Causes of the Wealth of Nations*, ed. W. Playfair (London, 1818), II, 132.

6 Ibid., p. 144.
7 Ibid., pp. 364–65.
8 Denis Diderot, *Correspondance*, ed. G. Roth (Paris: Editions de Minuit, 1955–70), IX, 211.
9 Quoted in ibid., X, 129.
10 Ferdinando Galiani, *Correspondance*, ed. L. Percy and G. Maugras (Paris: Calmann Lévy, 1881), I, 412.
11 Reproductions and a schematic outline of the various forms of the "Tableau économique" may be found in Ronald L. Meek, *The Economics of Physiocracy* (Cambridge, Mass.: Harvard University Press, 1963).
12 Friedrich Melchior, baron de Grimm, *Correspondance littéraire, philosophique et critique*, ed. M. Tourneux (Paris: Garnier, 1877–82), VIII, 417–21.
13 Alan C. Kors, *D'Holbach's Coterie: An Enlightenment in Paris* (Princeton, N.J.: Princeton University Press, 1976).
14 Ellen M. Strenski, "Diderot for and against the Physiocrats," *Studies on Voltaire and the Eighteenth Century*, 57 (1967), 1435–55.
15 Elizabeth Fox-Genovese, *The Origins of Physiocracy* (Ithaca, N.Y.: Cornell University Press, 1976), p. 201.
16 See Diderot's letter to Damilaville in which he lists eighteen reasons for his approval of *L'Ordre naturel* in *Correspondance*, ed. Roth, VII, 74.
17 Unpublished sixteen-page rough draft of a letter contained in the Dupont de Nemours papers at Eleutherian Mills Historical Library and quoted with their kind permission.
18 This can be easily verified by reference to the *Correspondance littéraire* of October 1 and 15, 1767, and February 15, 1768.
19 Diderot, *Correspondance*, X, 34.
20 Ibid., p. 140.
21 Ibid., XIV, 121–22.
22 Ibid., pp. 145–46.

The Useful Myth of Gothic Ancestry

MARK MADOFF

A myth of gothic ancestry did not simply mean bad history. Those who perpetuated the myth usually obeyed a stronger call than that of accuracy to historical evidence.[1] The ancestry in question was a product of fantasy invented to serve specific political and emotional purposes. Established as popular belief, the idea of gothic ancestry offered a way of revising the features of the past in order to satisfy the imaginative needs of the present. It flourished in response to current anxieties and desires, taking its mythic substance from their objects, its appeal from their urgency. By translating such powerful motives into otherworldly terms, gothic myth permitted a close approach to otherwise forbidden themes.

The process of translation began early. Even in Elizabethan times nostalgic castle-building enjoyed a vogue in England.[2] The castles, like Spenser's *Faerie Queene*, were reversions to a lost cultural moment, and they retained that symbolic value throughout the early decades of the eighteenth century. The same age that produced such monuments of antiquarian diligence as Camden's *Britannia* (1586) and Dugdale's *Monasticon* (1655)[3] also witnessed a renewed reverence for purely imaginary ancestors. The cultivation of a tribal pseudohistory became at least as important as any archaeological work. Actual historical research into the character of medieval society and feudal institutions certainly stimulated this imaginative activity. To a greater degree, however, it followed an independent course. Creating a mythical—as opposed to a historical—sense of ancestry implied an attempt to answer two crucial questions: What was the previous state of society? What is the essential, primal condition of man? The lines of origin led back to the gothic.

Naturally, the world of gothic myth was a convenient site for testing social ideals and their negations. Modern customs and attitudes could be compared with the gothic originals. In that sense, the eighteenth-century gothic, as crude and escapist as it often appears, cannot be isolated from later gothicism. The early interest in alternative ancestral societies anticipated the overtly Utopian thinking of Ruskin, Pugin, Morris, or Carlyle. In High Victorian gothic, the disillusionment became more radical, and playfulness was largely exchanged for earnest experiment. But the roots of the "serious" movements lie in the eighteenth century.

Even a quick survey of gothic fiction titles will show that the imaginary gothic world had very generous boundaries. Who were the Goths to whom the term *gothic* referred? Would-be historical answers have ranged from the Germans, Normans, Britons, and Saxons to the Arabs and Moors.[4] Italian Renaissance polemic, following the line of Giorgio Vasari's *Lives of the Painters* (1550), identified them broadly as the barbarian destroyers of Greco-Roman civilization. But the Italians also called *Gothic* the later Germanic invaders who ineptly tried to restore Roman art, law, and custom.[5] As a descriptive or generic label, *gothic* is very confusing. Architectural usage has been only slightly more orderly. Is it possible to determine the meaning of this elusive word? Many etymological accounts have tried to do so.[6] Reviewing them in relation to the sensibility of gothic fiction, one finds a common meaning for all variants: the gothic is *ancestral.*

It was a concern for ancestry that excited the enduring controversy over the gothic. At issue was the source of cultural standards. The Italian humanists, for example, who sought to reconstruct a classical vocabulary of style, detested the gothic because it seemed a desecration of their true heritage. They argued that the imaginary Goths, like the real tribes of that name, had supplanted the legitimate ancestors, having no style of their own. Embedded in the theory of the Three

Ages of Civilization, this outlook persisted even in the face of obvious contradiction. So, in a treatise on poetry and rhetoric of 1727, the German critic Johann Ulrich König attacked gothicism in all aspects as a corrupt inheritance:

> The so-called Nordic peoples flooded the whole of Europe with their ignorance and with that Bad Taste which clung permanently to their descendants; this can still be recognized today from the remains, among other things, of their badly composed writings, rambling romances, immoderate passion for rhyming, clumsy monkish script, coarse-sounding speech, barbarous music, graceless costumes, badly-drawn paintings, and above all from their Gothic architecture.[7]

Perhaps it never occurred to König that he was one of those "descendants" and that his condemnation included himself.

Though the targets changed, these sentiments were regularly echoed in condemnations of the gothic in art, politics, and manners. *Gothic* was a partisan, abusive catchword, its social and political meaning paralleling its aesthetic one. Arguments from aesthetic principles were easily mixed with *ad hominem* arguments—that is, with arguments about ancestry. By the mid-eighteenth century, when the gothic taste was gaining a respectable following in England, the unruly character of the putative gothic ancestors could be turned into a reflection upon the new enthusiasts and upstart social movements in general. Thus, William Whitehead, writing in *The World* in 1753, neatly joined a love for the gothic with other forms of licence:

> This, however odd it might seem, and however unworthy the name of Taste, was cultivated, was admired, and still has its professors in different parts of England. There is something in it, they say, congenial to our old Gothic constitution; I should rather think, to our modern idea of liberty, which allows everyone the privilege of playing the fool, and of making himself ridiculous in whatever way he pleases.[8]

Similarly, in the opposing camp, although there was no reliable correlation between political affiliation and stylistic preference, there was something that sounded like a whiggish aesthetics. Defenders of the gothic argued for its essential congeniality on account of its native origin and associations.

In *The Goths in England,* Samuel Kliger describes a clearly partisan, positive use of the concept of gothic ancestry. He notes that "the term 'Gothic' came into extensive use in the seventeenth century as an epithet employed by the Parliamentary leaders to defend the prerogatives of Parliament against the pretensions of the King to absolute right to govern England."[9] Writing of the "ancient constitution" and immemorial custom adduced in favor of Parliamentary privilege, Pocock comments on the results of this political advocacy for mythmaking: "The concept of the immemorial encouraged the fabrication of myths about immensely remote times, and the fact that the appeal to early national history took the form of partisan controversy between sovereign and constitution enhanced this tendency."[10]

Searching for the source of noble British institutions in increasingly obscure regions, the inventive Parliamentary advocates had to find ancestral myths, and hence support for their claims, wherever they could. The notion of a virtuous "Gothic folk" often provided the simple category needed to embrace this great expanse of pseudohistory. By a careful reworking of depictions of northern Germanic tribes by Tacitus, Jordanes, and Saint Augustine, they invested the gothic people with the image of a militant yet enlightened race. The Goths, they believed, were noble, vigorous, physically hardy, intellectually and morally superior to the Romans and other Latins. They were particularly famous for prizing their liberty.[11]

Along with this favorable picture of the imaginary gothic ancestors came an unfavorable one, which, oddly enough, was also prompted by the necessities of Whig polemic. Lovejoy has recorded a common use of *gothic* as a synonym for *anachronistic.* In this sense, he suggests, "it performed much the same function that, in certain circles, the adjective 'Victorian' performs today... since it not only vaguely suggested 'the old-fashioned' in general, but, more specifically, the political and social system of the Middle Ages.... It sometimes served the progressives of the period as an unpleasant way of referring to anything the Tories approved."[12]

The inconsistencies in usage corresponded exactly to the inconsistencies in attitude toward the gothic and the Goths. A conjunction of aesthetic preferences, political sentiments, and antiquarian fancies produced two conflicting descriptions of gothic ancestors. It did not matter whether they had ever held a place in British history; they still led a vigorous, autonomous existence in the popular imagination. On the one side was an imaginary epoch that surpassed the eighteenth century in elegance of manners, chivalry, chastity, social stability, proper hierarchical relations, vivid pageantry, and faith. On the other side, the material insecurity, tyranny, superstition, and sudden violence of dim ancestral times were potent objects of fear and fascination.

The full effect of either mythic pattern could be summoned up effectively in fiction, political rhetoric, or architectural associations. The latter were especially well marked by those who disputed the nature of the gothic ancestors. They read into the tangible monuments of gothic life—the abbeys, castles, cathedrals, and manor houses—an entire pseudohistory of the goths. They carried over their interpretations to later imitations or survivals of the gothic style.

An illuminating example of the gothic building's mythic value appears in the third of Bishop Richard Hurd's *Moral and Political Dialogues* (1759), that "on the Golden Age of Queen Elisabeth between the Hon. Robert Digby, Dr. Arbuthnot, and Mr. Addison."[13] Hurd imagined the three travellers' conversation during an excursion to "Kenelworth Castle" in 1716. He supplied each with a characteristic, and typical, motive for the journey: Arbuthnot, "for the pleasure of recollecting the ancient times"; Addison, "on account of some political reflexions, he was fond of indulging on such occasions"; and Digby, to feed "an ingenuous curiosity" (p. 37). Having thoroughly studied the castle's features, with the aid of "Dugdale's plans and descriptions" of it, they turn from architectural to moral and political considerations. Arbuthnot, overcome by "a melancholy of so delightful a kind, that I would not exchange it, methinks for any brisker sensation," wonders "how it is that the mind, even while it laments, finds so great pleasure in visiting these scenes of desolation." Addison does not wonder at this at all, for he feels unmixed pleasure, "a fiction of the imagination, which makes me think I am taking revenge on the once prosperous and overshadowing height... of inordinate Greatness" (pp. 40–41). For him, the castle awakens an indignation against the prosperous tyranny of those wretched times, and creates a generous pleasure in reflecting on the happiness we enjoy under a juster and more equal government.... I never see the remains of that greatness which arose in past ages on the ruins of public freedom and private property, but I congratulate with myself on living at a time, when the meanest subject is as free and independent as those royal minions; and when his property, whatever it be, is as secure from oppression, as that of the first minister. (Pp. 44–45)

For his part, Arbuthnot defends Elizabethan *culture* by comparing it with Greco-Roman culture. He likens the organized combat of tournaments to the Olympic Games and emphasizes the classical content of the court masques.

There are two significant points about these "readings" of the castle. The first is that Arbuthnot is made to refer to it and the age it represents as "gothic" and that *gothic* is employed as a relatively neutral term for an imaginary division of history. The second is that the mystique surrounding the building is so powerful that each viewer is encouraged to respond to it by reciting a myth of gothic ancestry. Thus gothic buildings assumed both sinister and reverential colorings which were meaningful to political partisans, landscape gardeners, illustrators, fiction-writers, and, of course, readers.[14]

The competing, sometimes converging myths formed the basis of gothic fiction. In the popular novels, the same contradictions between positive and negative meanings of *gothic* applied to characterization and setting. The sure sign of this ambivalence was the transformation of the repulsive, terrifying picture of the Goths into an attractive one. That change yielded the majority of the genre of sensational writing called "gothic."

In order to appreciate the uses of the two main myths of gothic ancestry in fiction, two representative novels will be examined: Clara Reeve's *Old English Baron* (1777) and M. G. Lewis's *Monk* (1795).[15] I have chosen these particular works for what they illustrate about the connection between early and later gothicism: one is recognizably Utopian in its use of gothic myth, the other anti-Utopian. In addition, the novels occupy the extremes of gothic style and technique. *The Old English Baron* is decorous, unromantic, and rationalistic; *The Monk* is obscene, wildly playful, violent, and psychologically harrowing. Through its own telling of gothic myth, however, each work undertakes an investigation of the origins of the eighteenth-century world, and each tries out an alternative to that world.

In *The Old English Baron* the alternative is idyllic yet dull. Reeve reduces the myth of gothic splendor and superiority until it is insipid. In line with a moralistic revulsion that grew during her literary career, Reeve opposed the excesses of Horace Walpole's *Castle of Otranto* (1764). She sought to observe the rules of probability and decorum in her own gothic novel, bringing the gothic closer to the mainstream of fiction.[16] Most present-day readers will agree with Walpole's judgment of her attempt, that "what makes one doze, seldom makes one merry."[17] Nevertheless, *The Old English Baron* reached a large audience, reinforced earlier gothic work,[18] and acquired a school of imitators. Its version of the myth of gothic ancestry, therefore, cannot be dismissed.

Like most others who had been engaged by the gothic taste, Reeve had a polemical interest in it. In her hands, the positive gothic myth became a means of vindicating bourgeois values. Reeve has adapted the myth so that the imaginary Goths, famous for their pride and independence, are also equipped with modern commercial instincts. She has caused the ethics of a Puritan merchant to walk about in thin romantic garb, with which neither she nor the characters are comfortable. All the usual elements of the laudatory ancestral myth are present in *The Old English Baron*—piety, obedience, loyalty, nobility of sentiment, cooperation—but they are diminished by Reeve's shift in emphasis. Frequent invocations of the "overruling hand of Providence" and the "certainty of Retribution" are deceptive. The central matter of the novel is the restoration of decent, stable family connections and the settlement of competitive claims for wealth and power. Thus, the total effect is more Grandisonian than wild, romantic, or medieval. But Reeve does extrapolate an ideal. For that reason, the total effect of her novel is also Utopian. Reeve implies that the closer one gets to the original gothic state, the closer one approaches a moment of perfect social balance.

It was always a nonhistorical direction that Reeve took, whatever her ostensible subjects and settings, and not only because, as Sir

Walter Scott proposed, her imagination was undernourished.[19] J. M. S. Tompkins has explained that Reeve saw in ancient times "the heroic days of pristine morality, and as such she described them, to rebuke her own degenerate age, to stimulate its ideals and to counteract the debilitating influence of pessimists and levellers."[20] That view of the gothic period drew directly on the positive ancestral myth. Like many gothic-myth makers, however, Reeve was more eager to allay her own fears and doubts than to discover what was worth conserving in the authentic past.

Consequently, in *The Old English Baron* Reeve avoided history inasmuch as history revealed exotic, exciting, and forbidden images. Her depiction of gothic life was confined to models of superior conduct. She did not rely on chauvinism (despite the "Old English" of the title), nor on speculative mingling of history with fiction (as in Sophia Lee's *Recess* of 1783-85), nor on exploitation of sex and brutality.

The myth of gothic ancestry was useful to Clara Reeve because it was almost infinitely adaptable. All that had to be retained was its core: the notion that an ideal society had once existed in England, before the onset of urban sophistication and the intrusion of alien free-thinking. The precise outlines of that imaginary society, though based on received patterns, were the work of the dreamer. In the case of *The Old English Baron,* the Goths inhabit a fairly neutral territory where the ethical principles are familiar and congenial.

Unfortunately, the moral excellence of Reeve's putative gothic ancestors did not allow for the action and emotion from which adventure and romance are created. Since Reeve deplored excessive show of emotion, *The Old English Baron* contains more nobility of expression than strength of sentiment. There is courtship by strict rule of negotiation and cash value. There are cautious words of chivalry, occasional allusions to feudal law and custom, and a crucial tournament dispatched in three sentences!

Opposed to this reassuring image of ancestral gothic purity was "Monk" Lewis's vision of attractive depravity. Lewis drew chiefly upon the other myth of the Goths, which declared their essential brutality, ignorance, and destructiveness. Such a message acquired a tone of urgency with the severe social and cultural disruptions of the 1780's and 1790's. It embodied fears of the alien, the irrational, and the chaotic. Most of its elements Lewis did not challenge, but one he altered radically. He refused to affirm the Goths' otherness, that safe distance beloved by enlightened modern readers that made the gothic era an intrusion into the smooth forward flow of civilization.

On the contrary, while encouraging the reader to believe the myth in most other respects, Lewis turned a sinister trick. The Goths, he eventually shows, are not so much strange, savage ancestors as alienated parts of the so-called normal personality. They are removed from the rational world of the eighteenth-century reader not by time but by denial. As much as Lewis's *gaucherie*, this distinction helps to account for the outrage caused by publication of The Monk.[21]

No other gothic novelist except Charles Robert Maturin, author of *Melmoth the Wanderer* (1820), was so dedicated to the twin projects of demolishing the myth of gothic superiority and proving the reality of gothic barbarism as a constant presence beneath the veneer of social convention. Lewis's principal tools were parody, a treacherous humor, and a facility with multiple ironic meanings. His masterstroke was the discovery that the same chaotic subconscious forces drove his villain and his heroes. With this stroke, Lewis effaced the customary distinction between the violent Goth and the decent modern. While he consistently denied the romance of gothic life, Lewis also undermined the protection offered by the contemptuous myth about the Goths, by demonstrating the difference between its historical and psychological validity. The true picture of gothic savagery is a picture of the repressed soul, without reference, finally, to time or place. (The novel's Spanish setting, then, is yet another of Lewis's elaborate jokes, irrelevant to its meaning.) Lewis has conflated the two myths of ancestry and has shown both to be misleading or incomplete. This observation is the source of much of the humor in The Monk, often directed at the readers' expectations, first encouraged, then shattered.

Like the virtue of those who try to enjoy them, the rare idyllic moments in The Monk seem ripe for corruption, for conversion into a gross burlesque. It is appropriate, for example, that the lush garden of Ambrosio's Capuchin Abbey, the closest thing to pastoral in the tormented landscape of The Monk, becomes the site of his temptation, and thus, the entrance to the wasteland where he suffers and dies.[22] The psychological rationale of the novel requires that such positive forces as heroism, sensibility, and domestic harmony be especially marked for reversal and ruin.

Normally pure actions—prayer, courtship, charity, marriage, rescue—are crossed with ambiguities. For example, the mission that frees the heroine Agnes simultaneously provokes mob sadism of a typically gothic fury. Elvira's unfortunate marriage produces a daughter and that daughter's murderer. Raymond's scheme to legitimize his child leads to its death by starvation in a dank cell and to the temporary madness of its mother. Lorenzo's concern for the niceties of courtship throws Antonia back into a fatal reliance on Ambrosio that destroys her. Even a reader who has managed to dismiss each separate episode as the crudity one would expect from mere Goths must eventually be disturbed by the universality of the blight on existence, as Lewis describes it.

The myth of gothic barbarism served Lewis's purposes in two ways. It gave readers a familiar means of identifying, and thereby dismissing, whatever was disturbing or repugnant in the novel. But inasmuch as the barbarism itself seemed attractive, the myth gave readers a vicarious alternative to the decent and the conventional.

Lewis has arranged Ambrosio's career mainly to suit this second meaning. According to the commonplace of antimonastic, anti-Catholic ridicule, repression ruins Ambrosio. Still, the excesses which he dares commit in rebellion possess a magnificence of their own, and he gains a provisional freedom. At least he does not subside into the attenuated existence of the survivors. Perhaps Lewis's contemporaries realized the implications of this dangerous contrast, even as they condemned him for blasphemy, indecency, and abuse of Parliamentary privilege. It is certain that the Marquis de Sade and, later, André Breton understood Lewis's experiment.[23] The real charge against him should have been that he had opened to wistful scrutiny a vast life of the unconscious, and that he had tricked many readers into looking. The existing myths of gothic ancestry made the task of revealing that hidden life much easier for him.

For works of gothic imagination which, like *The Old English Baron,* relied on a positive myth, the link with later Utopian thought and activity was obvious. The desire to find a corrective for the ills and weaknesses of modern man in the imaginary virtues of the Goths not only persisted but deepened. The basic features of the myth were readily accommodated to various ideological ends. If Clara Reeve was able to emphasize the Goths' courtesy and love of justice, Pugin could cite the precedent of their piety and Ruskin, the example of their cooperation and personal integrity. In short, a belief in gothic superiority was a refuge for unrealized hopes. As Horace Walpole confided to his friend George Montagu (January 5, 1766): "Old castles, old pictures, old histories, and the babble of old people make one live back into centuries that cannot disappoint one."[24]

It is somewhat more difficult to relate *The Monk* to ideas of perfection or amelioration. Certainly the novel does not describe a Utopia, in the usual sense, nor does it attempt, through the negative mythic pattern, to identify some important evil. Lewis's view of the ancestral (i.e., the deep personality) suggests that the gothic aspect of the self is, paradoxically, both an obstacle to moral improvement and a seat of exceptional power. The only perfection admitted within *The Monk* is of a psychological type, not a social order. Lewis began refinement of a creature that would dominate this branch of gothic imagination: man as victim and slave of his compulsions, natural man cast more in the model of Hobbes than of Rousseau. It is a monstrous creature, acting out its imprisoned will violently, at a preethical level. The reader can afford to admire it because he approaches it only vicariously, in dream or dreamlike art. Yet, if this satisfaction of dark motives—for power, for sexual conquest, for secrecy—is the limit of the novel's attainment, its conclusions are anti-Utopian and implicitly antisocial. No one would want to reestablish the gothic world animated by Lewis. The problem that he poses, however, is that such a world survives, internally, beyond the ability of fantasy to summon or dismiss it.

The unusual potency and longevity of gothic ancestral myths have been explained with reference to middle-class upward mobility, the rise of Anglo-Catholicism, the Reign of Terror in France, and reaction against mechanization and urban settlement.[25] Without denying the validity of such explanations, I would propose a common factor. The idea of gothic ancestry endured because it was useful. The Goths, and the relics attributed to them, acted as symbols of racial pride, communal solidarity, political controversy, cultural disintegration (or revival), and internal revolution. The imaginary Goths could bear the staggering load because they were completely subject to the variable needs of their inventors. There was no ancestral depth they could not populate.

NOTES

1 George Germann, *Gothic Revival in Europe and Britain: Sources, Influences and Ideas*, trans. Gerald Onn (Cambridge, Mass.: M.I.T. Press, 1972), Part I, "The Gothic in Vitruvianism," chs. 1 and 6.
2 J. Mordaunt Crook, ed., *A History of the Gothic Revival* by Charles L. Eastlake (1872; rpt. Leicester: Leicester University Press, 1970), pp. <27-28> (Crook's introduction).
3 William Camden (1551-1623) was the pioneer antiquary in whose honor the nineteenth-century Cambridge Camden Society was named. The *Monasticon Anglicanum*, a result of collaboration between Sir William Dugdale (1605-86) and Roger Dodsworth, appeared in 1655 with illustrations by Hollar. Further editions were published in 1664 and 1673.
4 Germann, *Gothic Revival*, Part I, ch. 6.
5 William Douglas Robson-Scott, *The Literary Background of the Gothic Revival in Germany* (Oxford: Clarendon Press, 1965), p. 6; Germann, *Gothic Revival*, p. 12; Paul Frankl, *The Gothic: Literary Sources and Interpretations through Eight Centuries* (Princeton: Princeton University Press, 1960), pp. 237-315.
6 Germann, *Gothic Revival*; Robson-Scott, *Literary Background*; B. Sprague Allen, *Tides in English Taste* (Cambridge, Mass.: Harvard University Press, 1937), vol. II, chs. XIV-XV; E. S. de Beer, "Gothic: Origin and Diffusion of the Term; the Idea of Style in Architecture," *Journal of the Warburg and Courtald Institutes*, 11 (1948), 143-62, "Gothic and Some Other Architectural Terms," *The Diary of John Evelyn*, ed. E. S. de Beer (Oxford: Oxford University Press, 1955), I, 1-7; Alfred E. Longueil, "The Word 'Gothic' in Eighteenth-Century Criticism," *Modern Language Notes*, 38, no. 8 (1923), 453-60; Arthur O. Lovejoy, "The First Gothic Revival and the Return to Nature," ibid., 27 (1932), rpt. in *Essays in the History of Ideas* (1948; rpt. New York: Capricorn, 1960), pp. 136-65.
7 Quoted in Robson-Scott, *Literary Background*, pp. 10-11.
8 Quoted in Lovejoy, "The First Gothic Revival," p. 145.
9 Samuel Kliger, *The Goths in England* (Cambridge, Mass.: Harvard University Press, 1952), p. 1.

10 J. G. A. Pocock, *The Ancient Constitution and the Feudal Law: A Study of English Historical Thought in the Seventeenth Century* (Cambridge: Cambridge University Press, 1957), p. 19.
11 Kliger particularly cites the doctrine of *translatio imperii ad Teutonicos*, which had been promulgated in the North since the Protestant Reformation as a polemical instrument. The *translatio* predicted "the triumph of Gothic humanity, honor, and simplicity over invertebrate Roman urbanism, effeminacy, and luxury" (*Goths in England*, p. 2; also see pp. 7-34).
12 Lovejoy, "The First Gothic Revival," p. 136.
13 Richard Hurd, *Letters on Chivalry and Romance, with the Third Elizabethan Dialogue*, ed. Edith J. Morley (London: Henry Frowde, 1911). Subsequent page references are given within the text.
14 For the meaning of gothic ruins, for example, see Devendra P. Varma, *The Gothic Flame* (London: Arthur Barker, 1957), p. 19, and Bertrand Evans, *Gothic Drama from Walpole to Shelley* (Berkeley and Los Angeles: University of California Press, 1947), p. 7. A more extensive discussion of gothic buildings as symbols is contained in Warren Hunting Smith, *Architecture in English Fiction* (1934; rpt. Ann Arbor: University Microfilms, 1966).
15 Clara Reeve, *The Old English Baron*, ed. James Trainer (London: Oxford University Press, 1967); an earlier version appeared anonymously as *The Champion of Virtue*, a more indicative title. Matthew Gregory Lewis, *The Monk: A Romance*, ed. Howard Anderson (London: Oxford University Press, 1973).
16 Reeve, p. 5 (Preface).
17 Horace Walpole to the Rev. William Cole, August 22, 1778, quoted by Montague Summers in the Preface to his edition of *The Castle of Otranto and The Mysterious Mother* (London: Constable, 1924), pp. xxxii-xxxiii.
18 For example, Thomas Leland's *Longsword, Earl of Salisbury* (1762), highly praised by Reeve in her critical survey *The Progress of Romance* (1785).
19 Scott attempted to explain what he regarded as the failure of Reeve's imagination through the limitations of her life: "In her secluded situation, and with acquaintance of events and characters derived from books alone," he argued, she could not avoid falling into "a certain creeping and low line of narrative and sentiment" (Scott, "Life of Reeve," in *Sir Walter Scott on Novelists and Fiction*, ed. Ioan Williams [London: Routledge and Kegan Paul, 1968], p. 100).
20 J. M. S. Tompkins, *The Popular Novel in England, 1770-1800* (London: Constable, 1932), p. 231.
21 Contemporary reaction to *The Monk* and the harassment of its author are described in André Parreaux, *The Publication of "The Monk"* (Paris: Marcel Didier, 1960), and in Louis F. Peck, *A Life of Matthew G. Lewis* (Cambridge, Mass.: Harvard University Press, 1961).
22 It is surprising that Lewis's parodies and inversions of Christian myth or doctrine went unnoticed by his otherwise hostile, blasphemy-seeking audience. Had his allusions to a Christ-parallel been observed, he might have had to do more than revise and recant.

23 Donatien A. F. de Sade, "Idées sur les Romans," *Selected Writings*, ed. and trans. Margaret Crosland (London: Peter Owen, 1964), p. 287. Sade admires Lewis's decision not to rationalize the horrors depicted in *The Monk* but does not excuse him from absurdities of style. For appreciation of the gothic among French Surrealists, see Montague Summers, *The Gothic Quest* (1938; rpt. New York: Russell & Russell, 1964), and Maurice Lévy, *Le Roman gothique anglais, 1764-1824* (Toulouse: Association des publications de la Faculté des lettres et sciences humaines de Toulouse, 1968).
24 *Horace Walpole's Correspondence*, ed. W. S. Lewis et al. (New Haven: Yale University Press, 1931-), X, 192.
25 See, for example, Lévy, *Le Roman gothique anglais*, pp. 613-14, for an argument connecting the gothic myth with the Revolution of 1688. Lévy offers a political reading of the gothic ruin almost identical with what Hurd has Addison present in the Third Dialogue. The gothic ruin reminds the viewer of past tyranny and present liberty; it is a memorial to the guarantees that support the religious and political establishment, guarantees reinforced by the Revolution.

Strawberry Hill:
Architecture of the "as if"

DIANNE S. AMES

In 1750 Horace Walpole began the renovation of his lately acquired country house. He had a grand design for the place, and as he tells us, "gilders, carvers, upholsterers, and picture cleaners are labouring at their respective forges, and I do not love to trust a hammer or a brush without my own supervisal."[1] In the course of some sixteen years he exercised his prerogatives as a gentleman builder in this manner and constructed a twenty-two room house in the gothic style at an approximate cost of £15,250.[2] How are we to regard the enterprise? In his own estimation Walpole had succeeded: he had "realized" his dreams. In the estimation of his contemporaries he had succeeded: Thomas Gray the poet, no mean critic of the Gothic style, praised Strawberry Hill for "the purity and propriety" of its "gothicism"; William Pulteney, Sir Robert Walpole's old enemy, wrote verses in its honor; and scores of eighteenth-century tourists wrote for tickets to see it.[3]

The judgment of the twentieth century has not been as enthusiastic. The critics seem to have mixed feelings about Strawberry Hill. Whatever some, like Wilmarth Lewis, may say in its favor, many mock the place, calling its decorations "cheap imitations," as does Warren Hunting Smith, and deplore the use of lath and plaster, or worse, papier-mâché, in the construction of the house, as does Kenneth Clark.⁴ The use of stone, however, does not preclude a Gothic imitation's being a fake or a sham, though Pugin may have uttered syllogisms to the contrary, and Clark, writing in the twenties, should have inherited them. Can it be said that Walpole mistook papier-mâché for stone any more than he took what he called his "small capricious house" for a castle or a cathedral? It is often so inferred. I believe, instead, that Walpole may be said to have used his materials in a subjunctive way, and to have created an architecture of the "as if."

An architecture of the "as if," like the philosophy of the "as if" expounded by Hans Vaihinger in a book by the same name, is one that provokes us to make novel inferences.⁵ The buildings in this group, either in their forms or materials, lead the viewer to think about them as metaphors. In the case of Strawberry Hill, the house—which is in reality an eighteenth-century country villa—may be viewed *as* it would be *if* it were a Gothic castle. The word *as* signifies that it is comparable to an actual Gothic castle—Aston Hall in Dugdale's *The History of Warwickshire* (1656), the model for the façade—and the word *if*, that the analogy is a matter of make-believe. Other parts of Strawberry Hill are presented as if they were Gothic church architecture, and the New Offices, as if they were Gothic collegiate architecture. This whimsical congregation of analogies is not an attempt at archeological truth in the manner of nineteenth-century Gothic buildings, which failed to achieve it. At Strawberry Hill there are no failures, only fictions.

Although other styles of buildings may perform the same inspirational function, Gothic churches and their imitations are most consistently conceived of as architecture of the "as if." For example, Abbot Suger of Saint Denis (1081[?]–1151), the acknowledged originator of the Gothic style, said of his own project:

> When out of my delight in the beauty of the house of God—the loveliness of the many colored stones has led me away from external cares, and worthy meditation has induced me to reflect, transferring that which is material to that which is immaterial, on the diversity of the sacred virtues: then it seems to me that I see myself dwelling, *as it were*, in some strange region of the universe which neither exists entirely in the slime of the earth nor entirely in the purity of heaven.⁶

Notably Suger uses *quasi* ("as it were") to signify that he is making an analogy that is a fabrication, but one that, nevertheless, is a fruitful source of inferences. In the same vein, his contemporary Hugh of St. Victor declared that "the church in which the people come together to praise God signifies the Holy Cathedral Church which is built in heaven of living stones."[7] For such medieval interpreters, as Otto von Simson points out, stones are insignificant in themselves but serve to symbolize the spiritual and the imperceptible.[8]

Therefore, when Kenneth Clark states that the "essential Gothic character" lay in the materials, by way of denigrating "shams" like Strawberry Hill, he actually points to what may be said in its favor.[9] For Walpole uses artificial materials to create his gothic fiction with the same indifference to their merely physical substance as the medieval interpreters of the Gothic. In fact, he insists that we be aware of their insubstantiality: he paid a high price—£150—for the artificial stone of the main gates and points out to us in the *Description of the villa of Mr. Horace Walpole* (1784) that the garden piers are artificial. In this insistence lies his originality, for, as Clark states, a Gothic villa was not original in 1750 and, moreover, was associated with parvenus.[10] Walpole did not create a cheap forgery, but rather a visionary architecture akin in spirit as it is in form to its Gothic models.

Among all the provocative metaphors Walpole employed to characterize his house and his intentions, his allusion to it in the *Description* as "a paper Fabric and an assemblage of curious trifles" reveals his awareness of the essential illusion of his house, where, as in Gothic cathedrals, materials transcend their forms. The paper metaphor is a telling one because it is precisely that which occurs to both Vasari and Fénelon in their efforts to dismiss the Gothic cathedral's chief illusion, the illusion of defying gravity. Vasari writes that "on all the facades, wherever else there is enrichment, they build a malediction of little niches one above the other, with no end of pinnacles and points and leaves, so that not to speak of the whole erection seeming insecure, it appears impossible that the parts should not topple over at any moment. Indeed they have more the appearance of being made of paper than of stone or marble."[11] And Fénelon echoes him, declaring that "one expects it will all collapse... the stones seem to have been cut out like cardboard, everything is light, everything is in the air."[12] Clearly, this is not very far from Kenneth Clark's pronouncement that there is "nothing simple, natural, and solid" in Strawberry Hill.[13] Walpole surely knew Vasari's work and may in fact allude to Vasari's judgment. In any event, he consciously makes a virtue of what others deem a fault. The insubstantiality of Gothic architecture under his hand is also notable because he tolerated nothing less than stone for classical structures and deplored a sham antique.[14] The Gothic was to be something else entirely.

Strawberry Hill is, in part, literally paper—papier-mâché. The battlements and several ceilings are made of this material. This fact leads to a number of inferences. For one thing, the house may thereby be viewed as an extension, almost a transfer print, of Walpole's archeological pen-and-paper drawings copied from Dugdale. Like the engravings and text of *The History of Warwickshire*, Strawberry Hill records and preserves the commemorative architecture honoring British worthies like Edward the Confessor, Prince Arthur, Archbishop Warham, and others. Walpole himself declared that, because of decay and the careless alteration of Gothic buildings, prints were likely to be the "sole preservatives" of the Gothic style.[15]

Why was the much maligned style worthy of being preserved by Strawberry Hill? The *Anecdotes of Painting* (1762–71) may answer the question. There, Walpole professes that he has "great difficulty not connecting every inanimate thing with the idea of some person, or of not affixing some idea of imaginary persons to whatever" he sees.[16] This makes him prefer the Gothic to the Greek because it furnishes more points of association. Such an outlook suggests that Strawberry Hill, for Walpole and the readers who have the advantage of the meticulous promptings of the *Description*, is full of "memory places," to use Frances Yates's expression, which evoke the history of England and the history of Horace Walpole.

The grand historical design of the house and its objects is impressive. Not only does one see tombs and choir screens from English cathedrals in every room; there are also portraits and prints of kings, poets, and other notables, of Walpole's family, of his friends, and of himself in every room. Moreover, woven into the window pattern one finds the head of Elizabeth I, "ancient" aristocratic arms, and the arms of the principal owners of Strawberry Hill—all treated as if they were relics. In this manner, built into the fabric of the house is a scheme of British history which puts Walpole and his friends, representing recent history, on an equal footing with the representatives of "ancient" British history. The historical breadth of the house is supplemented by the geographical variety of "curious trifles" in the collection, which annex the Mediterranean, the Near East, the Far East, and the American colonies to the visionary province of the house.

As a result, some critics, like Wilmarth Lewis, have thought of Strawberry Hill as a museum. But bearing in mind Walpole's "paper fabric" metaphor and the fact that the house is autobiographical as well as historical, I would prefer to think of it as a kind of scrapbook in which many items have been pasted down—for example, the Cathedral of Gloucester tiles in the floor of the China Room. How are we to read this scrapbook? Perhaps we may let Ruskin prescribe for us as he did for the nineteenth-century reader who tried to comprehend the Gothic. He said that "the idea of reading a building as we would read Milton or Dante and getting the same kind of delight out of the stones as the stanzas never enters our mind for a moment"—though it should, because "we may, without offending any laws of good taste, require of an architect, as we do of a novelist, that he should be not only correct, but entertaining."[17] I think Walpole had this kind of significant entertainment in mind when he built and furnished Strawberry Hill. The whole display falls flat, as flat as the Gothic did for Vasari, unless we make an imaginative leap from the collection of objects to the realm of ideas.

Occasionally the allusions in the villa may seem perplexing. We may be perturbed by the tomb references that confront us wherever we turn at Strawberry Hill. Wilmarth Lewis has already answered this objection with Walpole's own words, "for you know, the great delicacy and richness of Gothic ornaments was exhausted on small chapels, oratories, and tombs."[18] Thus, it is largely the beautiful in the funereal that attracts him. Yet for Walpole, Gothic architecture also meant that one had "the satisfaction in imprinting the gloomth of abbeys and cathedrals on one's house."[19] In practice he "imprinted" not only the wallpaper of his "paper Fabric" with the "gloomth" of Arthur's tomb, but the furnishings as well. Generally this meant the use of black and ebony furniture of a Gothic design. The chairs and tables and staircase lanthorn, however, are not merely made somber; they are architecturalized. Walpole, for example, specified that the chairs were to have "three windows"—i.e., three pierced openings in the back of the chair. This feature clearly marks the chairs as part of the architecture of the "as if," because they are treated as they would be if they had walls. In short, "gloomth" and Gothic architecture are one and the same; at least, they are twin aspects of the impetus for furnishing ideas to the mind at Strawberry Hill.

Some have been perturbed by the eighteenth-century Goths' application of so much antiquarian study and such meticulous drawings to frivolous ornaments like looking-glasses and chair backs.[20] It may be said in Strawberry Hill's favor that it creatively reinterprets its models. The creative reworking of Spenser into "gothic" poems in the literary practice of the day is like Walpole's quotation of the tomb of Archbishop Warham at Canterbury in the screen of the Holbein Chamber, one of the *stanze* of Strawberry Hill. The rooms are "more the works of fancy than of imitation," to use Walpole's words.[21] In fact, there were no medieval mansions to constrain his fancy, and he was free to extemporize on the Gothic.[22] Thanks to Walpole's poetic license, we may get the same kind of delight in reading this building that we get from reading poetry, or even a novel like *The Castle of Otranto*.

Otranto and the supposed era of its composition are important clues to reading out the main theme of Strawberry Hill. Walpole makes the date of *Otranto* 1529 and attributes to the manuscript the same fruition of style as he does to the whole period.[23] He thought the perfection of the Gothic style to have been achieved in this, the Tudor period, and so it is fitting that he should have dedicated an entire room of his house to the principal artist in England at the time, Hans Holbein the Younger (1497[?]-1543), who was responsible both for architectural and portrait tasks during his tenure as court painter to Henry VIII (ca. 1536). Strawberry Hill displayed his famous drawing of a chimney, presumably from Nonsuch House, in addition to numerous portraits, terra cotta, and carving. If we assume that, as a kind of scrapbook for

Walpole, this "paper Fabric" is a self-dramatizing structure, then these details point to the role to which he aspired in his fancy.

Walpole dramatized himself in his "nutshell" as having the "airs of an old baron."[24] Because he modifies his aspirations with an impossible condition, that of being a baron in a nutshell, he exempts himself from charges of delusions of grandeur and demonstrates, once again, that he does not trespass beyond the subjunctive mode. As an old baron, he plays out the life of chivalry of the old romances and his own *Otranto*, a fact to which he was fond of drawing attention.[25] The one scene from *Otranto* in the house is of the Great Procession. When one compares this glamorous chivalric show with Strawberry Hill's efforts in the same direction—the armoury, Francis I's gorgeous armor at the top of the staircase, the Durer terra cotta of a single combat performed before Maximilian I—one sees that Walpole was attracted to the most colorful aspect of the medieval period, the jousts and fanfare of knighthood.

Kenneth Clark, however, states flatly that Strawberry Hill was not built to satisfy a literary mood. He is mistaken because he tries to reconcile the gaiety of Strawberry Hill with the wrong literary tradition: with the graveyard school of poets and not with that of Spenser, Malory, Ariosto, and Tasso. *Otranto* itself may clarify this point. Not only did Strawberry Hill contain a print of the "actual" castle of Otranto, but the castle in the novel is as spruce as Strawberry Hill itself, unlike those found in later gothic novels. Every one of Charlotte Smith's thirteen castles and five abbeys, for example, is partly in ruins.[26] Not so Otranto. The subterranean vaults excepted, it is simply not a dismal place, as Ann Radcliffe's *Udolpho* most pointedly is. Otranto Castle and Strawberry Hill satisfy a more cheerful literary mood, that of the romance. From this we may make another inference, that Walpole's "paper Fabric" is an extension of the printed word, and that Walpole would have us read its imaginary sign, "The Gothic Castle."[27]

Keeping our paper metaphor in mind, we will expect two-dimensional thinking at Strawberry Hill. And, indeed, critics like Kristine Gorrigan point out that surface is what matters at Strawberry Hill.[28] Walpole was interested in effect and not in constructional principles. Indeed, stone, would be an extravagant incursion into the third dimension for a make-believe battlement when only one side of a block is needed to achieve the effect. Papier-mâché served his purposes much better, as in the gallery, where the fan vaulting on the ceiling from the Henry VII Chapel at Westminster Abbey gives a truly wonderful effect of richness without having the impractical weight of stone. Richness is the effect Walpole sought throughout the house, with his damask and his gilding, and nowhere more so than the gallery, where the ceiling is supplemented by the wallcovering which is, as he put it, "gold network over looking glass."[29] Thomas Gray gave a name to this kind of effect: he called it "gothicism."[30]

The effects of this "gothicism" may be measured by an incident that occurred in the chapel (or tribune). Its Catholic air deceived the ambassador from France, who, perceiving an altar, removed his hat upon entering the room and was much chagrined to realize his mistake. The Duc de Nivernais's reaction suggests how charged architectural symbols are, especially those of gothicism: by contrast, no one was fooled by the Preface of *The Castle of Otranto*, which proclaims that the manuscript is a superstitious tract to gain converts. The materials of architecture make the statements of Walpole's "paper Fabric" a more potent rhetorical force for "superstition" than the novel. This kind of rhetorical force, moreover, is the ground on which he appreciated medieval church architecture. The priests, he said, "exhausted their knowledge of the passions in composing edifices whose pomp, mechanism, vaults, tombs, painted windows, gloom, and perspectives infused such sensations of romantic devotion."[31] He used nearly every device in the list, and to what purpose? To give pleasure, I think, by working on the passions. He may have said that one "only wants passions to feel Gothic," but he knew that in practice it helped to have Gothic to feel passion, and for this reason he made sure that everyone's first introduction to the house was by way of a "small gloomy hall paved with hexagon tiles, and lighted by two narrow windows of painted glass."[32] Strawberry Hill was intended to be an experience, and still is for us, even with the alterations of time, as Wilmarth Lewis and Peter Quennell attest, with their remarks on its "magic" and "make-believe."[33]

Thomas Gray and Walpole gave some consideration to the question of how far the Gothic illusion should be extended. Gray defined one parameter by remarking that "nobody will expect the inhabitants of an ancient house to wear ruffs and farthingales."[34] To dress as an antique oneself would spoil the subjunctive mode of the house with a tedious overworking of the illusion, which Walpole insisted should never intrude on comfort.

He was content that his Georgian building should "dress in Plantagenet clothes."[35] Just as we should not do him the injustice of charging that he tried to pass off a forgery of stone in papier-mâché, so we must do him the justice of having perfectly understood how far his "Gothic castle" metaphor should be extended. Unlike Sir Charles Barry, who wanted to gothicize everything in the Houses of Parliament, down to the ink wells and umbrella stands, Walpole concentrated on illusions, substituting wallpaper in a stucco or fret pattern for the materials themselves.[36] His taste for this ruse has also been deprecated. It does not seem quite fair, however, to praise Adam for the marble-painted stairwell of Home House (1773–74), in preference to marble itself when it could be afforded, and not grant Walpole the same indulgence.[37] Do not the efforts of both men transcend the materials, and likewise master *difficolta?* The delight afforded by the illusion of fretwork in wallpaper is akin to that derived from wall paintings that incorporate architectural details: a delight in fooling the eye by making flat walls look *as if* they were covered by a variegated terrain of architectural details.

Wallpaper was itself a luxury, the papering for the staircase, two small bedrooms, and the garret costing as much as the damask for the large gallery—£77 and £73, respectively. For the most part, Walpole employed the finest materials and craftsmen he could afford, including the architects Adam and Wyatt, and he succeeded with his Decorated Style where the nineteenth-century ecclesiastical versions failed for scrimping and negligent workmanship.[38] Whereas Ruskin rightly despised the vogue he himself created, because buildings failed to become "jewel cases for sweet sculpture,"[39] Walpole may well congratulate himself for achieving this image, which is an important Gothic illusion, as we may remember if we recall the words of Abbot Suger of Saint Denis, that it is the beauty of the *house* of God and its gems that inspires the subjunctive leap of the imagination. Not only did Walpole describe Strawberry Hill as "set in enamelled meadows and filigree hedges,"[40] much of it, like the tribune, *is* a jewel case, displaying in its niches sculpture, like the bronze bust of Caligula with silver eyes, and jewels and jewel-like objects. Among them are a missal set in enameled gold and adorned with rubies, turquoises, cornelian, and a large garnet clasp, and the armor of Francis I, inlaid with gold, silver, and ebony.

This last article may instruct us to view the whole effort with the eyes of a "true Goth," which were the eyes Walpole required to see his rooms perceptively. Walpole said of the armor, "a very little stretch of the imagination will give it all the visionary dignity of the gigantic hand in armour that I dreamt of seeing on the balustrade of the staircase at Otranto."[41] To true Goths, men of Suger's ilk, it is only a small stretch of the imagination to ascend in fancy from this world to the visionary realm. It is the function of the rich relics, as well as the architecture, to foster this imaginative leap.

It is well to bear in mind that the leap is never strenuous; one can, and one ought, to make it tongue-in-cheek, as Walpole's arch tone when he writes of his possessions clearly indicates *he* did. And yet, I would not go so far in qualifying the experience Strawberry Hill affords as to agree with Kenneth Clark when he asks, "Who could take seriously the bespangled gothicism of the Gallery or the papier-mâché rosettes of the Holbein Chamber? Who could have the heart to break this little plaything out of Mrs. Chevenix's toyshop [i.e., her jewelry store]?"[42] This suggests a kind of naïveté and dogmatism on Walpole's part that simply was not there. He was both architect and master of his amusing illusion, which accomplishes the really quite wonderful feat of making his home an extraordinary experience. For this reason we cannot simply dismiss Strawberry Hill's "bespangled gothicism," or condescend to its beauty.

Walpole achieved his illusion ultimately in the characteristic

Gothic way, through resplendent novelty. This is as true of Abbot Suger's splendid stained glass luminosity at Saint Denis as it is of Beckford's opulent Fonthill. As we read out the ciphers of Walpole's "paper Fabric," as when we read those of Suger and Beckford, the message of every stanza begins "as if..."

NOTES

1 Horace Walpole to George Montagu, July 1, 1763, *The Yale Edition of Horace Walpole's Correspondence*, ed. W. S. Lewis, 34 vols. (New Haven: Yale University Press, 1937–65), X (1941), 84–85. Hereafter cited as *Yale Walpole*.
2 A figure arrived at by adding Walpole's 1773 total in the *Strawberry Hill Accounts* (£14,945.16.2½) to the expenses for the new tower in 1776 (£296.19.5) and rounding off to the nearest half hundred.
3 Thomas Gray to Thomas Wharton, September 18, 1754. *Correspondence of Thomas Gray*, ed. Paget Toynbee, 3 vols. (Oxford: Oxford University Press, 1935), I, 406. Walpole alludes to the verses by William Pulteney, Earl of Bath, who was responsible for the downfall of Walpole's father's administration in the notes to *A Description of the villa of Mr. Horace Walpole* (1784; London: Gregg Press, 1964). One of the tickets, signed by Walpole, is reproduced in W. S. Lewis's *Horace Walpole* (New York: Pantheon Books, 1961), pl. 50. Lewis writes that "Strawberry Hill 'worked' for eighteenth-century visitors" (p. 113).
4 Lewis, *Walpole*, p. 113; Warren Hunting Smith, *Architecture in English Fiction* (1934; New Haven: Yale University Press, 1960), p. 23; Kenneth Clark, *The Gothic Revival* (London: Butler and Tanner, 1950), pp. 61–64.
5 Hans Vaihinger, *The Philosophy of the 'as if,'* trans. C. K. Ogden (1911; London: Routledge and Kegan Paul, 1952). Vaihinger describes fiction as a viable logical mode, which, like hypothesis, is an aid to "discursive thought" in all branches of knowledge, especially mathematics, science, and political science. Fiction has the advantage of not being tied to literal reality, and so leads to inferences that simply could not be attained by hypotheses, which must be verifiable. The phrase the "as if" is the key fictional phrase because it semantically stipulates an analogy that is not possible, but yet is fruitful. Such analogies need be neither self-consistent nor consistent with anything else. In the essay "Heavenly Mansions" (*Heavenly Mansions* [New York: W. W. Norton, 1963]), John Summerson describes the same phenomenon in architecture, calling it the "subjunctive mode."
6 Abbot Suger, *De administratione* (1145), quoted in Erwin Panofsky's "Abbot Suger of St. Denis" (1946), in *Meaning in the Visual Arts* (New York: Doubleday, 1955), p. 129. My emphasis.
7 Hugh of St. Victor, *Speculum misteriis ecclesiae*, quoted in George Henderson's *Gothic* (London: Penguin Books, 1967), p. 70.

8 Otto Georg von Simson, *The Gothic Cathedral* (New York: Pantheon Books, 1956), p. xxi.
9 Clark, *Gothic Revival*, p. 60.
10 Ibid., p. 46.
11 Giorgio Vasari, Introduction to *Le Vite*, I, 3, quoted in Paul Frankl's *The Gothic* (Princeton: Princeton University Press, 1960), pp. 290-91.
12 François de Salignac de la Mothe-Fénelon, "Lettres sur les occupations de l'Académie Française" (1714), quoted by Frankl, *The Gothic*, p. 375.
13 Clark, *Gothic Revival*, p. 64.
14 Ibid.
15 Walpole, *Description*, p. 11.
16 Horace Walpole, *Anecdotes of Painting in England*, V (New Haven: Yale University Press, 1937), 159.
17 John Ruskin, "The Nature of the Gothic," in *The Stones of Venice* (1751-53), ed. J. G. Links (New York: Hill & Wang, 1960), p. 164.
18 Walpole to William Cole, Aug. 11, 1769, quoted in Lewis, *Walpole*, p. 105.
19 Walpole to Horace Mann, April 27, 1753, *Yale Walpole*, XX, 371-74.
20 Clark is one who objects (*Gothic Revival*, p. 53).
21 Walpole wrote Miss Berry (Oct. 17, 1794) that "every true Goth must perceive that they [the rooms of Strawberry Hill] are more the works of fancy than of imitation" (*Yale Walpole*, XXI, 136-38).
22 Clark, *Gothic Revival*, p. 99.
23 Walpole writes, "Letters were then in their most flourishing state in Italy" ("The Translator's Preface," *The Castle of Otranto* [London: Lowndes, 1764]).
24 Quoted by Smith, *Architecture*, p. 23.
25 In *A Description* he suggests that the reader view Strawberry Hill as "a very proper habitation of, as it was the scene that inspired, the author of *The Castle of Otranto*" (p. iv). To Mann (Nov. 18, 1771) he writes that the armor of Francis I "will make a great figure here at Otranto" (*Yale Walpole*, XXIII, 349-51).
26 Smith, *Architecture*, p. 106.
27 Walpole writes to Montagu (Sept. 3, 1763): "My house is full of people... in short, I keep an inn: the sign, 'the Gothic Castle'" (*Yale Walpole*, X, 98-99).
28 Kristine O. Gorrigan, *Ruskin on Architecture: His Thoughts and Influence* (Madison: University of Wisconsin Press, 1973), p. 8.
29 Walpole, "A Description of the villa at Strawberry Hill," in *Letters of Horace Walpole... to Horace Mann*, 4 vols. (London: Richard Bentley, 1844), IV, 415.
30 Gray wrote Wharton (Aug. 4, 1763) that the gallery was "all gothicism, and gold, and crimson, and looking glass" (*Correspondence of Thomas Gray*, I, 805-9).
31 Walpole, *Anecdotes*, quoted by Clark, *Gothic Revival*, p. 42.
32 Walpole, *Description*, p. 3.
33 Lewis, *Walpole*, p. 116; Peter Quennell, *Romantic England: Writing and Painting, 1771-1851* (New York: Macmillan, 1971), p. 72.
34 Gray to Wharton, Nov. 13, 1761 (*Correspondence of Thomas Gray*, II, 765-66).
35 Clark's phrase, used in another connection, *Gothic Revival*, p. 88.
36 Observations on Barry, whose plans were executed by Pugin, by Clark, p. 118.

37 Adam also did sham stonework for Walpole: the ceiling of the Beauclerc room. See Damie Stillman, *The Decorative Work of Robert Adam* (New York: Transatlantic Arts, 1966), p. 111.
38 James Wyatt designed the New Offices (Lewis, *Walpole,* p. 118). Clark discusses this fact of nineteenth-century Gothic churches (*Gothic Revival,* pp. 95–107).
39 Quoted from *Arata Pentelici* by Gorrigan, *Ruskin on Architecture,* p. 48.
40 Quoted by Clark, *Gothic Revival,* p. 64.
41 Walpole to Lady Ossory, Dec. 4, 1771, *Yale Walpole,* XXXII, 64–67.
42 Clark, p. 64.

Executive Board, 1977–78

President: J. G. A. POCOCK, Professor of History, The Johns Hopkins University

Past Presidents: GWIN J. KOLB, Professor of English, University of Chicago
VICTOR LANGE, John N. Woodhull Professor of German, Princeton University

First Vice-President: PHILLIP HARTH, Merritt Y. Hughes Professor of English, University of Wisconsin, Madison

Second Vice-President: MADELEINE B. THERRIEN, Professor of French, University of Maryland, College Park

Executive Secretary: PAUL J. KORSHIN, Associate Professor of English, University of Pennsylvania

Treasurer: JEAN A. PERKINS, Susan Lippincott Professor of French Literature, Swarthmore College

    SHIRLEY A. BILL (1978), Professor of History, University of Illinois, Chicago Circle

    ROBERT DARNTON (1980), Professor of History, Princeton University

    WALTER GROSSMANN (1979), Professor of History and Director of Libraries, University of Massachusetts, Boston

    ROBERT HALSBAND (1978), Professor of English, University of Illinois, Urbana

    JAN LA RUE (1980), Professor of Music, New York University

    JEANNE R. MONTY (1979), Professor of French, Tulane University

Institutional Members

of the American Society

for Eighteenth-Century Studies

Arizona State University
National Library of Australia
Bryn Mawr College
University of Calgary
University of California, Berkeley
University of California, Davis
University of California, Irvine
University of California, Los Angeles/William Andrews Clark Memorial Library
University of California, Riverside
University of California, San Diego
Carleton University
Case Western Reserve University
The Catholic University of America
University of Cincinnati
City College, CUNY
Claremont Graduate School
Cleveland State University
Colonial Williamsburg
University of Colorado, Denver Center
University of Connecticut
Dalhousie University
University of Deleware
Delta State University
Detroit Institute of Arts, Founder's Society
Institute of Early American History and Culture
Emory University
Fordham University
Libairie Gason, Verviers, Belgium
University of Georgia
Georgia Institute of Technology

Georgia State University
Herzog August Bibliothek, Wolfenbüttel
University of Illinois, Chicago Circle
University of Illinois, Urbana
Indiana University
The Johns Hopkins University
University of Kansas
University of Kentucky
Lehigh University
Lehman College, CUNY
The Lewis Walpole Library
University of Maryland
University of Massachusetts, Boston
McMaster University/Association for 18th Century Studies
The Metropolitan Museum of Art
University of Michigan, Ann Arbor
Michigan State University
Middle Tennessee State University
The Minneapolis Institute of Fine Arts
University of Minnesota
University of Mississippi
Mississippi State University
Université de Montréal
Mount Saint Vincent University
University of New Brunswick
State University of New York, Binghamton
State University of New York, Fredonia
State University of New York, Oswego
Noel Foundation Library, Shreveport, La.
University of North Carolina, Chapel Hill
North Georgia College

Northern Illinois University
Northwestern University
Ohio State University
University of Pennsylvania
University of Pittsburgh
Princeton University
Purdue University
Rice University
University of Rochester
Rockford College
Smith College
University of South Carolina
University of Southern California
Southern Illinois University
University of Southern Mississippi
Stanford University
Swarthmore College
Sweet Briar College
University of Tennessee
University of Texas
Texas Tech University
Toledo Museum of Art
Tulane University
University of Tulsa
University of Utrecht, Institute for Comparative and General Literature
University of Victoria
University of Virginia
Virginia Commonwealth University
The Voltaire Foundation
Washington University
Washington and Lee University
West Chester State College, Pennsylvania
Westfälische Wilhelms-Universität, Münster
West Virginia University
The Henry Francis du Pont Winterthur Museum
University of Wisconsin, Madison
University of Wisconsin, Milwaukee
The Yale Center for British Art and British Studies
Yale University

Index

Aaron, Richard, 162n9
Abrams, Meyer H., 183n6, 202n15
absolutism, 11, 29n24
Académie Française, 362n12
Adam, Robert, 359, 363n37
Adams, John, 95
Addison, Joseph, 6, 13, 16, 28n8, 113–14, 116–17, 120–21, 126–27, 129, 133n14, 159, 207, 341, 350n25
Adkins, A. W. H., 227n15
Aeneid (Vergil), 119
Aesop, 189, 201n5
Agulhon, Maurice, 20, 23, 30nn34, 39, 31nn46, 52, 32n59
Alfred the Great, 130–31
Allen, B. Sprague, 348n6
Allen, Ethan, 89, 97–98, 107n38
Amphion, 195
Anchor, P. E., 267n2
ancien régime, 33, 41, 61n1, 66n67
Ancients and Moderns, 187–200
Anderson, Howard, 349n15
Anderson, Paul Russell, 107n38
Anne, Queen, 163n27, 210
anticlericalism, 98
Antill, Edward, 80, 86n46
antimonasticism, 58
anti-Semitism, 27
Apollo, 197
Appleton, Jay, 134n27
Arbuthnot, John, 210, 212, 221–22, 225n3, 226n3, 228n30, 341–42
Ariosto, 357
Aristotle, 207–8, 226n15, 227nn15,16

Arkell, R. L., 228n28
Armogathe, J. R., 63nn39,41
Arthur, Prince, 354, 356
Asher, E. L., 29n23
Astell, Mary, 161
Auerbach, Erich, 31n54
Augustus, Gaius Julius Caesar Octavianus, 112, 189
Austin, J. L., 265, 268n9
Axtell, James, 162n4

Bachaumont, Louis Petit de, 313, 321n11, 324, 335n2
Bacon, Francis, 201n8, 202n8, 226n6
Bahner, Werner, 27n1
Baily, Bernard, 107n40
Bailyn, Bernard, 85n44, 92, 104n12, 105n14
Baker, Keith, 27n1
Baker, Sheridan, 233, 237, 241n4, 242n20
Banks, Joseph, 271, 277–78, 282
Banning, Lance, 106n28
Banton, M., 60n1
Barbeu-Dubourg, Jacques, 32n63
Baroque, 13, 29n27, 31n53, 237
Barrell, John, 134n24
Barry, Charles, 359, 363n36
Bathurst, Allen, Earl of [?], 117, 122–23, 128
Battestin, Martin C., 233–34, 237–38, 241n2, 242nn8,16,17
Baudeau, Nicolas, 332
Beaglehole, J. C., 289n4
Bearcroft, Philip, 81n4
Beaumarchais, Pierre-Augustin Caron de, 319
Beauroy, J., 61n1

369

Beck, Hanno, 289n14
Beck, L. W., 267n2
Beck, Robert N., 106n31
Becker, Carl, 105n20
Beckett, Samuel, 242n19
Beckford, William, 361
Behn, Aphra, 155
Belcher, Jonathan, 83n18
Bell, Sadie, 84n19
Bellori, Giovanni Pietro, 135n45
Benevolists, 242n19
Bengesco, Georges, 316
Bentham, Jeremy, 106nn26,32
Bentley, Richard, 189
Bercé, Y. M., 66n70
Berger, John, 114–15, 134n21
Bergier, Nicolas-S., 65nn61,62,64, 66n65
Berkeley, George, 83n16
Bernadau, Pierre, 44–47, 62n28
Berry, Agnes, 228n30, 326n21
Berry, Mary, 228n30
Bertrand, Elie [?], 319
Bertrand, M., 61n1
Besterman, Theodore, 320n4
Beutler, Ernst, 290n20
Billacois, F., 30n37
Blair, Samuel, 83n11, 84n19
Blake, E. V., 105n22
Bligh, William, 269
Bloom, Edward, 28n8
Bloom, Lilian, 28n8
Bloom, Lynn Z., 183n15
Blount, Charles, 103n2
Blount, Edward, 126, 135n42
Bois, P., 66n73
Bolingbroke, Henry Saint John, 210, 213, 221, 229n44, 232n73
Bollème, Geneviève, 32nn62,63, 61n13, 66n66
Bond, Donald F., 202n14, 226n12, 227nn18,19
Bonnaud, L., 63n28
Boos, Florence, 182n1, 184n28
Booth, Wayne C., 226n3
Borromée, Charles, 64n52
Boss, Ronald I., 30n40, 103n2
Bossuet, Jacques-Bénigne, 8–9, 15, 21–22, 28n13, 62n21
Boswell, James, 18–20, 24, 31n49
"Boulanger" [D'Holbach], 100
Bourde, André, 32n63

Boyle, Richard, Earl of Burlington, 123, 135n46
Bradley, Richard, 110, 133n5
Brantley, Richard E., 225
Braudy, Leo, 233–34, 236–37, 241nn4,5
Breton, André, 346
Bridenbaugh, Carl, 10, 29n20, 31nn46,48
Briggs, Asa, 28n12
Bristow, William, 83n16
Bronson, Walter C., 81n3, 85n39
Brown, Capability, 110, 113, 126, 128, 133n3
Browning, Robert, 206
Bruce, Lord, 130
Bruford, W. H., 28nn8,14, 30n39
Bruno, Giordano, 201nn5,8
Buckingham, John Sheffield, Duke of, 227n18
Budgell, Eustace, 227n18
Buel, Richard, 104n12
Buffon, Georges-Louis Leclerc, Comte de, 326–27
Bunyan, John, 185n32, 242n19
bureaucracy, 11–12, 30n31
Burlington, Richard Boyle, Earl of, 123, 135n46
Burnet, Gilbert, Bishop of Salisbury, 159, 163n22
Burnet, T., 156, 163n12
Burnet, Thomas, 272
Burney, James, 269
Burns, Robert, 206
Burr, Aaron [father], 72, 75, 78
Bute, Countess of, 158, 163nn18,21,24,27
Butler, Joseph, 242n19
Butler, Nicolas Murray, 267n2
Butt, John, 133n7, 202n18

Caesar, Gaius Julius, 7, 27
Cahuac, J., 108n52
Calame, Alexandre, 308nn4,6,16
Caligula, Gaius Caesar, 360
Calvinism, 77, 98, 154
Camden, William, 337, 348n3
Cameralists, 12, 29n27
Cameron, Kenneth Neill, 184n26
Campanella, Tommasco, 202n12
Capuchins, 46–47
Carlile, Richard, 90, 102–3, 108n52
Carlyle, Thomas, 338
Caroline, Queen [wife of George IV], xii,

131, 206, 208–9, 211–15, 217–20, 222, 227n28, 228nn28,30, 229n51, 230n51, 231n59
Carozzi, Albert V., 289nn6,11, 290nn26,29
Carswell, John, 289nn2,5, 290nn18,21
Casaubon, Meric, 196
Castan, Yves, 32n60
Cathelineau, L., 66n73
Catherine, Queen [wife of Charles II], 125
Catherine II, Empress of Russia, 32n63, 334
Catholicism, 40, 49, 65n61, 244
Caudwell, Christopher, 132
Certeau, M. de, 40, 62nn15,28, 63nn29–33,42, 67n74
Chabanon, Michel-Paul-Guy de, 309n30
Chabot, François, 46–47
Chambers, William, 121
Charteris, Francis, 220
Chartier, R., 64n46
Chase, Frederick, 81n3
Chaucer, Geoffrey, 206
Chaunu, P., 62n15, 64n49
Chayney, Edward P., 81n3
Chill, Emmanuel, 29n16
Chisick, Harvey, 28n5, 30n33, 64n46
Cholvy, G., 66n67
Chudleigh, Mary, 151, 156, 161, 163n13
Church, F., 28n4
Cicero, Marcus Tullius, 195
Clare, John, 134n24
Clarissa (Richardson), 238
Clark, H. F., 135n43
Clark, Kenneth, 352–54, 357, 360, 361n4, 362nn9,10,13,14,20,22,31,35, 363nn36,38,40,42
Clarke, George, 133n6, 135n50
classicism, 6, 202n14
Cleopatra, 112, 122
clergy, 33–60
Clerk, John, 121
Cleveland, Barbara Villiers, Duchess of, 142
Clifford, Derek, 133n6, 135n39
Clifford, James L., 203n18
Coats, A. W., 27n1
Cobham, Richard Temple, Viscount, 113–14, 128, 131, 135n50
Cockburn, Catherine Trotter, 151, 155–56, 163nn11,12
Coke, Thomas, Earl of Leicester, 135n46
Colbert, Jean-Baptiste, 11
Colden, Cadwallader, 79, 85n45

Cole, William, 349n17, 362n18
Coleman, Elliott, 184n28
Coleman, W., 61n9
Coleridge, Samuel Taylor, 200, 206
Colie, Rosalie, 162n3
Collet, Pierre, 43–44, 52, 62n26, 65nn54–57
Collin d'Harleville, Jean-François, xiii, 291–307
Collini, Côme-Alexandre, 311, 320n3
Collins, Varnum L., 81n3
Collins, William, 206
Collinson, Peter, 86n47
Colman, Francis, 227n26
Colman, George, 227n26
Comédie Française, 291
Compère, M. M., 64n46
Compton, Henry, 229n47
Condillac, Etienne Bonnot de, 331–32
Condorcet, Marie-Jean-Antoine-Nicolas Caritat, Marquis de, 13, 27n1, 28n1, 92, 325, 334
Convention, La, 46, 63n34
convulsionaries, 15
Conway, Moncure D., 108n53
Cook, Elizabeth, 288
Cook, James, 269–89
Cooper, Anthony Ashley, Earl of Shaftesbury, 227n18
Cooper, Samuel, 107n38
Copernicus, Nicolaus, 192
cosmopolitanism, 21, 24
Coton, Pierre, 44
Cotton, Charles, 132
Coulet, Henri, 62n27, 63n39
Couturier, H., 67n73
Cowper, William, 206
Coxe, William, 227nn28,30,32
Coyer, Gabriel-François, 3–4
Cramer, Carl Friedrich, 317
Crane, R. S., 237
Cranston, Maurice, 155, 162nn5–8
Cremin, Lawrence A., 84n28
Croismare, Marc-Antoine-Nicolas, Marquis de, 334
Croker, John Wilson, 228n32, 230n59
Crook, J. Mordaunt, 348n2
Crosland, Margaret, 350n23
Cudworth, Ralph, 155, 162n9, 192, 202n10
Cumberland, Prince William, Duke of, 231n59
Curti, Merle, 98, 107n39

D'Aguesseau, Henri François, 28n4
D'Alembert, Jean Le Rond, 32n62, 303, 305, 309nn20,24,26,30, 312, 318, 324, 326–27
Damaris, Lady Cudworth Masham, 151, 154–55, 158, 162nn4,8,10
Damilaville, Etienne-Noël, 336n16
Dancourt, Florent Carton, 302–4, 308n17, 309n18
D'Angeville, Claude, 332
D'Angerville, M., 335n2
Dante Alighieri, 355
D'Argenville, Antoine-Joseph Dezallier, 126
Darnton, R., 65n61
Darwin, Charles, 101, 106n32
Davidow, Lawrence Lee, 226n3
Davies, Samuel, 82nn5,6,11, 84n19
Davis, Herbert, 149n11, 225n3, 226n13, 228n43
Davis, N. Z., 60n1, 61n12
Day, Robert Adams, 163n12
Deacon, Margaret, 289n12, 290n25
Dearing, Vinton A., 230n56
De Beer, E. S., 162n8, 348n6
Deffand, Marie, Marquise du, 312
Degert, A., 62n16
deism, xi, 65n61, 87–103
Delany, Patrick, 221, 226n3
Delaruelle, Etienne, 35
Delumeau, J., 61n1, 64n50
Demarest, William H. S., 81n3
Denis, Marie-Louise Mignot, 319
Denniston, David, 93
Depauw, J., 65n60
D'Epinay, Louise Tardieu d'Esclavelles, dite Madame, 334
Descartes, René, 192, 202n9
Desmarest, Nicolas, 277, 285, 289n17, 290n19
despotism, 29n24, 30n31, 330
Deventer, Heinrich van, 249n3
Dewey, John, 101
Dewhurst, Kenneth, 162n5
Dexter, Franklin B., 84n27
Deyon, Pierre, 29n18
D'Holbach, Paul-Henri Thiry, 13, 23, 25, 100–101, 103n2, 106nn26,31, 326, 331–32, 334, 336n13
Dhotel, J. C., 63n37
Diderot, Denis, 25, 28n1, 32n63, 291, 303, 306, 318, 324–27, 332–34, 336nn8,9,14,16,19–22

Dieckmann, Herbert, 28n8
Digby, Robert, 134n33, 341
Dixon, P., 226n3
Dodsworth, Roger, 348n3
Donati, Vitaliano, 274
Don Juan, 137–38
Donne, John, 206
Dott, R. H., 289n7
Draper, Marie P. G., 228n32
Drapier [Swift, Jonathan], 212
Driscol, Dennis, 95, 106n26
Dryden, John, 125, 129, 135n45
Du Bos, Jean-Baptiste, 20
Duchè, Jacob, 85n34
Duclos, Charles, 5, 13–14, 30n35, 326
Dufresny, Charles, 303
Dugdale, William, 337, 341, 348n3, 352, 354
Dunkin, William, 231n67
Dunn, E. Catherine, 227n18
Dupont de Nemours, Pierre-Samuel, 326, 329, 332–34, 336n17
Durant, W. Clark, 184n24
Durkheim, E., 36, 61n5
Dwight, Timothy, 102

Eastlake, Charles L., 348n2
eclecticism, 22, 91
économistes, 323–35
Edict of Nantes, 15
education, 11–13, 15–17, 26, 28n5, 30nn30–32, 33–60, 64nn44,46,49, 69–81, 85n40, 151, 154, 156–58, 161, 162n1, 163nn13,14
Edward the Confessor, 354
Edwards, John, 154, 162n5
Edwards, Jonathan, 77, 83n18, 85n32
Edwards, Philip, 225n3
egalitarianism, xi, 91
Ehrenpreis, Irvin, 27n1, 31n54, 224, 226n3, 232n74, 242n13
Eisenstein, Elizabeth, 31n56, 32n57
Elioseff, Lee, 28n8
elitism, 3–27, 27n1, 33–60, 67n74
Elizabeth I, 355
Elkin, P. K., 225n3
Elwin, Whitwell, 230n54
Emerson, Ralph Waldo, 206
empiricism, x, 6–7, 21, 106n32, 151–52, 156, 161, 198, 201n8, 202n16
Empson, William, xii, 233–34, 240, 241n1
Encyclopédie, 5, 16, 22, 25, 28n3, 30n34,

Index / 373

63n40, 277, 311-13, 317-19, 320n5, 321n7, 323-35
Encyclopedists, x, xiii, 323-35
Enlightenment, ix, 3, 7-8, 13, 16, 21, 23-24, 27n1, 28n5, 29nn17,24, 30nn31,40,41, 31n56, 41, 55, 62n15, 76, 79, 89, 100, 104n3, 303-4, 311-20
Epictetus, 159
Euripides, 201n5
Evangelicalism, 73-74, 77
Evans, Bertrand, 349n14
Evans, George H., 107n35
Evans, Nathaniel, 85n35
Evans-Pritchard, E. E., 35, 61n2
Evelyn, John, 348n6
Eyles, V. A., 290n24

Fabricant, Carole, 133n13
Fackenheim, E. L., 267n2
Faguet, Emile, xiii
Faucheux, M., 66n73
Faulkner, George, 211, 214, 225n2, 229n46
Febvre, Lucien, 33
Féline, Père, 43-44
Fellows, John, 90-91, 98, 105n25
feminism, 151, 163n16, 170-71
Fénelon, François de Salignac de la Mothe, 44, 353, 362n12
Fenn, R. K., 61n5
Ficino, Marsilio, 202n12
Fielding, Henry, ix-x, xii, 25, 233-40
Filmer, Robert, 161
Fisch, Max Harold, 107n38
Fischer, John Irwin, 225n3
Fitch, John, 90
Flandrin, J. L., 65n59
Fleury, Claude, 42-44, 62nn21-25, 65n58
Fleury, M., 63n43
Flexner, Eleanor, 172
Flitner, Andrew, 30n31, 32n63
Florenne, Yves, 314, 321nn12,21
Fonvielhe, Abbé, 46-47
Forbonnais, François Véron, Sieur de, 332
Ford, Franklin, 10, 29n20, 31nn44,46
Forster, George, 270-71, 282
Forster, Johann Reinhold, 270-71, 282, 287
Forster, R., 65n60
Foster, John, 90
Foucault, Michael, 253, 267nn1,3
Fouilleron, J., 64n49
Fox-Genovese, Elizabeth, 331, 336n15

Fracart, M. L., 62n17
Francis I, 357, 360, 362n25
Frankl, Paul, 348n5, 362nn11-12
Franklin, Benjamin, 75, 77, 79, 82n7, 83nn13,17, 84n24, 85nn29,45, 86n47, 99-100, 288
Franks, Augustus W., 230n59
Fraser, Alexander Campbell, 202n16
Frederick II, 12, 311-12, 316
Freemasonry, 15, 18, 20, 30nn34,39
French, Roderick S., 104n4
Freneau, Philip, 94, 103n1
Fréron, Elie, 332
Freud, Sigmund, 109, 137, 145, 148n2
Freylinghuysen, Theodore, 74, 84nn20,22, 85n38
Fritz, Paul, 30n41
Froeschlé-Chopard, M. H., 66n67
Fronde, La, 15
Frye, Northrop, 235
Furet, F., 64n43

Gagliardo, John, 28n10, 30n31
Gagnebin, B., 28n9
Galiani, Ferdinando, 326-27, 333-34, 336n10
Garden, Maurice, 29n18
Gardiner, Dorothy, 163nn13,20
Gargan, E. T., 61n1
Garlan, Y., 66n70
Gassendi, Pierre Gassend, dit, 202n9
Gay, John, 209-10, 212-13, 215, 218-22, 228n38, 230nn51,53,56, 231nn64,70, 232nn71,72
Gay, Peter, 29n24, 31n56, 106n31
Gazier, A., 63nn34-36, 67n74
Geertz, C., 60n1
Geikie, Archibald, 290nn28,29
Geoffrin, Marie-Thérèse Rodet, Madame, 326
George, Dorothy M., 29n28, 31n48
George I, 164n27, 215-16
George II, 210, 214, 219, 228n28, 230n59
Germain, Elizabeth, 216, 227n27, 228n29, 229nn45,46, 230n51
Germann, George, 348nn1,4-6
Gibbon, Edward, 169
Gibbon, Michael, 133n6
Gifford, A., 82n6
Gilpin, William, 183n8
Gleichen, Charles-Henri, Baron de, 332

Godwin, William, 99, 170–71, 174, 176, 183nn16,18, 184nn23–25, 185n32
Goethe, Johann Wolfgang, 8, 181, 277, 290n20
Goldgar, Bertrand, 231n66
Goldknopf, David, 233, 241n4
Goldoni, Carlo, 306
Gontard, M., 64n46
Goody, Jack, 32n57, 39, 60n1, 62n14
Gordon, Ann D., 81n3
Gorrigan, Kristine O., 357, 362n28, 363n39
Gothic, xiii, 337–48, 351–61
Goubert, Pierre, 29n18
Gouesse, J. M., 65n58
Graffigny, Françoise d'Issembourg d'Happoncourt, Madame de, 29n17
Grandval, François-Charles Racot de, 334
Gray, Thomas, 19, 128, 206, 351, 358–59, 361n3, 362nn30,34
Greene, Jack P., 85n42
Grégoire, H., 45, 48, 63nn34,42, 67n74
Grieve, A. J., 201n1
Griffin, Dustin, 149n10
Grimm, Friedrich Melchior, 313, 321n10, 325, 331–34, 336n12
Grob, Gerald N., 106n31
Groethuysen, Bernard, 29n15
Grotius, Hugo, 266
Grueber, Herbert A., 230n59
Gua de Malves, Jean-Paul de, 332
Gywnn, Nell, 141

Haarmann, Erich, 289n1
Hagelman, Charles W., 183n11
Hall, James, 285
Halsband, Robert, 163nn18,25, 164n27
Hamilton, William, 183n9
Harley, Edward, Earl of Oxford, 135n46
Harrison, Bernard, 241n7, 242n19
Harvey, William, 192, 196
Hassell, John, 185n30
Hastie, W., 267n2
Hastings, Hugh, 82n8
Havens, George R., 313, 321n9
Hawkesworth, John, 227n17
Hawkins, Edward, 230n59
Haywood, Eliza, 134n31
Healey, F. G., 27n1
Heimert, Alan, 85n32

Helvétius, Claude-Adrien, 25, 106nn26,32, 324, 326, 330–31
Henderson, George, 361n7
Henry VII, 358
Henry VIII, 356
Herbert, George, 206
Herbert, Henry, Earl of Pembroke, 135n46
Herder, Johann Gottfried von, 7, 17, 268nn7,8
Herr, R., 28n1
Hertz, Frederick, 30n31
Hervey, John, 214, 228nn28,41, 229n47, 231n63
Hesiod, 193
Hiller, Dana V., 133n13
Hinnant, Charles H., 202n16
Hoare, Henry, 113, 119, 128, 130–31, 133n12, 134n16, 135n44
Hobbes, Thomas, 192, 198, 202nn9,16, 221, 227n20, 242n19, 347
Hofstadter, Richard, 84n27
Holbein, Hans, 356, 360
Holder, Orlee, 183n15
Holdsworth, Winch, 163n12
Hollar, Wenceslaus, 348n3
Homer, 118, 188, 193, 208, 227n15
Hooke, Robert, 273, 284
Hooker, Edward Niles, 202n18, 203n18
Horace, Quintus Flaccus, 120, 134n28, 304
Housman, Alfred Edward, 206
Howard, Henrietta, Countess of Suffolk, xii, 206, 208, 211–20, 222, 227n28, 228nn30,32,39,43, 229nn44,49,51, 230n51, 231nn60,64
Hufton, Olwen, 29nn21,26
Hugh of Saint Victor, 353, 361n7
Hughes, Merritt Y., 135n47
humanism, 338
humanitarianism, 5, 7
Hume, David, 102, 106n26
Hume, Robert D., 225n3
Humphrey, David C., 81n3
Hunt, John Dixon, 119, 133n6, 134n30
Hurd, Richard, 341, 349n13, 350n25
Hussey, Christopher, 133n6, 135nn36,38
Hutchens, Eleanor, 241n7
Hutt, M. G., 64n51
Hutton, James, 276–77, 285, 288, 289n7, 290n29

idealism, xii
Imlay, Gilbert, 166, 168, 170-72, 174, 177, 182, 183nn18-20, 184nn23,25,27, 185n31
imperialism, 27
industrialism, 17
Iversen, Audrey Notvik, 289nn6,11, 290nn26,29

Jackson, Andrew, 102
Jacobins, 106n26
James, Henry, 146
James, John, 126
James, William, 107n38
Jansenism, 51, 62n26, 64n49
Jardine, Alexander, 183n10
Jay, James, 74-75
Jefferson, Thomas, 95, 99-100, 105n20, 106nn26,28
Jelinek, Estelle C., 183n15
Jesuits, 11, 45, 62n26, 64n49
Jewson, N. D., 61n10
Johnson, Maurice, 224-25, 225n3
Johnson, Samuel, 19, 31nn46,47, 73-74, 77, 83n16, 84n25, 85n29, 232n74, 242n18
Jones, Gareth, 225n3
Jones, M. G., 32n63
Jones, R. F., 201n2
Jordanes, 340
Jourdain, Margaret, 135n38
Juhasz, Suzanne, 183n15
Julia, D., 62nn17,18,28, 63nn29-33,42, 64nn46,49, 65n58, 67n74
Jung, Carl Gustav, 109

Kann, Robert A., 29n27
Kant, Immanuel, xi, xii, 31n50, 253-67
Kaplan, F., 241n7
Kaplow, Jeffry, 32nn58,60
Keats, John, 206
Kelly, G. D., 184n25
Kent, William, 111-12, 123, 132, 135n38
Ker, W. P., 135n45
Keteltas, William, 94, 105n25
Klein, Julie B., 225n3
Klein, Milton M., 83n17, 85nn29,30
Kliger, Samuel, 340, 348n9, 349n11
Kneeland, Abner, 104n4, 107n49
Knight, Charles A., 241n7
Koch, Adolph, 88-89, 104nn5,7, 106n31

Kolodny, Annette, 133n2
König, Johann Ulrich, 339
Kors, Alan C., 331, 336n13
Kramnick, Isaac, 232n73
Krauss, Werner, 28n5
Krikorian, Yervant H., 107n33
Kurz, Otto, 135n35

Labaree, Leonard W., 82n7
Labienus, Titus, 196
La Bruyère, Jean de, 303
Le Mare, Nicolas de, 36, 57, 61n6
Langet, M., 64n46
Langley, Batty, 117, 134n23
La Poix de Fréminville, Edme de, 57-58
La Rochefoucauld, François, Duc de, 206, 222, 226n4, 227n18
Larrabee, Harold A., 96, 107n33
La Salle, Jean-Baptiste de, 47, 63n38
Latt, David Jay, 231n65
Launay, Michael, 29n22
Lazaristes, 46
Lébarq, J., 28n13
La Bras, Gabriel, 33, 35
Lebrun, F., 66n66
Leclerc, Jean, 152
Lee, Sophia, 344
Lees-Milne, James, 129
Legault, Georges A., 268n10
Le Gros, Jean C. F., 323-25, 335nn1,3,4
Leibni(t)z, Gottfried Wilhelm von, 156, 270, 275
Leicester, Thomas Coke, Earl of, 135n46
Leland, Thomas, 349n18
Le Mercier de La Rivière, P.P.F.J.H., 5, 326, 329, 332-34
Lenient, Charles Félix, 296, 308n9
Lenin, Nikolai, 27
Lesage, Alain René, 303-4, 309n19
Lévy, Maurice, 350nn23,25
Lewis, Matthew Gregory, 342, 344-47, 349nn15,21,22, 350n23
Lewis, Wilmarth, 351, 355, 359
Lewis, W. S., 350n24, 361nn1,3,4, 362nn18,33, 363n38
Lewy, G., 61n5
Leyden, W. von, 162n7
liberalism, 27n1
libertinism, xi, 138, 148

376 / Index

Liebel, Helen, 30n31
Lind, James, 271
Linguet, Simon N. H., 323, 335n1
Link, Eugene Perry, 105nn20,24,25
Links, J. G., 362n17
Linnaeus, Carolus, 287
Linus, 193
Lispenard, Leonard, 80, 86n46
literacy, 16–17, 22–23, 30n30,32,42, 31n56, 32n57, 33–60, 60n1, 62n14, 64n46
Livingston, William, 72–74, 77–78, 83n12, 85nn29,36
Locke, John, x, xii, 76–77, 106n26, 151–62, 198, 200, 202n18, 203n18
Loftis, John, 232n71
Longueil, Alfred E., 348n6
Lorain fils, 46
Lord, John K., 81n3
Louis XIV, 11, 21, 63n43
Louisa, Princess, 218
Loupès, P., 62n17
Lovejoy, Arthur O., 103n2, 340, 348nn6,8, 349n12
Lucretius, Titus Carus, 267n5
Luke, Hugh J., 106n32
Lumberg, David, 100, 107n47
Lyell, Charles, 271, 273, 289n7
Lyon, John, 208–9, 227n17

Macaulay, Thomas Babington, 187, 195
Maccoby, Simon, 106n32, 108n52
Machiavelli, Niccolò di Bernardo, 145
Mack, Maynard, 134n28
MacLean, John, 81n3
Macpherson, C. B., 201n8, 227n20
Maggiolo, Louis, 49, 63n43
Maier, Pauline, 103n2
Maillet, Benoît ou Bernard de, 272
Malcolmson, Robert W., 23, 31n45, 32n59
Malins, Edward, 122, 133n6, 134n26
Malory, Thomas, 357
Mandeville, Bernard, 242n19
Mandroux, R., 61n13
Mann, Horace, 362nn19,25,29
Manwaring, Elizabeth W., 134n15
Marburg, Clara, 201n2, 202n15
Maria Theresa, 12, 17
Marivaux, Pierre Carlet de Chamblain de, 159, 305–6
Marlowe, Christopher, 206

Marrus, M. R., 30n34
Marsigli, Luigi Ferdinando, 274
Martin, Josiah, 83n11, 86n47
Marvell, Andrew, 130, 202n12
Marxism, 36
Mary, Lady Montagu Wortley, 151, 157–60, 163nn18,21–24,27, 164n27
Masham, Lady Damaris Cudworth, 151, 154–55, 158, 162nn4,8,10
Mason, William, 125
Masson, Margaret W., 81n3
materialism, 76, 100, 156, 329
Matilda, Queen, 174
Maturin, Charles Robert, 345
Maugras, G., 336n10
Maupeou, René Nicolas Charles Augustin de, 317
Maximilian I, 357
May, Henry F., 84n28, 88, 100, 104n3, 107n47
McAnear, Beverly, 81n2
McClure, David, 84n21
McCormick, Richard P., 81n3, 85n37
McEwen, Gilbert D., 162n10
McGuire, J. E., 202n10
McHugh, Roger, 225n3
Meare, John, 183n10
Meek, Ronald L., 336n11
Mell, Donald C., 226n3
Melville, Lewis, 228n32
Mendelssohn, Moses, 20
Mengs, Anton Raphael, 112
mercantilism, 18, 26
Meslier, Jean, 41
Methodism, 15
Meyer, Donald H., 89, 104nn3,9
Middendorf, John H., 225n3, 232n74
Migne, Jacques Paul, 62n26
Miles, Josephine, 206, 226n5
Mill, James, 106n32
Mill, John Stuart, 106n32, 185n32
Miller, Henry Knight, 233, 235, 241n2
Miller, Howard, 85n33
Miller, Perry, 85n32, 97, 107n34
Miller, Philip, 134n25
Millett, Kate, 137, 148n3
Milton, John, 113, 128–29, 135n47, 184n25, 206, 235, 239, 355
Mira [Eliza Haywood], 134n31
"Mirabaud" [D'Holbach], 100

Mirabeau, Honoré, Comte de, 325
Mirabeau, Victor Riqueti, Marquis de, 323–24, 326, 329, 331
Mirandola, Pico Della, 192
Mitchell, H., 64n49
Mitchell, Jonathan, 76–77, 84n27
Mithridate, Hippocrates, 82n12, 85n36
Moderns, Ancients and, 187–200
Moers, Ellen, 183n17
Moland, Louis, 313, 320n2
Molé, François-René, 307
Molesworth, William, 227n20
Molière, Jean-Baptiste Poquelin, 293, 297, 304, 309n24
Monk, Samuel Holt, 187, 201n2
Montagu, George, 347, 361n1, 362n27
Montagu, Lady Mary Wortley, 128, 151, 157–60, 163nn18,21–24,27, 164n27
Montesquieu, Charles-Louis de Secondat, Baron de la Brède et de, 313
Montgomery, Thomas H., 81n3, 83nn13, 14
Monty, Jeanne R., 314, 319, 321nn13,20
Moore, Lady Betty, 210
Morais, Herbert M., 89, 104n8
moralists, 5–6, 8, 14
More, Hannah, 151, 156–58, 163nn14–17,19
Morellet, André, 325–26, 333–34
Morley, Edith J., 349n13
Morris, John, 77, 83n12, 85n34, 86n47
Morris, John N., 185n32
Morris, William, 338
Mortier, Roland, 28n1
Moses, 190, 193
Mousnier, Roland, 28n4
Mulgrave, John Sheffield, Earl of, 140
Murry, John Middleton, 225n3, 228n42, 229n51, 232n74
Musaeus, 193

Napoleon, 64n43
naturalism, xi, 89, 91, 96, 100–101, 107n33
Naves, Raymond, 312–13, 321nn7,8
Necker, Jacques, 326, 334–35
Neo-Platonism, 21, 202n12
New, Melvyn, 242n9, 249n3
Newton, Isaac, 101, 162n4, 201n7, 202n10, 230n59, 255
Nicholes, Eleanor L., 184n26
Nichols, John, 227n17

Nicolas, J., 58, 66nn71,72
Nidditch, Peter H., 162n2
Nières, C., 66n70
Nin, Anaïs, 183n15
Nivernais, Louis-Jules Barbon Mancini-Mazarini, Duc de, 358
Norman, Sylva, 165, 176, 182n3
Norris, John, 155, 162n10
Nose, Karl, Wilhelm, 290n20

Oberman, H. A., 60n1
Ogden, C. K., 361n5
Onn, Gerald, 348n1
orality, 33–60
Oratoriens, 64n49
Orpheus, 188–90, 193, 195, 201n3, 202n12
Osborn, James M., 133n10
Ossian, 270
Ossory, Lady, 363n41
Ovid, Publius Naso, 122
Owen, Robert, 27
Oxford, Edward Harley, Earl of, 135n46

Paine, Thomas, 89, 97, 99, 102–3, 106n31, 107n41, 108nn49,50,53
Palacio, Jean de, 184n25
Palmer, Elihu, xi, 87–103
Palmer, E. Taiwo, 241n7
Palmer, R. R., 65n61
Pamela (Richardson), 238
Panckoucke, Charles-Joseph, 317–19
Panofsky, Erwin, 361n6
Parish, Elijah, 84n21
Parks, George B., 184n29
Parreaux, André, 349n21
Pascal, Roy, 173
Passmore, J. A., 162n9
Patriotes, 324
Paul, C. Kegan, 172, 183nn18–20
Paulson, Ronald, 133n6, 205, 207, 225n3, 226n7, 232n74
Payne, Harry C., 27n1, 28n5, 30n40, 31n43, 64nn46,48, 67n74
Peck, Louis F., 349n21
Pemberton, Ebenezer, 82n11
Pembroke, Henry Herbert, Earl of, 135n46
Percival, Geoffrey, 226n15
Percy, L., 336n10
Percy, Thomas, 270
Perkins, M. L., 315, 321nn14,15

378 / Index

Perrault, Charles, 61n13
Perronet, M., 66nn68–69
Persons, Stow, 85n43
Peterborough, Charles Mordaunt, Earl of, 111, 227n27
Peters, Richard, 77, 83n17, 84n29, 85n30, 86n47
Phalaris, Tyrant of Agrigente, 189, 201n5
Philipson, Nicholas, 30n41
Philomathes, 84n25, 86n47
philosophes, 5–8, 21–22, 24–26, 27n1, 28n8, 31n46, 38, 55–56, 64nn46,48, 65n61, 67n74, 100, 106n32, 303, 311, 314, 320, 334
Physiocrats, x, xiii, 323–35
Pidansat de Mairobert, F., 335n2
Pinkus, Philip, 225
Pintard, René, 320n5
Piozzi, Hester Lynch, 166, 183n7
Plato, 6, 201n4
Playfair, William, 325, 335n5, 336nn6,7
Plongeron, Bernard, 35, 61nn3,4,11, 62n19, 63n29, 64n49
Pluche, N., 42, 62n20
Plumb, J. H., 30n34, 31n46, 229n47, 231n63
Pocock, J. G. A., 340, 349n10
Poe, Edgar Allan, 206
Poitrineau, A., 29n26, 65n62
police, 11–12, 29nn26,27,29, 61n6, 66n68
Pomeau, René, 311, 320n1
Pompadour, Jeanne-Antoinette Poisson Le Normant D'Etioles, Marquise de, 326–27
Pontas, Jean, 46
Pope, Alexander, 110–14, 116–20, 122–27, 132, 133nn7,8,13, 134nn18,28,33, 135n42, 200, 202n18, 203n18, 206, 209–10, 213, 221–22, 225n3, 226n3, 228n38, 230n54, 231nn65,69,70, 237
popularism, 3–27, 33–60
Poston, Carol H., 166, 173–74, 182nn1,3, 184n28
Pottle, Frederick, 31n49
Poulet, Georges, 184n28
Poutet, Y., 63n38
Powell, Mary, 106n26
pragmatism, 101, 106n32
Presbyterianism, 81n3
Preston, John, 233, 241n4, 242n19
Prévost, Antoine-François, 303
Price, Richard, 184n26

Priestley, Joseph, 99
Prince, Thomas, 83n18
Prinz, Johannes, 149n12
Protestantism, 40, 44, 47, 49, 55–56
Puf(f)endorf, Samuel, 266
Pugin, Augustus Welby Northmore, 338, 347, 352, 363n36
Pulteney, William, Earl of Bath, 210–11, 213, 227n26, 351, 361n3
Puritanism, 12, 15, 18, 75, 79, 107n38
Pythagoras, 188, 190

Queensberry, Duchess of, 230nn51,53, 231n64
Queensberry, William Douglas, Duke of, 231n64
Quennell, Peter, 359, 362n33
Quérard, Joseph-Marie, 316, 321n17
Quesnay, François, 323–29, 331

Radcliffe, Ann, 165, 178, 357
radicalism, 87–103
Raeff, Marc, 29n27
Ranum, O., 65n60
Raspe, Rudolf Erich, xii, 269–89
rationalism, 77, 88, 96, 100, 102
Rattansi, P., 202n10
Rawson, C. J., 233
Raynal, Guillaume-Thomas-François, 332
Reck, Andrew J., 107n40
Redwood, J. S., 103n2
Reeve, Clara, 342–44, 347, 349nn15,16,19
Reformation, 13, 15, 26, 40, 349n11
Regnard, Jean-François, xiii, 291–307
Reichard, Hugo M., 225n3
religion, 33–60
religiosity, 15, 22
Renaissance, 21–22, 31n55, 60n1, 188, 201n8, 202n12, 209, 227n18, 338
Repton, Humphrey, 111, 133n9
republicanism, 88, 91, 94–95, 100, 103n2
Restoration, 139–40, 148n7, 151–54, 158, 160–61, 188, 196, 202n14
Rétif de la Bretonne, Nicolas-Edme, 45, 63n30
Revel, J., 62n28, 63nn29–33,42, 67n74
Revolution, American, 85n44, 87–88, 91–92, 104n5, 105n14, 107n40
Revolution, French, 31n48, 38, 45, 48–49, 61n3, 62nn16,28, 63nn29,34, 64nn46,49, 87, 93, 99, 106n28, 325

Rexroth, Kenneth, 242n20
Rezler, Marta, 320n5
Richardson, Leon B., 81n3
Richardson, Samuel, 234, 238
Richelieu, Armand-Jean du Plessis, Duc de, 14
Richerism, 64n51
Riley, I. Woodbridge, 106n31
Rittenhouse, David, 97, 103n1
Robbins, Caroline, 104n12
Robertson, J. Logie, 134n17
Robson-Scott, William Douglas, 348nn5–7
Rochester, John Wilmot, Earl of, x, xi, 130, 135n48, 137–48
romanticism, 29n27, 30n34, 165–82, 183n6, 184n28
Roppen, Georg, 183n6
Røstvig, Maren-Sofie, 134n28
Roth, G., 336nn8,16
Rousseau, Jean-Jacques, 6–7, 27n1, 29n17, 65n61, 174, 176, 178, 181, 184nn23,25,28, 303, 305, 309nn20,24,26,30, 324, 347
Rudé, George, 30n38
Rush, Benjamin, 97, 107n38
Ruskin, John, 338, 355, 359, 362nn17,28, 363n39
Russell, Bertrand, 161, 164nn29,30
Rutherford, Samuel, 163n11
Ruthven, K. K., 241n7
Rysbrack, (John) Michael, 122

Sachs, W., 64n43
Sade, Donatien A. F., Marquis de, 346, 350n23
Said, Edward, 207, 225n3, 226n8
Saint Augustine, 239, 340
Saint Jacob, Pierre de, 29n23
Saint-Simon, Louis de Rouvroy, Duc de, 27
Saisselin, Rémy, 31n51
Sales, François de, 42, 64n52
Salvesen, Christopher, 184n28
Sandys, Lord, 81n4
Sarramon, A., 67n73
Sartine, Antoine Gabriel de, 327, 332–34
Savile, Henry, 139, 142, 148nn5,8
Schakel, Peter J., 226n3, 232n73
Schmitt, Jean-Claude, 35–36, 61n4
Schneer, Cecil J., 289n7
Schneider, Carol, 83n16
Schneider, Herbert W., 83n16, 94, 97, 105n21, 107n36

Schnorrenberg, Barbara Brandon, 162n1
Schwarzbach, Bertram Eugene, 319, 321n20
scientism, 27n1
Scott, Temple, 229n43
Scott, Walter, 344, 349n19
Scottish Enlightenment, 84n28, 85n32
Scoular, Kitty, 202n12
Scouten, A. H., 225n3
Scroope, Carr, 142
Seccombe, Thomas, 289n3
secularism, 13, 99
Sedaine, Michel-Jean, 306
Seneca, Lucius Annaeus, 227nn16,18
Serle, John, 113
Serres, Michel, 267n5
Servan, Antoine-Joseph-Michel, 319
Settle, T., 60n1
Shafer, R. J., 30n31
Shaftesbury, Anthony Ashley, Earl of, 121, 227n18
Shakespeare, William, 114, 206
Shawcross, J., 202n17
Sheets, Robin Ann, 133n13
Sheffield, John, Duke of Buckingham, 227n18
Sheffield, John, Earl of Mulgrave, 140
Shelley, Percy Bysshe, 184n26, 206, 349n14
Shenstone, William, 115
Shepard, Paul, 132n1
Sherburn, George, 134n33, 135n42, 231n69
Sheridan, Richard Brinsley, 216, 229nn45,48
Shinagel, Michael, 226n5
Shorter, Edward, 23, 32n59
Shumaker, Wayne, 183n12
Sideall, John, 93
Sièyes, Emmanuel-Joseph, 325
Simson, Otto Georg von, 353, 362n8
Skinner, Laurence Hervey, 307n2, 308n8
Slepian, Barry, 225n3
Sloan, Douglas, 84n28, 85n32
Slotkin, Richard, 85n41
Small, Albion, 29n27
Smith, Adam, 12, 325, 335n5, 336nn6,7
Smith, Charlotte, 357
Smith, Gregory, 133n14
Smith, Horace W., 84n23
Smith, Warren Hunting, 349n14, 351, 361n4, 362nn24,26
Smith, William, 73–75, 77, 80, 82nn7, 11, 83n14, 84nn23,25,29, 85nn30,31, 86n47

Smith, William Peartree, 82n11
Smith, Wilson, 84n27
Soboul, Albert, 31n48
Socrates, 201n5
Solé, J., 62n27
Soliday, Gerald, 29n18
Sommer, Richard, 183n6
Soriano, M., 61n13
Spacks, Patricia Meyer, 169, 183nn13,14
Spectator, 16,19, 116, 121, 133n14, 159, 226n12, 227nn18,19
Spence, Joseph, 133n10
Spenser, Edmund, 202n12, 206, 337, 356–57
Spingarn, J. E., 193, 202n11
Stangos, Nikos, 134n21
Stanhope, William, 118
Steele, Richard, 16, 133n14
Steensma, Robert C., 225n3
Sterne, Laurence, xi, xii, 181, 243–49
Stillman, Damie, 363n37
Stokes, Adrian, 132n1
Stone, Lawrence, 30nn30,32
Stout, Gardner D., 244
Strenski, Ellen M., 331, 336n14
Stromberg, Roland N., 103n2
Stroud, Dorothy, 133n3
Suard, Jean-Baptiste-Antoine, 326
Suffolk, Henrietta Howard, Countess of, xii, 206, 208, 211–20, 222, 227n28, 228nn30,32,39,43, 229nn44,49,51, 230n51, 231nn59,64
Suger, Abbé, 352–53, 360–61, 361n6
Summers, Montague, 349n17, 350n23
Summerson, John, 361n5
surrealism, 350n23
Swain, J. W., 61n5
Swift, Jonathan, xii, 146, 159–60, 188, 205–25
Switzer, Stephen, 111, 116–17, 119–20, 128–29, 132, 134n19

Tacitus, Publius Cornelius, 22, 340
Tackett, T., 62n17
Tammany Society, 94, 105n22
Tasso, Torquato, 357
Tatler, 16
Taveneaux, R., 64n46
Taylor, Kenneth L., 289n17, 290nn17,19
Taylor, Mary Louise, 267n2
Taylor, Samuel, 316, 321n18

Temple, William, xii, 130, 187–200
Tennent, Gilbert, 82nn5,6,11
Tennyson, Alfred, 206
Terreur, La, 347
Themistocles, 201n5
Thiers, J.-B., 55, 65n63, 66n66
Thomas, Keith, 36–37, 60n1, 61nn7,8
Thompson, E. P., 9, 28n11, 29n19, 30nn36,38, 61n1
Thompson, Paul V., 228n33
Thomson, James, 113, 120, 134n17
Tilly, C., 66n73
Tissier, André, 304, 306, 307n2, 308nn8,10,15,16, 309nn21,25,27,28,30
Tomalin, Claire, 166, 183nn5,17
Tom Jones (Fielding), xii, 233–40
Tomplins, J. M. S., 344, 349n20
Tourneux, M., 336n12
Toynbee, Paget, 228n30, 361n3
Trainer, James, 349n15
Trapnell, William H., 321n19
Treglown, Jeremy, 148n6
Trénard, Louis, 30nn34,39, 64n46
Trinkaus, C., 60n1
Trinterud, Leonard J., 81n3
Tristram Shandy (Sterne), xii, 243–49
Tudor, House of, 14, 356
Turberville, A. S., 31nn46,47
Turgot, Anne-Robert-Jacques, 4, 25, 29n17, 326–27, 333–35
Turner, William, 242n16
Twomey, Richard J., 106n26
Tyne, James L., 225n3

Ultee, J. Maarten, 29n25, 31n45, 65n62
Unitarianism, 88
Uphaus, Robert W., 225n3, 232n74
urbanism, 10
utilitarianism, 106n32
utopia, 253–67, 338, 342–43, 347

Vaihinger, Hans, 352, 361n5
Valmary, P., 63n43
Van Amringe, John Howard, 81n3, 82n9
Vancouver, George, 269
Varagnac, André, 31n55
Varma, Devendra P., 349n14
Vasari, Giorgio, 338, 353–55, 362n11
Venturi, Franco, 30n31, 32n63
Vergil, 119, 159, 193

Vieth, David M., 139, 148nn1,7, 205, 207, 225n3, 226n8
Vine, Phyllis, 85n40
Voight, Henry, 90
Volney, Constantin-François de Chasseboeuf, Comte de, 100, 106n26
Voltaire, François-Marie Arouet de, x, xiii, 4, 6–7, 14, 17, 22, 24, 28n1, 29n17, 102, 106n26, 131, 311–20, 324, 326–27
Vovelle, Michel, 20, 31n53, 64n44,45,47

Wade, Ira O., 316, 321n16
Wagner, William, 201n5
Waingrow, Marshall, 205, 208, 225n3, 226n14
Wales, Caroline, Princess of, 212–13
Walker, D. P., 201nn4,6, 202nn10,12
Walpole, Horace, x, 110–12, 118, 122, 126, 128, 133nn11,12, 212, 228nn30,32, 229n44, 343, 347, 349nn14,17, 350n24, 351–61
Walpole, Robert, 210–12, 215–22, 228nn28,30, 229n47, 231nn63,66, 232nn71,73, 351
Warburton, William, 163n11
Wardle, Ralph M., 166, 182nn1,4, 183n20, 184nn23,28
Warham, William, 354, 356
Watson, Richard, 108n53
Watt, Ian, 29nn22,28, 30n42, 31n54, 32n57, 39, 60n1, 62n14, 233, 241nn2,3
Wattel, 266
Webb, R. K., 31n42
Weber, Eugen, 31n55
Weintraub, Karl J., 28n1, 183n12
Weischedel, Wilhelm, 267n2
Werner, Abraham Gottlob, 276
Wertenbaker, Thomas J., 81n3
Werther (Goethe), 166, 171, 174, 176, 180
West, Gilbert, 114
Westfall, Richard S., 201n7
Wharton, Thomas, 361n3, 362nn30,34
Whately, Thomas, 114, 116, 126
Wheelock, Eleazar, 70, 73–74, 82n6, 83n15, 84n21
Whistler, Laurence, 133n6
Whiston, William, 272
White, William, 90

Whitehead, William, 113, 339
Wieland, Christoph Martin, 6, 28n8
Wiener, Philip P., 106n32
Wilcoxon, Reba, 148n4
Wilkins, W. H., 228n28
William, Duke of Cumberland, 231n59
Williams, Aubrey, 233, 241n2
Williams, David, 30n41
Williams, Harold, 225n1, 226n4, 227nn20,25
Williams, Ioan, 349n19
Williams, Raymond, 125, 134n24
Williamson, George, 202n14
Willis, Peter, 133n6
Willis, Sue, 140
Wilmot, John, Earl of Rochester, x, xi, 130, 135n48, 137–48
Wilson, B., 60n1
Wilson, John Harold, 148n5
Wind, Edgar, 201n8
Witherspoon, John, 84n28
Wollstonecraft, Mary, xi–xii, 165–82
Wood, Gordon S., 85n44, 104n12
Wood, Paul Spencer, 202n14
Woodbridge, Homer E., 201n2, 202n15
Woodbridge, Kenneth, 123, 133nn6,12, 134n16, 135nn44,49
Woodman, David, 202n12
Woodward, John, 272
Woolley, David, 225
Woolley, James, 227n25
Wordsworth, William, 7, 23, 178, 183n6, 184n28, 206
Wortman, Tunis, 94
Wotton, William, 190, 201nn6,7, 202n9
Wright, Chauncy, 97, 106n32, 107n36
Wyatt, James, 359, 363n38

Xenophon, 227n16

Yates, Frances A., 191, 201n5, 354
Yolton, John, 162nn3,4, 163n12
Young, Alfred F., 94, 105nn18,20,23,25
Young, Thomas, 103n2
Yvon, Claude, 332

Zehbe, J., 31n50